Lecture Notes in Computer Science 15594

Founding Editors

Gerhard Goos
Juris Hartmanis

AF173482

The series Lecture Notes in Computer Science (LNCS), including its subseries Lecture Notes in Artificial Intelligence (LNAI) and Lecture Notes in Bioinformatics (LNBI), has established itself as a medium for the publication of new developments in computer science and information technology research, teaching, and education.

LNCS enjoys close cooperation with the computer science R & D community, the series counts many renowned academics among its volume editors and paper authors, and collaborates with prestigious societies. Its mission is to serve this international community by providing an invaluable service, mainly focused on the publication of conference and workshop proceedings and postproceedings. LNCS commenced publication in 1973.

Roberto Giorgi · Mirjana Stojilović ·
Dirk Stroobandt · Piedad Brox Jiménez ·
Ángel Barriga Barros
Editors

Applied Reconfigurable Computing

Architectures, Tools, and Applications

21st International Symposium, ARC 2025
Seville, Spain, April 9–11, 2025
Proceedings

 Springer

Editors
Roberto Giorgi 🆔
University of Siena
Siena, Italy

Mirjana Stojilović 🆔
EPFL
Lausanne, Switzerland

Dirk Stroobandt 🆔
Ghent University
Ghent, Belgium

Piedad Brox Jiménez 🆔
University of Seville
Seville, Spain

Ángel Barriga Barros 🆔
University of Seville
Seville, Spain

ISSN 0302-9743   ISSN 1611-3349 (electronic)
Lecture Notes in Computer Science
ISBN 978-3-031-87994-4   ISBN 978-3-031-87995-1 (eBook)
https://doi.org/10.1007/978-3-031-87995-1

Preface

The 21st International Symposium on Applied Reconfigurable Computing (ARC 2025) was organized by the Institute of Microelectronics of Seville, Spain, and took place in Seville, Spain from April 9th to 11th, 2025.

Message from the General Chairs

On behalf of the Organizing Committee, we would like to welcome you to the twenty-first edition of the International Symposium on Applied Reconfigurable Computing (ARC 2025). The objective of this symposium was to explore and advance applications leveraging cutting-edge reconfigurable computing technologies. The requirements of electronic systems, in terms of functionality, performance, costs, consumption, and reliability, make new processing paradigms, architectures, and technologies necessary. Reconfigurable computing is crucial in several application domains, such as artificial intelligence, cybersecurity, communication, and automotive, among many others.

We were particularly pleased to host the symposium in Seville, the capital of Andalusia in southern Spain. Beyond its academic significance, this event provided a unique platform for researchers and professionals to network, collaborate, and discuss the latest developments in applied reconfigurable computing. This edition was organized by the Institute of Microelectronics of Seville, with the support of the Spanish National Research Council (CSIC) and the University of Seville.

Piedad Brox Jiménez
Ángel Barriga Barros

Message from the Program Chairs

The 21st International Symposium on Applied Reconfigurable Computing (ARC 2025) continued its tradition of bringing together researchers and practitioners to share advancements, challenges, and future directions in reconfigurable computing. This year, ARC 2025 reinforced its commitment to impactful research and innovation, marking a significant milestone in the evolution of the symposium.

As in previous editions, ARC 2025 covered a wide range of topics, including hardware acceleration, security and fault tolerance, energy-efficient architectures, and emerging applications in artificial intelligence and high-performance computing. The symposium fostered collaboration and pushed the boundaries of state-of-the-art research.

We received 40 submissions this year, reflecting the community's strong engagement and ongoing research efforts. After a rigorous double-blind review process, with each submission receiving at least three and an average of 3.8 expert reviews, 12 papers were accepted, as well as a short paper. These high-quality contributions showcase both theoretical advancements and practical implementations in reconfigurable computing.

The ARC 2025 program featured oral and poster presentations, two insightful keynotes by leading experts, one full-day tutorial, two workshops, and a special session, "20 years of ARC: A selection of most representative papers." The special session consisted of talks by authors of the 10 papers with the most nominations from the selection of 26 representative papers presented and published in the first 20 editions of ARC. We hope this session was an important moment for ARC and contributed to the discussions regarding recent advancements in the topics presented by those papers.

The paper entitled "First Twenty Years of the International Symposium on Applied Reconfigurable Computing (ARC): A Selection of Papers" presents a curated list of 26 representative contributions presented and published in the first 20 editions of the ARC.

We sincerely thank all authors for their submissions, and the program committee members and external reviewers, whose expertise and dedication ensured a high-quality and well-balanced program. We also thank the sponsors and the organizing committee for their invaluable contributions to making ARC 2025 a successful and memorable event.

We hope that ARC 2025 served as an engaging and inspiring forum, sparking discussions and collaborations that will continue to drive the field of reconfigurable computing forward. We were excited about the authors' contributions and the vibrant exchange of ideas throughout the symposium.

Thank you for being part of ARC 2025!

February 2025

Roberto Giorgi
Mirjana Stojilović

Organization

General Chairs

Piedad Brox Jiménez   Instituto de Microelectrónica de Sevilla, Spain
Ángel Barriga Barros   Instituto de Microelectrónica de Sevilla, Spain

Program Committee Chairs

Roberto Giorgi   University of Siena, Italy
Mirjana Stojilović   EPFL, Switzerland

Proceedings Chair

Dirk Stroobandt   Ghent University, Belgium

Special Session and Issue (20 Years of ARC) Chairs

João M. P. Cardoso   University of Porto, Portugal
Walid Najjar   University of California Riverside, USA

Publicity Chairs

Martin Margala   University of Louisiana at Lafayette, USA
Kevin Martin   Université de Bretagne Sud, France
Madhura Purnaprajna   PES University, India

Local Chairs

Macarena C. Martínez-Rodríguez   Instituto de Microelectrónica de Sevilla, Spain
David Martín Sánchez   Instituto de Microelectrónica de Sevilla, Spain

Finance Chair

Víctor García Flores   Instituto de Microelectrónica de Sevilla, Spain

Workshops and Tutorials Chairs

Eros Camacho-Ruiz   Instituto de Microelectrónica de Sevilla, Spain
José Miguel Mora Gutiérrez   Instituto de Microelectrónica de Sevilla, Spain

Web Chair

Macarena C. Martínez-Rodríguez   Instituto de Microelectrónica de Sevilla, Spain

Program Committee

Michael Adler   Altera, USA
Hideharu Amano   Keio University, Japan
Caaliph Andriamisaina   Commissariat à l'Énergie Atomique et aux
                                        Énergies Alternatives, France
Nikolaos Bellas   University of Thessaly, Greece
Mladen Berekovic   University of Lübeck, Germany
João Bispo   University of Porto, Portugal
Vanderlei Bonato   Institute of Mathematical and Computer Sciences,
                                        Brazil
Alejandro Cabrera Aldaya   Tampere University, Finland
João Cardoso   University of Porto, Portugal
Luigi Carro   UFRGS, Brazil
Ray Cheung   City University of Hong Kong, China
Daniel Chillet   University of Rennes, France
Pedro Diniz   INESC-ID, Portugal
Ricardo Ferreira   Universidade Federal de Vicosa, Brazil
Darshan Gandhi   University of Texas at Austin, USA
Roberto Giorgi   University of Siena, Italy
Diana Göhringer   TU Dresden, Germany
Frank Hannig   Friedrich-Alexander-Universität
                                        Erlangen-Nürnberg, Germany
Christian Hochberger   TU Darmstadt, Germany
Michael Hübner   Brandenburg University of Technology Cottbus,
                                        Germany

Krzysztof Kepa	GE Global Research, USA
Georgios Keramidas	Aristotle University of Thessaloniki/Think Silicon S.A., Greece
Paris Kitsos	University of the Peloponnese, Greece
Andreas Koch	TU Darmstadt, Germany
Tomasz Kryjak	AGH University of Science and Technology, Poland
Francesco Leporati	University of Pavia, Italy
Konstantinos Masselos	University of the Peloponnese, Greece
Cathal McCabe	AMD, USA
Antonio Miele	Politecnico di Milano, Italy
Takefumi Miyoshi	e-trees.Japan, Inc., Japan
Horacio Neto	INESC-ID/IST/ULisboa, Portugal
Nuno Paulino	INESC TEC, Portugal
Marco Platzner	University of Paderborn, Germany
Dionisios Pnevmatikatos	National Technical University of Athens, Greece
Madhura Purnaprajna	PES University, India
Francesco Regazzoni	University of Amsterdam, the Netherlands and Università della Svizzera italiana, Italy
Martin Rönnbäck	Cobham Gaisler, Sweden
Kentaro Sano	Riken R-CCS, Japan
Marco D. Santambrogio	Politecnico di Milano, Italy
Antonio Carlos Schneider Beck Filho	Universidade Federal do Rio Grande do Sul, Brazil
Dimitrios Soudris	National Technical University of Athens, Greece
Ioannis Sourdis	Chalmers University of Technology, Sweden
Srdjan Stanković	University of Montenegro, Montenegro
Mirjana Stojilović	EPFL, Switzerland
Theocharis Theocharides	University of Cyprus, Cyprus
George Theodoridis	University of Patras, Greece
Markus Weinhardt	Osnabrück University of Applied Sciences, Germany

Additional Reviewers

Boma Anantasatya Adhi	Leon Dietrich
Georgios Alexandris	Christoph Flothow
Ensieh Aliagha	Manolis Galetakis
Christoph Berganski	Jonas Gehrunger
João Paulo S. Bertoncini	Paul Gottschaldt
Filippo Carloni	Lukas Groth
Panagiotis Chaidos	Fatma Jebali

Felix Jentzsch
Akira Jinguji
Stavros Kalapothas
Ahmed Kamaleldin
Jialin Liu
Leon Mayrhofer
Xinmin Meng
Anouar Nechi
Tim Noack
Magnus Östgren

Rohit Prasad
Domenico Ragusa
Aguimar Ribeiro Junior
Leonardo Solis-Vasquez
Florian Stock
Panagiotis Strikos
Emanuele Torti
Tomohiro Ueno
David Volz
Jason Zhang

Contents

Efficient AI and Stream Analytics on FPGAs

Fast and Adaptive AI on FPGAs

Short Paper

20 Years of ARC

First Twenty Years of the International Symposium on Applied Reconfigurable Computing (ARC): A Selection of Papers

João M. P. Cardoso[1]([⊠]) [iD] and Walid Najjar[2] [iD]

[1] Faculty of Engineering, University of Porto, Porto, Portugal
jmpc@fe.up.pt
[2] University of California Riverside, Riverside, USA
najjar@cs.ucr.edu

Abstract. The International Symposium on Applied Reconfigurable Computing (ARC) is an annual forum for the discussion and dissemination of research, notably applying the Reconfigurable Computing (RC) concept to real-world problems. The first edition of ARC took place in 2005, and in 2024, ARC celebrated its 20th edition. During those 20 years, the field of reconfigurable computing saw a tremendous growth in its underlying technology. ARC contributed very significantly to the presentation and dissemination of new ideas, innovative applications, and fruitful discussions, all of which have resulted in the shaping of novel lines of research. Here, we present selected papers from the first 20 years of ARC, that we believe represent the corpus of work and reflect the ARC spirit by covering a broad spectrum of RC applications, benchmarks, tools, and architectures.

Keywords: Reconfigurable Computing · FPGA · Applied Reconfigurable Computing · Reconfigurable Hardware

1 Introduction

Reconfigurable Computing (RC) [1, 2] is a form of computing that, by using reconfigurable hardware, combines the flexibility of software with the execution speed and energy efficiency of hardware. Although Gerald Estrin proposed the main reconfigurable computing concept in the 1960s [3, 4], the invention of Field-Programmable Gate Arrays (FPGAs) in the 1980s [5] provided the most successful technology for supporting reconfigurable computing.

FPGAs provide reconfigurable hardware with the capacity for customization and reconfiguration, two essential features for reconfigurable computing. Coarse-grained reconfigurable arrays (CGRAs) [6] are another technology with important contributions to the reconfigurable computing concept. The application domains for reconfigurable computing are vast, from high-performance to embedded and edge computing. Over the years, academia and industry have shown the benefits of reconfigurable computing by proposing more efficient computing systems, e.g., in terms of energy efficiency and processing speed.

R. Giorgi et al. (Eds.): ARC 2025, LNCS 15594, pp. 3–12, 2025.
https://doi.org/10.1007/978-3-031-87995-1_1

The annual Applied Reconfigurable Computing (ARC) scientific event [7, 8] has disseminated research work focused on applying reconfigurable computing to real-world problems. ARC started as the "International Workshop on Applied Reconfigurable Computing" and was associated with the IADIS International Conference on Applied Computing held in Carvoeiro, Algarve, Portugal, 2005. After the first edition, ARC became an independent workshop for another four editions. In 2010, ARC changed to the "International Symposium on Applied Reconfigurable Computing". The 20th edition of ARC was organized in 2024, in Aveiro, Portugal. During the first 20 years, ARC has been organized in ten countries and four continents, in Carvoeiro (Portugal), Delft (The Netherlands), Mangaratiba (Rio de Janeiro, Brazil), London (UK), Karlsruhe (Germany), Bangkok (Thailand), Belfast (UK), Hong Kong (P.R China), Marina del Rey (California, USA), Vilamoura (Algarve, Portugal), Bochum (Germany), Mangaratiba (Rio de Janeiro, Brazil), Delft (The Netherlands), Santorini (Greece), Darmstadt (Germany), Toledo (Spain, held virtually), Rennes (France, held virtually), Beijing (P.R. China, held virtually), Cottbus (Germany), and Aveiro (Portugal).

During the first 20 years of ARC, we witnessed significant advancements in reconfigurable computing in applications, tools, compilers, system software, devices, and architectures. This paper intends to celebrate the ARC's 20th anniversary by presenting some of the most representative research work and achievements presented at ARC and published in ARC proceedings (published by Springer LNCS since the 2nd ARC [9]) in the first 20 ARC editions. The selected papers presented herein show research on diverse topics spanning the broad spectrum of application domains and research topics of RC.

This paper is organized as follows. Section 2 describes the process followed for selecting the papers presented. Section 3 presents the selected papers. Finally, Sect. 4 concludes this paper.

2   Selection Process

The process of selecting the papers presented here involved the following two steps.

First, we have organized a first selection of 60 papers according to the following five categories:

1. Papers with Google Scholar citations, as of Oct. 2024, greater or equal to 70.
2. Papers not previously included and with Google Scholar citations of both the ARC paper and its extended version published in a Journal, namely a Special Issue/Section dedicated to selected ARC papers, as of Oct. 2024, greater or equal to 70. In this case, we also searched for other ARC papers that might have been extended and published in ACM TRETS as regular papers.
3. Papers not previously included, presented in ARC between 2010 and 2024, and with a number of citations per year greater or equal to 5.
4. Papers that received an ARC Best Paper Award.
5. Papers ranked in the top 3 according to reviewer's scores of the five most recent ARC editions (2019–2024).

Second, we asked the members of the Steering Committee (SC) of ARC, the Program Chairs/Co-Chairs, and the General Chairs/Co-Chairs of the first 20 editions of ARC, to nominate papers from this first list of 60 selected papers. In addition, we also asked them to nominate other papers if they thought it adequate.

3 Selected Papers

The previously described selection process resulted in the final selection consisting of the 26 papers in Tables 1, 2, and 3. They were the most voted papers, each one consisting of at least six nominations, and represent around 3.7% of all the papers presented in the first 20 editions of ARC.

For papers that, as far as we know, resulted in extended versions published in journals, we also include references to those journal versions in the tables.

Although we are conscious that this may not be a perfect selection and that many other papers could have been selected, we think that the selection of papers highlighted here provides a representative view of the research work presented at ARC.

Table 1. Selected papers (part I).

ARC year	Title of the paper	Reference	Main Topic	Main Application
2006	"Reconfigurable Modular Arithmetic Logic Unit for High-Performance Public-Key Cryptosystems"	[10, 11]	Arithmetic and cryptography	Security
2006	"Impact of Loop Unrolling on Area, Throughput and Clock Frequency in ROCCC: C to VHDL Compiler for FPGAs"	[12, 13]	HLS estimations	General
2007	"Architectural Exploration of the ADRES Coarse-Grained Reconfigurable Array"	[14]	Coarse-grained reconfigurable arrays (CGRAs)	General
2007	"Synthesis of Regular Expressions Targeting FPGAs: Current Status and Open Issues"	[15]	Synthesis techniques for regular expressions	Network Intrusion Detection Systems
2007	"Authentication of FPGA Bitstreams: Why and How"	[16]	Authentication	Security

(continued)

Table 1. (*continued*)

ARC year	Title of the paper	Reference	Main Topic	Main Application
2008	"A High Throughput FPGA-Based Floating Point Conjugate Gradient Implementation"	[17, 18]	Arithmetic accelerators	Numerical applications
2008	"The Instruction-Set Extension Problem: A Survey"	[19, 20]	Instruction-set extension	General
2008	"PARO: Synthesis of Hardware Accelerators for Multi-dimensional Dataflow-Intensive Applications"	[21]	Synthesis of hardware accelerators	General

Table 2. Selected papers (part II).

ARC year	Title of the paper	Reference	Main Topic	Main Application
2010	"Towards Rapid Dynamic Partial Reconfiguration in Video-Based Driver Assistance Systems"	[22]	Dynamic partial reconfiguration	Video-based driver assistance
2010	"Optimising Memory Bandwidth Use for Matrix-Vector Multiplication in Iterative Methods"	[23, 24]	Memory and arithmetic	Using matrix-vector multiplications
2011	"FaRM: Fast Reconfiguration Manager for Reducing Reconfiguration Time Overhead on FPGA"	[25, 26]	Hardware reconfiguration	General
2014	"Efficient Elliptic-Curve Cryptography Using Curve25519 on Reconfigurable Devices"	[27, 28]	Efficient support for cryptography	Security

(*continued*)

Table 2. (*continued*)

ARC year	Title of the paper	Reference	Main Topic	Main Application
2015	"Pyverilog: A Python-Based Hardware Design Processing Toolkit for Verilog HDL"	[29]	Hardware design with HDLs	General
2015	"Preemptive Hardware Multitasking in ReconOS"	[30]	Hardware multitasking	General
2017	"Optimizing CNN-Based Object Detection Algorithms on Embedded FPGA Platforms"	[31]	Optimizations for CNNs	Object Detection
2018	"Approximate FPGA-Based LSTMs Under Computation Time Constraints"	[32, 33]	Machine learning	Using LSTMs
2018	"Redundancy-Reduced MobileNet Acceleration on Reconfigurable Logic for ImageNet Classification"	[34]	Image classification	General
2019	"The TaPaSCo Open-Source Toolflow for the Automated Composition of Task-Based Parallel Reconfigurable Computing Systems"	[35, 36]	Tool flows for task-based programming	General
2019	"HiFlipVX: An Open Source High-Level Synthesis FPGA Library for Image Processing"	[37, 38]	Image processing HLS library	Image and video processing
2020	"Improving Performance Estimation for FPGA-Based Accelerators for Convolutional Neural Networks"	[39, 40]	Performance estimation	Using CNNs

(*continued*)

Table 2. (*continued*)

ARC year	Title of the paper	Reference	Main Topic	Main Application
2020	"A Parameterisable FPGA-Tailored Architecture for YOLOv3-Tiny"	[41]	Machine learning	Using Real-Time Object Detection
2020	"Judiciously Spreading Approximation Among Arithmetic Components with Top-Down Inexact Hardware Design"	[42]	Approximate arithmetic	General

Table 3. Selected papers (part III).

ARC year	Title of the paper	Reference	Main Topic	Main Application
2021	"Supporting On-Chip Dynamic Parallelism for Task-Based Hardware Accelerators"	[43, 44]	Dynamic parallelism	General
2023	"Increasing the Fault Tolerance of COTS FPGAs in Space: SEU Mitigation Techniques on MPSoC"	[45]	Dependability	General
2024	"SNN vs. CNN Implementations on FPGAs: An Empirical Evaluation"	[46]	Deep learning	Using SNNs and/or CNNs
2024	"Open-Source SpMV Multiplication Hardware Accelerator for FPGA-Based HPC Systems"	[47]	Arithmetic accelerators	Using matrix-vector multiplications

4   Conclusion

This paper presented a selection of the work published in the first 20 editions of the International Symposium on Applied Reconfigurable Computing (ARC). The selected papers resulted from a first set of papers chosen with predefined rules that mainly included the number of citations to each paper, best paper award assignments, followed by a selection refinement from nominations. By showcasing this selection of ARC papers, we aim to provide a representative view of some impactful research work presented at ARC.

Acknowledgments. We are grateful to the ARC Steering Committee members, the General, and the Program Committee Chairs and Co-Chairs of some of the ARC editions for their input regarding the nominations of the papers. We also acknowledge the support of the ARC'2025 General and Program Co-chairs for supporting us in highlighting at ARC2025 the selected papers presented here.

Disclosure of Interests.   The authors have no competing interests to declare relevant to this article's content.

References

1. Compton, K., Hauck, S.: Reconfigurable computing: a survey of systems and software. ACM Comput. Surv. **34**(2), 171–210 (2002). https://doi.org/10.1145/508352.508353
2. Gokhale, M., Graham, P.: Reconfigurable Computing: Accelerating Computation with Field-Programmable Gate Arrays, Springer, NY (2005). https://doi.org/10.1007/b136834
3. Estrin, G.: Organization of computer systems: the fixed plus variable structure computer. In: Papers presented at the 3–5 May 1960, Western Joint IRE-AIEE-ACM Computer Conference (IRE-AIEE-ACM '60 (Western)), pp. 33–40. Association for Computing Machinery, New York, NY, USA. https://doi.org/10.1145/1460361.1460365
4. Estrin, G.: Reconfigurable computer origins: the UCLA fixed-plus-variable (F+V) structure computer. IEEE Ann. Hist. Comput. **24**(4), 3–9 (2002). https://doi.org/10.1109/MAHC.2002.1114865.
5. Boutros, A., Betz, V.: FPGA architecture: principles and progression. IEEE Circuits Syst. Mag. **21**(2), 4–29, Second quarter 2021. https://doi.org/10.1109/MCAS.2021.3071607.
6. Li, Z., Wijerathne, D., Mitra, T.: Coarse-grained reconfigurable array (CGRA). In: Chattopadhyay, A. (ed.) Handbook of Computer Architecture. Springer, Singapore (2023). https://doi.org/10.1007/978-981-15-6401-7_50-1
7. International Symposium on Reconfigurable Computing (ARC) Homepage. http://www.arcsymposium.org/. Accessed 8 Jan 2025
8. DBLP Homepage, Computer Science Bibliography: International Symposium on Applied Reconfigurable Computing. Architectures, Tools, and Applications (ARC). https://dblp.org/db/conf/arc/index.html. Accessed 8 Jan 2025
9. ARC: International Symposium on Applied Reconfigurable Computing, © Springer Nature Switzerland AG. Part of Springer Nature. https://link.springer.com/conference/arc. Accessed 8 Jan 8 Jan 2025
10. Sakiyama, K., Mentens, N., Batina, L., Preneel, B., Verbauwhede, I.: Reconfigurable modular arithmetic logic unit for high-performance public-key cryptosystems. In: Bertels, K., Cardoso, J.M.P., Vassiliadis, S. (eds.) ARC 2006. LNCS, vol. 3985. Springer, Heidelberg (2006). https://doi.org/10.1007/11802839_43
11. Sakiyama, K., Mentens, N., Batina, L., Preneel, B., Verbauwhede, I.: Reconfigurable modular arithmetic logic unit supporting high-performance RSA and ECC over GF(p). Int. J. Electron. **94**(5), 501–514 (2007). https://doi.org/10.1080/00207210701293264

12. Buyukkurt, B., Guo, Z., Najjar, W.A.: Impact of loop unrolling on area, throughput and clock frequency in ROCCC: C to VHDL compiler for FPGAs. In: Bertels, K., Cardoso, J.M.P., Vassiliadis, S. (eds.) ARC 2006. LNCS, vol. 3985. Springer, Heidelberg (2006). https://doi. org/10.1007/11802839_48

13. Buyukkurt, B., Cortes, J., Villarreal, J., Najjar, W.A.: Impact of high-level transformations within the ROCCC framework. ACM Trans. Archit. Code Optim. **7**, 4, Article 17, 36 p. (2010). https://doi.org/10.1145/1880043.1880044

14. Bouwens, F., Berekovic, M., Kanstein, A., Gaydadjiev, G.: Architectural exploration of the ADRES coarse-grained reconfigurable array. In: Diniz, P.C., Marques, E., Bertels, K., Fernandes, M.M., Cardoso, J.M.P. (eds.) ARC 2007. LNCS, vol. 4419. Springer, Heidelberg (2007). https://doi.org/10.1007/978-3-540-71431-6_1

15. Bispo, J., Sourdis, I., Cardoso, J.M.P., Vassiliadis, S.: Synthesis of regular expressions targeting FPGAs: current status and open issues. In: Diniz, P.C., Marques, E., Bertels, K., Fernandes, M.M., Cardoso, J.M.P. (eds.) ARC 2007. LNCS, vol. 4419. Springer, Heidelberg (2007). https://doi.org/10.1007/978-3-540-71431-6_17

16. Drimer, S.: Authentication of FPGA bitstreams: why and how. In: Diniz, P.C., Marques, E., Bertels, K., Fernandes, M.M., Cardoso, J.M.P. (eds.) ARC 2007. LNCS, vol. 4419. Springer, Heidelberg (2007). https://doi.org/10.1007/978-3-540-71431-6_7

17. Lopes, A.R., Constantinides, G.A.: A high throughput FPGA-based floating point conjugate gradient implementation. In: Woods, R., Compton, K., Bouganis, C., Diniz, P.C. (eds) ARC 2008. LNCS, vol. 4943. Springer, Heidelberg (2008). https://doi.org/10.1007/978-3-540-78610-8_10

18. Lopes, A.R., Constantinides, G.A.: A high throughput FPGA-based floating point conjugate gradient implementation for dense matrices. ACM Trans. Reconfig. Technol. Syst. **3**(1), Article 1, 19 p. (2010). https://doi.org/10.1145/1661438.1661439

19. Galuzzi, C., Bertels, K.: The instruction-set extension problem: a survey. In: Woods, R., Compton, K., Bouganis, C., Diniz, P.C. (eds.) ARC 2008. LNCS, vol. 4943. Springer, Heidelberg (2008). https://doi.org/10.1007/978-3-540-78610-8_21

20. Galuzzi, C., Bertels, K.: The instruction-set extension problem: a survey. ACM Trans. Reconfig. Technol. Syst. **4**(2), Article 18, 28 p. (2011). https://doi.org/10.1145/1968502.196 8509

21. Hannig, F., Ruckdeschel, H., Dutta, H., Teich, J.: PARO: synthesis of hardware accelerators for multi-dimensional dataflow-intensive applications. In: Woods, R., Compton, K., Bouganis, C., Diniz, P.C. (eds.) ARC 2008. LNCS, vol. 4943. Springer, Heidelberg (2008). https://doi. org/10.1007/978-3-540-78610-8_30

22. Claus, C., Ahmed, R., Altenried, F., Stechele, W.: Towards rapid dynamic partial reconfiguration in video-based driver assistance systems. In: Sirisuk, P., Morgan, F., El-Ghazawi, T., Amano, H. (eds.) ARC 2010. LNCS, vol. 5992. Springer, Heidelberg (2010). https://doi.org/ 10.1007/978-3-642-12133-3_8

23. Boland, D., Constantinides, G.A.: Optimising memory bandwidth use for matrix-vector multiplication in iterative methods. In: Sirisuk, P., Morgan, F., El-Ghazawi, T., Amano, H. (eds.) ARC 2010. LNCS, vol. 5992. Springer, Heidelberg (2010). https://doi.org/10.1007/978-3-642-12133-3_17

24. Boland, D., Constantinides, G.A.: Optimizing memory bandwidth use and performance for matrix-vector multiplication in iterative methods. ACM Trans. Reconfig. Technol. Syst. **4**, 3, Article 22, 14 p. (2011). https://doi.org/10.1145/2000832.2000834

25. Duhem, F., Muller, F., Lorenzini, P.: FaRM: fast reconfiguration manager for reducing reconfiguration time overhead on FPGA. In: Koch, A., Krishnamurthy, R., McAllister, J., Woods, R., El-Ghazawi, T. (eds.) ARC 2011. LNCS, vol. 6578. Springer, Heidelberg (2011). https:// doi.org/10.1007/978-3-642-19475-7_26

26. Duhem, F., Muller, F., Lorenzini, P.: Reconfiguration time overhead on field programmable gate arrays: reduction and cost model. IET Comput. Digit. Tech. **6**(2), 105–113 (2012). https://doi.org/10.1049/iet-cdt.2011.0033

27. Sasdrich, P., Güneysu, T.: Efficient elliptic-curve cryptography using Curve25519 on reconfigurable devices. In: Goehringer, D., Santambrogio, M.D., Cardoso, J.M.P., Bertels, K. (eds.) ARC 2014. LNCS, vol. 8405. Springer, Cham (2014). https://doi.org/10.1007/978-3-319-059 60-0_3

28. Sasdrich, P., Güneysu, T.: Implementing Curve25519 for side-channel--protected elliptic curve cryptography. ACM Trans. Reconfigurable Technol. Syst. **9**(1), Article 3, 15 p. (2015). https://doi.org/10.1145/2700834

29. Takamaeda-Yamazaki, S.: Pyverilog: a Python-based hardware design processing toolkit for Verilog HDL. In: Sano, K., Soudris, D., Hübner, M., Diniz, P. (eds.) ARC 2015. LNCS, vol. 9040. Springer, Cham (2015). https://doi.org/10.1007/978-3-319-16214-0_42

30. Happe, M., Traber, A., Keller, A.: Preemptive hardware multitasking in ReconOS. In: Sano, K., Soudris, D., Hübner, M., Diniz, P. (eds.) ARC 2015. LNCS, vol. 9040. Springer, Cham (2015). https://doi.org/10.1007/978-3-319-16214-0_7

31. Zhao, R., Niu, X., Wu, Y., Luk, W., Liu, Q.: Optimizing CNN-based object detection algorithms on embedded FPGA platforms. In: Wong, S., Beck, A., Bertels, K., Carro, L. (eds.) ARC 2017. LNCS, vol. 10216. Springer, Cham (2017). https://doi.org/10.1007/978-3-319-56258-2_22

32. Rizakis, M., Venieris, S.I., Kouris, A., Bouganis, C.S.: Approximate FPGA-based LSTMs under computation time constraints. In: Voros, N., Huebner, M., Keramidas, G., Goehringer, D., Antonopoulos, C., Diniz, P. (eds.) ARC 2018. LNCS, vol. 10824. Springer, Cham (2018). https://doi.org/10.1007/978-3-319-78890-6_1

33. Kouris, A., Venieris, S.I., Rizakis, M., Bouganis, C.-S.: Approximate LSTMs for time-constrained inference: enabling fast reaction in self-driving cars. IEEE Consum. Electron. Mag. **9**(4), 11–26 (2020). https://doi.org/10.1109/MCE.2020.2969195.

34. Su, J., et al.: Redundancy-reduced MobileNet acceleration on reconfigurable logic for ImageNet classification. In: Voros, N., Huebner, M., Keramidas, G., Goehringer, D., Antonopoulos, C., Diniz, P. (eds.) ARC 2018. LNCS, vol. 10824. Springer, Cham (2018). https://doi.org/10.1007/978-3-319-78890-6_2

35. Korinth, J., Hofmann, J., Heinz, C., Koch, A.: The TaPaSCo open-source toolflow for the automated composition of task-based parallel reconfigurable computing systems. In: Hochberger, C., Nelson, B., Koch, A., Woods, R., Diniz, P. (eds.) ARC 2019. LNCS, vol. 11444. Springer, Cham (2019). https://doi.org/10.1007/978-3-030-17227-5_16

36. Heinz, C., Hofmann, J., Korinth, J., et al.: The TaPaSCo open-source toolflow. J. Sig. Process. Syst. **93**, 545–563 (2021). https://doi.org/10.1007/s11265-021-01640-8

37. Kalms, L., Podlubne, A., Göhringer, D.: HiFlipVX: an open source high-level synthesis FPGA library for image processing. In: Hochberger, C., Nelson, B., Koch, A., Woods, R., Diniz, P. (eds.) ARC 2019. LNCS, vol. 11444. Springer, Cham (2019). https://doi.org/10.1007/978-3-030-17227-5_12

38. Kalms, L., Rad, P.A., Ali, M., et al.: A parametrizable high-level synthesis library for accelerating neural networks on FPGAs. J. Sig. Process. Syst. **93**, 513–529 (2021). https://doi.org/10.1007/s11265-021-01651-5

39. Ferianc, M., Fan, H., Chu, R.S.W., Stano, J., Luk, W.: Improving performance estimation for FPGA-based accelerators for convolutional neural networks. In: Rincón, F., Barba, J., So, H., Diniz, P., Caba, J. (eds.) ARC 2020. LNCS, vol. 12083. Springer, Cham (2020). https://doi.org/10.1007/978-3-030-44534-8_1

40. Ferianc, M., et al.: Improving performance estimation for design space exploration for convolutional neural network accelerators. Electronics **10**, 520 (2021). https://doi.org/10.3390/electronics10040520

41. Yu, Z., Bouganis, C.S.: A parameterisable FPGA-tailored architecture for YOLOv3-tiny. In: Rincón, F., Barba, J., So, H., Diniz, P., Caba, J. (eds.) ARC 2020. LNCS, vol. 12083. Springer, Cham (2020). https://doi.org/10.1007/978-3-030-44534-8_25

42. Ansaloni, G., Scarabottolo, I., Pozzi, L.: Judiciously spreading approximation among arithmetic components with top-down inexact hardware design. In: Rincón, F., Barba, J., So, H., Diniz, P., Caba, J. (eds.) ARC 2020. LNCS, vol. 12083. Springer, Cham (2020). https://doi.org/10.1007/978-3-030-44534-8_2

43. Heinz, C., Koch, A.: Supporting on-chip dynamic parallelism for task-based hardware accelerators. In: Derrien, S., Hannig, F., Diniz, P.C., Chillet, D. (eds.) ARC 2021. LNCS, vol. 12700. Springer, Cham (2021). https://doi.org/10.1007/978-3-030-79025-7_6

44. Heinz, C., Koch, A.: On-chip and distributed dynamic parallelism for task-based hardware accelerators. J. Sig. Process. Syst. (2022). https://doi.org/10.1007/s11265-022-01759-2

45. Pagonis, G., Leon, V., Soudris, D., Lentaris, G.: Increasing the fault tolerance of COTS FPGAs in space: SEU mitigation techniques on MPSoC. In: Palumbo, F., Keramidas, G., Voros, N., Diniz, P.C. (eds.) ARC 2023. LNCS, vol. 14251. Springer, Cham (2023). https://doi.org/10.1007/978-3-031-42921-7_15

46. Plagwitz, P., Hannig, F., Teich, J., Keszocze, O.: SNN vs. CNN implementations on FPGAs: an empirical evaluation. In: Skliarova, I., Brox Jiménez, P., Véstias, M., Diniz, P.C. (eds.) ARC 2024. LNCS, vol. 14553. Springer, Cham (2024). https://doi.org/10.1007/978-3-031-55673-9_1

47. Mpakos, P., et al.: Open-source SpMV multiplication hardware accelerator for FPGA-based HPC systems. In: Skliarova, I., Brox Jiménez, P., Véstias, M., Diniz, P.C. (eds.) ARC 2024. LNCS, vol. 14553. Springer, Cham (2024). https://doi.org/10.1007/978-3-031-55673-9_2

Hardware Acceleration Frontiers

HT-NoC: Reconfigurable High Throughput Network-on-Chip for AI Dataflow Accelerators

Mohamed Amine Zhiri[1,3]([✉]) [iD], Hana Krichene[1] [iD], Chiara Sandionigi[2] [iD], and Sébastien Pillement[3] [iD]

[1] Université Paris-Saclay, CEA, LIST, 91120 Palaiseau, France
{mohamed-amine.zhiri,hana.krichene}@cea.fr
[2] Université Grenoble Alpes, CEA, LIST, 38000 Grenoble, France
chiara.sandionigi@cea.fr
[3] Nantes Université, CNRS, IETR, UMR 6164, 44000 Nantes, France
{mohamed-amine.zhiri,sebastien.pillement}@univ-nantes.fr

Abstract. Fully Connected (FC) layers are a bottleneck for many Deep Neural Networks (DNN) algorithms due to their high bandwidth requirements, which makes their hardware acceleration particularly challenging. In this paper, we address this challenge from a communication-centric approach. We propose HT-NoC (High Throughput Network-on-Chip), a reconfigurable NoC to accelerate FC layers. HT-NoC features reconfigurable router connections that adapt to varying data traffic patterns. This enables the utilization of available unused bandwidth and router resources to transport more packets simultaneously. Compared to a baseline mesh NoC, HT-NoC achieves a 4× reduction in latency and a 2.7× decrease in energy consumption in the propagation of time-consuming FC layer weight parameters. HT-NoC also achieves favorable performance for some Convolution (CONV) layers. When integrated into an AI dataflow accelerator, HT-NoC achieves a 3× speedup in executing Feed Forward Network (FFN) blocks in Transformers, outperforming state-of-the-art (SoA) systolic array (SA) based accelerators.

Keywords: Network-on-Chip · AI accelerators · Fully connected layers · Transformers

1 Introduction

DNNs have shown enormous potential in recent years, with architectures such as Convolutional Neural Networks (CNN) and transformers leading the way in Computer Vision (CV) and Natural Language Processing (NLP). A common layer among those two architectures is the FC layer. Due to their large parameter count, FC layers are bandwidth bound, making efficient communication critical for their acceleration. To accelerate various DNN algorithms, numerous DNN accelerators have been developed. Among these, NoC-based accelerators

[1] have gained considerable attention. NoCs enable efficient communication between multiple processing units, effectively reducing bottlenecks commonly associated with traditional bus-based systems. Furthermore, some accelerators [2–5] have taken the next step by incorporating reconfigurable NoCs. These accelerators offer enhanced flexibility and support multiple dataflows, making them adaptable to a wide range of DNN types. Many DNN accelerators [6] focus on accelerating FC layers by employing compression techniques that exploit sparsity to bypass the computation of zero values. While effective, this approach tackles FC layer acceleration from a purely computational perspective. In this work, we leverage the potential of reconfigurable NoCs to address that problem. We propose HT-NoC, a reconfigurable NoC that dynamically adjusts its throughput to match the bandwidth needs of FC layers. To achieve this, HT-NoC uses a reconfiguration mechanism that revolves around rerouting router ports to fully utilize unused NoC resources -such as channels, buffers, and routing logic blocks-thereby taking profit from available unused bandwidth. HT-NoC achieves a 4× speedup and a 2.7× energy saving factor when propagating FC layer weights compared to a baseline mesh NoC. The significant performance gains relative to the overhead are the results of the efficient utilization of NoC resources. HT-NoC also shows promising results in some CONV layers.

The remainder of the paper is as follows. Section 2 provides the background of this work. Section 3 presents related works. Section 4 describes the architecture of HT-NoC and the reconfiguration mechanism. Section 5 evaluates the performance of HT-NoC, with an analysis of latency and energy consumption. Next, we integrate HT-NoC into an AI dataflow accelerator and compare the performance with SoA solutions. The paper is finally concluded in Sect. 6.

2   Background

In this section, we first define FC layers, as they are the primary focus of this work. Then, we briefly introduce transformers to highlight the specific block we aim to accelerate. Since our reconfiguration mechanism can also be applied to CONV layers, we provide a brief definition of CONV layers as well. Finally, we present some dataflows used in AI accelerators.

2.1   AI Background

An FC layer is a linear transformation applied to an input vector X^{Nin} through a weight matrix $W^{Nout \times Nin}$ to which a bias vector b is added to obtain an output vector Y^{Nout}. Nin refers to the number of input neurons, and $Nout$ is the number of output neurons. The computation of an FC layer is described in Eq. 1:

$$Y^{Nout} = W^{Nout \times Nin} \times X^{Nin} + b \tag{1}$$

FC layers are used in many DNN architectures such as CNNs and transformers. Transformers [7] are a branch of DNNs that have revolutionized the field of NLP. As shown in Fig. 1, a transformer has an encoder and a decoder. An encoder has two sub-layers that are : the multi-head attention and the fully connected FFN. A decoder has additionally the masked multi-head attention as a third sub-layer. The FFN consists of two FC layers, and accounts for the majority of parameters of a transformer model. Therefore, accelerating the FFN is crucial for improving the overall execution speed of transformers.

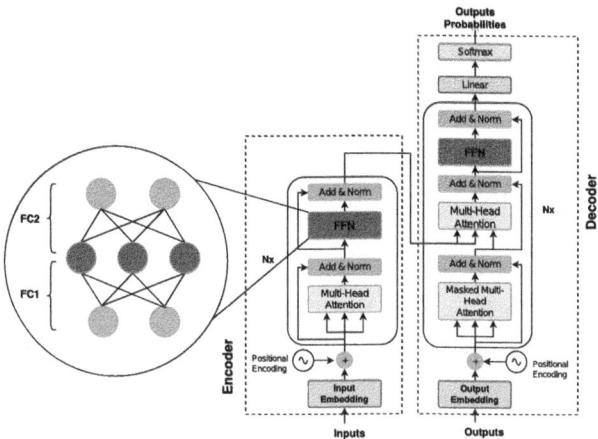

Fig. 1. The Transformer architecture adapted from [7] with an emphasis on the FFN block

CONV layers are used for feature extraction in CNNs. A CONV layer con-volves a striding filter over an input feature map (ifmap) to obtain an output feature map (ofmap) as described in Eq. 2

$$\mathbf{O}[z][u][x][y] = \mathbf{B}[u] + \sum_{k=0}^{M-1}\sum_{i=0}^{H-1}\sum_{j=0}^{C-1}\mathbf{I}[z][k][Sx+i][Sy+j] \times \mathbf{F}[u][k][i][j],$$

$$0 \le z < BS,\ 0 \le u < OC,\ 0 \le x < OW,\ 0 \le y < OH.$$

(2)

In Eq. 2, $\mathbf{O}$, $\mathbf{I}$, $\mathbf{F}$, and $\mathbf{B}$ represent ofmap, ifmap, filter, and bias matrices respec-tively. S is the stride size. M, H, and C are the depth, height and width of the filters respectively. Similarly, OC, OW, and OH correspond to the depth, width, and height of the ofmap respectively. Finally, BS denotes the batch size.

2.2 Dataflows in AI Accelerators

In AI accelerators, dataflow refers to the way data moves and is processed during training or inference. Chen et al. [8] classified dataflows into the following:

- Output Stationary (OS) : A Processing Element (PE) computes a given out-put pixel. Weight and ifmap pixels needed to compute the given output pixel are sent to that PE. The final result of the accumulation is obtained locally at the PE. This minimizes the movement of Partial Sums (psum). This dataflow is used by many accelerators such as ShiDianNao [9].

- Weight Stationary (WS): A given PE fetches a unique weight and keeps it until all operations involving that weight are completed. Ifmaps used to compute psums related to that weight are sent to that PE. This minimizes the movement of weights. This dataflow is used in Google's TPU [10].
- Row Stationary (RS) : In this dataflow, filters are propagated horizontally through the PE 2D-mesh. Ifmaps are sent diagonally. Psums are collected using vertical accumulation. This is the dataflow used in Eyeriss [11].

Figure 2 illustrates an example of executing a 2D convolution using a 3×3 filter on a 5×5 ifmap to produce a 3×3 ofmap over a 3×3 PE grid. Each PE is assumed to consist of a register file (RF) and a multiply-accumulate (MAC) unit. The green, blue, and red arrows represent the flows of ifmaps, filters, and psums, respectively. In Fig. 2a, IP are the pixels of the ifmap and FP are the pixels of the filter. Each pixel of the 9 ofmap pixels (O1 to O9) is obtained in the RF of a given PE. For the WS dataflow, each pixel of the 9 pixel filter (W1 to W9) is stored in a given PE RF. Lastly, in Fig. 2c, FRx, IRx, and ORx refer the pixels of the row x of filter, ifmap, and ofmap respectively. Each ofmap row is obtained in the RF of the PEs of the top.

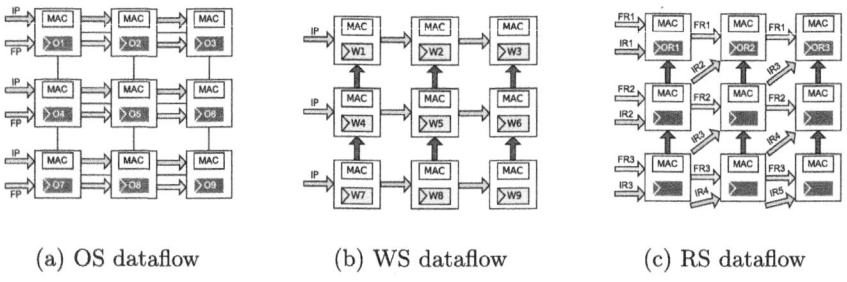

(a) OS dataflow   (b) WS dataflow   (c) RS dataflow

Fig. 2. 5×5 ifmap 3×3 kernel matrix multiplication under 0S, WS, and RS dataflows

3   Related Work

As the communication backbone of modern systems on chip, NoCs should guarantee the desired Quality of Service (QoS) to ensure that performance requirements for different applications are met. In this section, we present different strategies used in NoCs to enhance the QoS, with a particular focus on improving latency and bandwidth.

Duplicating NoC resource techniques are commonly employed to achieve higher throughput. These techniques include widening links [12,13], utilizing multiple planes [14,15], or employing multiple routers, as seen in Eyeriss v2 [2], which assigns a dedicated router to each of ifmaps, weights, and psums. Additionally, increasing the number of buffers in routers, as in Virtual Channels (VC) [16], also falls into this category. Although VCs are among the most efficient and widely used flow control mechanisms to mitigate congestion, the addition of extra pipeline stages in each router increases latency, especially when handling large data burst traffic, as in DNNs. To reduce latency in mesh NoCs, [17–19] propose multi-hop mechanisms to connect non neighboring routers and hence enable long distance communications to be performed in one clock cycle only. Nevertheless, this approach may result in longer critical paths thus reducing the operating frequency, which raises many concerns regarding the scalability of the multihop concept. Finally, improving performance through the duplication of resources is not always feasible, particularly in constrained environments, due to the associated power and area overhead.

In this context, reconfigurable NoCs present a viable solution to these limitations. By reusing existing NoC resources such as links and router's buffers and logic blocks, reconfigurable NoCs can help meeting QoS targets in constrained devices. For instance, link sharing has been investigated in [20] where congestion information is propagated in data links during their idle cycles to congestion aware routers. Additionally, [21–23] propose to enhance performance by using bi-directional channels. Those works however did not investigate buffer reuse potential. In this regard, [24] proposes to use a unified shared buffer among input ports. However, this required a serialization of concurrent entries leading to latency increase. To overcome the serialization overhead, [25] introduces reconfigurable input ports, each with its own buffers, to support buffer sharing between adjacent ports. Buffer sharing is also used by [26] to improve efficiency for 3D-NoC, and in [27] that integrates already present design-for-debug trace buffers into the router architecture to reclaim its storage space for functional purposes. Even though area and power are saved by reusing available hardware resources, the overall performance of this approach can be limited. Optimizing buffers without addressing channel inefficiencies, or vice versa, restricts the overall improvement. Therefore, for optimal results, it is necessary to reuse all available NoC resources, including channels, buffers, and routing logic.

While duplicating resources can improve performance with large overhead, reusing available resources can mitigate area overhead but with limited impact on overall performance. Our solution, however, optimally utilizes available NoC resources, achieving better overall performance with minimal overhead.

4   Architecture and Data Propagation

This section provides an in-depth description of HT-NoC. It begins with a general overview of HT-NoC, followed by a presentation of the architecture of the router and the reconfiguration mechanism. Next, we explain how HT-NoC manages the traffic pattern of FC layers. The section is finally concluded by a similar analysis on CONV layers.

4.1   HT-NoC Architecture

HT-NoC features a 2D-mesh topology and utilizes the XY routing algorithm alongside wormhole flow control, with a channel width of 32 bits. As depicted in Fig. 3, the routers in the westernmost column serve as the entry points to the NoC. Each of these routers has four entry point connections: I_N, I_E, I_S, and I_W. Bottom row routers serve as the exit points. HT-NoC supports unicast, multicast, and broadcast communications. Each router in HT-NoC operates in one of two distinct modes as will be detailed in Sect. 4.2. Communication packets are categorized into three types: configuration packets, control packets, and payload packets. Configuration packets specify the router's operating mode. Control packets indicate the type of communication (unicast, multicast, or broadcast) and the number of payload packets to transfer. Control packets are followed by one or more payload packets, each of which contains only data. In Fig. 4, which depicts the structure of communication packets, the header flit specifies the type of packet and communication. Mode flit of configuration packets defines the desired operating mode. A_D_X and A_D_Y represent the X and Y coordinates of the destination node for unicast communication, while A_S_X and A_S_Y denote the source coordinates in multicast and broadcast communications. NP is the number of payload packets.

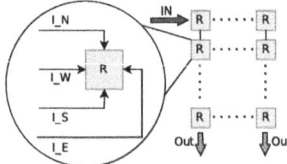

Fig. 3. HT_NoC architecture

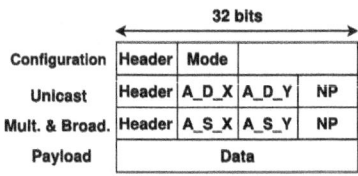

Fig. 4. Communication packets

4.2   Router Architecture

As shown in Fig. 5, each router has five ports : north, south, west, east, and local. Incoming packets are first stored in input FIFOs of their respective entry ports. Afterwards, they are processed at the corresponding Routing Logic Block (RLB) of the entry port that decides the packet destination. Finally, packets are forwarded to the central crossbar and subsequently to the output port. To introduce dynamic flexibility to the NoC, the router operates in one of two modes: Normal mode or HT (High Throughput) mode. Surrounding each router are four HT switches: N_HT, E_HT, S_HT, and W_HT. To operate on a specific mode, a router first receives a configuration packet that specifies the desired mode. After processing the packet, the router sets the Mode Select signal for each switch accordingly, thereby controlling the HT swiches to operate in the selected mode.

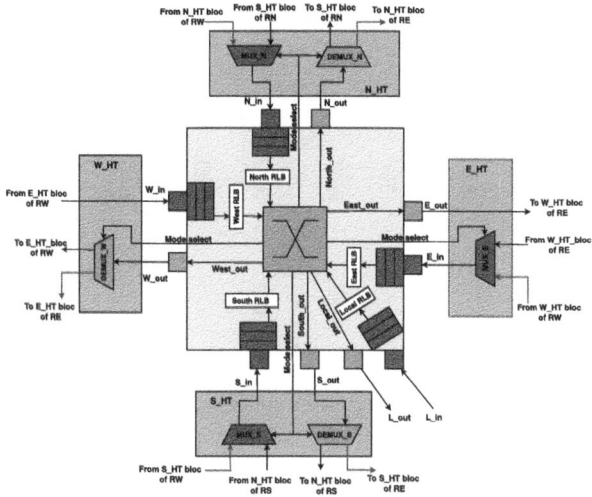

Fig. 5. Router architecture

The Normal Mode serves as the default mode in which each router is directly connected to its four neighboring routers. In this mode, the router's available output bandwidth is evenly distributed across its five output ports. This mode is ideal for applications that require diverse output ports by default. It is also suitable for traffic patterns with modest bandwidth demands, where the limited bandwidth per port is compensated by data reuse. Data reuse refers to scenarios where a single piece of data is utilized by multiple nodes. In such cases, the data is only fetched once from the source node and subsequently propagated to all destination nodes.

The HT Mode is designed for persistent high-bandwidth traffic patterns that maintain a consistent direction, either from west to east, east to west, north to south, or south to north. A prime example of this is the propagation of weights in FC layers. For the remainder of this paper, our study and results will focus on data traffic moving from west to east, as input data is injected into HT-NoC through the westernmost column and transmitted to nodes in the east. However, this technique can also be adapted for other traffic directions. To fully utilize the available bandwidth of each router, unused output ports are reconfigured to transmit data in the same direction (west to east). Consequently, a router in HT Mode can process up to four packets from the same neighboring router simultaneously. This contrasts with Normal Mode, where a router can process only one packet from a given neighboring router at a time. Since the four packets arrive at different input ports, they are handled by four separate input FIFOs and RLBs, thereby maximizing the internal resource utilization of the router.

Figure 6 illustrates the connections of a router. The black arrows indicate the connections used in the Normal mode, where the router R is connected to all its neighboring routers. The blue arrows represent connections in the HT

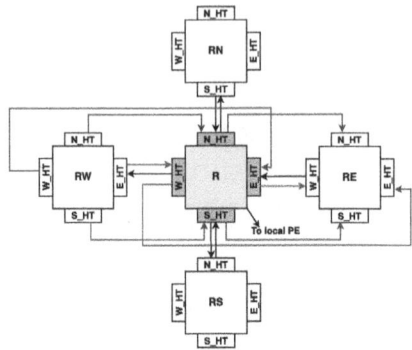

Fig. 6. Router connections

mode, where R is disconnected from its northern RN and southern RS neighbors. Instead, the northern and southern connections of R are rerouted to connect with RW and RE. The red arrows denote the connections used in both modes. For entry-point routers in the farthest western column, in Normal mode, connections I_N, I_E, and I_S are linked to neighboring routers RN, RE, and RS, respectively, while only I_W functions as an entry point to the NoC. In HT mode, however, I_N, I_S, and I_E are disconnected from neighboring routers and instead serve as additional entry points alongside I_W.

4.3   FC Traffic in HT-NoC

FC Layer Mapping. To map a given FC layer onto HT-NoC, we adopt the OS dataflow model [8], where each output neuron is assigned to a specific node. Ifmaps and weights required to compute a given output neuron are first sent to the corresponding node. For a given $X \times Y$ configuration of HT-NoC, the first X output neurons are mapped to the first row. If the number of output neurons exceeds the number of nodes, only the first XY neurons will be mapped concurrently. Neurons ranked higher than XY will have to wait until the initial nodes are freed before being mapped onto the grid. Figure 7a illustrates the mapping of an FC layer with M input neurons and N output neurons onto a $X \times Y$ accelerator. Output neurons and their corresponding nodes are purposely colored with the same color for clarity.

In the first row, the weights for nodes 1, 5, and 9 are injected into HT-NoC through the I_N port of router 1, while the weights for nodes 2, 6, and 10 are injected through the I_E port. The weights for nodes 3, 7, and 11 are injected via the I_S port, and the weights for nodes 4, 8, and 12 are injected through the I_W port. This mechanism enables the injection of weight packets of four consecutive nodes into HT-NoC simultaneously. The same process applies to the remaining rows.

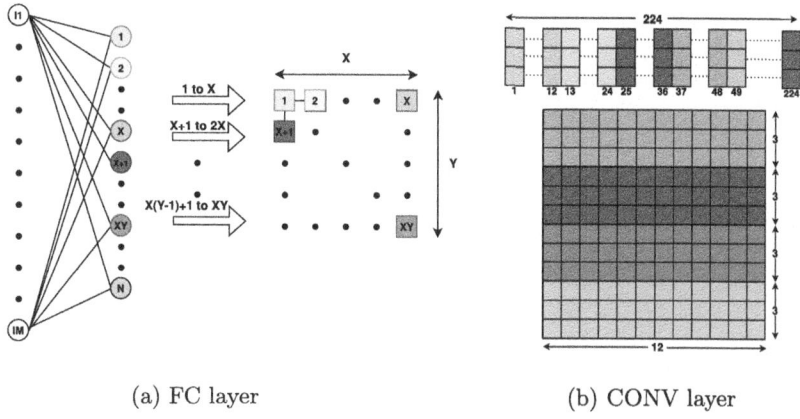

(a) FC layer   (b) CONV layer

Fig. 7. Mapping of FC and CONV layers

Data Propagation Phases. The data propagation phases of FC layers consist of three stages, as shown in Table 1 that are: ifmap propagation, weight propagation, and ofmap collection. In addition to these phases, we can also include the computation phase, even though no communication occurs during computation, as it is not managed by the NoC.

Table 1. Data propagation phases for FC and CONV layers

Phase	FC Layers		CONV Layers	
	Comm. type	Mode	Comm. type	Mode
Ifmap propagation	Broadcast	Normal	Diag. Multicast	HT
Weight propagation	Unicast	HT	Horiz. Multicast	Normal
Computation	No communication		No communication	
Ofmap collection	Unicast	Normal	Unicast	Normal

In the first phase, input neurons are propagated to all nodes of the mesh. All input neurons I1 to IM of Fig. 7a are injected through I_W port. The propagation is characterized by data reuse property. Thus, this first phase is performed in the normal mode. During weight propagation, each node receives the weights needed to compute the corresponding output neuron. In contrast to input neurons, weights are injected from all input ports I_N, I_E, I_S, and I_W of the routers of the westernmost column. Due to the huge traffic load, this phase is performed under the HT mode, since for each row, four packets destined to four different nodes are simultaneously injected to HT-NoC. The ofmap collection is the last phase. Each node of a given column of the accelerator sends its output neuron to the external output port of that column. The ofmap collection is performed using unicasts in the normal mode. Since packets intended for four different nodes in the same row can be transferred simultaneously, we must ensure that four packets are sent to different nodes each time; otherwise, we will not fully utilize the available bandwidth. Therefore, the number of nodes in a row should be a multiple of four, resulting in HT-NoC being configured with 12 columns.

4.4   CONV Traffic in HT-NoC

In this section, we propose to explore the application of the reconfiguration mechanism for CONV layers. To map a given CONV layer, we adopt the RS dataflow model. Virtually, the execution of a 2D-CONV layer in RS fashion, requires a mesh of dimension $O \times K$, K being the number of rows of the filter and O representing the number of columns of the ofmap. However, this virtual configuration does not necessarily correspond to the physical dimension of the mesh. It is then necessary to map this virtual configuration on the physical one. For instance, the first CONV layer of VGG-16 [28] convolves a 3×3 filter over a 224×224 input image to generate a 224×224 ofmap. In this case, the virtual configuration is 224×3. To map this layer onto a physical 12×12 mesh, we cut the virtual configuration into sections of size 12×3. Figure 7b shows that the first yellow section, comprising columns ranked 1 to 12, is mapped to the yellow zone. Following sections are mapped to physical columns of the same color. Once the first 48 columns are processed, the next columns are mapped to the mesh and executed. This process continues until all virtual columns are handled. The data propagation for a CONV layer follows the same phases as those of FC layers, as illustrated in Table 1. Since weights are reused across nodes within the same row, weight propagation occurs in Normal mode. However, because ifmaps are not reused horizontally, HT mode is utilized for their propagation.

In modern CNNs, 3x3 filters are commonly used due to their effectiveness in feature extraction. To enhance data propagation efficiency in HT-NoC, we designed it with a number of rows that is a multiple of 3, hence the choice 12.

5   Experimental Results

5.1   Experimental Setup

In this section, we present the experimental results of HT-NoC. First, we synthesize HT-NoC using the Xilinx Vivado Design Suite (Version 2021.2), targeting the AMD Versal XCVC1902 device [29]. Next, we evaluate the performance of HT-NoC on various FC and CONV layers from SoA DNN models, as summarized in Table 2. Additionally, we analyze the latency and dynamic energy associated with propagating input data (weights and ifmaps) for the benchmarked layers. Results of Sect. 5.2 are obtained after running post-implementation simulation of the RTL model of HT-NoC. In Sect. 5.3, we integrate HT-NoC into the AI dataflow accelerator used in [30], to compute the total execution time of FFN layers. For this purpose, we developed a cycle-accurate simulator for the accelerator, which was validated against its RTL model. The simulator allows us to explore NoC configurations of different sizes and enables a fair comparison with results from Marino et al. [31] and Lu et al. [32]. All results in Sect. 5.3 are generated using this simulator.

Table 2. Layer benchmark

Network	Layer	Input size	Output size
Transformer [7]	FC1	512	2048
	FC2	2048	512
ViT-Base [33]	FC1	768	3078
	FC2	3078	768
DeiT-S [34]	FC1	384	1536
	FC2	1536	384
VGG-16 [28]	CONV 2	$224 \times 224 \times 64$	$224 \times 224 \times 64$
	CONV 3	$112 \times 112 \times 64$	$112 \times 112 \times 128$
	CONV 4	$112 \times 112 \times 128$	$112 \times 112 \times 128$
	CONV 5	$56 \times 56 \times 128$	$56 \times 56 \times 256$
	CONV 6	$56 \times 56 \times 256$	$56 \times 56 \times 256$
	CONV 10	$28 \times 28 \times 512$	$28 \times 28 \times 512$
	CONV 11	$14 \times 14 \times 512$	$14 \times 14 \times 512$
	FC 16	4096	1000

5.2 Hardware Results

Area. We present the FPGA synthesis results for a 12×12 HT-NoC configuration operating at 100 MHz in Table 3. The baseline router, which shares the same functionalities as the HT-NoC router but operates only in normal mode without HT switches, serves as a comparison. The results show that HT-NoC increased LUT usage by 17% and Flip Flops by 4% compared to the baseline, mainly due to the addition of HT switches and the logic required to decode configuration words for mode switching.

Table 3. Hardware resource utilization

	Baseline router	HT router	Baseline NoC (12×12)	HT_NoC (12×12)
CLB LUTs	2064	2137	290810	339549
Flip Flops	1142	1146	158620	164996

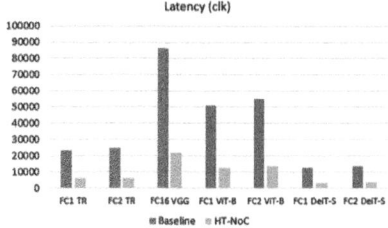

FC latency in clock cycles

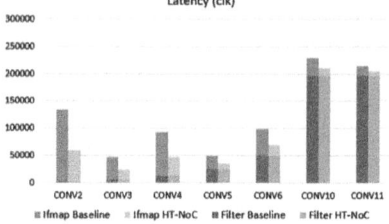

CONV latency in clock cycles

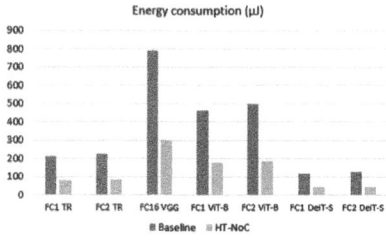

FC dynamic energy in (μJ)

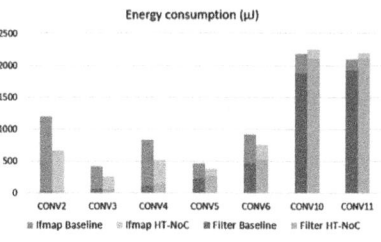

CONV dynamic energy in (μJ)

Fig. 8. Propagation of FC and CONV layers input parameters latency and dynamic energy consumption

FC Results. Figure 8 illustrates input data propagation time and energy consumption for benchmarked FC and CONV layers. FC layers are dominated by weight parameters, which are up to three orders of magnitude larger than input neuron parameters. Therefore, the results in Fig. 8 focus on weight parameters only for input data. Regarding latency, HT-NoC speeds up data propagation by a factor of four for all layers, compared to the baseline NoC. This is due to the utilization of the northern, southern, eastern, and western ports for communication. Energy-wise, HT-NoC achieves an average reduction of 2.7$\times$ for each FC layer.

CONV Results. For each CONV layer, we expose latency of ifmap and filter propagation for both the baseline NoC and HT-NoC. Blue and orange bars represent filter propagation metrics for the baseline NoC and HT-NoC respectively, whereas grey and yellow bars represent ifmap results of the baseline NoC and HT-NoC respectively. For all CONV layers, filter propagation has the same latency in both NoCs, since HT-NoC does not accelerate the filter data sending. However, the energy consumption for filter propagation was slightly increased for HT-NoC which is attributed to the reconfiguration mechanism. For ifmaps, HT-NoC achieves a 2.35$\times$ acceleration and an average energy saving factor of 2 compared to the baseline NoC.

Unlike FC layers, the performance of HT-NoC for CONV layers depends widely on the data size in each layer. For instance, latency reductions reach up to 55% for CONV2, 30% for CONV5 and CONV6, and as low as 5% for CONV11. Energy reduction ratios vary from 45% for CONV2, 18% for CONV5 and CONV6, to a slight 5% increase for CONV11. This variability is due to the different sizes of the ifmaps and filters in each layer. In earlier layers, ifmaps are substantially larger than filters. For example, CONV2 which shows the greatest acceleration and energy reduction, has a large ifmap of 1,225,824 pixels compared to a much smaller filter of 36,864 pixels. In contrast, CONV11 has a much larger filter size of 2,359,296 pixels applied to a smaller ifmap of 100,352 pixels. These pixel counts reflect the total number of pixels across all channels for both filters and ifmaps in each layer. Therefore, the performance of HT-NoC in CONV layers is influenced by the size of the ifmap relative to the filter. Optimal results are obtained when the ifmap is considerably larger than the filter.

5.3   Integration Into an AI Accelerator

Accelerator Architecture. In this work, we have integrated HT-NoC into AI dataflow accelerator used in [30] as shown in Fig. 9. The architecture consists of an $X \times Y$ grid of neural compute nodes, interconnected via HT-NoC and surrounded by a set of distributed input and output memories. The accelerator includes a global controller responsible for managing the various phases of DNN execution. Input Buffers (IBs) store HT-NoC configuration packets, weights and ifmaps of the neural network layer to execute. Output Buffers (OB) store the ofmap of the executed layer. To take full profit of high throughput capabilities of HT-NoC, each entry point router of the westernmost column is connected to four IBs that are: IB_N, IB_E, IB_W, and IB_S. Each node consists of a router connected to a PE and a local memory. A PE operates on 8-bits data. It can perform 3 simultaneous multiplications per cycle. After all multiplications are completed, the resulting partial sums are accumulated one-by-one over successive clock cycles. As such, computing the scalar product of two vectors of size N takes $\lceil N/3 \rceil + N$ clock cycles. Consequently, the PE achieves a MAC throughput of 0.75 MACs per cycle.

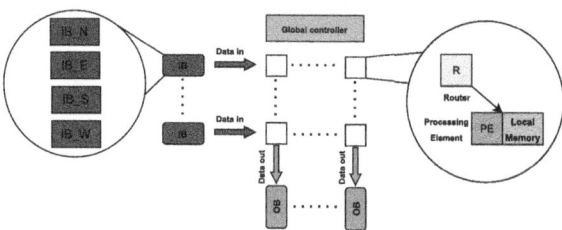

Fig. 9. Architecture of the accelerator

Execution Time Breakdown. In this section, we propose to analyze the execution time of the DeiT-S [34] FFN block over two configurations of the accelerator, with 16×16 and 64×64 sizes, using baseline mesh NoC and HT-NoC. The execution phases of DNN layers are as follows: weight propagation, ifmap propagation, computation, and ofmap collection. Note that, for simplicity, we did not include the configuration phases managed by the global controller because the transmission of configuration packets is negligible compared to other execution phases.

Figure 10 shows the execution time by phase. In both configurations, the use of HT-NoC has induced an acceleration of the weight propagation phase by a $4\times$ factor. The execution time of other phases remained the same with both the baseline NoC and HT-NoC. We can notice that, for all configurations, the ifmap propagation and ofmap collection phases have little impact on the total execution time. This can be explained by the fact that weights are larger than ifmaps and ofmaps in FC layers. Regarding the execution with the 16×16 configuration, the weight contribution shrank from 73% using the baseline NoC to only 41% when using HT-NoC. The computation phase rose from 24% to 54%, thus becoming the most time-consuming phase in the HT-NoC-based accelerator. Overall, HT-NoC accelerated the execution of the FNN block by a $2.22\times$ factor. In larger configurations, like 64×64, more output neurons can be mapped and computed simultaneously. Hence, the computation time becomes less impactful compared to the first configuration, moving from 7% with the baseline NoC to 23% using HT-NoC. The execution is dominated by the weight propagation phase, which accounts for 90% with the baseline NoC and 71% with HT-NoC. This weight predominance induced a greater acceleration factor of 3.1x.

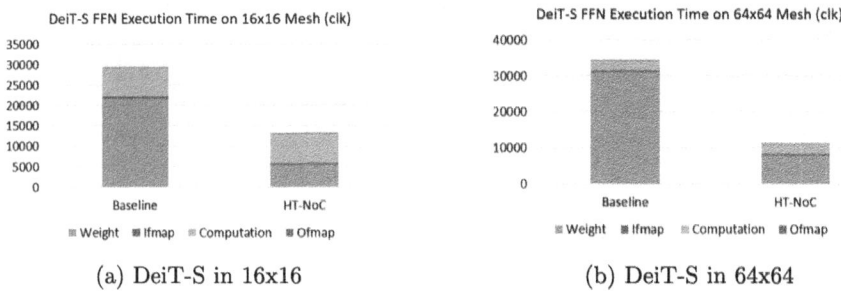

(a) DeiT-S in 16x16   (b) DeiT-S in 64x64

Fig. 10. Execution time breakdown of FFN layers of DeiT-S on 16x16 and 64x64 configurations of the accelerator

Comparison with the SoA Results. In this section, we compare the execution time of FFN layers from DeiT-S [34] and the original Transformer [7] models on the accelerator simulated using our custom cycle-accurate simulator, with the performance of Me-ViT [31] and the Transformer accelerator [32]. Both

Me-ViT and the Transformer accelerator are FPGA-based solutions designed for transformer models, built on a SA architecture that utilizes direct communication between PEs and operates on 8-bit data. These accelerators do not rely on a NoC for communication. Me-ViT uses a 32 × 32 SA, while the Transformer accelerator employs a larger 64 × 64 SA. To ensure a fair comparison, we use a 32 × 32 configuration of the simulated accelerator when comparing with Me-ViT and a 64 × 64 configuration when comparing with the Transformer accelerator.

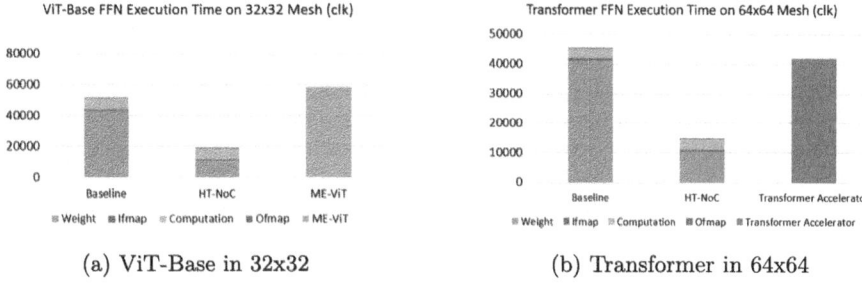

(a) ViT-Base in 32x32   (b) Transformer in 64x64

Fig. 11. Execution time breakdown of FFN layers of Vit-Base, transformer over different configurations of the accelerator

In Fig. 11, the execution time of both Me-ViT and the Transformer accelerator, represented by the gray bars, are directly taken from their respective papers. However, the execution phase details are not provided in these papers. For both the ViT-Base and Transformer models, we observe that the accelerator with the baseline NoC performs comparably to Me-ViT and the Transformer accelerator. This similarity can be explained by the fact that the baseline mesh NoC operates like a SA, where data is forwarded from one compute node to another through fixed-bandwidth connections.

By using HT-NoC, we achieve acceleration factors of 2.7× and 3× compared to the 32 × 32 baseline accelerator and Me-ViT, respectively, when executing the FFN block of the ViT-Base model. Furthermore, HT-NoC delivers a speedup of 3.1× and 2.8× over the 64 × 64 baseline accelerator and the Transformer accelerator, respectively, when executing the FFN block of the original Transformer model. This speedup is attributed to the use of reconfigurable-throughput connections.

6 Conclusion

In this paper, we presented HT-NoC, a reconfigurable NoC that adjusts its throughput to accelerate the execution of FC layers. Depending on the traffic, HT-NoC can switch between Normal and HT modes by reconfiguring connections between neighboring routers to leverage unused bandwidth. This maximizes NoC resource utilization, achieving a 4× speedup and a 2.7× reduction in energy consumption when transmitting weights of FC layers. HT-NoC was also evaluated for CONV layers, showing promising results, especially in layers where ifmaps are significantly larger than filters. For example, in the CONV2 layer of VGG-16, HT-NoC reduced latency and energy consumption by 55% and 45%, respectively. Lastly, we integrated HT-NoC into an AI dataflow accelerator and showed that HT-NoC can accelerate the execution time of FNN blocks of transformers by a 3× factor, thus yielding favorable results compared to SoA SA-based solutions.

References

1. Chen, K.-C.(J.), Ebrahimi, M., Wang, T.-Y., Yang, Y.-C.: NoC-based DNN accelerator: a future design paradigm. In: Proceedings of the 13th IEEE/ACM International Symposium on Networks-on-Chip, New York, NY, USA, articleno, vol. 11, pp. 1–8 (2019). https://doi.org/10.1145/3313231.3352376
2. Chen, Y.-H., Yang, T.-J., Emer, J., Sze, V.: Eyeriss v2: a flexible accelerator for emerging deep neural networks on mobile devices. IEEE J. Emerg. Sel. Top. Circ. Syst. **9**(2), 292–308 (2019). https://doi.org/10.1109/JETCAS.2019.2910232
3. Kwon, H., Samajdar, A., Krishna, T.: MAERI: enabling flexible dataflow mapping over DNN accelerators via reconfigurable interconnects. In: Proceedings of the Twenty-Third International Conference on Architectural Support for Programming Languages and Operating Systems, Williamsburg, VA, USA, pp. 461–475 (2018). https://doi.org/10.1145/3173162.3173176
4. Tong, J., Itagi, A., Chatarasi, P., Krishna, T.: FEATHER: a reconfigurable accelerator with data reordering support for low-cost on-chip dataflow switching. In: 2024 ACM/IEEE 51st Annual International Symposium on Computer Architecture (ISCA), New York, NY, USA, pp. 198–214 (2024). https://doi.org/10.1109/ISCA59077.2024.00024
5. Muñoz-Martínez, F., Garg, R., Pellauer, M., Abellán, J.L., Acacio, M.E, Krishna, T.: Flexagon: a multi-dataflow sparse-sparse matrix multiplication accelerator for efficient DNN processing. In: Proceedings of the 28th ACM International Conference on Architectural Support for Programming Languages and Operating Systems, vol. 3, Vancouver, BC, Canada, pp. 252–265 (2023). https://doi.org/10.1145/3582016.3582069
6. Han, S., et al.: EIE: efficient inference engine on compressed deep neural network. In: 2016 ACM/IEEE 43rd Annual International Symposium on Computer Architecture (ISCA), pp. 243–254 (2016). https://doi.org/10.1109/ISCA.2016.30
7. Vaswani, A., et al.: Attention is all you need. In: Advances in Neural Information Processing Systems, vol. 30 (2017). https://proceedings.neurips.cc/paper_files/paper/2017/file/3f5ee243547dee91fbd053c1c4a845aa-Paper.pdf
8. Chen, Y.-H., Emer, J. S., Sze, V.: Eyeriss: a spatial architecture for energy-efficient dataflow for convolutional neural networks. In: 2016 ACM/IEEE 43rd Annual International Symposium on Computer Architecture (ISCA), pp. 367–379 (2016). https://doi.org/10.1109/ISCA.2016.40
9. Du, Z., et al.: ShiDianNao: shifting vision processing closer to the sensor. In: 2015 ACM/IEEE 42nd Annual International Symposium on Computer Architecture (ISCA), pp. 92–104 (2015). https://doi.org/10.1145/2749469.2750389
10. Jouppi, N.P., et al.: In-datacenter performance analysis of a tensor processing unit. SIGARCH Comput. Archit. News **45**(2), 1–12 (2017). https://doi.org/10.1145/3140659.3080246

11. Chen, Y.-H., Krishna, T., Emer, J.S., Sze, V.: Eyeriss: an energy-efficient reconfigurable accelerator for deep convolutional neural networks. IEEE J. Solid-State Circ. **52**(1), 127–138 (2017). https://doi.org/10.1109/JSSC.2016.2616357
12. Petrisko, D., et al.: NoC symbiosis (Special Session Paper). In: 2020 14th IEEE/ACM International Symposium on Networks-on-Chip (NOCS), pp. 1–8 (2020). https://doi.org/10.1109/NOCS50636.2020.9241584
13. Fischer, T., Rogenmoser, M., Cavalcante, M., Gürkaynak, F.K., Benini, L.: FlooNoC: a multi-tb/s wide NoC for heterogeneous AXI4 traffic. IEEE Des. Test **40**(6), 7–17 (2023). https://doi.org/10.1109/MDAT.2023.3306720
14. Giri, D., Mantovani, P., Carloni, L.P.: NoC-based support of heterogeneous cache-coherence models for accelerators. In: 2018 Twelfth IEEE/ACM International Symposium on Networks-on-Chip (NOCS), pp. 1–8 (2018). https://doi.org/10.1109/NOCS.2018.8512153
15. Wang, L., Wang, Y., Wang, X.: An approximate multiplane network-on-chip. In: 2020 Design, Automation & Test in Europe Conference & Exhibition (DATE), pp. 234–239 (2020). https://doi.org/10.23919/DATE48585.2020.9116377
16. Dally, W.J.: Virtual-channel flow control. IEEE Trans. Parall. Distrib. Syst. **3**(2), 194–205 (1992). https://doi.org/10.1109/71.127260
17. Monemi, A., Pérez, I., Leyva, N., Vallejo, E., Beivide, R., Moretó, M.: PlugSMART: a pluggable open-source module to implement multihop bypass in networks-on-chip. In: Proceedings of the 15th IEEE/ACM International Symposium on Networks-on-Chip, pp. 41–48 (2021). https://doi.org/10.1145/3479876.3481601
18. Kwon, H., Krishna, T.: OpenSMART: single-cycle multi-hop NoC generator in BSV and Chisel. In: 2017 IEEE International Symposium on Performance Analysis of Systems and Software (ISPASS), pp. 195–204 (2017). https://doi.org/10.1109/ISPASS.2017.7975291
19. Ou, Y., Agwa, S., Batten, C.: Implementing low-diameter on-chip networks for manycore processors using a tiled physical design methodology. In: 2020 14th IEEE/ACM International Symposium on Networks-on-Chip (NOCS), pp. 1–8 (2020). https://doi.org/10.1109/NOCS50636.2020.9241710
20. Chen, C., Li, Q., Li, N., Liu, H., Dai, Y.: Link-sharing: regional congestion aware routing in 2D NoC by propagating congestion information on idle links. In: 2018 IEEE 3rd International Conference on Integrated Circuits and Microsystems (ICICM), pp. 291–297 (2018). https://doi.org/10.1109/ICAM.2018.8596400
21. Lan, Y.-C., Lo, S.-H., Lin, Y.-C., Hu, Y.-H., Chen, S.-J.: BiNoC: a bidirectional NoC architecture with dynamic self-reconfigurable channel. In: 2009 3rd ACM/IEEE International Symposium on Networks-on-Chip, pp. 266–275 (2009). https://doi.org/10.1109/NOCS.2009.5071476
22. Qian, Z., Abbas, S.M., Tsui, C.-Y.: FSNoC: a flit-level speedup scheme for network on-chips using self-reconfigurable bidirectional channels. IEEE Trans. Very Large Scale Integr. (VLSI) Syst. **23**(9), 1854–1867 (2015). https://doi.org/10.1109/TVLSI.2014.2351833
23. Tsai, W.C., Lin, H.E., Lan, Y.C., Chen, S.J.: Anticipative QoS control: a self-reconfigurable on-chip communication. Micromachines **13**(10), 1669 (2022). https://doi.org/10.3390/mi13101669
24. Farrokhbakht, H., Kao, H., Jerger, N.E.: UBERNoC: unified buffer power-efficient router for network-on-chip. In: Proceedings of the 13th IEEE/ACM International Symposium on Networks-on-Chip, article no. 1, pp. 1–8 (2019). https://doi.org/10.1145/3313231.3352362

25. Sun, C., Ouyang, Y., Liang, H.: Traffic-oriented reconfigurable NoC with augmented inter-port buffer sharing. Front. Inf. Technol. Electron. Eng. (2024). https://doi.org/10.1631/FITEE.2300458

26. Said, M., Sarihi, A., Patooghy, A., El-Mohandes, A.M., Badawy, A.-H.A., Gebali, F.: Novel flexible buffering architectures for 3D-NoCs. Sustain. Comput. Inf. Syst. **29**, 100472 (2021). https://doi.org/10.1016/j.suscom.2020.100472

27. Jindal, N., Gupta, S., Ravipati, D.P., Panda, P.R., Sarangi, S.R.: Enhancing network-on-chip performance by reusing trace buffers. IEEE Trans. Comput.-Aided Des. Integr. Circ. Syst. **39**(4), 922–935 (2020). https://doi.org/10.1109/TCAD.2019.2907909

28. Simonyan, K., Zisserman, A.: Very deep convolutional networks for large-scale image recognition. arXiv preprint arXiv:1409.1556 (2014)

29. Versal AI Core Series. https://www.amd.com/en/products/adaptive-socs-and-fpgas/versal/ai-core-series.html Accessed 23 Dec 2024

30. Krichene, H., Prasad, R., Mouhagir, A.: AINoC: new interconnect for future deep neural network accelerators. In: Chavarrías, M., Rodríguez, A. (eds.) Design and Architecture for Signal and Image Processing. DASIP 2023. Lecture Notes in Computer Science, vol. 13879. Springer, Cham (2023). https://doi.org/10.1007/978-3-031-29970-4_5

31. Marino, K., Zhang, P., Prasanna, V.K.: ME-ViT: a single-load memory-efficient FPGA accelerator for vision transformers. In: 2023 IEEE 30th International Conference on High Performance Computing, Data, and Analytics (HiPC), pp. 213–223 (2023). https://doi.org/10.1109/HiPC58850.2023.00039

32. Lu, S., Wang, M., Liang, S., Lin, J., Wang, Z.: Hardware accelerator for multi-head attention and position-wise feed-forward in the transformer. In: 2020 IEEE 33rd International System-on-Chip Conference (SOCC), pp. 84–89 (2020). https://doi.org/10.1109/SOCC49529.2020.9524802

33. Dosovitskiy, A., et al.: An Image is worth 16x16 words: transformers for image recognition at scale. In: 9th International Conference on Learning Representations, ICLR 2021, Virtual Event, Austria, 3–7 May 2021, OpenReview.net (2021) https://openreview.net/forum?id=YicbFdNTTy

34. Touvron, H., et al.: Training data-efficient image transformers & distillation through attention. In: Proceedings of the 38th International Conference on Machine Learning, edited by Meila, Marina and Zhang, Tong, volume 139 of Proceedings of Machine Learning Research, PMLR, pp. 10347–10357 (2021). https://proceedings.mlr.press/v139/touvron21a.html

An MLIR-Based Compilation Framework for CGRA Application Deployment

Yuxuan Wang[1]([✉]), Cristian Tirelli[2], Lara Orlandic[1], Juan Sapriza[1],
Rubén Rodríguez Álvarez[1], Giovanni Ansaloni[1], Laura Pozzi[2],
and David Atienza[1]

[1] EPFL, Lausanne, Switzerland
`yuxuan.wang@epfl.ch`
[2] Università della Svizzera italiana, Lugano, Switzerland

Abstract. Coarse-Grained Reconfigurable Arrays (CGRAs) are a programmable architectural solution that efficiently supports the execution of computation-intensive application functions (kernels). Compilers for CGRAs typically focus on optimizing the mapping of single loops, whose body can be expressed in a basic block produced by a compiler front-end. This approach, while effective in leveraging spatial parallelism within data flows, restricts the scope of deployment and neglects opportunities stemming from control flow analysis.

To enhance the code coverage of CGRA compilers, the end-to-end compilation framework presented in this paper operates at the kernel level, considering both Data Flow Graph (DFG)-based and Control Flow Graph (CFG)-based optimizations. Its implementation, based on the MLIR infrastructure, includes a front-end for Intermediate Representation (IR) abstraction, an optional middle-end reshaping the IR to facilitate modulo scheduling, a kernel mapper for operation allocation that supports both DFG and CFG mapping optimizations, and a backend that performs register allocation and generates assembly with the mapped solution. The entire framework pipeline is fully automated and is released as open-source software (Code available at https://github.com/esl-epfl/Compigra.git).

1 Introduction

Coarse-Grained Reconfigurable Arrays (CGRAs) offer a trade-off between energy efficiency and versatility by connecting several programmable Processing Elements (PEs) in a mesh topology to obtain computational parallelism at a low hardware cost [1]. Time-multiplexed CGRAs provide high hardware flexibility by allowing their PEs to perform different operations in each clock cycle but require substantial effort to deploy applications, as operations must be mapped both in the space and time dimensions [2,3].

Most existing works aim to map data flow graphs (DFGs) extracted from compute-intensive functions onto PEs. To this end, a common approach is modulo scheduling (MS) [4,5]. This technique aims to overlap loop iterations, thereby

© The Author(s), under exclusive license to Springer Nature Switzerland AG 2025
R. Giorgi et al. (Eds.): ARC 2025, LNCS 15594, pp. 33–50, 2025.
https://doi.org/10.1007/978-3-031-87995-1_3

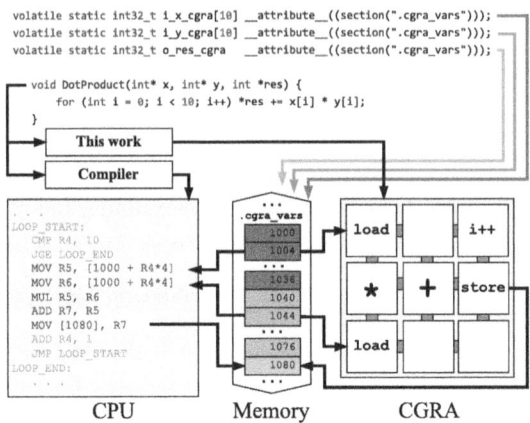

Fig. 1. Overview of the proposed framework. On a microcontroller environment, a general-purpose compiler (e.g., gcc) translates C-code for the system's CPU, while our work compiles the accelerated kernels for the CGRA. The CPU and CGRA can access the same variables placed on a pre-defined memory region.

minimizing the initiation intervals (II) - the time gap between the start of consecutive loop iterations [6]. A modulo-scheduled loop is divided into three stages: a prologue for data preparation, a steady state that overlaps iterations, and an epilogue for finalization. Although DFG-based mapping strategies effectively leverage loop-level parallelism [7], they do not fully automate the function kernel deployment, including instructions outside loops, which hinders their usability.

These shortcomings can be attributed to the lack of support for control-flow graph (CFG) mapping. Although most CGRA instruction set architectures (ISAs) support simple branch operations utilized for loop control in DFG mapping [8,9], compilers do not exploit their full potential for control flow management. Approaches that consider CFG mapping [10,11] often rely on additional hardware components to handle basic block branching, which is not general enough to be applicable across all CGRA architectures.

In contrast, here we present an open-source and end-to-end compilation framework that automatically processes the C code to generate a configuration bitstream, i.e. a binary representation of the CGRA assembly, mapped on hardware resources. Considering a system that contains shared memory between the host and the CGRA, we reserve an exclusive memory region for users to declare the data exchange, as shown in Fig. 1. Our framework, based on MLIR [12], directly supports the abstraction of DFG and CFG at the intermediate representation (IR) level. This approach facilitates front-end optimizations, such as converting operations to CGRA ISAs and automating memory access, as well as middle-end transformations to support modulo scheduling. Our mapper leverages DFG and CFG management to enable full function kernel mapping, with the back-end generating assembly code for hardware execution. By integrating

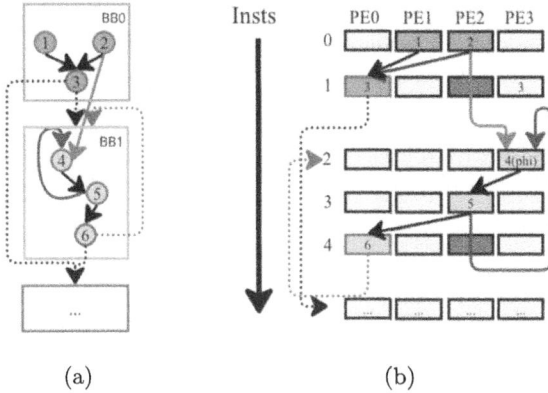

(a)   (b)

Fig. 2. a) Graph representation of a computational kernel, highlighting the DFG and CFG. The phi node (Op4) selects a value produced by the predecessor BBs. b) A valid mapping on a time-multiplexed 2×2 CGRA, with PEs unfolded in the horizontal dimension and different instruction executing on each row. (Color figure online)

front-, middle- and back-end components, we aim to bridge the usability gap in deploying CGRAs as accelerators in embedded systems.

2   Related Work

2.1   Compilation

MLIR (Multi-Level Intermediate Representation) is a compilation infrastructure built on top of LLVM, designed to represent and transform IR with customized needs. As a sub-project of LLVM, it ensures compatibility with the LLVM front end. MLIR supports dialects (including LLVM itself), allowing developers to define domain-specific operations, types, and attributes. Our framework indeed embeds a custom dialect for abstract operations and basic blocks within the IR.

Figure 2a presents a graph representation of an idealized kernel at the IR level, where the DFG consists of IR operations (circles) and their dependencies (solid edges), while the CFG is represented by control-free code sections (basic blocks, enclosed in rectangles) and control paths among them (plotted as dashed edges). The compilation aims to find a feasible mapping solution to the PEs that make up a CGRA, given the constraints of the DFG and CFG, as shown in Fig. 2. The example shows a mapping solution for 2×2 grid-connected CGRAs, whose elements are unrolled on each row, while the instruction flow is depicted in the vertical dimension. Control operation may cause branches to out-of-sequence instructions.

In DFGs, nodes connected by a directed edge are referred to as the producer (source node) and consumer (destination node). Consumers rely on the results of their producers for computation or control operations. In contrast, in CFGs, nodes connected via a directed edge are called predecessors and successors. A basic block is executed when its predecessor branches to it through the control flow. In the case of loops, a basic block branches to itself if the loop condition is satisfied (as in the red dashed line in Fig. 2a).

Table 1. Comparison with state-of-the-art CGRA mapping methods.

Features		AA-ILP[13]	SAT-MapIt[14]	E2EMap[15]	4D-CGRA[10]	RipTide[11]	Ours
Memory interface	Memory interface config	✗	✗	✗	✓	✓	✓
	Automate data mapping	✗	✗	✗	✓	✓	✓
Front end	ISA support	✗	✗	✗	✗	✗	✓
	Imm refactoring	✗	✗	✗	✗	✗	✓
DFG mapping	DFG generation	✓	✓	✓	✓	✓	✓
	loop level parallelism	✓	✓	✓	✓	✓	✓
CFG mapping	CFG generation	✗	✗	✗	✓	✓	✓
	No extra hardware	-	-	-	✗	✗	✓

2.2 CGRA Mappers

In CGRA compilation, the mapper's task is to assign each instruction to the appropriate time step and PE, taking into account the topology of the target architecture Table 1 lists the various features supported by state-of-the-art (SoA) mappers. Mapping frameworks such as AA-ILP [13], SAT-MapIt [14], and E2EMap [15] all perform DFG-based modulo scheduling to reduce II and improve runtime efficiency. However, in these works, data transfer operations are not automated, and the DFG mappers can process only one basic block, as they do not support CFG generation, thus limiting CGRA code coverage.

Among the few works that address these shortcomings, 4D-CGRA [10] and RipTide [11] provide strategies to manage the memory interface and CFG generation, but both require extra hardware dedicated to control operations. Moreover, their mapping strategies are tailored to specific architectures by mandating hardware controllers, resulting in larger II than DFG mappers. Finally, in contrast to our proposed work in this paper, they do not support CGRA-specific ISAs and immediate field refactoring.

3 Motivation

Most existing works focus on efficiency optimization while neglecting the usability of end-to-end automated compilation. Figure 3 shows the C source code and IR of benchmarks GSM. The MS mappers working on the highlighted blue area of the LLVM IR (as shown in the Fig. 3b) face two primary challenges in automation: IR incompatibility and limited compilation scope.

(a) C source code

```
# define GSM_ABS(a) ((a) < 0 ? ((a) ==
MIN_WORD ? MAX_WORD : -(a)) : (a))
#define MIN_WORD ((-32767)-1)
#define MAX_WORD ( 32767)

int GSM(int *dmax_ptr, int *d){

int dmax = *dmax_ptr;
int temp = 0;

for (int k = 0; k <= 39; k++) {
  temp = d[k];
  temp = GSM_ABS( temp );
  if (temp > dmax) dmax = temp;
}

*dmax_ptr = dmax;

return 0;
}
```

(b) LLVM IR

```
define dso_local i32 @GSM(i32* ) {
%3 = load i32, i32* %0, align 4, !tbaa !4
br label %5

4:                          ; preds = %5
store i32 %16, i32* %0, align 4, !tbaa !4
ret i32 0

5:                          ; preds = %2, %5
%6 = phi i32 [ 0, %2 ], [ %17, %5 ]
%7 = phi i32 [ %3, %2 ], [ %16, %5 ]
%8 = getelementptr inbounds i32, i32* %1,
i32 %6
%9 = load i32, i32* %8, align 4, !tbaa !4
%10 = icmp slt i32 %9, 0
%11 = icmp eq i32 %9, -32768
%12 = sub nsw i32 0, %9
%13 = select i1 %11, i32 32767, i32 %12
%14 = select i1 %10, i32 %13, i32 %9
%15 = icmp sgt i32 %14, %7
%16 = select i1 %15, i32 %14, i32 %7
%17 = add nuw nsw i32 %6, 1
%18 = icmp eq i32 %17, 40
br i1 %18, label %4, label %5, !llvm.loop !8
}
```

(c) MLIR with customized cgra dialect

```
cgra.func @GSM{
  %0 = llvm.add 12, 0 : i32
  %1 = llvm.shl %0, 12 : i32
  %2 = llvm.add %1, 2048 {constant = 51200 : i32} : i32
  %3 = llvm.add %5, %6 : i32
  %4 = llvm.shl 12, 0 : i32
  %5 = llvm.add %4, %32 {constant = 51204 : i32} : i32
  %6 = llvm.add 2052, 0 : i32
  %7 = llvm.shl %6, 12 : i32
  %8 = llvm.add %7, 0 : i32
  %9 = llvm.add -1, 0 : i32
  %10 = llvm.shl %9, 24 : i32
  %11 = llvm.add %8, %10 {constant = -32768 : i32} : i32
  %12 = llvm.add 7, 0 : i32
  %13 = llvm.shl %12, 12 : i32
  %14 = llvm.add 4095, %13 {constant = 32767 : i32} :
i32
  %15 = lwi %2 : i32->i32
  %16 = llvm.add 0, 0 {constant = 0 : i32} : i32
  %17 = llvm.add 0, 40 {constant = 40 : i32} : i32
  llvm.br ^bb1(%16, %15 : i32, i32)
^bb1(%18: i32, %19: i32): // 2 preds: ^bb0, ^bb1
  %20 = llvm.mul %18, 4 : i32
  %21 = llvm.add %5, %20 : i32
  %22 = cgra.lwi %21 : i32->i32
  %23 = llvm.sub %22, 0 : i32
  %24 = llvm.sub %22, %11 : i32
  %25 = llvm.sub 0, %22 : i32
  %26 = cgra.bzfa %24 : i32 [%14, %25] : i32
  %27 = cgra.bsfa %23 : i32 [%26, %22] : i32
  %28 = llvm.sub %19, %27 : i32
  %29 = cgra.bsfa %28 : i32 [%27, %19] : i32
  %30 = llvm.add %18, 1 : i32
  cgra.cond_br<ne> [%30 : i32, %17 : i32], ^bb1(%30,
%29 : i32, i32), ^bb2
^bb2: // pred: ^bb1
  llvm.br ^bb3
^bb3: // pred: ^bb2
  %31 = llvm.add 12, 0 : i32
  %32 = llvm.shl %31, 12 : i32
  %33 = llvm.add 2048, %32 {constant = 51200 : i32} :
i32
  swi %29, %33 : i32, i32
  llvm.return
}
```

Fig. 3. C source code and IR of GSM: the original IR is produced by LLVM and adapted hardware compatible IR by MLIR.

ISA discrepancy and hardware constraints require the additional IR transformation for the benchmarks to be deployed onto CGRAs. Decoupling the IR transformation and the operation mapping is critical because the IR for the mapper should satisfy an important prerequisite before mapping: *all operations are executable on hardware*. LLVM's designed for various architectures with target-independent IR often fail to meet this prerequisite directly. In contrast, MLIR's customized dialects enable vendor-defined operations and provide direct IR-level

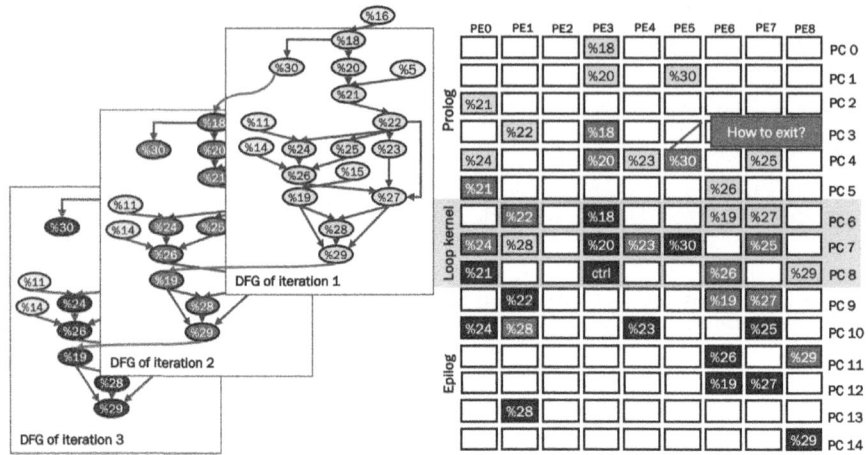

Fig. 4. Mapping result from modulo scheduling for the highlighted block in Fig. 3. (Color figure online)

abstraction. This allows advanced features like type and dominance checking, minimizing illegal middle-end transformations.

Figure 3 motivates our use of MLIR, showing (a) a snippet of C code, (b) the corresponding LLVM code, and (c) the generated MLIR code in a dialect supporting OpenEdgeCGRA ISA [8] that we adopt as an architectural target in this work. Details on the conversion between LLVM and the CGRA dialect are provided in Sect. 4.1. Figure 4.1 also shows the limitations of state-of-the-art DFG-based MS mappers, as they only support the compilation of the IR statements highlighted in blue, corresponding to a loop body. Therefore, they require manual effort to map operations beyond this scope, including the ones required for data initialization and result write-back (marked in yellow in Fig. 4-left).

Moreover, DFG-based modulo scheduling can only allow the execution of loops whose iteration count is known at compile time, where an explicit jump to an epilogue can be done. Such issue is exemplified in Fig. 4-right, which shows an example mapping on a 9-PEs CGRA of the gsm benchmark[1] with an $II = 3$. In this mapping, operation %30 is a data-dependent branch that indicates whether the current iteration should be the last one. If this condition is true, all operations of the current iterations should be executed, but none of the ones belonging to successive iterations. Nevertheless, this is not possible from DFG analysis alone, because in modulo scheduling operations from different iterations can be executed concurrently (on different PEs).

Our work provides a *fully automated end-to-end* compilation framework for kernel deployment to address the aforementioned limitations. The compiler focuses on expanding the mapping scope from basic block to kernel through CFG

---

[1] Details on adopted benchmarks are provided in Sect. 5.

management, while exploiting CGRA inherent hardware parallelism to accelerate application kernels. The specific MS algorithm is *not* a primary concern of this work. Instead, assuming a feasible solution from an existing MS mapper as shown in Fig. 4, the framework can still expand the mapping scope while strictly following the original MS solution without adapting the hardware or compromising the obtained II.

4   Methodology

Figure 5 plots the proposed CGRA compilation flow from C to the CGRA assembly. Firstly, the pre-processing component converts high-level languages to the LLVM dialect in MLIR, employing clang and mlir-translate [12]. The front end generates IR with operations supported by the target CGRA instruction set. While we assume C as a source code, llvm supports multiple source language including C, C++, and Object C. Then, a modulo scheduler (e.g. [16]) can be used to increase parallelism. In this case, a CFG transformation pass is performed to efficiently represent the schedule. Furthermore, in both cases where modulo scheduling is used (Route 2 in Fig. 5) or not (Route 1), the IR mapper performs the placement of operations in space and time. Lastly, the back end allocates registers within each PE and outputs the CGRA assembly. We detail each of these components as follows.

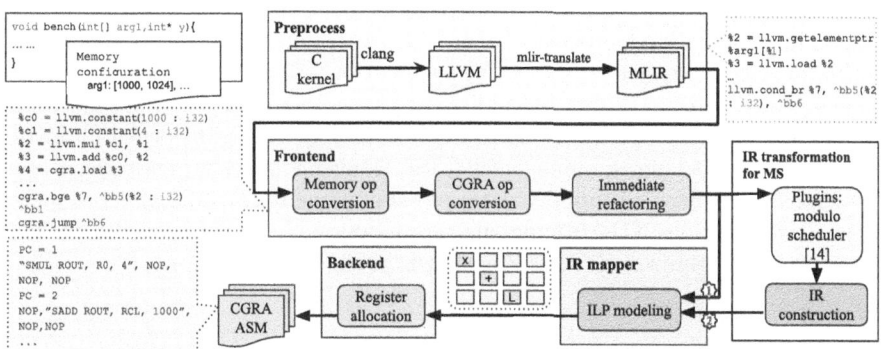

Fig. 5. Birds-eye view of the compilation flow for deploying a kernel function on a CGRA with MLIR-based pre-processing front-end, back-end passes, ILP-based mapping, and optional CFG transformations to support modulo scheduling.

4.1   Front-End

The front end employs a custom CGRA dialect, extending the LLVM dialect, to ensure compatibility between ISA and CGRA operations such as conditional branches and load and store operations. This extension allows for maintaining a high level of abstraction, enabling compiler optimizations at the IR level before the generation of assembly code.

Memory Operation Conversion: The CPU reserves a memory space to place the variables that the CGRA will use. We achieve this by using the `section` directive during the variable declaration, as illustrated in Fig. 1. In such a space, our framework controls the placement of the data and provides the address for all the variables required by a kernel. After preprocessing, those are indexed through pointers relying on the *getelementptr* operation to retrieve the data address. On the CGRA side, this operation is decomposed into two parts for arrays, the first being the computation of the array element offset by multiplying its index with the stride, the second being the sum of the offset with the array base address. For scalars, only the base address is required. Those operations overwrite *getelementptrs* in the CGRA dialect.

IR Optimization for Hardware Compatibility: Each CGRA implements its own ISA based on the supported operations and optimizations. We here consider the ISA in [14] as a concrete example. Our compiler automatically translates illegal instructions into instructions the CGRA supports through the `cgra` dialect, leveraging the ISA's advantages. For instance, it translates the LLVM's "compare" and "select" instructions into the CGRA's corresponding instructions that use the zero and sign flags from the previous instruction. Similarly, we connect basic blocks by leveraging the CGRA's specific "branch" and "jump" instructions. This feature allows our solution to adapt to any CGRA particularities and optimizations based on the targeted hardware.

The intermediate refactoring pass also checks if immediate values encoded in instructions are compatible with ISA specifications, never exceeding the size of immediate fields (e.g., 12 bits for additions for the ISA in Sect. 5), decomposing them across multiple operations if required. The front-end transformation introduces memory load/store management, ISA conversion, which uses executable operations to replace unsupported types, and immediate value generation by arithmetic operations if the original operation does not support immediate fields. The complete optimized IR of GSM is shown in Fig. 3c.

4.2   IR Mapper

Employing an Integer Linear Programming (ILP) formulation, the IR mapper arranges each operation on hardware resources, considering the constraints deriving from the control flow graph (CFG) and the data flow graph (DFG) of the IR generated by the front end.

CFG Constraints: The control constraints specify the placement of the instruction of the basic blocks, where the start and end instructions of the entire CGRA kernel should include all its basic blocks. For a basic block b, its start and end instruction are notated as t_b^0 and t_b^1, which are constrained by the kernel start and end instruction, notated as t^0 and t^1 respectively:

$$t_b^0 \geq t^0, \; t^1 \geq t_b^1, \; \forall b \tag{1}$$

The block start and end instruction range constrains operations within it. The operation set in basic block b is notated as $\mathbb{I}^b$:

$$t_b^0 \leq t_i \leq t_b^1, \ i \in \mathbb{I}^b \tag{2}$$

Each basic block has one and only one control operation to determine where to branch after its execution. The destination must be the first instruction of another basic block or of itself. Hence, the following constraints hold:

$$t_b^1 = t_b^{\{term\}} \tag{3}$$

$$t_b^1 \leq t_{next(b)}^0 - 1 \tag{4}$$

Algorithm 1. Path seeker

1: Input: I_i, I_j and their belong blocks B_i, B_j
2: Init empty path intervals ϕ
3: **if** $B_i == B_j$ **then**
4:     $\phi \leftarrow [t_{I_j}, t_{B_j}^1], [t_{B_j}^0, t_{I_i})$ if $I_i \rightarrow I_j$ is back edge,
        else $\phi \leftarrow [t_{I_i}, t_{I_j})$
5: **else**
6:     DFS CFG from B_i to B_j to obtain all routes $\xi_{I_i \rightarrow I_j}$
7:     $\phi \leftarrow [t_{I_i}, t_{B_i}^1], [t_{B_k}^0, t_{B_k}^1], \ldots, [t_{B_j}^0, t_{I_j})$, where $B_k \in \xi_{I_i \rightarrow I_j}$
8:     $\phi \leftarrow [t_{I_j}, t_{B_j}^1]$, if B_j is a loop block and I_j is not a *phi* node.
9: **end if**
10: Return ϕ.

---

where $t_b^{\{term\}}$ is the control operation that terminates the block to which it belongs. Constraint 4 forces the last instruction of a basic block to be placed before the first instruction of another basic block, resulting in their sequential scheduling.

Lastly, if a *phi* node receives multiple result operands from different basic blocks, they must be executed at the same PE, shown in the intersection PE of blue and purple arrows in Fig. 2b.

$$p_{I_m} == p_{I_n} \ \forall I_m, I_n \in \Phi \tag{5}$$

where Φ notated instruction aggregation for the *phi* node, and p_{I_m} is the execution unit for an operation I_m.

DFG Dominance Constraint: The dominance constraint regulates the execution order of the operations. The execution time of t_{I_m} an operation I_m should be before its consumer in the same basic block, notated as $t_{Cons(I_m)}$:

$$t_{I_m} \leq t_{Cons(I_m)} - 1 \tag{6}$$

We only consider this constraint in the same basic block because control constraints handle the dominance relationship in the CFG. From the entry point of the function execution, the predecessor block is always executed before its successors.

DFG Liveness Constraint: An operation executed afterward in the same PE would overwrite the pre-produced value. This constraint ensures the liveness of the produced results of operation I_i before its consumption by I_j:

$$|p_{I_k} - p_{I_i}| > 0 \ \forall I_k \in \mathbb{I}, \text{if } p_{I_i} \neq p_{I_j} \ \& \ t_{I_k} \in path_t\{I_i \rightarrow I_j\} \tag{7}$$

where $\mathbb{I}$ is the full operation sets. This constraint blocks certain PEs use, as shown in the dark gray units of Fig. 2b. If instead the producer and consumer are allocated in the same PE, e.g., $p_{I_i} = p_{I_j}$, register allocation handles liveness analysis. Hence, there is no need to block the PE from execution.

Algorithm 1 shows how to identify the execution path from the producer to the consumer through depth-first search (DFS) along a CFG.

Routing Constraints: Operations should be assigned to physical PEs. In a CGRA configuration with R rows and C columns, the placement p_{I_m} of operation I_m is cannot exceed the CGRA size:

$$0 \leq p_{I_m} \leq RC - 1 \tag{8}$$

The consumer should access the producer's result, which is constrained by the hardware connectivity. If the CGRA is grid-connected, p_{I_m} is constraint by the producer units p_{I_n}:

$$\begin{aligned} p_{I_m} = \ & \text{top}(p_{I_n}) \ ||\text{bottom}(p_{I_n}) \ || \\ & \text{left}(p_{I_n}) \ ||\text{right}(p_{I_n})||p_{I_n} \ , \forall j \in Prod(I_n) \end{aligned} \tag{9}$$

A PE can execute at most one operation one time, which makes the combination of p_{I_m} and t_{I_n} unique:

$$|p_{I_m} - p_{I_n}| > 0 \ \forall m, n \in \mathbb{I}, \text{if } t_{I_m} == t_{I_n} \tag{10}$$

Problem Formulation: Under Constraints 1 to 10, the objective of the ILP is to minimize the IR runtime and compact the output assembly:

$$\min \ (t^1 - t^0) \tag{11}$$

where t^0, t^1 is the start and end instruction of the kernel. The ILP returns the execution instruction t_{I_m} and unit p_{I_m} for each operation I_m, mapping all operations onto the target CGRA.

4.3   IR Transformation with Modulo Scheduling

The IR mapper illustrated in the previous section is limited to scheduling basic blocks sequentially. Hence, if directly operating on the CFG produced by the front end, it considers each iteration of the loop kernel in isolation, neglecting opportunities stemming from modulo scheduling. Though not compulsory for deployment, we in this section showcase that modulo-scheduling strategies can instead be embedded in our framework via CFG rewriting, without requiring modification to upstream (front-end) or downstream (IR mapper) passes. In addition to providing modulo scheduling and the CFG transformation described in the following, the IR transformation phase also retrieves the placements of operations in the targeted loop. This additional information is used to reduce the workload of the IR mapper, as the placement of operations in modulo scheduled loops is fixed before solving the ILP formulation in Sect. 4.2.

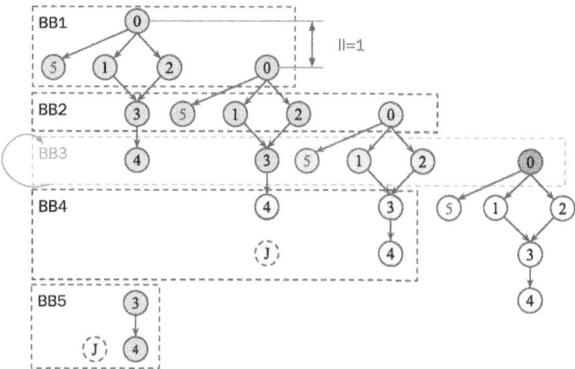

(a) Unrolled loop for MS, with BBs grouping operation from different iterations.

```
%0 = llvm.mlir.constant(1 : i32) : i32
%1 = llvm.mlir.constant(2 : i32) : i32
%2 = llvm.mlir.constant(0 : i32) : i32
%3 = llvm.mlir.constant(100 : i32) : i32
%4 = llvm.mlir.constant(256 : i32) : i32
br ^bb1(%2 : i32)
^bb1(%5 : i32):  // pred: ^bb2
⓪ %6 = llvm.add %5, %1 : i32
① %7 = llvm.shl %6, %0 : i32
② %8 = llvm.sub %6, %0 : i32
③ %9 = llvm.mul %7, %8 : i32
④ cgra.swi %9, %4 : i32, i32
⑤ cgra.cond_br<ge> [%6 : i32, %3 : i32], ^bb1(%6 :
   i32), ^bb2
...
```

(b) IR code before CFG transformation.

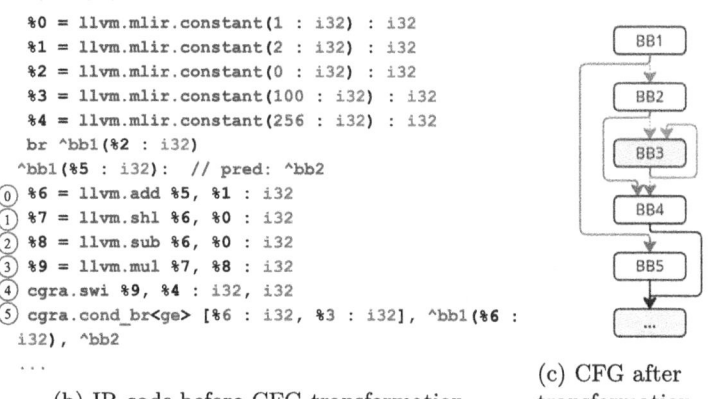

(c) CFG after transformation.

Fig. 6. Running example: CFG transformation for modulo scheduling (MS). Arrows in (a) illustrate data dependencies, and arrows in (c) show the control flow of the IR after the transformation. (Color figure online)

We illustrate the CFG rewriting pass with the help of a running example. Figure 6b shows an IR snippet after the front-end passes. Its DFG is plotted in Fig. 6a in blue, where each circle represents an operation. Modulo scheduling unfolds the loops, maps operations to architecture PEs, and accelerates execution by overlapping multiple iterations, with each iteration beginning II (Initiation Interval) clock cycles after the previous one. Lower IIs hence result in shorter runtimes. An example with $II = 1$ is shown in Fig. 6a. Our IR transformation approach considers a solution generated by a modulo scheduler as input and builds its DFG and CFG to enable its deployment. It transforms the CFG in order to allow the execution of loops whose iteration count is data dependent, so that it can be determined at runtime.

The transformation pass creates basic blocks formed by grouped operations, as shown in the dashed rectangles in Fig. 6a. The standard basic blocks only present one control operation (at their end), but include operations from multiple loop iterations. Control operations (such as ⑤) dictate whether to continue (green arrows in Fig. 6c) or quit (red arrows) a loop execution. The control operation initiates branches to the successor block when the conditional flag is set (e.g., from BB3 to itself). Otherwise, the PC increments one by default and passively branches to the basic block below, indicated by the dashed lines. Such an approach allows us to support the execution of loops with variables and even a data-dependent number of iterations. As an example, if only one iteration is required for the loop in Fig. 6c, execution immediately branches from BB1 to BB5 while, if the loop should end after two iterations, the control path from BB2 to BB4 is taken. Execution enters the steady state in BB3 if three or more loop iterations are required. Note that the transformed CFG includes the basic exit blocks, e.g., BB5 is the exit block for BB1 in Fig. 6a. When the operations in the basic blocks with different data arguments are the same, they are merged to make the code compact, as shown by BB4 being the exit block for both BB2 and BB3. All exit blocks end with an unconditional jump to the successor basic block of the entire modulo scheduled loop, depicted in grey in Fig. 6c.

The operations mapping produced by the modulo scheduler are employed as additional constraints in the CFG-level mapper described in Sect. 4.2:

$$p_{I_m} = s_m, \ t_{I_m} = t_m, \tag{12}$$

where I_m belongs to the aggregate of scheduled operations, s_m, t_m are the spatial and temporal results respectively. Such additional constraints tangibly decrease the CFG compile time, as presented in Sect. 5.

4.4   Back End

Once the IR mapper returns a valid mapping result, the corresponding interference graph is built, indicating the liveness of operands within each PE considering the entire PC control flow. The register allocation is performed PE-wise, which follows the traditional single processor register allocation [17]. Operands from neighboring PEs are retrieved from their output registers, eliminating the need for internal register allocation. After register allocation, a final rewriting pass converts the MLIR code to the input needed for the CGRA assembler. During the MLIR-to-CGRA assembler conversion, redundant jumps to basic blocks placed immediately afterwards in the instruction placements are removed. The assembler is then translated into binaries for execution on the target hardware.

5   Evaluation

We evaluate our compilation framework using a representative set of benchmarks from the MiBench suite [18]. We also consider a dot product benchmark with a size of 16, as this is a common computational pattern, e.g., in machine learning. The selected benchmarks are compiled to evaluate the compilation time as well as the runtime achieved on the target hardware. Although our framework can employ any modulo scheduling strategy, for experiments, we employ the open-source SAT-based DFG mapper [14].

We target a heterogeneous system composed with a low-power RISC-V Ibex CPU [19] and a 4×4 OpenEdgeCGRA [8], as illustrated in Fig. 1. The CGRA is a grid-connected architecture with a single program counter that manages the execution of all PEs. The CGRA and CPU are programmed with separate source files implemented in C. A reserved memory space is used to store data variables shared by the CPU and the CGRA.

5.1   IR Scope Analysis

Table 2 lists the number of operations and basic blocks generated on the front-end with or without modulo scheduling. Data refers to the IR after the IR mapper passes because it relates to instructions that can be directly deployed on hardware. The last column reports the number of operations that do not belong to the loop and therefore require manual placement when employing DFG-based CGRA compilers [13–15], but are automatically mapped by our compiler.

The number of operations and basic blocks is influenced by the CFG-based transformation for modulo scheduling. Modulo scheduling could increase the number of operations and basic blocks if it unrolls the loop to overlap the iteration, as shown in Fig. 6. Although the modulo scheduler can produce in some cases a solution without loop unrolling (II equals the iteration length), the number of operations generated using modulo scheduling is still larger than the number obtained by the strategy without MS. This is because the *phi* IR instruction used for operand selection must explicitly be replaced with a MOV operation in the w/ MS case, while it can be discarded in the w/o MS one (constraint 3 in Sect. 4.2).

5.2   Compilation Time

Figure 7 shows the compilation time of the selected benchmarks for different CGRA sizes. The blue bar with slashes is the compilation time in IR generated by the front-end without loop runtime optimization (Route 1 in Fig. 5). When

Table 2. Number of operations and basic blocks for each benchmark and scheduling strategy.

	# ops w/o MS	# BBs w/o MS	# ops w/ MS	# BBs w/ MS	# ops (non loop)
reverse_bits	32	5	35	5	26
gsm	42	4	81	6	28
isqrt	25	4	27	4	19
sha1	42	4	121	6	18
dot_product	32	4	49	5	20

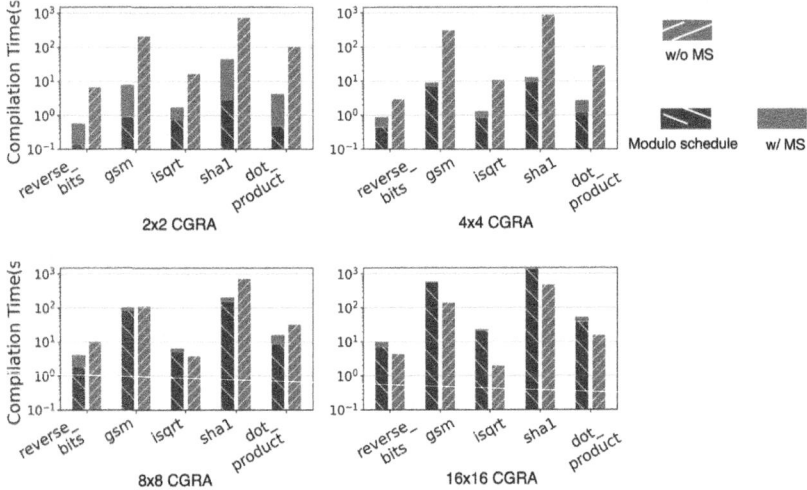

Fig. 7. Compilation time on Intel(R) i7-13700H. (Color figure online)

modulo scheduling is employed (Route 2), the compilation time consists of the time spent by the modulo scheduler, represented in green, and the time taken by the IR mapper, represented in blue.

Regardless of the compilation methodologies, the compilation time increases exponentially with the number of operations to be mapped. As an example, the compilation time of sha1 is significantly longer than that of other benchmarks, as it has more operations in the basic loop blocks. The CFG structure also affects the compilation time. Indeed, in the reverse_bits benchmark, most operations are not in the loop block, reducing the complexity of the ILP formulation and shortening the compilation time.

Instead, the CGRA size does not significantly influence the compilation time in the ILP model. This is because ILP is a sparse problem with multiple solutions, and hence the optimizer stops immediately when one is found. When the CGRA size is small, finding a solution could be more challenging due to the limited available resources. However, the search space is reduced accordingly, potentially shortening the search time. Those two effects tend to cancel each other out in our experiments.

Counter-intuitively, modulo scheduling can reduce compile time for small-size CGRAs. This effect is caused by decoupling the compilation problem between modulo-scheduled and non-modulo-scheduled operations, which reduces the mapping complexity (as explained in Sect. 4.3). The opposite is true for large CGRAs because the SAT-based modulo scheduler's compile time increases with the CGRA size, exponentially affecting the number of Boolean expressions.

5.3   Runtime Analysis on OpenEdgeCGRA

The runtime experiments are executed on HEEPsilon, a synthesizable open-source MCU consisting of the X-HEEP platform [20]. Latency measurements are extracted from pre-synthesis simulations conducted at 100 MHz. We benchmark the performance of the CGRA against executions on the CPU, on which the C code is compiled using GCC with the highest optimization level ($-O3$). The results, summarized in Table 3, compare our two approaches -with and without MS - against CPU execution.

The CGRA provides higher speedups for benchmarks with more operation-level parallelism which requires less data dependencies. Indeed, for benchmarks such as `reversebits, dot_product`, where the number of operations is many times higher than the loop length (LL), CGRA implementations provides speedup compared to the CPU executions even when MS is not employed. For `isqrt`, we observed that the CPU execution outperforms the CGRA one. This outcome is caused by a loop-carrying dependency that covers the entire benchmark, reducing parallelism.

Moreover, results produced with modulo scheduling achieve, as expected, higher speedups when II is lower than LL. For benchmarks where the II achieved by modulo scheduling equals the loop length, the w/o MS strategy results in lower runtime, as it does not mandate explicit *phi* operations, hence resulting in fewer instructions.

Table 3. Execution latency, in clock-cycles (cc)- for different compilation approaches.

Kernel	LL*/II	CPU	w/o MS		w/ MS	
		cc	cc	speedup	cc	speedup
isqrt	5/5	101	103	-2%	118	-17%
gsm	9/3	487	489	0%	337	31%
sha1	9/3	946	987	-4%	591	38%
dot_product	6/2	215	189	12%	115	47%
reversebits	3/3	264	79	70%	111	58%

6   Conclusion

By combining efficiency and reprogrammability, CGRAs can support acceleration of computationally intensive edge applications. The key to their mainstream
adoption is the availability of a compilation framework that enables the autom-
atization of the deployment of compute kernels on available hardware resources.

Against this backdrop, we have proposed in this paper a novel end-to-end
framework that, by leveraging and extending the MLIR infrastructure, is able to
generate CGRA assembly from source code. We broadened the scope of CGRA
scheduling by considering control flow as well as data flow in the compilation
process, showcasing how this approach can be employed to efficiently compile
kernels, with or without employing modulo scheduling. Moreover, we introduced
a strategy for the memory management for kernel variables, automating their
placement in a shared host-CGRA space, and providing compiler passes for the
lowering of the LLVM intermediate representation to a CGRA-specific IR dialect.

When applied to benchmark computational kernels and targeting an open-
hardware CGRA instance, our framework allowed us to automatically map complex kernels in their entirety, including operations outside of the basic block of
their main loop body.

Acknowledgment. This work was supported in part by the Swiss NSF Edge-
Companions project (GA No. 10002812); in part by the EC H2020 FVLLMONTI
Project under Grant 101016776; in part by the ACCESS-AI Chip Center for Emerging
Smart Systems, sponsored by InnoHK funding, Hong Kong, SAR; and in part by the
Swiss State Secretariat for Education, Research, and Innovation (SERI) through the
SwissChips Research Project. This work was in part supported by the Swiss National
Science Foundation via project ADApprox (Grant 200020_188613).

References

1. Chen, S., Cai, C., Zheng, S., et al.: Hiercgra: a novel framework for large-scale
   CGRA with hierarchical modeling and automated design space exploration. ACM
   Trans. Reconfigurable Technol. Syst. **17**(2), 1–31 (2024)
2. Bandara, T.K., Wijerathne, D., Mitra, T., Peh, L.S.: Revamp: a systematic framework for heterogeneous CGRA realization. In: Proceedings of the 27th ACM International Conference on Architectural Support for Programming Languages and
   Operating Systems, pp. 918–932 (2022)
3. Das, S., Rossi, D., Martin, K.J.M., Coussy, P., Benini, L.: A 142MOPS/mW integrated programmable array accelerator for smart visual processing. In: 2017 IEEE
   International Symposium on Circuits and Systems (ISCAS), pp. 1–4 (2017)
4. Mei, B., Vernalde, S., Verkest, D., De Man, H., Lauwereins, R.: Exploiting
   loop-level parallelism on coarse-grained reconfigurable architectures using modulo scheduling. In: 2003 Design, Automation and Test in Europe Conference and
   Exhibition, pp. 296–301 (2003)

5. Mei, B.: Dresc: a retargetable compiler for coarse-grained reconfigurable architectures. In: Proceedings of 2002 IEEE International Conference on Field-Programmable Technology (FPT), pp. 166–173. IEEE (2002)

6. Friedman, S., Carroll, A., Van Essen, B., Ylvisaker, B., Ebeling, C., Hauck, S.: SPR: an architecture-adaptive CGRA mapping tool. In: Proceedings of the ACM/SIGDA International Symposium on Field Programmable Gate Arrays, ser. FPGA 2009, pp. 191–200 (2009)

7. Chin, S.A., Sakamoto, N., Rui, A., et al.: CGRA-ME: a unified framework for CGRA modelling and exploration. In: 2017 IEEE 28th International Conference on Application-specific Systems, Architectures and Processors (ASAP), pp. 184–189 (2017)

8. Álvarez, R.R., Denkinger, B., Sapriza, J., Calero, J.M., Ansaloni, G., Alonso, D.A.: An open-hardware coarse-grained reconfigurable array for edge computing. In: Proceedings of the 20th ACM International Conference on Computing Frontiers, pp. 391–392 (2023)

9. Denkinger, B.W., Peón-Quirós, M., Konijnenburg, M., Atienza, D., Catthoor, F.: VWR2A: a very-wide-register reconfigurable-array architecture for low-power embedded devices. In: Proceedings of the 59th ACM/IEEE Design Automation Conference, pp. 895–900 (2022)

10. Karunaratne, M., Wijerathne, D., Mitra, T., Peh, L.S.: 4D-CGRA: introducing branch dimension to spatio-temporal application mapping on CGRAs. In: 2019 IEEE/ACM International Conference on Computer-Aided Design (ICCAD), pp. 1–8 (2019)

11. Gobieski, G., Ghosh, S., Heule, M., et al.: RipTide: a programmable, energy-minimal dataflow compiler and architecture. In: 2022 55th IEEE/ACM International Symposium on Microarchitecture (MICRO), pp. 546–564 (2022)

12. Lattner, C., Amini, M., Bondhugula, U., et al.: MLIR: scaling compiler infrastructure for domain specific computation. In: 2021 IEEE/ACM International Symposium on Code Generation and Optimization (CGO), pp. 2–14 (2021)

13. Chin, S.A., Anderson, J.H.: An architecture-agnostic integer linear programming approach to CGRA mapping. In: 2018 55th ACM/IEEE Design Automation Conference (DAC), pp. 1–6 (2018)

14. Tirelli, C., Sapriza, J., Álvarez, R.R., et al.: Sat-based exact modulo scheduling mapping for resource-constrained CGRAS. J. Emerg. Technol. Comput. Syst. **20**(3), 1–26 (2024)

15. Liu, D., Xia, Y., Shang, J., Zhong, J., Ouyang, P., Yin, S.: E2EMap: end-to-end reinforcement learning for CGRA compilation via reverse mapping. In: 2024 IEEE International Symposium on High-Performance Computer Architecture (HPCA), pp. 46–60 (2024)

16. Tirelli, C., Ferretti, L., Pozzi, L.: SAT-mapIt: a SAT-based modulo scheduling mapper for coarse grain reconfigurable architectures. In: 2023 Design, Automation and Test in Europe Conference and Exhibition (DATE), pp. 1–6 (2023)

17. Hack, S., Grund, D., Goos, G.: Register allocation for programs in SSA-form. In: Mycroft, A., Zeller, A. (eds.) CC 2006. LNCS, vol. 3923, pp. 247–262. Springer, Heidelberg (2006). https://doi.org/10.1007/11688839_20

18. Guthaus, M., Ringenberg, J., Ernst, D., Austin, T., Mudge, T., Brown, R.: Mibench: a free, commercially representative embedded benchmark suite. In: Proceedings of the Fourth Annual IEEE International Workshop on Workload Characterization. WWC-4 (Cat. No. 01EX538), pp. 3–14 (2001)

19. Schiavone, P.D., Conti, F., Rossi, D., et al.: Slow and steady wins the race? A comparison of ultra-low-power RISC-V cores for internet-of-things applications. In: 2017 27th International Symposium on Power and Timing Modeling, Optimization and Simulation (PATMOS), pp. 1–8 (2017)
20. Machetti, S., Schiavone, P.D., Müller, T.C., Peón-Quirós, M., Atienza, D.: X-heep: an open-source, configurable and extendible RISC-V microcontroller for the exploration of ultra-low-power edge accelerators, arXiv preprint arXiv:2401.05548 (2024)

Hardware-Accelerated Event-Graph Neural Networks for Low-Latency Time-Series Classification on SoC FPGA

Hiroshi Nakano[1] , Krzysztof Blachut[2] , Kamil Jeziorek[2] , Piotr Wzorek[2] ,
Manon Dampfhoffer[3] , Thomas Mesquida[3] , Hiroaki Nishi[1] ,
Tomasz Kryjak[2]([✉]) , and Thomas Dalgaty[3]

[1] Graduate School of Science and Technology, Keio University, Tokyo, Japan
nakano@west.sd.keio.ac.jp, west@keio.jp
[2] Embedded Vision Systems Group, Computer Vision Laboratory,
AGH University of Krakow, Krakow, Poland
{kblachut,kjeziorek,pwzorek,tomasz.kryjak}@agh.edu.pl
[3] CEA-List, Université Grenoble Alpes, Grenoble, France
{Manon.DAMPFHOFFER,thomas.mesquida,Thomas.DALGATY}@cea.fr

Abstract. As the quantities of data recorded by embedded edge sensors grow, so too does the need for intelligent local processing. Such data often comes in the form of time-series signals, based on which real-time predictions can be made locally using an AI model. However, a hardware-software approach capable of making low-latency predictions with low power consumption is required. In this paper, we present a hardware implementation of an event-graph neural network for time-series classification. We leverage an artificial cochlea model to convert the input time-series signals into a sparse event-data format that allows the event-graph to drastically reduce the number of calculations relative to other AI methods. We implemented the design on a SoC FPGA and applied it to the real-time processing of the Spiking Heidelberg Digits (SHD) dataset to benchmark our approach against competitive solutions. Our method achieves a floating-point accuracy of 92.7% on the SHD dataset for the base model, which is only 2.4% and 2% less than the state-of-the-art models with over $10\times$ and $67\times$ fewer model parameters, respectively. It also outperforms FPGA-based spiking neural network implementations by 19.3% and 4.5%, achieving 92.3% accuracy for the quantised model while using fewer computational resources and reducing latency.

Keywords: FPGA · event-based audio processing · graph convolutional neural networks dynamic audio sensor artificial cochlea

1 Introduction

As the Internet of Things expands, distributed sensors are collecting ever-increasing quantities of data. This has driven the need for efficient edge computing systems capable of processing this data locally, for example, to make

R. Giorgi et al. (Eds.): ARC 2025, LNCS 15594, pp. 51–68, 2025.
https://doi.org/10.1007/978-3-031-87995-1_4

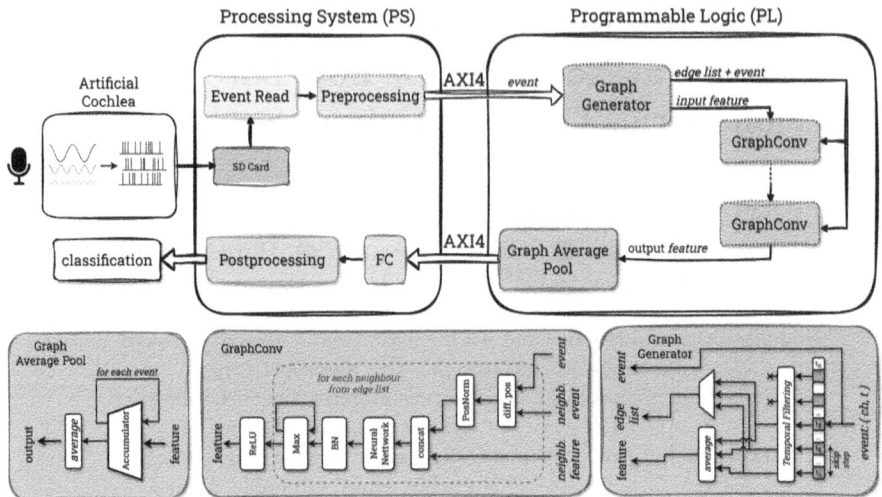

Fig. 1. Overview of our hardware-accelerated event-graph neural network implementation. Dotted modules indicate event-by-event operation. For testing, we read data from an SD card and simulate real intervals between events.

predictions [1]. The energy consumption and latency of these systems are of particular importance.

In most cases, the raw data produced by the sensors is time-series – continuous signals following the evolution of environmental variables [2]. For example, sensors that monitor the vibration of mechanical parts have been used to predict failures in gearboxes [3], or implantable cardioverter-defibrillators monitor the state of a patient's heart in order to apply an electric shock in the event of dangerous fibrillation [4].

It is becoming increasingly common to use AI methods to process this time-series data. However, using conventional hardware, such as GPUs (graphics processing units), consumes too much power, and microprocessors may struggle to meet the latency requirements of many applications. FPGAs (field programmable gate arrays) and custom integrated circuits offer a means of implementing architectures optimised to specific AI methods that are capable of meeting latency requirements while minimising power consumption [5–7].

A particularly promising method is event-based AI, which operates on the sparse data generated by event-based sensors and allows reducing power consumption and prediction latency [8]. Event-based sensors, instead of regularly sampling an environmental variable, generate "events" in case of the changes in the signal. Event-based time-series data is generated by a class of sensors known as artificial cochleas (AC) (also referred to as dynamic audio sensors or silicon cochleas) [9,10]. Their operating principle is to apply a bank of band-pass filters to separate the signal into multiple frequency channels. A digital pulse (i.e. an event) is generated per channel in an asynchronous manner when the signal intensity changes by a pre-defined threshold. This results in a sparse spectrogram, which an event-based AI method exploits to perform efficient computation.

Processing AC-generated event-data has been the subject of many publications. The most common approach is to apply spiking neural networks (SNNs) implemented for specialised hardware [11–13]. However, it is not clear how event-data sparsity can be truly exploited due to the nondeterministic pattern of synaptic weight-memory access [14,15] inherent to SNNs.

Recently, event-graph neural networks have been proposed as an alternative way of processing event-data [16–20]. The event-graph approach consists of a dynamically updated graph generated by an event-sensor, and it involves applying graph convolutions on the resulting data structure. Unlike SNNs, the weight access pattern for many event-graph models is deterministic. This may provide an opportunity to develop new event-based AI hardware that is truly capable of exploiting the inherent sparsity of data to reduce power consumption and latency. Although digital architectures for accelerating event-graphs have been proposed in the context of computer vision [21,22], a dedicated architecture for time-series audio applications has not yet been considered.

In this paper, we propose, for the first time, a hardware accelerator implemented on a SoC FPGA device for event-graph AC data classification (Fig. 1). Specifically, we consider a recently proposed spectro-temporal model [20] developed for keyword spotting and evaluated on the Spiking Heidelberg Digits (SHD) dataset [23], which is a representative for time-series data.

We summarise our main contribution as follows:

- We use the hardware-aware design method to propose optimisations required to implement spectro-temporal event-graphs in reconfigurable hardware with low power, low latency and low resource utilisation.
- We propose the first embedded system for event-graph-based audio processing on a SoC FPGA and also the first hardware implementation that supports fully asynchronous event-by-event processing with conservation of data's temporal sparsity.
- We achieve a new state-of-the-art performance for FPGA solutions applied to the Spiking Heidelberg Digits dataset, demonstrating significant improvements in resource utilisation, latency reduction and accuracy compared to previous SNN-based approaches.

The remainder of this paper is organised as follows. In Sect. 2 we present an overview of the related work. In Sect. 3 we introduce the proposed embedded audio processing system. In Sect. 4 we provide hardware implementation details and present the results of ablation studies. We conclude with a discussion on future research directions.

2   Related Work

2.1   Event-Audio Data

The advent of artificial cochlea models, especially dynamic audio sensors (DAS) [9,10], has highlighted an opportunity to apply event-based AI methods, extensively explored in computer vision, for time-series applications. A popular benchmark for evaluating event-based time-series AI models is the Spiking Heidelberg Digits dataset [23]. SHD simulates an AC by filtering recordings with a computational model of the inner-ear. The dataset contains over 10k recordings (8156 train and 2264 test samples) consisting of spoken digits in English and German from zero to nine. This results in a set of sparse 700-channel spectrograms, each 750 ms in length on average (Fig. 2). In order to compare our SoC FPGA implementation of an event-graph neural network to previous state-of-the-art software models and hardware realisations, we use the SHD dataset with the same train/test split as a benchmark in this paper.

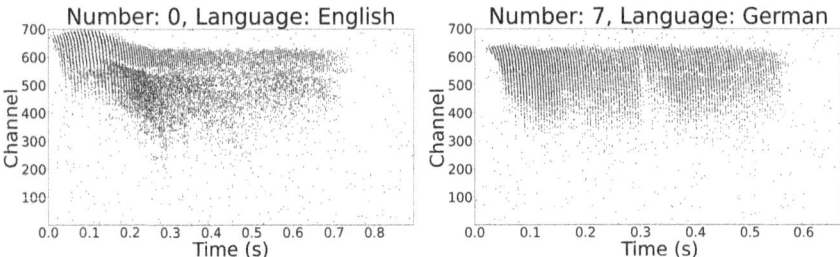

Fig. 2. Spectro-Temporal Spike Rasters from the SHD dataset.

2.2   Event-Based AI Applied to the SHD Dataset

In Table 1 existing works applied to the SHD dataset are summarised. They mostly correspond to software implementations of recurrent spiking neural networks [23–26] and feed-forward models leveraging learned synaptic delays [27–31].

Recently, an alternative approach was proposed in [20] based on a radically different idea. Instead of applying a spiking neural network to raw data, an event-stream is first transformed into a graph data structure, which is then processed using graph neural networks (GNNs). This event-graph neural network approach achieved a performance close to the state-of-the-art synaptic delay-based SNNs on the SHD benchmark, although requiring between one and two orders of magnitude fewer synaptic weights in many cases. Notably, a tiny model comprising only 17k parameters obtained a test accuracy of over 90%.

These findings suggest that the event-graph approach holds great promise for processing event-based time-series data. While it is believed that event-graphs, due to their deterministic synaptic weight access pattern and their natively asynchronous operation, may translate well into a dedicated hardware, this has yet to be investigated.

2.3 FPGA-Based Event-Sensor Data Processing

In contrast, numerous dedicated implementations of SNNs on application specific integrated circuits [33] as well as FPGAs [34] have been proposed. The majority of these works have focussed on event-vision applications. To the best of the authors' knowledge, there are three research papers describing FPGA-based SNN implementations for AC time-series processing [12,32,35] – only two of them report benchmarking results on the SHD dataset and are therefore included in Table 1. The last article [35] reports the results on custom-generated events from TIDIGITS audio dataset only, therefore it cannot be directly compared.

The Spiker+ framework [12] and QUANTISENC tool [32] both target efficient SNN accelerators for FPGA-based edge computing, with Spiker+ achieving 72.9% accuracy on the SHD benchmark at 430 mW and 540 μs latency, while QUANTISENC demonstrated 87.8% accuracy and 1.6 W peak power consumption. A summary of these results is provided in Table 4.

The main objective of this paper was to propose an FPGA event-graph implementation and compare the task accuracy, power consumption, latency and resource utilisation relative to these two papers on the SHD benchmark. This would provide an understanding of whether the promised performance of event-graph neural network can be achieved in hardware and how such an approach compares relative to SNNs. An additional goal of the implemented system was to enable fully asynchronous, event-by-event processing.

Table 1. Model comparison on the SHD dataset. The symbol | indicates that only two models are present, while "–" denotes several intermediate values.

Author(s)	Year	Acc. (%)	#Params	Features/Details
Cramer et al. [23]	2020	83.2	–	Recurrent SNN (RSNN)
Yu et al. [31]	2022	92.4	2.1 M	RSNN with synaptic dynamics
Dampfhoffer et al. [25]	2022	87.8	139 k	RSNN
Bittar et al. [24]	2022	94.6	3.9M	RSNN
Rossbroich et al. [26]	2022	83.5	209k	Convolutional RSNN
Hammouamri et al. [28]	2023	95.1	200 k	FF SNN with delay learning
Sun et al. [30]	2023	92.4	140 k	FF SNN with delay learning
Rafeldt et al. [20]	2024	90.0 | 94.3	17.1 | 217 k	Spectro-temporal graph
D'Agostino et al. [27]	2024	87.6	224 k	FF SNN with dendritic delays
Malettira et al. [29]	2024	94.7	1.3 M	Temporal Skips with delay learning
Carpegna et al. [12]	2024	72.9	–	RSNN on FPGA
Matinizadeh et al. [32]	2024	87.8	–	Fully configurable FPGA SNN
The proposed system	2025	88.8–94.5	8.6–272 k	Spectro-temporal graph on SoC FPGA

3 FPGA Implementation of an Event-Graph for Time-Series Classification

The principle of the event-graph approach is to generate a graph from the raw events generated by an event-sensor – in this case the artificial cochlea. Formally, a graph is defined as $\mathcal{G} = (\mathcal{V}, \mathcal{E})$, where $\mathcal{V}$ is the set of vertices (events) and $\mathcal{E}$ is the set of edges. Each vertex $v \in \mathcal{V}$ is associated with a position $\mathcal{P}$ and feature vector $\mathcal{X}$, both of which characterise the underlying entity that the event represents, while edges represent the connections between pairs of these entities.

Spectro-temporal event-graphs are a specific form of event-graphs constructed from AC time-series data. They are typically created by performing a hemispherical search in the channel-time domain (Fig. 2), establishing edges between events that lie within defined distance. This neighbourhood can be determined by spatial and temporal radius thresholds, or, alternatively, edges can be assigned randomly within the search volume. Each new event generated by the sensor forms directed edges from previously recorded events found within a semi-circle defined by a channel radius r_{ch} and a time radius r_t.

In earlier work [20], PointNetConv graph convolutions [36] were applied to spectro-temporal event-graphs. In this publication, the feature vector $\mathcal{X}$ of each event consisted of two components of a normal vector estimated by fitting a local surface to the event-data using a least-squares approach. The position $\mathcal{P}$ comprised a channel index and a timestamp. The relative positions between events defined edge vectors, creating an $\mathcal{N}(i)$ neighbourhood set for each node i.

Given an event-graph, we can apply PointNetConv operations across L convolutional layers. Each layer uses a unique weight matrix shared across all events. Within each layer, the following operation is performed to update the embedding of the ith event:

$$\hat{\mathcal{X}}_i = \max_{j \in \mathcal{N}(i)} \left(\phi([\mathcal{X}_j \, || \, (\mathcal{P}_j - \mathcal{P}_i)]) \right), \qquad (1)$$

where $\hat{\mathcal{X}}_i$ is the updated feature vector for event i, and $\phi(\cdot)$ represents a fully-connected layer. The notation $||$ indicates the concatenation of the feature vector $\mathcal{X}_j$ with the relative position vector $\mathcal{P}_j - \mathcal{P}_i$. After this transformation, a feature-wise max-pooling aggregates the neighbour contributions into a single output vector per event, and a ReLU activation is applied to introduce nonlinearity.

To generate a final prediction for an entire time-series, global average pooling is applied across all event embeddings from the last convolutional layer. The resulting vector is then fed into a small multi-layer perceptron, which produces the desired output (e.g. a class prediction) for the time-series under consideration.

The following subsections detail the adaptations and optimisations performed in order to map this software baseline [20] to a hardware accelerator architecture on FPGA. To achieve more flexible and scalable implementation, computational tasks were distributed between the processing system (PS) and the programmable logic (PL) of the SoC FPGA device, as illustrated in Fig. 1.

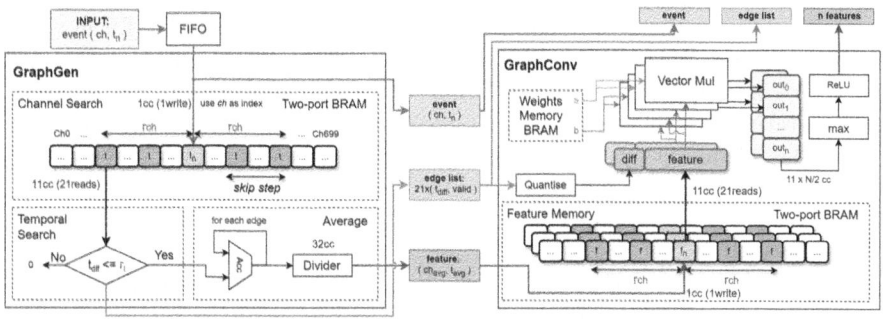

Fig. 3. Overview of the graph generation and convolution modules. The *skip step* is set to 10 and r_{ch} is set to 100. The number of output features is denoted as n.

3.1   Graph Generator

The baseline model presented in [20] has proven effective in capturing spectro-temporal relationships within event-graphs. However, it faces significant challenges when considering hardware implementation. First, the calculation of a normal vector requires fitting regression lines to the event-data that has a high computational complexity. Second, identifying neighbouring vertices requires storing all vertex vectors in memory and performing sequential searches, resulting in high latency and significant memory overhead.

To address these limitations, a novel graph generation was designed to optimise memory usage, reduce latency, and minimise computational overhead. The following key modifications were introduced:

1. Drawing inspiration from FPGA-based event camera data processing implementations [21, 22], events are stored in 1D context memory (implemented as a block RAM memory (BRAM)) using their channel ch as the address and timestamps t as the data. Only the most recent event generated per channel is stored, continuously overwriting timestamps at each channel index. Each new event can be connected only to the ones already processed, creating a directed graph.
2. Event-normal vectors were replaced with simpler features based on the average timestamp and channel coordinates of neighbouring events, massively reducing the computational cost.
3. To improve the efficiency of neighbour search, we introduce a method called *skip step connection*. This corresponds to a pre-defined deterministic pattern regarding how edges can be formed between vertices.

Figure 3 illustrates the main components and data flow of the graph generation module. Asynchronous events, defined by their time t and channel index ch, enter a first-in first-out (FIFO) buffer, ensuring a stable data stream. Each event then moves to a 1D context memory indexed by the channel.

The module performs a neighbour search using the *skip step connection* method. Instead of scanning all possible neighbours, the system reads events at fixed intervals along the channel dimension from the BRAM. Events that meet the *temporal search* criteria (based on r_t radius) are added to an edge list, and their corresponding time and channel indices are fed into an accumulator. After iterating over all channels, this accumulator computes the average position of the neighbours using a simple divider. The resulting averaged features, together with the newly stored event and the edge list, are then passed to the first stage of the graph convolution pipeline, where the time in channel index (*ch*) is updated.

The total number of clock cycles N_{cycles} required for graph generation depends on the channel radius (r_{ch}), the *skip step* (s), and the additional cycles for feature computation (N_{div}). Assuming dual-port memory (two reads per clock cycle), this can be expressed as:

$$N_{\text{cycles}} = \frac{1 + 2 \cdot \frac{r_{ch}}{s}}{2} + N_{\text{div}} \tag{2}$$

Here, 1 corresponds to the central channel read, $2 \cdot \frac{r_{ch}}{s}$ represents the reads from the upper and lower channels, and N_{div} accounts for division.

3.2   Graph Convolution

In the baseline approach, the PointNetConv [36] convolutional layer was used, which extends the classical *message passing mechanism* commonly used in graph convolutions. As highlighted in [19,21], these layers are lightweight and well-suited for hardware acceleration, making them a natural choice for adoption in our work. However, we introduce two key modifications.

First, we integrate a *batch normalisation (BN)* layer into ϕ to ensure stable training. Notably, during quantisation these layers are folded [37], which prevents any increase in the model parameters for hardware deployment. The second and more important change involves an additional normalisation step for the positional differences used on the event-graph edges. Input data is initially normalised to $(0, 1)$ range, while neighbours are determined within the radius r_{ch} and r_t. Consequently, channel index differences are within $(-r_{ch}, r_{ch})$, and time index differences are within $(-r_t, 0)$ due to the use of a time-based directed graph generator. These values occupy only a small fraction of $(0, 1)$ range, which adversely affects training and reduces precision during quantisation. To address this, we apply *positional normalisation (PN)* after computing position differences, rescaling the values back to $(0, 1)$ range, by multiplying time differences by $-\frac{1}{r_t}$, and channel differences by adding r_{ch} and multiplying by $\frac{2}{r_{ch}}$.

The modified model is expressed as:

$$\hat{\mathcal{X}}_i = \max_{j \in N(i)} \left(BN \; \phi([\mathcal{X}_j || PN(\mathcal{P}_j - \mathcal{P}_i)]) \right). \tag{3}$$

For hardware implementation each graph convolution assumes fully asynchronous event-by-event processing and can be executed in parallel. Each incoming event with its edge list and input features is processed independently. The module must also access the features of each vertex connected with an edge and the difference between the neighbour and the processed event. For this purpose, we implemented one 2-port BRAM memory that stores the features of the last processed event for each channel, and another one for storing the weights.

To determine the final output feature, the linear layer must be applied for the vertex itself (so-called self-loop) and for each of its neighbours (a maximum of MAX_EDGE = 21 times with the r_{ch}=100 and *skip step* s=10). The key part of the graph convolution is the vector multiplication module – in order to reduce resource utilisation, the module was implemented in a way that some of the calculations were performed sequentially (as inspired by [21]).

Taking advantage of two-port memories, we process two feature vectors and calculate two elements of the output vector (OUT_DIM = 64) at the same time (cf. Fig. 3). The total number of clock cycles required to perform the convolution for a single event can be determined with the following formula:

$$N_{\text{cycles}} = \frac{MAX\_EDGE + 1}{2} \cdot \frac{OUT\_DIM}{2} \tag{4}$$

The graph convolution module can be considered a bottleneck of the proposed method. The throughput of the system is dependent on the maximum number of clock cycles required per single event. For our baseline model implemented for a 200 MHz clock, the theoretical throughput was thus calculated to be 555 kEPS (thousand events per second). At the same time, the average in the SHD dataset is around 20 kEPS. However, it should be noted that the number of parallel vector multiplication modules could be increased to improve latency and throughput (using additional resources), or decreased with an opposite effect.

An essential part of the system is the quantisation. In our work, the precision of calculations on integer values can be selected per layer. Both feature map elements and weights are stored in memory as unsigned integers, and rescaled before (quantisation) and after (re-quantisation) of multiplications. For scaling we use DSP multiplication and bit-shifting or look-up tables (depending on the number of possible quantised values).

3.3   Graph Average Pool

The final step of the baseline method requires global average pooling to aggregate all of the vertex-level features of the last layer into a single fixed-length vector to be processed by fully-connected layers. Our experiments with simpler alternatives, such as global maximum pooling or global sum pooling, revealed that these approaches result in significantly degraded quality results (by 7 pps for max and 5 pps for sum). Therefore, we decided to keep the original method.

We implemented a global average pooling module which receives the features from the last stage of the graph convolution (Fig. 1) to the input. The mean value is calculated by accumulating the sum of each vector feature in a given register. To determine the number of events that have been accumulated, a simple counter is used. When the output vector corresponding to the last event in a spoken word is calculated, the accumulator register values are divided by the current value of the counter. These values are then output by the module and stored in a BRAM memory.

3.4 System Integration

To test the architecture on the target platform, it was necessary to provide the data from an AC to the input and receive the output features to classify it. As we currently do not have the access to the real AC sensor, we decided to use test data samples from the SHD dataset written into separate text files on an SD card, which were read using the SoC FPGA processing system. The subsequent events were sent to the programmable logic via an AXI4 bus. To simulate AC, it was required to provide events to the architecture at the moments that respect the event timestamps. In the processing system a delay function was implemented in order to achieve this based on the differences of successive timestamps.

When the average pooling output is fully written into the BRAM memory, an interrupt flag is raised, which triggers a function in the SoC FPGA processing system. The BRAM contents are read into the PS and two multi-layer perceptron functions are executed. Each layer was implemented using a pair of nested loops and is highly sequential. For a future work, these calculations could also be realised with a greater parallelism in the programmable logic.

4 Evaluation

In order to evaluate the event-graph model, we consider three key metrics: top-1 accuracy, model size and FLOPs per event on the SHD dataset [23]. This permits the runtime performance, power consumption and resource utilisation of the hardware implemented model to be compared with previous SNN FPGA implementations. We conducted preliminary ablation studies concerning graph generation and graph convolution hyper-parameters to evaluate several model configurations and select the best one for the implementation in hardware.

4.1 Setup

For implementation and training, we used PyTorch and PyTorch Geometric libraries [38]. All prepared models were trained for 100 epochs in floating-point precision, followed by 20 epochs of quantisation-aware training [37] with a batch size of 16 on a single A100 GPU. The Adam optimiser was configured with a learning rate of 2e–4, weight decay of 1e–4, and a ReduceLROnPlateau scheduler with a 0.5 reduction factor and patience of 10. The best model weights were saved based on the minimum training loss and subsequently evaluated on the test set.

All models consist of four PointNetConv convolutional layers, a graph average pooling layer, and two fully-connected layers. To preserve the input temporal resolution, we applied 16-bit quantisation on the first convolution. The remaining convolutional layers were quantised with 8-bit precision. The final two fully-connected layers, implemented in the processing system of the SoC FPGA device, were not quantised and therefore use 32-bit floating-point.

The hardware architecture of the network was implemented in the SystemVerilog language using Vivado 2022.2, while the processing system was programmed using Vitis 2022.2 in the C++ language. After verifying the compatibility with PyTorch software model via Vivado simulation, it was implemented on a Zynq UltraScale+ ZCU104 FPGA platform with XCZU7EV chip from AMD Xilinx.

4.2 Ablation Studies

In this section, we present the results of experiments designed to evaluate the impact of hyper-parameters on the proposed architecture. First, we study the impact of the graph generator parameters. We then compare the performance and number of parameters required for different variants of the model in order to evaluate the scalability of the proposed approach. Unless stated otherwise, the base model was configured with all output channels set to 64, a graph generator with an r_{ch} of 100, a *skip step* of 10 and an r_t of 20 ms.

Graph Generation Configurations. In Table 2 we present the results of our accuracy analysis for the base model as a function of the r_{ch} and *skip step* parameters. The experiment was carried out in two stages. In the first one, we varied the r_{ch} parameter from 30 to 300 while keeping the *skip step* fixed at 10. In the second stage, using the best r_{ch} value identified in the first stage, we varied the *skip step* parameter from 1 to 20. A "-" score indicates configurations excluded from the analysis due to excessively large tensor sizes that could not fit in the GPU memory.

Table 2. The impact of search radius r_{ch} and *skip step* parameters on top-1 accuracy. The best results, highlighted in **bold**, were obtained for moderate parameters.

r_{ch}	skip step	top-1 acc. float	top-1 acc. quantised	r_{ch}	skip step	top-1 acc. float	top-1 acc. quantised
100	1	90.95%	–	30	10	85.43%	84.23%
100	5	91.37%	90.10%	50	10	88.25%	87.60%
100	**10**	**92.74%**	**92.30%**	200	10	91.23%	90.05%
100	15	90.63%	89.22%	250	10	90.47%	89.72%
100	20	90.05%	88.91%	300	10	89.66%	88.62%

We observed that too few edges – caused by either a high *skip step* or a low r_{ch} – negatively affect the model accuracy. Conversely, an excessively large r_{ch} or too small *skip step* can also degrade classification performance. This is due to the sensitivity of PointNetConv layers to outliers, which become more noticeable with a large number of edges – a consequence of using a max-type aggregation.

The best results were achieved with moderate parameter values: an r_{ch} of 100 and a *skip step* of 10, yielding 92.74% accuracy for the floating-point model.

It is also important to emphasise that the computational cost of graph convolutions is proportional to the number of edges. As illustrated in Fig. 4a, the number of floating-point operations (FLOPs) required per event – for all convolutions, averaged across the entire test dataset – is influenced by the *skip step* parameter. This analysis indicates that using connections with a *skip step* of 10 reduces FLOPs by a factor of ten (3.568 vs 0.368 MFLOPs/ev), confirming a linear relationship between computational demands and the number of generated edges. The role of our novel *skip step* method is crucial for reducing the calculation complexity. Note that this is not specific to the context of FPGA implementations.

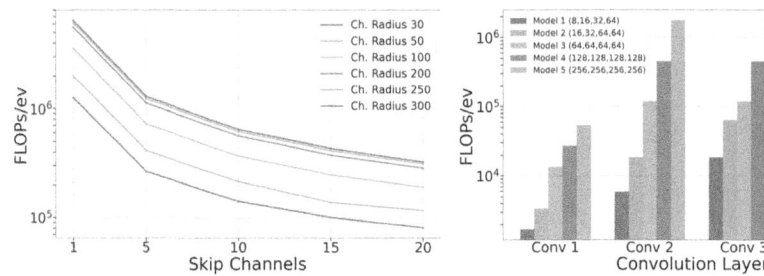

(a) Average FLOPs per event for different graph generation configurations.

(b) Average FLOPs per event for model configurations (outputs per convolution).

Fig. 4. Model complexity analysis in term of FLOPs. The figures illustrate not only the significant impact of model size on computational complexity, but also the parameters of the graph generator.

Model Configurations. In this subsection, we examine how varying the dimensions of the convolutional layers affects model performance. As a reference, we used two model configurations described in [20]: small – with all layer dimensions set to 64 and large – with all layer dimensions set to 256. To explore a broader range of options, we study three additional models: one with all layer sizes set to 128, and two variants with increasing layer size. The results, including layer dimensions, total number of parameters, and classification accuracy, are summarised in Table 3.

The results demonstrate that increasing the number of parameters improves classification accuracy, highlighting the scalability of our method. Importantly, compared to the baseline (achieving 90.0% and 94.3% accuracy for the small and large models), the equivalent models based on our proposed approach (minor differences in parameter number are due to BatchNorm layers) achieve accuracies of 92.74% and 94.63%, respectively. This indicates that the proposed solutions not only facilitate efficient hardware implementation, but also enhance performance.

Table 3. Layer configurations (number of output features) with number of parameters and top-1 accuracy. Increasing the number of parameters improves classification results, demonstrating the scalability of our approach.

Conv 1	Conv 2	Conv 3	Conv 4	FC	Params (k)	top-1 acc. float	top-1 acc. quantised
8	16	32	64	64	8.6	89.22%	88.78%
16	32	64	64	64	12.9	90.54%	90.98%
64	64	64	64	64	18.9	92.74%	92.30%
128	128	128	128	128	70.5	93.93%	93.31%
256	256	256	256	256	272.0	94.64%	94.45%

Similar to the number of edges, another key factor influencing model complexity is the dimensionality of event feature vectors processed by the network. To address this, we conducted an analysis of the average number of FLOPs per event for each convolutional layer, depending on its configuration. The results are presented in Fig. 4b. They show that the computational complexity of the first convolutional layer increases linearly with its dimension due to the fixed size of input data (13.516 vs 27.032 kFLOPs/ev for Model 3 vs Model 4), while for subsequent layers in models with uniform dimensions, complexity grows quadratically (118.269 vs 452.801 kFLOPs/ev for Conv 2). Consequently, the total FLOPs for the evaluated models are 0.091, 0.204, 0.368, 1.385, and 5.366 MFLOPs/ev, respectively. These results underline the importance of careful selection of network parameters to optimise memory and computational costs.

4.3   Comparison with the State-of-the-Art

In order to position our work relative to the state-of-the-art, we first compare accuracy and parameter count of our event-graph neural network software model to other event-based AI approaches on the SHD dataset. Next, we compare our hardware implementation with two FPGA works of spiking neural networks with consideration of power consumption, latency and resource utilisation.

The results in Table 1 show that our models are among the smallest in the state-of-the-art. Our base model, with only 18.9k parameters, in terms of size is surpassed only by the small model from [20], which served as our baseline inspiration, and by some optimised variants of our network (from Table 3). The test accuracy of 92.31% is comparable to those reported by [30,31], while drastically reducing the number of parameters by 86.5% and over 99%, respectively. Our largest model achieves an accuracy of 94.45%. This result is lower than only three models. It should be noted that two of these models [24,29] require millions of parameters compared to only 272k in our case. Furthermore, it should be noted that our event-graph approach underwent significant hardware-aware modifications and quantisation. The high performance achieved is a testament to the suitability of GNNs for event-data processing.

A direct comparison of our hardware implementation with solutions from the literature (SNNs) is presented in Table 4. We implemented base and tiny variants (the latter refers to the smallest model in Table 3) for Zynq US+ ZCU104 board.

Table 4. Comparison of state-of-the-art hardware implementations. The values in parentheses take into account the PS part (classification head). The values marked with "-" were not mentioned in the respective papers.

	Matinizadeh [32]	Carpegna [12]	Ours (base)	Ours (tiny)
Device/Board	Zynq ZCU104	Zynq Z7-20	Zynq ZCU104	Zynq ZCU104
Logic cells	–	18,268	–	–
LUT	149,760	–	81,567	34,474
FF	92,160	–	47,699	23,713
BRAM	75	51	70	28
DSP	–	–	318	106
Frequency	100 MHz	100 MHz	200 MHz	200 MHz
Latency [µs]	–	540	8 (179)	4 (175)
Power [W]	–	0.43	1.20 (3.94)	1.05 (3.79)
Peak power [W]	1.629	–	–	–
Accuracy	87.80%	72.99%	**92.30%**	88.78%

With our approach, we established a new state-of-the-art accuracy for an FPGA solution applied to the SHD benchmark by a considerable 4.5% margin. Our base model uses available logic resources more evenly than [32] (fewer LUTs/FFs, more DSPs), thus avoiding potential routing delays. We achieved this through executing some of the multiplications sequentially and leveraging the DSP multipliers. Furthermore, with the tiny model we achieved 0.8% higher accuracy with just 23% of LUTs and 37% of BRAMs compared to [32].

An important advantage of our solution is its asynchronous event-by-event processing and the intrinsic ability of event-graphs to exploit temporal sparsity for rapid and efficient calculations. However, this makes it difficult to compare it with other solutions in terms of latency. Our base hardware module's (graph generation and graph convolution) per-event latency was measured at 8 µs for a 200 MHz clock with 555 kEPS throughput (4 µs and 277 kEPS for tiny model). After taking into account the PS-PL communication and the determination of the value of classification results by the network's head in the processing part of the heterogeneous system, we obtain the predicted class 179 µs after the occurrence of the last event. In [12] the reported latency of 0.54 ms assumes the processing of the entire data sample after its encoding in 100 time steps. Our solution, which requires no prior data aggregation, maintains high throughput and low latency for edge applications by exploiting data's temporal sparsity.

The power estimation provided by the Vivado software for the PL part of the system (base model) is 1.20 W (0.60 W dynamic and 0.60 W static). With the

PS part included energy usage increases to 3.94 W (3.25 W dynamic and 0.7 W static) for the entire base architecture.

For an additional ablation study we implemented the resource-optimised variant of the base model for decreased number of parallel multiplications (from 4 per convolution to 2). With this modification, we were able to achieve 49% decrease in both DSP and LUT utilisation and 35% for FFs with a simultaneous increase of latency for a single event (in the PL) to 15.2 μs (theoretical throughput of 277 kEPS). This experiment confirms that the amount of resources depends on the latency – the choice of the final solution should be based on the requirements of the specific task and the size of the target platform.

5   Summary

In this work we present the first hardware-software co-design of an event-graph neural network for time-series audio classification. Because our approach exploits the inherent sparsity of event-data to reduce the computational complexity and latency, it is highly promising for near-sensor AI processing at the edge.

We proposed adaptations and optimisations permitting an event-graph to be implemented efficiently on a SoC FPGA. In particular, we presented the novel *skip step* graph generation method with simplified and computationally efficient features. In spite of this, our quantised hardware-aware event-graph model achieved a test accuracy extremely close to floating-point precision software models from the state-of-the-art while requiring almost two orders of magnitude fewer parameters. Crucially, our method outperformed all previous FPGA implementations of hardware-aware spiking neural networks on the same benchmark achieving improvements of up to 4.5% and 19.3% in accuracy. Relative to these works, the utilisation of FPGA resources and the latency were also reduced. Our smallest model (tiny) achieves comparable accuracy to previous state-of-the-art while utilising only 23% of logic and 37% of memory resources.

We have confirmed that the hardware implementation of graph neural networks applied to event data from artificial cochlea sensors is both highly efficient and capable of achieving superior task accuracy compared to spiking neural network alternatives.

In future work we intend to improve our system by making it compatible with continuously streamed events. Currently, we classify the samples, in which only one word is spoken. However, in real-life case there may be multiple words in a recorded sentence that need to be separated and recognised, thus making this task more difficult. Additionally, while input for our system was simulated using event-data written to an SD card, our goal is to integrate a real event-sensor for a fully end-to-end demonstrator. This may not necessarily be an audio sensor, our approach is generally applicable to any time-series application. Furthermore, in the current version of the system the multi-layer perceptron that outputs the final prediction result is implemented in the processing system of the used SoC FPGA for a higher flexibility and scalability of the solution. Not only we intend to perform this function in the programmable logic or in the AI cores available in the Versal SoC FPGA for a greater parallelism and lower latency, but we also plan to explore different neural network architectures that may be better adapted. For example, recurrent neural networks like LSTMs may be more naturally able to exploit temporal dependencies extracted by the event-graph.

Acknowledgments. This work was supported by The Horizon Europe (dAIedge, grant 101120726), the "Excellence initiative – research university" programme for the AGH University of Krakow, the Polish National Science Centre projects 2024/53/N/ST6/04254 and 2024/53/N/ST6/04331 and Polish high-performance computing infrastructure PLGrid (HPC Center: ACK Cyfronet AGH – grant no. PLG/2023/016897).

References

1. Ren, L., Jia, Z., Laili, Y., Huang, D.: Deep learning for time-series prediction in IIoT: progress, challenges, and prospects. IEEE Trans. Neural Netw. Learn. Syst. (2023). https://doi.org/10.1109/TNNLS.2023.3291371
2. Lim, B., Zohren, S.: Time-series forecasting with deep learning: a survey. Phil. Trans. R. Soc. A **379**(2194), 20200209 (2021). https://doi.org/10.1098/rsta.2020.0209
3. Saufi, S.R., Ahmad, Z., Leong, M.S., Lim, M.H.: Gearbox fault diagnosis using a deep learning model with limited data sample. IEEE Trans. Industr. Inf. **16**(10), 6263–6271 (2020). https://doi.org/10.1109/TII.2020.2967822
4. DiMarco, J.P.: Implantable cardioverter-defibrillators. N. Engl. J. Med. **349**(19), 1836–1847 (2003). https://doi.org/10.1056/NEJMra035432
5. Al-Ameri, Y., Nguyen, M., Westerlund, T.: Fpga-based hardware acceleration for deep learning in mobile robotics. In: 2024 IEEE Nordic Circuits and Systems Conference (NorCAS), pp. 1–7 (2024). https://doi.org/10.1109/NorCAS64408.2024.10752450
6. Al-Ali, F., Gamage, T.D., Nanayakkara, H.W., Mehdipour, F., Ray, S.K.: Novel casestudy and benchmarking of alexnet for edge AI: From cpu and gpu to fpga. In: 2020 IEEE Canadian Conference on Electrical and Computer Engineering (CCECE), pp. 1–4 (2020). https://doi.org/10.1109/CCECE47787.2020.9255739
7. Guo, K., Zeng, S., Yu, J., Wang, Y., Yang, H.: [dl] a survey of fpga-based neural network inference accelerators. ACM Trans. Reconfigurable Technol. Syst. **12**(1) (2019). https://doi.org/10.1145/3289185
8. Gallego, G., et al.: Event-based vision: a survey. IEEE Trans. Pattern Anal. Mach. Intell. **44**(1), 154–180 (2020). https://doi.org/10.1109/TPAMI.2020.3008413
9. Liu, S.C., van Schaik, A., Minch, B.A., Delbruck, T.: Asynchronous binaural spatial audition sensor with 2 ×64×4 channel output. IEEE Trans. Biomed. Circuits Syst. **8**(4), 453–464 (2013). https://doi.org/10.1109/TBCAS.2013.2281834
10. Mostafa, A., Hardy, E., Badets, F.: 17.8 0.4 v 988nw time-domain audio feature extraction for keyword spotting using injection-locked oscillators. In: 2024 IEEE International Solid-State Circuits Conference (ISSCC), vol. 67, pp. 328–330. IEEE (2024). https://doi.org/10.1109/ISSCC49657.2024.10454389
11. Ortner, T., Pes, L., Gentinetta, J., Frenkel, C., Pantazi, A.: Online spatio-temporal learning with target projection. In: 2023 IEEE 5th International Conference on Artificial Intelligence Circuits and Systems (AICAS), pp. 1–5. IEEE (2023). https://doi.org/10.1109/AICAS57966.2023.10168623

12. Carpegna, A., Savino, A., Carlo, S.D.: Spiker+: a framework for the generation of efficient spiking neural networks FPGA accelerators for inference at the edge. IEEE Trans. Emerg. Top. Comput. **01**, 1–15 (2024). https://doi.org/10.1109/TETC.2024.3511676

13. Dalgaty, T., et al.: Mosaic: in-memory computing and routing for small-world spike-based neuromorphic systems. Nat. Commun. **15**(1), 142 (2024). https://doi.org/10.1038/s41467-023-44365-x

14. Dampfhoffer, M., Mesquida, T., Valentian, A., Anghel, L.: Are SNNs really more energy-efficient than ANNs? an in-depth hardware-aware study. IEEE Trans. Emerg. Top. Comput. Intell. **7**(3), 731–741 (2023). https://doi.org/10.1109/TETCI.2022.3214509

15. Dalgaty, T., et al.: The CNN vs. SNN event-camera dichotomy and perspectives for event-graph neural networks. In: 2023 Design, Automation & Test in Europe Conference & Exhibition (DATE), pp. 1–6. IEEE (2023). https://doi.org/10.23919/DATE56975.2023.10137023

16. Li, Y., et al.: Graph-based asynchronous event processing for rapid object recognition. In: Proceedings of the IEEE/CVF International Conference on Computer Vision, pp. 934–943 (2021). https://doi.org/10.1109/ICCV48922.2021.00097

17. Dalgaty, T., Mesquida, T., Joubert, D., Sironi, A., Vivet, P., Posch, C.: Hugnet: hemi-spherical update graph neural network applied to low-latency event-based optical flow. In: Proceedings of the IEEE/CVF Conference on Computer Vision and Pattern Recognition (CVPR) Workshops, pp. 3952–3961, June 2023. https://doi.org/10.1109/CVPRW59228.2023.00411

18. Mesquida, T., Dampfhoffer, M., Dalgaty, T., Vivet, P., Sironi, A., Posch, C.: G2N2: lightweight event stream classification with GRU graph neural networks. In: https://proceedings.bmvc2023.org/, https://proceedings.bmvc2023.org/, Aberdeen, United Kingdom, p. 660, November 2023. https://cea.hal.science/cea-04321175

19. Jeziorek, K., Pinna, A., Kryjak, T.: Memory-efficient graph convolutional networks for object classification and detection with event cameras. In: 2023 Signal Processing: Algorithms, Architectures, Arrangements, and Applications (SPA), pp. 160–165. IEEE (2023). https://doi.org/10.23919/SPA59660.2023.10274464

20. Rafeldt, L., et al.: Event-based audio prediction with spectro-temporal event-graphs (2025)

21. Jeziorek, K., Wzorek, P., Blachut, K., Pinna, A., Kryjak, T.: Embedded graph convolutional networks for real-time event data processing on SoC FPGAs (2024). https://arxiv.org/abs/2406.07318

22. Yang, Y., Kneip, A., Frenkel, C.: Evgnn: an event-driven graph neural network accelerator for edge vision. arXiv preprint arXiv:2404.19489 (2024). https://doi.org/10.48550/arXiv.2404.19489

23. Cramer, B., Stradmann, Y., Schemmel, J., Zenke, F.: The heidelberg spiking data sets for the systematic evaluation of spiking neural networks. IEEE Trans. Neural Netw. Learn. Syst. **33**(7), 2744–2757 (2022). https://doi.org/10.1109/TNNLS.2020.3044364

24. Bittar, A., Garner, P.N.: A surrogate gradient spiking baseline for speech command recognition. Front. Neurosci. **16** (2022). https://doi.org/10.3389/fnins.2022.865897

25. Dampfhoffer, M., Mesquida, T., Valentian, A., Anghel, L.: Investigating current-based and gating approaches for accurate and energy-efficient spiking recurrent neural networks. In: Pimenidis, E., Angelov, P., Jayne, C., Papaleonidas, A., Aydin, M. (eds.) Artificial Neural Networks and Machine Learning – ICANN 2022, pp. 359–370. Springer Nature Switzerland, Cham (2022). https://doi.org/10.1007/978-3-031-15934-3_30

26. Rossbroich, J., Gygax, J., Zenke, F.: Fluctuation-driven initialization for spiking neural network training. Neuromorphic Comput. Eng. **2**(4), 044016 (2022). https://doi.org/10.1088/2634-4386/ac97bb

27. D'Agostino, S., et al.: Denram: neuromorphic dendritic architecture with rram for efficient temporal processing with delays. Nature Commun. **15**(3446) (2024). https://doi.org/10.1038/s41467-024-47764-w

28. Hammouamri, I., Khalfaoui-Hassani, I., Masquelier, T.: Learning delays in spiking neural networks using dilated convolutions with learnable spacings (2023). https://arxiv.org/abs/2306.17670

29. Malettira, P.G., Negi, S., Ponghiran, W., Roy, K.: TSkips: Efficiency through explicit temporal delay connections in spiking neural networks (2024). https://arxiv.org/abs/2411.16711

30. Sun, P., Chua, Y., Devos, P., Botteldooren, D.: Learnable axonal delay in spiking neural networks improves spoken word recognition. Front. Neurosci. **17** (2023). https://doi.org/10.3389/fnins.2023.1275944

31. Yu, C., Gu, Z., Li, D., Wang, G., Wang, A., Li, E.: Stsc-snn: Spatio-temporal synaptic connection with temporal convolution and attention for spiking neural networks. Front. Neurosci. **16** (2022). https://doi.org/10.3389/fnins.2022.1079357

32. Matinizadeh, S., et al.: A fully-configurable open-source software-defined digital quantized spiking neural core architecture (2024). https://arxiv.org/abs/2404.02248

33. Basu, A., Deng, L., Frenkel, C., Zhang, X.: Spiking neural network integrated circuits: a review of trends and future directions. In: 2022 IEEE Custom Integrated Circuits Conference (CICC), pp. 1–8. IEEE (2022). https://doi.org/10.1109/CICC53496.2022.9772783

34. Kryjak, T.: Event-based vision on fpgas-a survey. In: 2024 27th Euromicro Conference on Digital System Design (DSD), pp. 541–550. IEEE (2024). https://doi.org/10.1109/DSD64264.2024.00078

35. Xu, Y., Perera, S., Bethi, Y., Afshar, S., van Schaik, A.: Event-driven spectrotemporal feature extraction and classification using a silicon cochlea model. Front. Neurosci. **17**, 1125210 (2023). https://doi.org/10.3389/fnins.2023.1125210

36. Charles, R.Q., Su, H., Kaichun, M., Guibas, L.J.: Pointnet: deep learning on point sets for 3d classification and segmentation. In: 2017 IEEE Conference on Computer Vision and Pattern Recognition (CVPR), pp. 77–85 (2017). https://doi.org/10.1109/CVPR.2017.16

37. Jacob, B., et al.: Quantization and training of neural networks for efficient integer-arithmetic-only inference. In: Proceedings of the IEEE Conference on Computer Vision and Pattern Recognition, pp. 2704–2713 (2018). https://doi.org/10.1109/CVPR.2018.00286

38. Fey, M., Lenssen, J.E.: Fast graph representation learning with pytorch geometric. ArXiv **abs/1903.02428** (2019). https://api.semanticscholar.org/CorpusID:70349949

Security and Resilience in FPGA Systems

RePAIR: Reconfigurable Platform for AI Resilience Within RISC-V Ecosystem

Giorgio Cora$^{(\boxtimes)}$ ⓘ, Eleonora Vacca ⓘ, Corrado De Sio ⓘ, Sarah Azimi ⓘ,
and Luca Sterpone ⓘ

Politecnico di Torino, Torino, Italy
{giorgio.cora,eleonora.vacca,corrado.desio,sarah.azimi,
luca.sterpone}@polito.it

Abstract. Recently, platforms combining RISC-V processors with accelerators for deep-learning applications have gained popularity even for high-reliability applications such as avionics and space. However, for high-performance safety-critical systems, it is mandatory to couple high-performance architecture with reliable mechanisms for coping with errors and faults. We propose the first FPGA-based architecture that combines a RISC-V processor with a systolic array-based accelerator, a fault detection, fault correction, and an execution recovery mechanism. The proposed solution corrects faults in the systolic array datapath by exploiting a partial reconfiguration mechanism. When an error is detected, the RISC-V processor can trigger the accelerator reconfiguration, correcting the fault. Furthermore, the approach allows resuming the inference from the last correctly executed step, significantly reducing the availability overhead. The approach results in a high-performance and high-reliable platform that can autonomously detect and correct faults, providing execution continuity and minimal system downtime.

Keywords: RISC-V · Systolic Arrays · Fault Detection · Partial Reconfiguration · AI

1 Introduction

The widespread adoption of Deep Learning (DL) techniques, combined with the increase in model complexity, has driven the development of high-performance platforms capable of delivering the computational power required for efficient and rapid inference. Due to the open-source nature of the RISC-V Instruction Set Architecture (ISA), researchers are increasingly focusing on enhancing RISC-V-based solutions to meet these computational demands. The predominant strategies involve either extending the ISA [1] or coupling RISC-V with application-specific accelerators [2]. Since most DL workloads involve large-scale matrix multiplications, many proposed solutions integrate methods for executing neural networks, such as general matrix multiplications (GEMM), within the RISC-V environment [3, 4], which has renewed interest in Systolic Array (SA) architectures. Solutions based on SA employ a grid-like structure of processing elements (PEs) for efficient parallel computation, minimizing memory access, maximizing

© The Author(s), under exclusive license to Springer Nature Switzerland AG 2025
R. Giorgi et al. (Eds.): ARC 2025, LNCS 15594, pp. 71–87, 2025.
https://doi.org/10.1007/978-3-031-87995-1_5

data reuse, and performing on-chip computation. These aspects are appealing for deep neural networks (DNNs)-based applications, where minimizing data movement becomes a priority to achieve high computation efficiency. Due to the complexity of DNN, modern SA-based accelerators, with Google's Tensor Processing Unit being a pioneering example [5], are equipped with their own ISA supporting single-instruction multiple data execution to process large vectors of data in one clock cycle.

However, when DNN models are employed in safety-critical applications, focusing only on computational efficiency is insufficient. Indeed, ensuring the correctness of the inference execution is as important as the performance. For this reason, several works proposed methodologies to address hardware fault detection in the SA accelerator [6] or fault masking acting on the DNN model [7, 8]. Still, there's a lack of solutions that target reconfigurable platforms, such as FPGA, when adopted to implement such kinds of AI accelerators.

The demand for fault-tolerance solutions for SRAM-based FPGAs is also exacerbated by the fact that they are susceptible to errors in configuration memory caused by external factors, such as ionizing radiation, which is the primary concern for space and avionics systems and can also occur at sea level [9]. A trivial way to address hardware faults in the implemented circuit due to configuration memory (CRAM) corruption is to reload the configuration data (CDATA) to restore the correct circuit functionalities using the unfaulty configuration bitstream. However, this approach has substantial limitations since it takes several seconds, which results in a reduction of system availability. Moreover, runtime fault detection in FPGA devices is often invasive to applications and computational systems. Standard fault detection methodologies may require additional modules allocated along with the implemented circuit, like SEM-IP [10], or to perform periodic memory readback to compare with a golden configuration, eventually triggering complete reconfiguration upon error detection. The former approach also diminishes the resources dedicated to computational units, and additionally, correcting the error does not consider errors already propagated in the user logic between the error and the correction. The latter fails to meet the real-time constraints of DNN, as it can take several seconds to detect and correct an error—potentially leading to catastrophic failures or service disruption in safety-critical systems.

1.1 Main Contributions

This work presents RePAIR, a heterogeneous computing platform integrating and extending an open-source RISC-V processor [11] and an open-source TPU-like accelerator [12]. RePAIR targets reconfigurable devices and offers fault detection, fault correction, and recovery capability, preserving high performance and minimum overhead.

To the best of our knowledge, this is the first platform to combine performance optimization and fault tolerance in this manner. The main innovations and contributions are as follows:

- Design and implementation of the RePAIR platform, integrating a RISC-V processor with a systolic array-based accelerator.

- Extension of tinyTPU ISA [12] for Runtime Self-Test: The ISA of the AI accelerator is extended to enable runtime self-test capabilities. This feature allows the detection of structural faults in the accelerator datapath with minimal impact on the inference process.
- Dual Inference Modes: the computational platform can execute either in a *plain mode* for standard inference operation without additional overhead or in *testing mode*, which introduces a checksum test for the current inference workload at the cost of three additional clock cycles per matrix multiplication. This mechanism enables fault detection during inference without disrupting the normal operational flow with an accelerator area overhead of only 0.31%.
- Fault Detection, Correction, and Recovery: When a fault is detected in the TPU datapath, the accelerator notifies the RISC-V processor. The processor triggers a dynamic partial reconfiguration to reload the bitstream section associated with the faulty accelerator while preserving its ongoing correct workload. By utilizing partial reconfiguration, the RePAIR platform implemented on the AMD KCU105 device can reduce system downtime by up to 900 times compared to traditional methods. This ensures rapid fault recovery and enhances system availability. The recovery mechanism resumes the workload from the last correctly executed instructions. This approach limits the inference execution overhead to 30% in the worst-case scenario, compared to full device reconfiguration, which can result in up to 96% overhead.

The content of the paper is structured as follows. Section 2 introduces the related works. Section 3 details the SA fault detection mechanism, while Sect. 4 outlines the integration of the RISC-V processor with the accelerator. Finally, Sect. 5 presents the experimental results, and Sect. 6 concludes.

2 State of the Art

Over the years, the introduction of the RISC-V ISA has led to the development of various computing platforms [13], addressing the needs of many domains of targeting DNN applications [14, 16], with remarkable results. For instance, authors in [3] propose a custom, high-performance, and multithread library for convolutional operations targeting RISC-V processors. Results show extremely good performance in terms of Floating-Point Operations Per Second (FLOPS), even when compared to other processors such as ARM ones, proving their suitability for carrying out DNN operations. One of the main characteristics of RISC-V processors is the open-source nature of the ISA, allowing for easier pipeline modification to support custom instruction execution and efficient coupling with external modules. Following this trend, authors in [17] propose a custom architecture that couples a 64-bit RISC-V architecture, Ariane, with a co-processor for DNN inference applications. The possibility of extending the ISA of the RISC grants faster and more efficient DDR access, improving the overall execution time. Authors in [4] developed an architecture that embeds custom modules and co-processors in the RI5CY processor pipeline to support GEMM operations. The acceleration of GEMM operation is achieved through the ISA extension, which provides three custom SIMD instructions to be executed depending on the selected parallelism. Similarly, authors in [18] propose and compare two similar designs, evaluating the differences in terms of execution speedup when co-processors are instantiated inside or outside the RISC-V pipeline. In the first approach, the co-processor is coupled with the 64-bit Rocket architecture through the TileLink Bus, while in the latter solution, the Matrix multiply unit is directly instantiated inside the soft-processor pipeline. Results show a speedup of 1.3x for the latter method with respect to the external coupling, while both grant improved performances against the plain version of Rocket architecture.

However, these RISCV-based platforms solely focus on performance, leaving a gap in the adoption of DNN reliability in a critical domain. We fill such a gap by proposing a platform combining a RISCV processor and a TPU accelerator oriented to enhance the system's dependability by combining three features: an error detection technique based on checksum, a fault correction mechanism based on FPGA reconfiguration capability, and an execution recovery mechanism for resuming execution from the last correct computation. In our proposed approach, we assure runtime error detection capabilities in the DNN accelerator by extending the ISA of a TPU coupled with a processor system with custom instructions that detect and notify faults. We do not only notify the RISC-V processor system that a fault is affecting the datapath, but we also trigger a dynamic partial reconfiguration of the accelerator to correct the soft errors and recover the DNN inference from the last correct operation. As a result, we proposed the RePAIR platform that targets performance and reliability with a minimal performance penalty and resource overhead.

3   The Proposed Error Detection Mechanism

3.1   Fault Model

The proposed methodology introduces a novel approach for detecting computational errors caused by structural faults in the datapath of systolic arrays. When considering designs implemented in reconfigurable computing platforms, these faults typically arise from the corruption of CRAM —a common issue in harsh environments like space [19], further exacerbated by increased sensitivity as technology scales down [20]. Radiation-induced errors in the CRAM of a reconfigurable system, such as FPGA, may introduce errors corrupting the hardware design implementation. Since CRAM is usually written only during the system boot, errors accumulating in the CRAM will cause errors and eventually lead to system failure [21, 22].

3.2   Limitation of Traditional Approaches

Traditional reliability enhancement techniques adopted in such kinds of platforms based on hardware and/or software redundancy impose significant overheads on computation, memory, and energy, making them impractical for DNN applications. For instance, while AMD's Soft Error Mitigation (SEM) IP can detect and restore CRAM faults in runtime, the detection latency, ranging from 25 ms for Kintex-7 to 13 ms for KU040 [23] devices, is incompatible with the real-time detection demands of DNN inference. Furthermore, SEM IP is resource-intensive, consuming up to 835 LUTs, 506 FFs, and multiple BRAM blocks, reducing resources available for application-specific designs. Another aspect to consider is that using SEM-IP provokes operational frequency design constraints. Indeed, the vendor datasheet imposes a max frequency of 100 MHz, which is incompatible with high-performance computing platforms [23]. Finally, correcting configuration memory will not correct previously erroneous generated output or faulty state, creating transient errors that could manifest unexpectedly in the future. Another potential scenario is full device reconfiguration, which does not require additional hardware resources but has two significant drawbacks. First, since the FPGA reboots during this process, the program restarts from the beginning, resulting in the loss of all previously completed computations, therefore increasing the inference execution overhead. Second, full device reconfiguration is time-intensive, taking several seconds to complete—a duration that grows with the device size—substantially prolonging system downtime. Considering KCU105 device, the full board reconfiguration takes 13 s while moving to a smaller device as the Ultrascale+ PYNQ-ZU, it requires 6.9 s.

3.3 Proposed Approach

Our proposed method addresses issues that make traditional approaches unsuitable for high-performance safety-critical systems, particularly in ensuring reliable execution of DNN inference. It significantly reduces the resource overhead by exploiting the computational resources already existing within the accelerator datapath. Furthermore, it is specifically designed to enable rapid fault detection and recovery during runtime, ensuring compatibility with real-time performance requirements, exploiting dynamic partial reconfiguration for error correction, and the RISC-V for enabling the TPU computational flow recovery.

The methodology combines key elements of ABFT for systolic arrays and scan chain techniques. Similar to systolic array-oriented ABFT [6, 24], the proposed method detects faults by computing checksum values on the data processed by the accelerator, but without using additional hardware resources. Indeed, drawing on the scan chain approach [25, 26], the checksums are computed by propagating specific test patterns through the functional path of the systolic array.

In detail, let's consider the normal operation executed by the processing element $PE_{i,j}$ of a SA grid. After the neural network weight loading in the PEs grid, each $PE_{i,j}$ performs a Multiply-and-Accumulate (MAC) operation. Specifically, it multiplies one input data for the weight value $w_{i,j}$ stored in its weight register and accumulates the partial product produced with that coming from the $PE_{i-1,j}$. In the next clock cycle, a new input data feeds the $PE_{i,j}$, while the previous input data is propagated to the $PE_{i,j+1}$. To summarize, we have input data propagation from left edge to the right edge of the array, and partial product accumulation that propagates from top to bottom in each SA column, while weights stay fixed on the PEs.

Our proposed approach exploits these functional paths to propagate test patterns across the PEs. These test patterns are chosen to produce a checksum value and its complement of the weights currently loaded in each column of SA. Hence, base and complemented checksums are produced in consecutive clock cycles. They enable to distinguish between transient faults or soft errors and structural faults induced by CRAM corruption. Such distinction is important since correcting the source of the error for the former only requires re-loading the weight matrix in the SA, and a fresh execution, so correction is made at the software level. In contrast, the structural faults require CRAM refresh with the unfaulty CDATA.

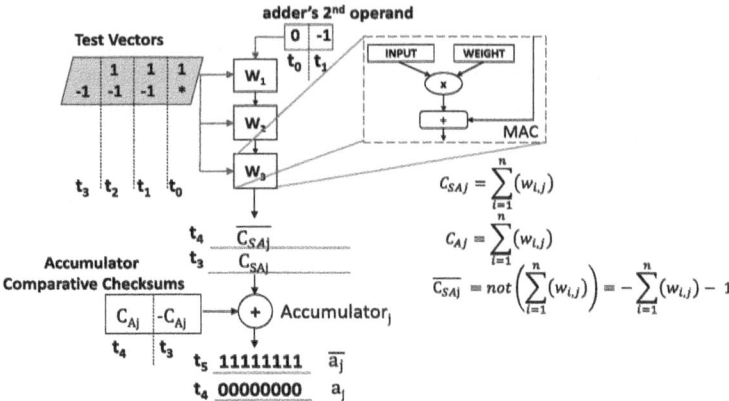

Fig. 1. Dataflow of the proposed fault detection mechanism considering the j column of MACs and the j Accumulator.

Going into detail on the checksum generation shown in Fig. 1, two test patterns are applied as input vectors to the SA in two consecutive clock cycles. These test vectors have n elements when considering a PE grid of size $n \times m$. These test vectors are built to produce checksum values C_{SAj}, corresponding to the sum of the weights loaded in the processing grid at column j, and its complementary value $\overline{C_{SAj}}$ as reported in Eq. 1 and Eq. 2. To compute C_{SAj} it is sufficient to have all the elements of the first vector equal to 1. In contrast, to produce $\overline{C_{SAj}}$ all elements of the second vector are equal to -1, and the second operand of the adders of the SA first MACs row is fed with -1.

$$C_{SAj} = \sum_{i=1}^{n}(w_{i,j}) \qquad \text{with } j\, 0, 1 \ldots m \tag{1}$$

$$\overline{C_{SAj}} = not\left(\sum_{i=1}^{n}(w_{i,j})\right) = -\sum_{i=1}^{n}(w_{i,j}) - 1 \qquad \text{with } j\, 0, 1 \ldots m \tag{2}$$

Since the two test vectors used for checksum computation have their LSB set to 1, an additional vector of 0s must be propagated to evaluate the flipping of this bit. This ensures that no stuck-at-1 fault affects it. The SA will produce all 0s in case no fault affects this bit. For the ABFT approach to be effective, we must compare the generated checksums to those produced by another unit to detect any mismatch signaling a possible error. Commonly, TPU architecture is equipped with an external bank of accumulators adjacent to the MAC grid to support tiling when the matrix multiplication does not fit in with the available resources. Our proposed approach exploits these external accumulators to compute the comparative checksum value. To do so, when the weights are loaded in the SA one vector at a time, they will also flow through the accumulators, which sum the weights data, generating C_{Aj}, as in Eq. 3. The comparison between the checksum values produced by the SA and those produced by the accumulators will happen by exploiting the accumulators themselves.

$$C_{Aj} = \sum_{i=1}^{n} (w_{i,j}) \tag{3}$$

As soon as the SA checksums are produced, they are accumulated with those produced by the accumulators, following the traditional datapath of the accelerator. Hence, what changes with respect to the canonical use of the accumulation process is only the meaning of the operands. Indeed, these will not be the results of consecutive matrix multiplications to be merged but checksums values accumulated. Specifically, consider C_{SAj} and $\overline{C_{SAj}}$ as checksum values direct and complemented produced by the column j of the SA, and C_{Aj} as the one produced by the accumulator j. Each accumulator A_j will perform the following operation:

$$a_j = C_{SAj} - C_{Aj} \tag{4}$$

$$a_j^* = \overline{C_{SAj}} + C_{Aj} \tag{5}$$

In the absence of faults, regardless of the weights' values, each a_j will assume value 0, and each $\overline{a_j}$ the value -1 (i.e. all 1s in binary). By examining the values assumed by each pair of $(a_j, \overline{a_j})$, for each column of PEs, we can identify and distinguish either the presence of a bitflip in a weight register when the pair a_j, a_j^* differs from the fault-free values, and values are complementary or a structural fault. Specifically if a_j, $\overline{a_j}$ differs from the fault-free values and are not complementary, then we have a structural fault in datapath. To identify fault location, we need to look at the checksums produced by the SA. Specifically, if the pair a_j, $\overline{a_j}$ is not complementary while C_{SAj} and $\overline{C_{SAj}}$ are complementary, then the structural fault is located in the j accumulator. Otherwise, the fault is located in the j column of the SA.

With respect to previous works that required N adders [1], and 2N + 1 adders +1 MAC [24] to compute checksum values in an SA of size N x N, our proposed approach does not require any additional resources while inducing a penalty of just 3 clock cycles to process the test vectors.

4 The RePAIR Platform

The RePAIR platform is based on a pair of open-source computing cores: the NEORV32 RISC-V processor [11] and the tinyTPU accelerator [12]. In the context of DNN applications, the platform implements a traditional processor-coprocessor paradigm, where the NEORV32 orchestrates the execution by supplying the tinyTPU accelerator with a microcode transmitted via the accelerator's instruction FIFO to perform computation layer-by-layer. Upon completing the computation of a layer, NEORV32 retrieves the results and reforms the data to suit the requirements of the subsequent layer. Each layer execution can be conducted in a testing mode, employing the fault detection methodology described in Subsect. 3.3. If a fault is detected in the tinyTPU datapath, the NEORV32 triggers and manages the dynamic partial reconfiguration of the accelerator to correct the faulty datapath. Once the accelerator is operational again, NEORV32 resumes computation from the last successful execution. This mechanism ensures continuity of application execution while minimizing system downtime.

4.1 Proposed Platform

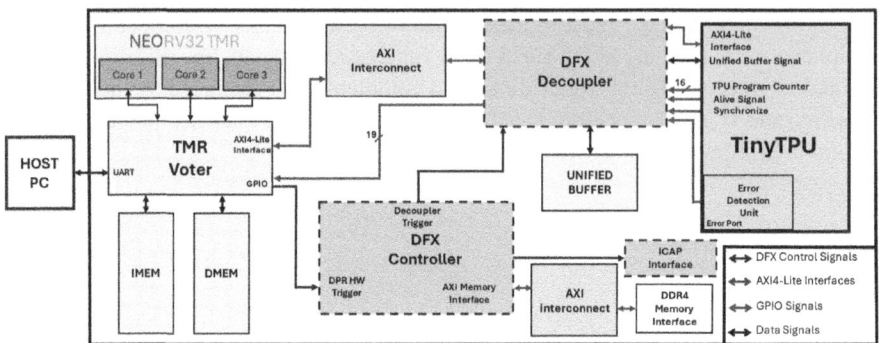

Fig. 2. The RePAIR platform.

Figure 2 provides a schematic view of the implemented architecture and the internal connections, including the UART connection that can be used for interfacing with an external host PC. The data exchange between the processor and the accelerator is handled through AXI interfacing and memory. The TPU can notify fault detection through interrupts, and the TPU status is provided to NEORV using GPIOs. Upon detecting a fault, the NEORV is responsible for initiating the dynamic partial reconfiguration of the accelerator. The dynamic partial reconfiguration [27] is handled by controlling the DFX modules. In particular, the DFX Controller [28] oversees the reconfiguration itself, fetching the CDATA from DDR and writing configuration memory. A DFX decoupler between the TPU and the rest of the system ensures that the interface signals are kept at a stable low value while partial reconfiguration is performed. Finally, if the partial reconfiguration of the TPU fails to correct the error in the datapath, a full FPGA reconfiguration is triggered as a last effort to restore functionality.

4.2 NEORV32

The NEORV32 [11] is an open-source RISC-V processor based on a 4-stage pipelined multi-cycle architecture with a maximum operating frequency of 250 MHz supporting the base RV32I ISA. It is highly customizable with various additional modules and extensions. To include NEORV32 in the RePAIR platform, the AXI-Lite communication to interface the system with the TPU has been enabled. Moreover, the UART module has been enabled to support debugging and communication with a host PC. No ALU extensions have been enabled for our platform since most of the computational work in DNN inference is carried out by the TPU accelerator, which performs matrix multiplications and applies activation functions. Since the platform's main goal is to provide performance and highly reliable execution, the NEORV processor has been hardened by design, applying TMR.

4.3 tinyTPU

The tinyTPU [12] is an open-source, VHDL-based machine learning co-processor resembling the behavior and architecture of Google's TPU version 1. It consists of a parametric design, where the size of a systolic array core can be modified from a minimum size of 6×6 MAC units to a maximum size of 14×14. Along with SA, the accelerator is equipped with an external accumulator bank. Since it is implemented to execute DNN, it embeds hardwired quantized activation units supporting the ReLu and Sigmoid activation functions. Additionally, it comes with its own weight and input/output buffer where DNN weights and input images/output of each layer are stored. The tinyTPU is a co-processor offering a custom ISA designed for 80-bit instruction parallelism. This instruction format integrates multiple elements, including opcode, memory addresses for source and destination operands, and a field specifying the number of data vectors to be processed in a single instruction. The instructions used to perform DNN inference can be summarized as *read_weights*, *matrix_multiply*, and *activate*.

4.4 Recovery Routine

A new version of the *read_weight* and *matrix_multiply* instructions, *t_read_weight*, and *t_matrix_multiply*, respectively, has been added to the TPU ISA to support the fault detection methodology. The *t_read_weight* instruction performs two tasks. First, it loads weight values from memory into the SA. Second, it propagates these weights through the accumulators to compute the weight C_{Aj} checksums. At the moment of weight flowing, the accumulators could be busy accumulating the previous matrix multiplication results if needed by the program code, like when tiling is performed. To avoid delaying the pipeline execution or allocating additional hardware resources, we exploit the mapping of the accumulators on the on-chip DSP to operate the accumulators in Single Instruction Multiple Data (SIMD) mode. Indeed, modern FPGA devices support DSP operands on more than 48 bits (AMD Ultrascale 48 bits, AMD Versal 58 bits, Intel Agilex 54 bits). By doing so, while matrix multiplication results on 32 bits are accumulated (baseline behavior), the weights, represented on 8 bits, are accumulated to produce the checksums (testing behavior). Once all the weights for the instruction are read, the computed checksum values are stored in a dedicated location of the registers file, referred to as R0 and R1. The *matrix multiply* instruction always follows the *read weight* instruction, and similarly, *t_matrix_multiply* always follows the *t_read_weight*. In the testing mode, additional test vectors, required to compute the SA checksum C_{SAj} and $\overline{C_{SAj}}$, detailed in the previous section, are appended to the input vectors, generating the checksums. Once the SA checksums are computed, they flow through the accumulators, just like partial products from the SA. However, they are always summed up with R0 and R1 content. This sum follows the operations described by Eq. (4) and Eq. (5) in Sect. 3. Without faults, the results must be all 0s and all 1s, which are written back to R0 and R1.

A XOR-based detection unit compares the contents of R0, R1, C_{SAj} and $\overline{C_{SAj}}$ to detect faults and to perform diagnosis as explained in Subsect. 3.3. The diagnosis unit notifies any detected error to NEORV using interruption, as well as the detailed information in the status. When the accelerator triggers the interruption, it needs to be reconfigured to fix errors in the datapath.

Considering the DNN workload, a single network layer is typically decomposed in hundreds of matrix multiplications. It is a programmer's choice to execute the full layer in testing mode, hence executing each matrix multiplication with the additional checksum computation or just some operations during the overall layer executions. When required by NEORV, the TPU starts fetching instructions from its instruction FIFO, prepared by the NEORV processor. In the testing mode, while a new instruction is fetched and executed, a stage of the TPU pipeline will evaluate the testing checksums produced by the previous instruction. If no errors are detected, the pipeline operation will continue normally. Differently, when an error is detected, the TPU triggers an interruption to the RISCV that starts the recovery procedure. In the recovery procedure, the TPU pipeline is flushed first, as no further instructions should be executed while the datapath is compromised. Simultaneously, the NEORV32 acquires detailed information about the specific instruction execution that triggered the error. This fault information is crucial for recovery: after reconfiguration, the program resumes from a correctly executed instruction. This approach ensures that the execution continues from the remaining instructions of the current DNN layer, avoiding a full restart.

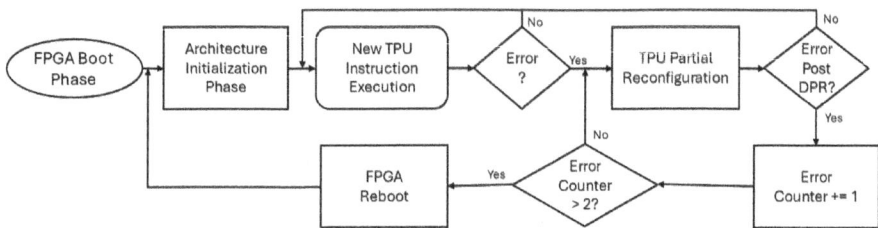

Fig. 3. Error Detection and Correction Flow.

If computations within a layer are fully executed in testing mode, the fault detection latency is confined to a single matrix multiplication operation, allowing all preceding executed instructions to be considered correct. However, if the layer is not processed entirely in testing mode—except for key operations like the first and last matrix multiplications (ensuring correct datapath behavior at entry and exit points of the layer)—the program must restart from the beginning of the faulty layer. This conservative strategy minimizes the potential propagation of undetected faults across layers.

The RISCV processor requests the dynamic partial reconfiguration of the TPU through the DFX controller. Once the partial reconfiguration process is triggered, the NEORV32 waits for its completion. In the proposed design, this is achieved by including in the TPU architecture an *alive* signal that activates as soon as the accelerator becomes operational. The soft processor continuously polls this signal, and as soon as it transitions to 1, indicating that the TPU is functional again, the interrupt subroutine concludes, and normal execution flow resumes. However, if the partial reconfiguration fails, meaning the soft processor detects consecutive TPU errors during two reconfiguration attempts, the system initiates a full-board reprogramming process to restore the correct behavior. Because the device undergoes complete reconfiguration, the memory content is not retained. This means that the platform performs a cold start. Figure 3 highlights the flow describe above.

5 Experimental Analysis

5.1 RePAIR Implementation Details

The RePAIR platform has been implemented on an AMD KCU105 Evaluation Board. The TPU accelerator uses the on-chip DSP blocks to implement all MACs and accumulator units. The weight buffers and unified buffers are mapped to BRAM resources. Minimal LUT usage is required for implementing control logic and glue logic. Table 1 reports the implementation details for the two processing cores.

Table 1. RePAIR Resource Utilization on KCU105.

RePAIR Modules	LUTs	FFs	BRAMs	DSP
tinyTPU	4,294	7,211	181	210
TMR NEORV32	3,219	3180	3	0
DPR Logic	1,185	989	0	0
Glue Logic Resources	13,874	17,670	95.5	3
Total [%]	9.31%	5.99%	46.58%	11.09%

Table 2. Benchmark CNNs Characteristics.

Dataset	Convolutional Layers [#]	Fully Connected layers [#]	Parameters [#]	Accuracy [%]
MNIST	3	1	40,874	97
CIFAR10	6	1	91,648	83.4

The area overhead introduced by interfacing the dynamic partial reconfiguration (DPR) and the two cores, listed as *glue logic* in the table, remain within acceptable limits. All the resources in the design operate at 100MHz. To further increase the reliability of the design, we enabled the ECC in the BRAMs to prevent data corruption due to radiation-induced Single Event Upset (SEU).

5.2 Experiment Analysis

The experimental analysis focuses on two primary aspects of the platform: fault detection capability and dynamic reconfiguration properties. These have been evaluated with experiments using the actual hardware platform. SEU-induced structural faults in the TPU Datapath have been emulated by bitstream corruption to reproduce faults.

To test fault detection capability, a fault injection campaign targeting the resources of the systolic array was conducted. The campaign injected 20,000 distinct faults in the configuration memory. Each fault has been evaluated singularly. Bitflips in the CRAM were used to emulate various fault types, including stuck-at, bridge, conflict, and open faults. As a benchmark, two classification tasks—MNIST digit recognition and CIFAR-10—served as benchmark applications. The CNNs performing classification were implemented using the quantized Qkeras TensorFlow library and trained from scratch to align with the hardware characteristics of the tinyTPU accelerators, especially regarding the quantized activation functions integrated within the core. The details of the models' implementation are provided in Table 2. For each injected fault, inference was performed on a random sample of 10 images selected from the test dataset to analyze possible data-induced fault-masking effects during processing. The inferences have been executed in testing mode for all the computations operations.

5.3 Experimental Results and Discussion

The experimental results for fault detection are shown in Fig. 4a. A major concern when evaluating this kind of application is that faults may affect the confidence level of the prediction without changing the results to classification. However, such errors are still relevant since they modify the expected behavior and could eventually lead to misclassification with different inputs. In the chart, we indicated that these errors are Silent Data Corruption (SDC), while the change of the classification output is defined as *misclassification*.

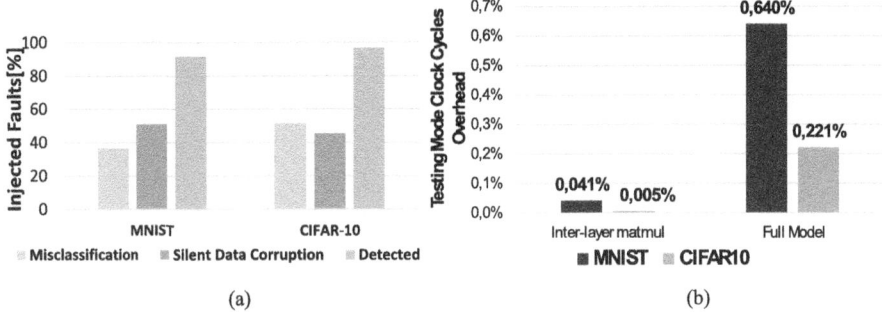

Fig. 4. (a) Fault Injection Results over 20,000 injected faults and (b) Maximum and Minimum Clock Cycles Overhead

We want to emphasize that the faults that affect designs implemented within the FPGAs due to CRAM corruption are multiple and challenging to detect due to the lack of documentation on CRAM and CDATA, which are not provided by vendors. The proposed approach demonstrated robust fault resilience, achieving an average detection rate of approximately 94%, as shown in Fig. 4a. Regarding performance overhead, it is important to highlight that it is related to the inference execution time, which is different for different inference tasks, in particular 0.23 ms for MNIST and 1.8ms for CIFAR10, respectively. Additionally, the fault detection mechanism introduces an overhead, but this overhead depends on how many instructions the developer want to execute in testing mode. Reminding that the testing procedure introduces 3 clock cycles of penalty, the execution overhead is *3 clock cycles * number of matmul instructions per layer * number of layers,* in the worst case, i.e. when all the matrix multiplication in all the DNN's layers are executed in testing mode. If the test mode is activated only during the last *matmul* of the layer, we have an overhead with *3 clock cycles * number of layers* while still detecting fault in each layer computation. The minimum and maximum relative overhead for the benchmark models is reported in Fig. 4b. In both cases, the overhead is negligible, and it decreases as the model complexity increases. The disadvantage of having a coarser fault detection is that in case of fault, we need to recompute the computation of the whole layer instead of repeating only the last matrix multiplication, as will be discussed further. By applying our methodology to the CNN inference, the computational overhead incurred was about 100 clock cycles per layer when executing full testing mode for both architectures, underscoring the platform's efficiency in maintaining fault tolerance and performance.

The advantage regarding system downtime strictly relates to the amount of time required to apply DPR to the accelerator compared to the time required for reconfiguring the full device. The time required for DPR depends on the size of the systolic array since the larger the accelerator, the higher the DPR time, while the time for complete reconfiguration depends on the device size since larger devices require longer reconfiguration times. Specifically, the DPR time resulted in scaling linearly with the systolic array size, as shown in Fig. 5a. For instance, a DPR time of 14 ms is necessary to complete the reconfiguration of a 14×14 SA, the maximum SA size allowed by tinyTPU architecture. In contrast, considering the KCU105 device, its full board reconfiguration requires almost 13 s. Therefore, when mapping the accelerator to KCU105, we can benefit of an 872.1x reduction in time exploiting DPR. When implementing the platform on different devices, the order of magnitudes remains the same. Indeed, smaller devices have shorter reconfiguration time and fewer resources available, which constrain a smaller SA, reducing the DPR time as well.

In the case of full reconfiguration, the program needs to start the inference process from the beginning, assuming it can retrieve the input data again. Consequently, the execution overhead depends on the timing of the fault. In the best-case scenario, the fault is detected during the execution of the first instruction in the first layer of the DNN. Here, the system discards the result after executing the first instruction, reconfigures the board, and then completes the full inference process starting from the beginning. Conversely, in the worst-case scenario, the fault is detected at the end of the inference process, requiring the entire process to be repeated twice. In addition, some time is also required by the NEORV to boot before starting computation. Figure 5b shows the

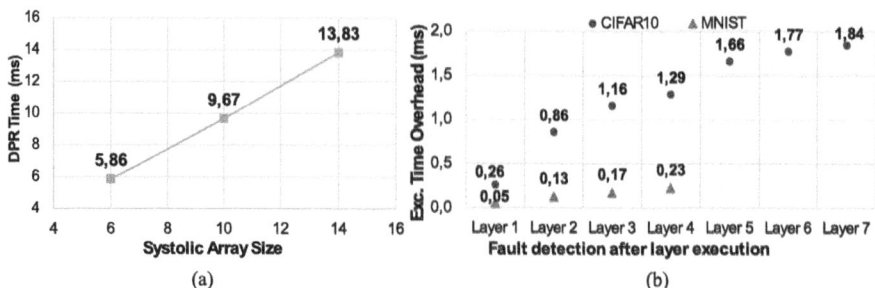

Fig. 5. (a) TPU DPR time related to the SA size; (b) the execution time overhead in full board reconfiguration, depending on when the fault is detected during the inference.

execution overhead depending on when the fault occurs during the inference, considering the two benchmark CNNs.

When DPR is enabled, the inference process does not start from the beginning after the reconfiguration. When the whole model is executed in testing mode, i.e. every matmul of each layer is executed in testing mode, the process resumes from the last correct instruction. This approach avoids discarding and executing computations that were correct again. The testing mode ensures the correctness of results up to the fault occurrence. The recovery of the execution from the last correct instructions is achieved by excluding the TPU input/output buffer from the DPR process. The buffer is hardened with ECC, preserving the TPU context during reconfiguration while protecting it from SEU.

The cost of the recovery procedure depends on the cost of the failed instruction, particularly the number of vectors processed by the instruction. Figure 6 illustrates the time overhead associated with executing the faulty instruction as a function of the processed vector count, ranging from a matrix multiplication with the size of operands of 14 × 14 (matching the TPU dimensions) to operands up to eight times larger. However, the additional time required for processing again the same instruction after DPR, compared to a scenario where no fault is detected, is below 2 μs, which is negligible considering that the entire inference process for the simplest CNN model is 100 times longer.

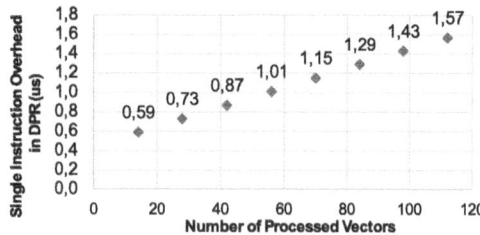

Fig. 6. Faulty instruction overhead in DPR as a function of processed vectors.

However, if the layers are not fully executed in testing mode, for instance, only the first and last instructions are checked to ensure correct inter-layer processing, the program must restart from the last correctly executed layer. Consequently, the total execution time with DPR differs from the previous case and depends on the layers' complexity and the CNN model itself, as explained further.

Figure 7 illustrates a quantitative comparison of inference execution scenarios, focusing on the closest comparable cases involving testing instructions at each layer's entry and exit points, under full reconfiguration versus DPR. In the chart, the No-Fault scenario serves as the baseline, representing the execution with two testing instructions per layer with no fault detected; hence, the inference is executed with no interruptions. The other scenarios depict the total execution time when a fault occurs during different layers, that have different computational costs. These values account only for the computational overhead caused by restarting the program, excluding reconfiguration time. This exclusion is due to the significantly longer duration of full device reconfiguration—on the order of seconds—making it incomparable to the other measured values. The graphs show that the inference execution overhead introduced by partial or full re-execution of the program during inference exhibits similar trends for both CNN benchmarks. If the fault occurs during the execution of the first layer, the computational overhead is the same for both DPR and full reconfiguration. In this case, the only differentiating factors between the two techniques are the total reconfiguration time, which depends on the device's characteristics (e.g., size, ICAP port speed), and the partial reconfiguration time, which is influenced by the size of the accelerator.

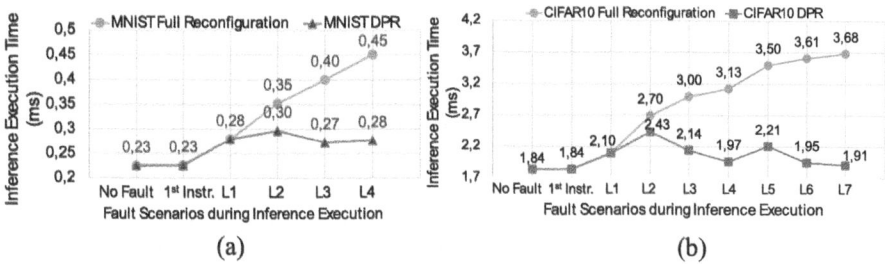

(a)   (b)

Fig. 7. Total inference execution time considering fault occurrences at different stages of the inference process with and without DPR for MNIST (a) and CIFAR10 (b).

Starting from the second layer, the use of DPR becomes significantly more advantageous. DPR allows the computations completed before the fault to be preserved, enabling the process to resume from the last successfully executed layer. In contrast, with full reconfiguration, the overhead increases as more layers are processed, as all computations must be restarted. For DPR, the worst-case scenario involves re-executing the most complex layer. For the benchmarks under study, this corresponds to the second layer, which results in an increase in inference execution of almost 30% for both MNIST and CIFAR10. In both cases, this is significantly less than the overhead induced by the worst-case scenario in full reconfiguration, which is a more than 96% increase.

Additionally, DPR offers the advantage of significantly shorter reconfiguration times—on the order of milliseconds—compared to full reconfiguration, which can take several seconds for a medium-sized device. These benefits further highlight the efficiency of DPR in mitigating inference overheads during fault recovery.

6   Conclusions

This research introduces RePAIR, a highly reliable and high-performance FPGA-based platform specifically designed for DNN execution in safety-critical applications. RePAIR integrates the NEORV32 RISC-V core, enhanced with TMR for fault tolerance, and tinyTPU, a systolic array-based accelerator augmented with ISA extensions for runtime fault detection during inference. The proposed platform goes beyond fault detection by incorporating fault correction through dynamic partial reconfiguration of the DNN accelerator, managed by the RISC-V core. The platform was tested using hardware fault emulation by corrupting the device configuration memory to simulate radiation-induced single-event upsets affecting the datapath. Experimental results demonstrated a 94% runtime fault detection accuracy across two benchmark CNNs, with a worst-case computational overhead of only 0.6%. Furthermore, employing dynamic partial reconfiguration significantly reduced system downtime, achieving a nearly 900x improvement on medium-to-large-scale FPGA devices.

Disclosure of Interests.   The authors have no competing interests to declare that are relevant to the content of this article.

References

1. Waterman, A., Asanović, K. (eds.): The RISC-V Instruction Set Manual, Volume I: User-Level ISA, Document Version 2.2. RISC-V Foundation, May 2017
2. Li, D.-Z., Gong, H.-R., Chang, Y.-C.: Implementing RISCV system-on-chip for acceleration of convolution operation and activation function based on FPGA. In: 2018 14th IEEE International Conference on Solid-State and Integrated Circuit Technology (ICSICT), Qingdao, China, pp. 1–3 (2018). https://doi.org/10.1109/ICSICT.2018.8564810
3. Martínez, H., et al.: Parallel GEMM-based convolutions for deep learning on multicore ARM and RISC-V architectures. J. Syst. Archit. **153** (2024). j.sysarc.2024.103186
4. Wang, X., et al.: RV-GEMM: neural network inference acceleration with near-memory GEMM instructions on RISC-V. In: 21st ACM International Conference on Computing Frontiers (CF '24), pp. 302–305 (2024). https://doi.org/10.1145/3649153.3649181
5. Jouppi, N.P., et al.: In-datacenter performance analysis of a tensor processing unit. In: ACM/IEEE 44th Annual International Symposium on Computer Architecture (ISCA), pp. 1–12 (2017)
6. Libano, F., et al.: Efficient error detection for matrix multiplication with systolic arrays on FPGAs. IEEE Trans. Comput. **72**(8), 2390–2403A
7. Burel, S., et al.: MOZART: masking outputs with zeros for architectural robustness and testing of DNN Accelerators. In: 2021 IEEE 27th International Symposium on On-Line Testing and Robust System Design (IOLTS), Torino, Italy, pp. 1–6 (2021)
8. Vacca, E., et al.: ZOR: zero overhead reliability strategies for AI accelerators. In: 2024 22nd IEEE Interregional NEWCAS Conference (NEWCAS), Sherbrooke, QC, Canada, pp. 248–252 (2024). https://doi.org/10.1109/NewCAS58973.2024.10666350
9. Dodd, P.E., et al.: Current and future challenges in radiation effects on CMOS electronics. IEEE Trans. Nucl. Sci. **57**(4), 1747–1763 (2010)
10. AMD: Soft Error Mitigation Controller v4.1, (PG036) (2018)
11. Nolting, S., et al.: The NEORV32 RISC-V Processor. Zenodo, 18 August 2023. https://doi.org/10.5281/zenodo.8260609

12. Fuhrmann, J.: Implementierung einer Tensor Processing Unit mit dem Fokus auf Embedded Systems und das Internet of Things, Germany (2018). http://hdl.handle.net/20.500.12738/8527
13. Sanchez-Flores, A., Alvarez, L., Alorda-Ladaria, B.: Accelerators in embedded systems for machine learning: a RISCV view. In: 2023 38th Conference on Design of Circuits and Integrated Systems (DCIS), Málaga, Spain, pp. 1–6 (2023). https://doi.org/10.1109/DCIS58620.2023.10335969
14. Parisi, E., et al.: TitanCFI: toward enforcing control-flow integrity in the root-of-trust. In: 2024 Design, Automation and Test in Europe Conference and Exhibition (DATE), Valencia, Spain, pp. 1–6 (2024). https://doi.org/10.23919/DATE58400.2024.10546873.
15. Nikiema, P.R., et al.: Towards dependable RISC-V cores for edge computing devices. In: 2023 IEEE 29th International Symposium on On-Line Testing and Robust System Design (IOLTS), Crete, Greece, pp. 1–7 (2023), https://doi.org/10.1109/IOLTS59296.2023.10224862.
16. Gewehr, C., Luza, L., Moraes, F.G.: Hardware acceleration of crystals-Kyber in low-complexity embedded systems with RISC-V instruction set extensions. IEEE Access **12**, 94477–94495 (2024). https://doi.org/10.1109/ACCESS.2024.3416812
17. Wang, Z., et al.: RTPE: a high energy efficiency inference processor with RISC-V based transformation mechanism. In: 2024 IEEE 6th International Conference on AI Circuits and Systems (AICAS), Abu Dhabi, United Arab Emirates, pp. 297–301 (2024). https://doi.org/10.1109/AICAS59952.2024.10595923
18. Wei, J., Zhang, L., Yu, Z., Liu, D.: Design space exploration for heterogenous SoC integrated with matrix accelerator. In: 2020 IEEE 2nd International Conference on Circuits and Systems (ICCS), Chengdu, China, pp. 40–43 (2020)
19. Vacca, E., et al.: Failure rate analysis of radiation tolerant design techniques on SRAM-based FPGAs. Microelectron. Reliab. **138** (2022). j.microrel.2022.114778
20. Azimi, S., et al.: A comparative radiation analysis of reconfigurable memory technologies: FinFET versus bulk CMOS. Microelectron. Reliab. **138** (2022). j.microrel.2022.114733
21. Aguilar, E.M., Benevenuti, F., Kastensmidt, F.L.: Hardening a RISC-V softcore for embedded aerospace applications in SRAM-based FPGA. In: 2024 37th SBC/SBMicro/IEEE Symposium on Integrated Circuits and Systems Design (SBCCI), Joao Pessoa, Brazil, pp. 1–5 (2024). https://doi.org/10.1109/SBCCI62366.2024.10703996
22. de Oliveira, Á.B., et al.: Evaluating soft core RISC-V processor in SRAM-based FPGA under radiation effects. IEEE Trans. Nucl. Sci. **67**(7), 1503–1510 (2020). https://doi.org/10.1109/TNS.2020.2995729
23. AMD UltraScale Architecture Soft Error Mitigation Controller LogiCORE IP Product Guide (PG187)
24. Safarpour, M., et al.: Algorithm level error detection in low voltage systolic array. IEEE Trans. Circuits Syst. II Express Briefs **69**(2), 569–573 (2022)
25. Kim, J., et al.: ZOS: zero overhead scan for systolic array-based AI accelerator. In: 2022 19th International SoC Design Conference (ISOCC), pp. 360–361 (2022)
26. Lee, H., et al.: STRAIT: self-test and self-recovery for AI accelerator. IEEE Trans. Comput.-Aided Des. Integr. Circuits Syst. 3092–3104 (2023)
27. AMD, Vivado Design Suite User Guide: Dynamic Function eXchange (UG909)
28. AMD, Dynamic Function eXchange Controller v1.0 Product Guide (PG374)

ROBoost: A Study of FPGA Logic-Based Power-Wasting Primitives

Dina G. Mahmoud[1](✉)[ID], Simone Andreani[2], Vincent Lenders[3][ID], and Mirjana Stojilović[2][ID]

[1] The American University in Cairo, Cairo, Egypt
dina-mahmoud@aucegypt.edu
[2] EPFL, Lausanne, Switzerland
{simone.andreani,mirjana.stojilovic}@epfl.ch
[3] Cyber-Defence Campus, armasuisse, Thun, Switzerland
vincent.lenders@armasuisse.ch

Abstract. Heterogeneous computing systems increasingly leverage FPGAs in the cloud and embedded use cases. With cloud FPGAs being remotely accessible, security is a critical concern. Recent studies show adversaries can exploit FPGA logic to create and remotely deploy malicious power-wasting circuits that consume excessive dynamic power, potentially injecting faults or causing denial of service. This work analyzes the most common reconfigurable power-wasting primitives to assess their power consumption, detection challenges, and attack effectiveness. We further propose new, logic-based, and resource-efficient variations of these circuits and experimentally evaluate them on two families of AMD FPGAs. Finally, we discuss factors influencing attack effectiveness and compare the studied designs' trade-offs.

Keywords: FPGAs · remote attacks · voltage drop · hardware security

1 Introduction

The rising demand for accelerated computing has outpaced general-purpose CPUs, pushing embedded and cloud systems to adopt specialized processing units. Field-programmable gate arrays (FPGAs) are favored for their fine-grained parallelism and reconfigurability. Cloud service providers (CSPs) like Amazon and Alibaba now offer FPGA-accelerated instances [27], while AMD and Intel integrate FPGAs with CPUs in systems-on-chip (SoCs).

The growing adoption and remote accessibility of FPGAs in the cloud have made their security critical [27]. Users with low-level control on the FPGA fabric can deploy malicious bitstreams, creating *power wasters*—FPGA circuits that draw excessive power. These circuits can overwhelm power supplies, causing voltage drops and, in turn, timing violations or even FPGA resets [12]. Other remote exploits include passive circuits monitoring activity for side-channel attacks [10].

This paper focuses on FPGA logic-based power-wasting primitives. While prior research explores their use in attacks and defenses [11,12,15,17,19], implementation details and voltage drop capabilities remain underexplored. To effectively counter current and future threats, a deeper understanding of power waster

© The Author(s), under exclusive license to Springer Nature Switzerland AG 2025
R. Giorgi et al. (Eds.): ARC 2025, LNCS 15594, pp. 88–105, 2025.
https://doi.org/10.1007/978-3-031-87995-1_6

characteristics and the extent of possible improvements is needed. Additionally, evaluating the ease of implementation, portability, and associated constraints is vital to assess their risk to cloud and remote FPGA applications.

In this work, we compare known logic-based power-wasting primitives on two AMD FPGAs [8,24] and examine the factors influencing their success. Building on these findings, we propose new variations that validate these factors, including the ability to confine primitives to specific logic regions[1]. Some of these variations rival the best-known designs while bypassing design rule check (DRC) warnings used by CSPs like Amazon (offering AMD FPGA instances) to block malicious circuits [14]. This makes them deployable in current cloud environments.

The paper is structured as follows: Sect. 2 provides background on power-wasting attacks and voltage measurement. Section 3 reviews power waster types. Section 4 details the experimental setup. Section 5 presents the results. We discuss findings in Sect. 6 and conclude in Sect. 7.

2 Background

2.1 Power-Wasting Attacks

Power consumption in electronic circuits depends on static leakage and dynamic signal changes. Dynamic power varies with the circuit implementation and operations, in the function of voltage, switching frequency, and load capacitance:

$$P_{\mathrm{dyn}} \propto C_{\mathrm{L}} \times V_{\mathrm{cc}}^2 \times f. \tag{1}$$

Here, P_{dyn} is the dynamic power consumption, C_{L} the load capacitance, V_{cc} the supply voltage, and f the switching frequency [7]. The clock frequency and the frequencies of combinational signals toggling determine the switching frequency.

Remote power-wasting exploits on FPGAs attracted attention after Gnad et al. demonstrated the first DoS attack using ring oscillators (ROs) [12]. These attacks leverage short combinational feedback paths, creating high-frequency oscillations that increase power consumption. Power-wasting primitives can also target higher load capacitance to amplify power consumption further. Current variations caused by signal switching lead to voltage drops in the power distribution network (PDN), affecting signal propagation delays and potentially causing faults in memory elements [5,13,22,25,32]. Voltage drops also increase flip-flop (FF) setup and hold times [6], potentially causing unsafe operating conditions.

To combat malicious combinational loops, Amazon prevents their use in cloud FPGAs by using AMD Vivado's DRCs [3], but exploits still exist. Later research employs FFs and latches to break the combinational loop and bypass these checks [15,23]. Continuing research efforts are devoted to detecting power wasters on one side and developing stealthier malicious designs on the other [27].

---

[1] For the reproducibility of the experiments and the results of this work, we make the associated artifacts openly available [16].

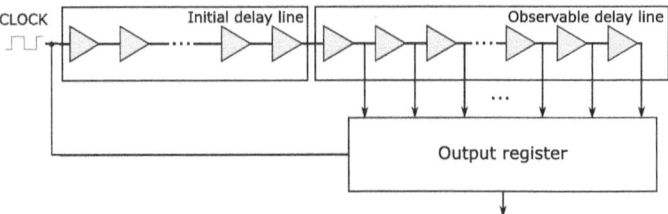

Fig. 1. High-level view of a TDC sensor for FPGA on-chip voltage variations [26].

2.2 On-Chip Voltage Measurement

Similarly to power-wasting primitives, FPGA logic can turn into sensors capturing delay changes that correlate with PDN voltage variations caused by on-chip activity [10,26]. These sensors are typically used in remote power side-channel attacks, where an adversary steals secrets or detects voltage drops [10,32]. The most common sensor is the time-to-digital converter (TDC, Fig. 1). It measures the propagation depth of a clock signal edge while it travels down a fine-grained delay line. This delay line, sensitive to voltage variations, is typically implemented using the carry chain logic. The delay line is tapped, meaning the sensor has an output register that periodically captures the clock's propagation depth. The output register value is converted to the Hamming weight (HW) to obtain one sensor *sample*, which directly correlates with the on-chip voltage. Finally, the on-chip voltage profile can be reconstructed by collecting the sequence of sensor samples for a given time. We use on-chip TDC sensors to measure voltage drops caused by the power wasters, mimicking the real remote undervolting attack scenario [10].

3   Types of Power Wasters

Early power wasters, known as *combinational power wasters*, used only combinational elements in FPGAs to create self-oscillating circuits that rely on feedback loops around combinational logic (e.g., lookup tables (LUTs)). However, FPGAs also offer flip-flops. Accordingly, a second category of power wasters, noncombinational or *FF-based power wasters*, becomes a possibility. FF-based power-wasting primitives introduce sequential elements into the feedback path and may require a clock signal. Next, *improved power wasters* refine previous designs to enhance resource utilization, stealth, and power consumption by leveraging FPGA fabric properties. Finally, there are *hidden power wasters* that embed malicious designs within circuits that appear benign; hiding techniques are beyond the scope of this work.

Effective power wasters maximize dynamic power consumption by increasing switching frequency, load capacitance, or both, as shown by Eq. (1). High switching frequencies can be achieved through fast clocks, feedback loops, or glitches, while high fanout boosts load capacitance. We discuss these categories of power-wasting primitives in detail in the following subsections.

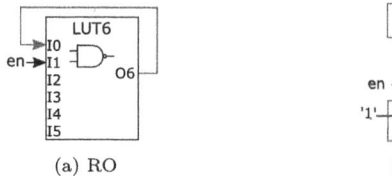

(a) RO   (b) RO2-*cf*

Fig. 2. A ring oscillator implemented with (a) one six-input LUT and (b) two five-input LUTs (I5 needs to be a logical 1 for the two outputs to be independent). The combinational feedback connections are highlighted in red. (Color figure online)

3.1   Combinational Power Wasters

Combinational power wasters use only combinational logic elements within the FPGA fabric. Targeting the goal of high switching frequency, a combinational RO (RO-*cf*) is the most straightforward design of a power waster; here, *cf* stands for the combinational feedback. An RO-*cf* consists of an odd number of inverters in a loop. In the simplest FPGA-based implementation, one LUT implementing an inverter is sufficient and would result in the lowest combinational delay. Consequently, the oscillation frequency of one such RO-*cf* would be extremely high, leading to a high power draw with enough instances of RO-*cf*s. In practical attack scenarios, the attacker needs control over when the RO-*cf*s should start (and stop) oscillating [19]. Therefore, typical RO-*cf* designs resemble the circuit in Fig. 2a, where a NAND gate replaces the inverter and is controlled by an enable input. As many FPGAs now support fracturable LUTs, it is also possible to implement two ROs in one LUT for more efficient use of logic resources [23]. Figure 2b illustrates the design of the corresponding *dual* RO (RO2-*cf*).

Modern FPGAs contain combinational logic elements other than LUTs that can also be programmed to create a self-oscillating circuit. Depending on the target FPGA, users can control MUXes, carry chain elements (CARRY), or digital signal processing (DSP) blocks, creating MUX-based ROs, CARRY-based ROs, and DSP-based ROs [15]. These designs bypass the design rule checks on commercial tools such as AMD Vivado, which can detect the feedback loop only through a LUT [15].

3.2   FF-Based Power Wasters

FF- and latch-based power wasters are designed to break the combinational loop using a flip-flop or a latch to avoid detection. Inserting these elements increases the feedback path length, effectively decreasing the oscillation frequency. It also results in higher resource usage. However, the additional connections increase the load capacitance and FF-based power wasters still prove effective for DoS attacks on cloud FPGA instances [14].

Figure 3a shows an example design of the FF-based power waster proposed by Giechaskiel et al., who used it not as an attack primitive but as a power side-channel attack sensor [9]. The LUT part is identical to the combinational RO.

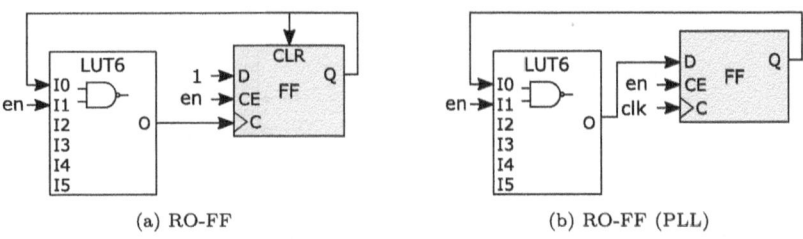

(a) RO-FF   (b) RO-FF (PLL)

Fig. 3. FF-based RO with (a) self-oscillations and (b) clock signal from a PLL.

However, the output of the RO LUT acts as the clock for the FF. The D input of the FF is fixed to 1, and according to the states of the clock and the clear signals, the output oscillates. The oscillating FF output acts as an input to the LUT and controls the clear signal of the FF. The continuous change of the FF output due to the back and forth between it being cleared and it becoming a 1 at the rising edge of the clock results in the oscillating behavior of this design [23].

Another variation of FF-based ROs, shown in Fig. 3b, uses a high-frequency clock generated from a phase-locked loop (PLL) on the FPGA. In this case, the D input of the FF is the output of the LUT, and the enable signal is used to control both the FF and the LUT [23]. Suppose a latch is available in the programmable logic. In that case, the design may be simplified by controlling the latch's enable with the enable signal, connecting the D input to the output of an inverter LUT, and connecting a constant 1 to the clock of the latch. The input of the LUT would be driven by the latch, creating the RO-L design [9].

Additionally, modern FPGAs can implement shift registers in their programmable fabric. Suppose the clock that controls the FFs of the shift register is fast, and the register is initialized with a sequence of values to ensure the outputs change every clock cycle (an alternating sequence of 1s and 0s). In that case, the outputs of each FF will oscillate at the high clock frequency, resulting in considerable power consumption [23].

FF-based power wasters are not limited to the patterns of FFs and LUTs. For instance, deliberately created long routing paths with different delays, when connected to a logic gate, can result in inputs taking a long time to stabilize and, consequently, multiple transitions (i.e., glitches) at the output. Matas et al. [20] proposed and evaluated an example of such a design with XOR logic.

3.3   Improved Power Wasters

While effective, the typical primitives with ROs and FFs can be improved to increase the dynamic power consumption further. High switching frequency is the main feature of RO-cfs and RO2-cfs, making them suitable for power attacks. Therefore, ROs can be enhanced to take advantage of the other characteristic of good power wasters: the load capacitance. La et al. proposed a design for enhanced ring oscillators (EROs), increasing the fanout of each RO and the routing used to consume more power [15]. One instance of an ERO-cf is shown in Fig. 4; it comprises four LUTs implementing a NAND of the enable and the feedback signals. The enable signal of the ERO-cf drives one input of each LUT.

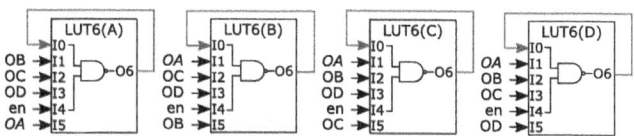

Fig. 4. Enhanced ring oscillator (ERO). The feedback connections are in red. The output of the first LUT is in italic to highlight its connections to the other LUTs. (Color figure online)

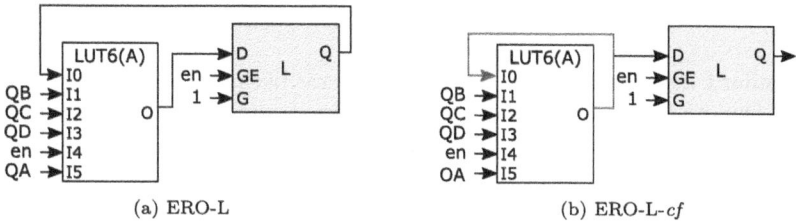

Fig. 5. Latch-based ERO with (a) latch feedback and (b) combinational feedback.

Two LUT inputs are connected to the output of the same LUT, forming a combinational loop. The remaining three inputs are driven by the outputs of the other three LUTs in the ERO-cf. Compared to the traditional ROs, LUTs in the ERO-cf drive a higher capacitive load, resulting in increased power consumption [15].

Following the same reasoning behind the design of the EROs and the use of FFs and latches in the RO-FF and RO-L primitives, we design new variations that aim to combine the best features of existing designs:

- We combine EROs with latches, once breaking the combinational loop using the latch and preserving the increased routing of the EROs (ERO-L, Fig. 5a), and once maintaining the combinational loop of the EROs (ERO-L-cf, Fig. 5b).
- We combine EROs with FFs, instead of latches. Two variations are designed and tested, one breaking the combinational feedback with an FF (ERO-FF, Fig. 6a) and one preserving it (ERO-FF-cf, Fig. 6b).

For the versions preserving the feedback loop, we configure the additional inputs of the LUTs to be driven by the FF outputs due to the constraints on routing the LUT outputs when all the FFs are used (i.e., if both FFs are used, only one LUT output, O6 in Fig. 6, can be routed out of the slice back to the LUT inputs). Typically, a PLL drives the FF clock input. We also propose a variation clocked from an RO-L, avoiding the requirement of a PLL.

4 System Design

We implement several power waster designs to compare them. The first designs we consider are RO-cf and RO2-cf (Figs. 2a and 2b). These two designs are

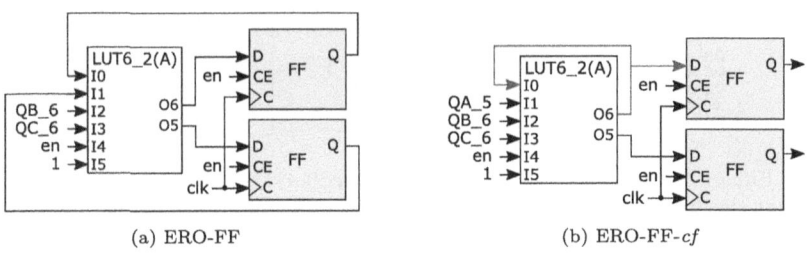

(a) ERO-FF   (b) ERO-FF-*cf*

Fig. 6. FF-based ERO with (a) FF feedback and (b) combinational feedback.

the standard baseline against which to compare because many of the demonstrated DoS and fault-injection exploits leveraged combinational ROs [27]. Our analysis also considers ERO-*cf* circuits, representing the most effective power wasters in literature [11,15]. Additionally, we consider two designs without combinational loops: latch-based ROs (RO-L) [15] and FF-based ROs clocked from a phase-locked loop (RO-FF (PLL)) [23]. Neither of these two designs generates DRC warnings. We do not consider self-oscillating FF-based wasters for two reasons: first, they generate a gated clock warning [15] and, second, they cannot be densely packed because the FFs within a slice on an AMD FPGA must share the clock signal if they are to be used simultaneously [29]. We also evaluate our new variations of power wasters: ERO-L (Fig. 5a), ERO-L-*cf* (Fig. 5b), ERO-FF (Fig. 6a), and ERO-FF-*cf* (Fig. 6b). For the two FF-based designs, we evaluate them when (a) a PLL or (b) an ERO-L generates the clock.

The key result of power wasters activity is a voltage drop. An effective power waster causes a more significant voltage drop than other designs. To compare malicious designs, we monitor the on-chip FPGA voltage variations during their activity. The design causing the most variation and the largest voltage drop is deemed the most effective. While external measurements are possible, internal FPGA-based measurements avoid external equipment and directly capture the power wasters' impact on the collocated and concurrently executing FPGA applications. We use TDC on-chip voltage-variations sensors, described in Sect. 2, whose readings directly correlate with voltage changes [21].

We perform experiments on Pynq Z1 and Genesys-ZU boards, covering two AMD FPGA families. The variety helps assess design portability and how FPGA fabric features affect power waster implementation.

4.1   Pynq-Z1 Setup

The FPGA PL of the PYNQ-Z1 SoC is of the AMD 7-series. It contains 13,300 logic slices, each with four six-input LUTs and eight flip-flops [24]. Four of the eight FFs per slice can act as latches. The SoC also includes a dual-core Cortex-A9 processing system (PS). We use the PS to control the PL, and the two parts communicate through advanced extensible interface (AXI) general-purpose inputs/outputs (GPIOs). The PL clock frequency is 100 MHz. This frequency ensured the correct operation of all circuits implemented within the PL. An

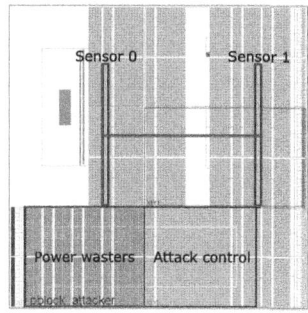

Fig. 7. Design floorplan on the Pynq-Z1.

experimental attack run lasts for 256 clock cycles (2.56 μs). Vivado 2020.1 was used to generate all of the tested hardware circuits. The enable signal of the power wasters has a period of 150 clock cycles and a duty cycle of 50%.

To mimic the limitations on the region available to an adversary and to avoid accidental reset, we limit the testing of all of our power wasters to the clock region X0Y0, which contains 50 columns, where each column has 50 slices, as shown in Fig. 7. The power wasters' control is limited to the region adjacent to it. Two TDC sensors are used, one placed on the same side as the power wasters on top of X0Y0 (sensor 0) and the second (sensor 1) placed on the other side of the PL farther away from the wasters. Each sensor uses 64 CARRY4 elements, resulting in 256 bits in the sensor output (sensor readings—i.e., the Hamming weight of the output register—lie in the 0–256 range).

We organize the power wasters in *blocks*, each covering one column of the chosen region. Depending on the number of primitives we can use in an FPGA slice, we either group two blocks in one *node* or restrict the node size to one block. The PS sends the signals to the control circuit to determine how many power waster nodes are active in an experimental run. The nodes are activated one by one in a staggered manner with 25 steps at most (for designs with 50 nodes, two nodes are activated at each step). The staggered activation makes the effect of the attack gradual. Additionally, it has been shown to be more effective because it reduces the magnitude of the sudden voltage changes occurring when the power wasters are activated and deactivated [18].

4.2 Genesys-ZU Setup

The second testing platform is the Genesys-ZU board, which includes a Zynq UltraScale+ MPSoC [8]. The FPGA PL contains 71,000 LUTs, organized in slices of eight, where each slice also contains 16 FFs, for a total of 8,875 logic slices. Unlike the Pynq-Z1, all the FFs within a slice can act as latches. The MPSoC includes a quad-core ARM Cortex-A53 application processing unit (APU). We leverage this APU to control the PL through the AXI GPIOs. The PL clock frequency is 150 MHz, which guarantees correct design operation and takes advantage of the faster logic within the Zynq UltraScale fabric. One experimental attack run corresponds to 384 clock cycles (2.56 μs).

The enable signal of the power wasters has a period of 800 clock cycles and a duty cycle of 50% (i.e., circuits are active for 400 clock cycles). This period is longer than the attack duration, thus we do not get the full-length voltage trace captured. However, this choice improves the likelihood of getting reasonably accurate voltage readings from the on-chip system monitor so that we can compare them to the TDC sensor readings. The analog-to-digital converter (ADC) used in the system monitor operates at 0.2 MHz [28], a much lower rate compared to the TDC sensor (150 MHz). Hence, we take the readings from the system monitor only as an indication of the voltage values rather than an accurate measure of the minimum voltage. This is because the minimum value may be skipped due to the reduced sampling speed of the ADC with respect to the TDC. Having the power wasters active for the entire attack duration means that the lowest voltage is expected to last longer, improving the likelihood of the system monitor capturing it.

The power wasters and their control are constrained to the clock regions X0Y0 and X1Y0. The only constraint on the power wasters within the two clock regions is that each group of logic elements forming power wasters that can fit into one slice is packed and not spread across slices. We implement 25 nodes of 400 LUTs each (and 800 FFs when FFs are used). The power wasters are also activated in a staggered fashion. We use one TDC sensor constrained to the right side of the FPGA. The TDC comprises 64 CARRY8 elements, resulting in a sensor reading in the 0–512 range.

5   Comparison of Power Wasters

The experiments commence with recording the sensors' calibration parameters (for reproducibility), followed by baseline readings from the sensor when no power wasters are active. Then, we repeat the power waster's activity ten times to ensure the repeatability and consistency of the results. Each run records the sensor's average, maximum, and minimum readings. We then compute the sample-wise averages across all runs, noting the combined results' maximum, minimum, and average sensor readings. All values are reported relative to the baseline sensor average (e.g., negative value means the activity resulted in lower voltage compared to the baseline in the absence of activity).

Voltage and power variations depend on the circuit design, which determines its frequency of oscillation and load capacitance. Measuring or estimating the oscillation frequency using the synthesis tools are two ways to assess that comparison metric. Regarding capacitance, even though it is not immediately available, the designs can be compared based on their fanout and use of routing resources (e.g., higher fanout increases routing demand and load capacitance).

Table 1. FPGA resource use and DRC warnings on Pynq-Z1. Critical warnings are italicized. Parentheses show the clock source. In gray, wasters introduced in this work.

Power waster	LUTs	Flip-Flops (FFs)	Warnings
RO [12]	10k	0	*LUTLP-1*
RO2 [15]	10k	0	*LUTLP-1*
ERO [15]	10k	0	*LUTLP-1*
RO-L [15]	10k	10k	N/A
RO-FF (PLL) [23]	10k	20k	N/A
ERO-L-*cf*	10k	10k	*LUTLP-1*
ERO-L	10k	10k	PDCN-1569
ERO-FF-*cf* (PLL)	10k	20k	*LUTLP-1*
ERO-FF (PLL)	10k	20k	PDCN-1569
ERO-FF-*cf* (L)	10k	19.8k	*LUTLP-1*
ERO-FF (L)	10k	19.8k	PDCN-1569

5.1   Experimental Results on Pynq-Z1

Packing of Power Wasters. Within clock region X0Y0, we implement the power wasters listed in Table 1. Since they use local routing, Vivado reports no routing congestion. Therefore, Table 1 reports only logic resources used. We also report DRC warnings, as they correlate with the ease of detection and deployment within a cloud environment. All power wasters use all LUTs within the slice. RO2-*cf* uses each LUT as two LUT5s, but while each LUT generates two outputs, the number of LUTs remains unchanged. Aside from purely combinational power wasters, the designs use the FFs within the slice. Given the limitation of the 7-series FPGAs that only four of each eight FFs in a slice can act as latches, all latch-based designs use half of the available FFs. The FF-based power wasters use all available FFs. Versions of ERO-FF-*cf* and ERO-FF clocked using a RO-L (last two rows) can use only half the registers within in slices where a clock signal is generated. With one clock signal per column and 50 columns, the design uses only 19,800 FFs (50×4 FFs unused).

The designs without a latch or an FF in the feedback path generate a critical DRC warning (LUTLP-1), pointing to the combinational loop. All designs with increased routing following the ERO design generate a warning (PDCN-1569) related to unused inputs of the LUT. Such a warning is not critical and can occur for many designs, including AMD IPs, and can be safely ignored [4]. All other designs have no DRC warnings, making them suitable for generating oscillations when the target platform forbids combinational loops. One of the designs we excluded is the self-oscillating FF, where the clock for the FF is generated from its inverted output. This circuit generated a gated clock warning, removing the stealth advantage [15]. Moreover, in 7-series FPGAs, the FFs within a slice must use the same clock signal to be all used simultaneously, making the self-oscillating FF unable to fully utilize the resources [29]. Similar constraints exist for other architectures, including the UltraScale [30].

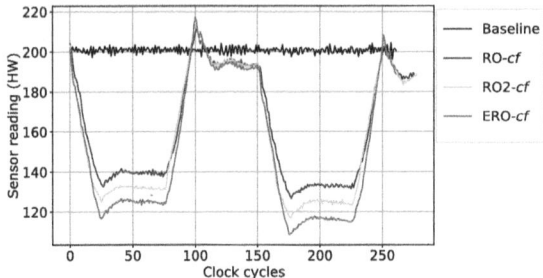

Fig. 8. Comparison of the sensor readings for the combinational power wasters.

Table 2. Max, min, average, and peak-to-peak Sensor 0 readings relative to the baseline (Pynq-Z1). Wasters are sorted from the most to the least effective. The best values are highlighted in italic if the waster generates DRC warnings and in bold if it does not. The parentheses specify the clock source. In gray, wasters introduced in this work.

Power waster	Max. reading*	Min. reading*	Avg. reading*	Peak-to-peak
ERO-L-cf	*21.83*	*-118.07*	*-62.47*	*139.9*
ERO	16.79	-95.61	-50.07	112.40
ERO-FF-*cf* (L)	6.78	-94.82	-49.63	101.6
ERO-L	**16.00**	**-92.90**	**-47.83**	**108.9**
ERO-FF-*cf* (PLL)	6.88	-92.72	-48.02	99.6
RO2	5.21	-82.09	-41.61	87.3
RO	11.84	-76.16	-38.55	88.00
ERO-FF (L)	4.66	-71.44	-36.87	76.1
RO-L	12.52	-69.88	-34.64	82.40
RO-FF (PLL)	3.78	-60.02	-27.02	63.80
ERO-FF (PLL)	4.00	-59.60	-27.37	63.60

*Relative to the baseline average obtained before each experiment

Sensor Readings. Starting with combinational power wasters, we compare them to understand how their features affect power consumption and to establish a baseline against which to measure other wasters' effectiveness. As expected, our results show that Sensor 0, being closer, is more sensitive to the changes induced by the power wasters. Therefore, the results we report are those from Sensor 0. Figure 8 shows the drop in the TDC sensor readings for the averaged ten runs when using all attacker nodes. All three designs have comparably high oscillation frequencies, as the combinational loop in all cases includes one LUT. However, the additional routing within ERO-*cf*s and the resulting increase in capacitance make the ERO-*cf*s more effective at wasting power. The denser packing of the RO2-*cf*s results in a more significant voltage drop than the RO-*cf*s. The results in Fig. 8 are consistent with what we expected and the previous work [15].

    Table 2 shows the maximum, minimum, and average sensor readings relative to the baseline when the power wasters are using all the available resources

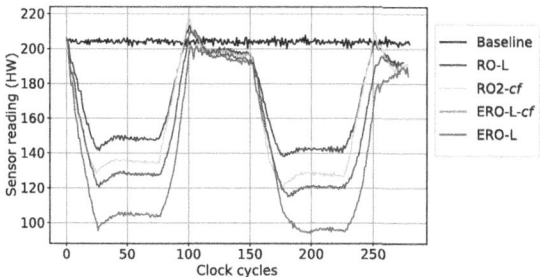

Fig. 9. Comparison of the sensor readings for the latch-based power wasters.

within the clock region. Each value in Table 2 is the average of the corresponding quantity over the ten experimental runs. We find that the variations between the runs are minimal. The peak-to-peak is the difference between the averaged maximum and minimum readings, indicating the effectiveness of the power waster. A power waster that causes a substantial drop with respect to the baseline will likely cause a noticeable peak in the voltage when the activity is stopped due to the reaction of the voltage regulator. The peak-to-peak captures the extent of that voltage swing. However, we base our analysis on the drop with respect to the baseline, because the drop is important for the success of a fault-injection or denial-of-service exploit.

For the FF-based power wasters, we first examine the self-oscillating latch (RO-L), where the latch is constantly enabled when the enable signal of the waster is high. The latch's existence on the path decreases the oscillation frequency with respect to the RO designs. While the reduced frequency affects the voltage drop, the effect is not detrimental to the power-wasting capability, as can be seen in Fig. 9 (RO2-*cf* and RO-L lines). Also, given the additional routing and logic elements involved, some additional capacitance is added, resulting in a design with power-wasting capabilities comparable to the ROs, but that is also implemented without generating any warnings (Table 1). The RO-FF power waster fares worse. The decrease in oscillation frequency is only in part caused by the increased path length, due to passing through the register. In this case, the frequency is governed by the maximum frequency that the PLL can generate, which in our case is 465 MHz. The frequency of self-oscillating designs is much higher than that, usually more than double that frequency [15]. Therefore, the FF-based designs clocked from the PLL always perform the worst.

While the RO-L power wasters are a good alternative for combinational power wasters, their power consumption is slightly lower. If an exploit requires a specific voltage drop and the adversary is limited to a particular region, latch-based variants may not generate the needed voltage drop when their combinational counterparts would. Therefore, we explore new design variations, where we combine latches and FFs with EROs to increase the load capacitance. The frequency, minimally affected, is not a primary factor to consider since it is either limited by the PLL or the delay of the feedback path. We also implement versions of these improved power wasters with combinational feedback to be able to analyze the effect of the combinational loops.

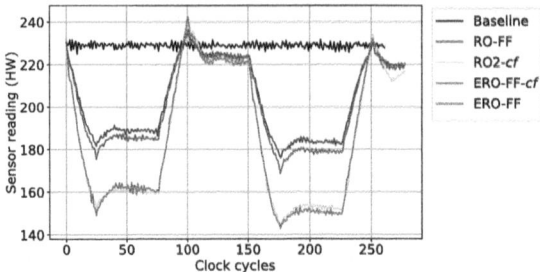

Fig. 10. Comparison of the sensor readings for the PLL-clocked FF-based power wasters.

Figure 9 shows the sensor readings obtained for the latch-based designs, compared against those for the RO2-*cf*. Combining the ERO with the latch while maintaining the combinational feedback means that the latch only adds extra routing and load capacitance while not breaking the feedback loop. Therefore, this achieves the most significant voltage drop. Looking at Table 2, we can see that it even outperforms the ERO-*cf*. The version without the combinational feedback breaks the loop using the latch. While that decreases the oscillation frequency and makes it consume less power than the ERO-*cf*, the additional routing and capacitance more than compensate for it, and we observe that it performs better than the ROs.

Including an ERO with sequential elements while maintaining the feedback loop preserves the effectiveness of the EROs for the FF-based designs as well, as shown in Fig. 10. Using the PLL clock or the latch clock induces minimal differences. This is not unexpected, as the delays of passing through the latch are much more significant than those of only passing through a LUT, as reported in the device datasheet [31]. Therefore, the frequency achievable by an RO-L is not significantly higher than that of the PLL. The limited frequency of the change of the FF output compared to the transparent latch makes the improved FF-based designs induce a less significant voltage drop. They also perform slightly worse than standard ERO-*cf*s, potentially because the increased capacitance at the LUT output decreases the ERO oscillation frequency. Removing the feedback loop makes the FF-based EROs comparable to and slightly better than the RO-FF power waster. The version using a latch clock benefits from the slightly increased frequency of the clock and the increased routing from the ERO, and thus performs somewhat better.

5.2 Experimental Results on Genesys-ZU

Packing of Power Wasters. Within the clock regions for the attacker, we instantiate the same number of power wasters as for the Pynq-Z1. As a result, the utilization numbers are similar to those in Table 1. However, there are a few differences. First, all of the FFs within a slice can act as latches, so the number of utilized FFs in all designs that are not purely combinational is the same. Second, a slice contains eight LUTs and 16 FFs, so fewer slices are needed to have the same resource utilization. Our designs use the same hardware description as

Table 3. Max, min, average, and peak-to-peak Sensor 0 readings relative to the baseline, along with the min and max voltage reported by Vivado (Genesys-ZU). Wasters are ranked by effectiveness. The best values are in italics if triggering critical DRC warnings and in bold if not. In gray, wasters introduced in this work.

Power waster	Max. reading*	Min. reading*	Avg. reading*	Peak-to-peak	Min. Voltage	Max. Voltage
ERO-L-cf	*1.32*	*-371.28*	*-311.03*	*372.60*	*0.762 V*	*0.864 V*
ERO-*cf*	-1.29	-294.29	-244.73	293.00	0.797 V	0.864 V
ERO-L	**1.51**	**-261.69**	**-214.77**	**263.20**	**0.785 V**	**0.864 V**
ERO-FF-*cf* (L)	5.03	-216.37	-177.04	221.40	0.803 V	0.861 V
RO2	5.52	-196.09	-161.19	201.61	0.803 V	0.864 V
ERO-FF-*cf* (PLL)	2.82	-173.38	-132.31	176.20	0.812 V	0.861 V
RO-L	-5.00	-186.51	-154.25	181.51	0.812 V	0.864 V
RO	2.26	-139.44	-112.75	141.70	0.844 V	0.864 V
ERO-FF (L)	11.23	-95.77	-74.72	107.00	0.820 V	0.861 V
ERO-FF (PLL)	-1.49	-48.79	-36.38	47.30	0.844 V	0.864 V
RO-FF (PLL)	3.06	-32.44	-22.61	35.50	0.844 V	0.861 V

*Relative to the baseline average obtained before each experiment

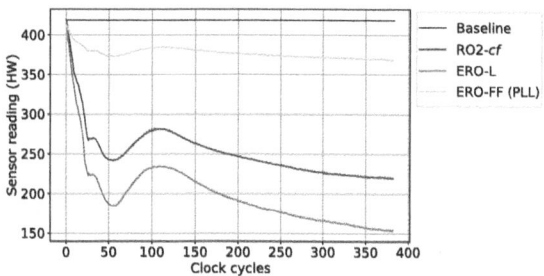

Fig. 11. Comparison of the sensor readings on the Genesys-ZU.

for the other board, with the only variation being the constraint of two power waster instances (four LUTs and eight FFs each) per slice to ensure that the wasters are packed effectively.

Sensor Readings. The results for the Genesys-ZU board are summarized in Table 3. The power wasters' performance follows the same trends as for the Pynq-Z1. The results correspond to the enable signal period of 800 clock cycles, but an attack duration of 384 clock cycles (we have tested the power wasters with various enable signal periods and validated that they remain consistent). We note that the sensor calibration is board-specific and, hence, different (the range for the readings is also different); accordingly, the readings also differ with respect to those on the Pynq-Z1. Figure 11 shows a sample of the sensor readings for three power wasters on the Genesys-ZU. The main difference between the Pynq-Z1 and the Genesys-ZU is due to the number of latches used in a slice. Therefore, we see latch-based power wasters ranking better in Table 3 than in Table 2.

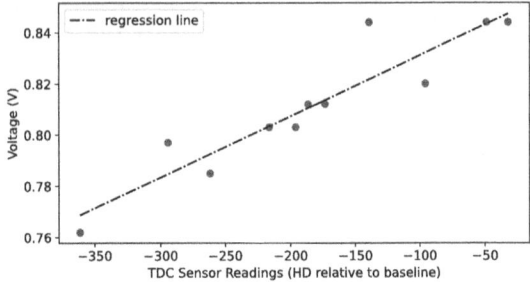

Fig. 12. Minimum TDC sensor readings relative to the baseline vs. minimum voltage readings reported by the system monitor (SYSMON). The figure also shows the regression line to underscore the correlation between the two values.

We also report the voltages collected from the system monitor on the chip. The reported voltage values make use of the fact that the supply voltage and the corresponding voltage regulator for the programmable logic are shared with the processing system and the BRAM. Therefore, Table 3 reports the minimum voltage values across these three components as recorded by Vivado. We choose to do this as the limited sampling frequency of the ADC sometimes leads to the minimum reading on one of the monitored voltages not changing after the ten experimental runs despite the other voltage values changing. The effect of the low sampling frequency of the ADC is apparent in Table 3. While the most effective power waster (ERO-L-*cf*) also results in the lowest voltage, corresponding to a drop of about 10% of the nominal voltage, not all voltage readings are consistent. For example, the ERO-L design has a minimum recorded voltage lower than the ERO-*cf*, despite the TDC sensor readings, which are directly correlated with the voltage [21], showing the opposite trend. However, we validate the correlation between the TDC readings and the voltage and find that the Pearson correlation coefficient is 0.97385. Figure 12 shows how the minimum voltage and the minimum TDC readings (as Hamming distance (HD) from the baseline) are correlated. In agreement with that, the voltage readings still show that the effect of the top half of the table, i.e., the more effective wasters, is more significant and affects the voltage in a way that the on-chip sensors can measure.

Overall, the results highlight how the expected effect of a power waster can be predicted based on its implementation details. This understanding allowed us to build new power wasters (e.g., ERO-L-*cf* and ERO-L) that outperform existing ones and work with and without combinational loops. The results also show that the designs are portable across FPGA families and that combinational loops are unnecessary for an effective FPGA-based voltage-drop attack.

6   Discussion

On an FPGA, the fine granularity and variety of hardware primitives translate to possible extreme variations in circuit power consumption, as demonstrated by the power-wasting primitives we examined in this work. Consequently, an adversary has a plethora of options to choose from in the function on the desired exploit, the target FPGA platform, and the available resources.

Attack Circuits' Effectiveness: As expected from Eq. (1), the most effective power wasters are those that combine signals switching at a high frequency with a large fanout and a lot of routing. Therefore, all variants that use combinational feedback loops cause more significant variations in the sensor readings than their counterparts that break the combinational loop. Increasing the routing and the fanout also make a substantial difference, with ERO-cf and similar designs performing better than those using only one LUT with the corresponding FFs. The only case where the capacitance effect is not apparent is when the designs are significantly limited by the oscillation frequency, such as those in the last two rows of Table 2. Additionally, due to the limits on the clocks generated by the clock managers within an FPGA, self-oscillating designs tend to perform better than those that use a PLL clock.

Portability: Modern FPGAs share similar organization and resources, facilitating the portability of power-wasting primitives across platforms. LUT-based designs are simple to port, as most FPGAs support similar LUTs with two outputs. On the other hand, ERO-cfs may need adjustments for LUT input counts and grouping. Designs using latches and FFs require more effort to be adapted to available FFs and control signal origins. Routing LUT and FF outputs might offer different options for synchronous and combinational outputs. For all designs, the control mechanism will also need to be adapted to the platform. As shown in Sect. 5, porting designs across FPGA families is feasible, requiring only adjustments to account for the potentially different organization of resources.

Stealth: Oscillating circuits can enable side-channel, fault-injection, and DoS attacks, leading to efforts to detect them. Amazon leverages Vivado to detect the loops to prevent the deployment of ROs [2]. FF-based power wasters, which break the combinational loop, can be deployed on commercial cloud FPGA instances and, as a result, they offer more stealth than their combinational counterparts. Despite the potential for detection [1,15], the threat remains critical, and studying these exploits is essential for developing future robust protections.

7 Conclusion

Due to their widespread deployment, the security of remotely accessible FPGAs is increasingly critical. This paper explores the potential for implementing power wasters using logic primitives within FPGA programmable fabrics. We classify FPGA-based power-wasting circuits as combinational, FF-based, improved, and hidden. Key comparison features include power consumption, voltage drop, resource efficiency, and the severity of design rule check warnings. We implemented known logic-based power wasters, analyzed them, and proposed new variations. Our analysis validated the factors influencing power consumption, with some proposed designs outperforming the standard ring oscillator. Evaluation on two hardware platforms demonstrated the portability of these designs and validated findings across FPGA families. Our results reveal the potential for new waster designs that evade critical warnings while causing significant voltage drops, posing a threat to remotely accessible systems. Future work can explore hiding wasters within benign designs and developing countermeasures to detect and disable these malicious circuits while preserving legitimate functionality.

Acknowledgments. This research is supported by armasuisse Science and Technology.

References

1. Alrahis, L., Nassar, H., Krautter, J., Gnad, D., Bauer, L., Henkel, J., Tahoori, M.: MaliGNNoma: GNN-based malicious circuit classifier for secure cloud FPGAs. arXiv, March 2024. arXiv:2403.01860 [cs]
2. AWS EC2 FPGA HDK+SDK errata (2019). https://github.com/aws/aws-fpga/blob/master/ERRATA.md
3. FPGA-based Amazon EC2 F1 computing instances (2022). https://aws.amazon.com/ec2/instance-types/f1/
4. 66906 - UltraScale soft error mitigation (SEM) IP - [DRC 23-20] rule violation (PDCN-1569) LUT equation term check, September 2021. https://support.xilinx.com/s/article/66906?language=en_US
5. Amer, H.H.: Behavior of memory elements in the presence of power supply disturbances. In: 34th Annual Spring Reliability Symposium, "Reliability - Investing in the Future, pp. 45–51. Boxborough, MA, USA, April 1996
6. Chen, C.H., Bowman, K., Augustine, C., Zhang, Z., Tschanz, J.: Minimum supply voltage for sequential logic circuits in a 22nm technology. In: International Symposium on Low Power Electronics and Design, pp. 181–186. Beijing, China, September 2013
7. García, A.D.G., Pérez, L.F.G., Acuña, R.F.: Power consumption management on FPGAs. In: 15th International Conference on Electronics, Communications and Computers, pp. 240—245, February 2005
8. Genesys ZU: Zynq UltraScale+ MPSoC development board (2022). https://digilent.com/reference/programmable-logic/genesys-zu/reference-manual
9. Giechaskiel, I., Rasmussen, K.B., Szefer, J.: Measuring long wire leakage with ring oscillators in cloud FPGAs. In: 29th International Conference on Field-Programmable Logic and Applications, pp. 45–50. Barcelona, Spain, September 2019
10. Glamočanin, O., Coulon, L., Regazzoni, F., Stojilović, M.: Are cloud FPGAs really vulnerable to power analysis attacks? In: Design, Automation & Test in Europe Conference & Exhibition (DATE), pp. 1–4. Grenoble, France, March 2020
11. Glamočanin, O., Kostić, A., Kostić, S., Stojilović, M.: Active wire fences for multitenant FPGAs. In: DDECS, pp. 13–20, May 2023
12. Gnad, D.R.E., Oboril, F., Tahoori, M.B.: Voltage drop-based fault attacks on FPGAs using valid bitstreams. In: FPL, pp. 1–7. Ghent, Belgium, September 2017
13. Gupta, M.S., Oatley, J.L., Joseph, R., Wei, G.Y., Brooks, D.M.: Understanding voltage variations in chip multiprocessors using a distributed power-delivery network. In: Design, Automation & Test in Europe Conference & Exhibition (DATE), pp. 1–6. Nice, France, April 2007
14. La, T., Pham, K., Powell, J., Koch, D.: Denial-of-Service on FPGA-based cloud infrastructures - attack and defense. IACR Trans. Cryptographic Hardware Embedded Syst. **2021**(3), 441–464 (2021)

15. La, T.M., Matas, K., Grunchevski, N., Pham, K.D., Koch, D.: FPGADefender: malicious self-oscillator scanning for Xilinx UltraScale + FPGAs. ACM Trans. Reconfigurable Technol. Syst. **13**(3), 15:1–15:31 (2020)

16. Mahmoud, D.G., Andreani, S., Lenders, V., Stojilović, M.: ROBoost: a study of FPGA logic-based power-wasting primitives. Artifacts (2025). https://doi.org/10.5281/zenodo.14840696

17. Mahmoud, D.G., Dervishi, D., Hussein, S., Lenders, V., Stojilović, M.: DFAulted: Analyzing and exploiting CPU software faults caused by FPGA-driven undervolting attacks. IEEE Access **10**, 134199–216 (2022)

18. Mahmoud, D.G., Hussein, S., Lenders, V., Stojilović, M.: FPGA-to-CPU undervolting attacks. In: Design, Automation & Test in Europe Conference & Exhibition (DATE), pp. 999–1004, March 2022

19. Mahmoud, D.G., Shokry, B., Lenders, V., Hu, W., Stojilović, M.: X-Attack 2.0: the risk of power wasters and satisfiability don't-care hardware trojans to shared cloud FPGAs. IEEE Access **12**, 8983–9011 (2024)

20. Matas, K., La, T.M., Pham, K.D., Koch, D.: Power-hammering through glitch amplification - attacks and mitigation. In: 28th Symposium on Field-Programmable Custom Computing Machines. pp. 65–69. Fayetteville, AR, USA, May 2020

21. Moini, S., Deric, A., Li, X., Provelengios, G., Burleson, W., Tessier, R., Holcomb, D.: Voltage sensor implementations for remote power attacks on FPGAs. ACM Trans. Reconfigurable Technol. Syst. **16**(1) (2022)

22. Pant, S.: Design and analysis of power distribution networks in VLSI Circuits. Ph.D. thesis, The University of Michigan (2008). https://deepblue.lib.umich.edu/bitstream/handle/2027.42/58508/spant_1.pdf%3Fsequence%3D1

23. Provelengios, G., Holcomb, D., Tessier, R.: Power wasting circuits for cloud FPGA attacks. In: 30th International Conference on Field-Programmable Logic and Applications, pp. 231–35. Gothenburg, Sweden, August 2020

24. Digilent reference for PYNQ-Z1. https://digilent.com/reference/programmable-logic/pynq-z1/start

25. Salman, E., Dasdan, A., Taraporevala, F., Kucukcakar, K., Friedman, E.G.: Exploiting setup-hold-time interdependence in static timing analysis. IEEE Trans. Comput. Aided Des. Integr. Circuits Syst. **26**(6), 1114–25 (2007)

26. Spielmann, D., Glamočanin, O., Stojilović, M.: RDS: FPGA routing delay sensors for effective remote power analysis attacks. IACR Trans. Cryptographic Hardware Embedded Syst. **2023**(2), 543–567 (2023)

27. Stojilović, M., Rasmussen, K., Regazzoni, F., Tahoori, M.B., Tessier, R.: A visionary look at the security of reconfigurable cloud computing. Proc. IEEE **111**(12), 1548–71 (2023)

28. UltraScale architecture system monitor user guide, September 2021

29. Xilinx Inc.: 7 series FPGAs configurable logic block user guide (UG474), September 2016

30. Xilinx Inc.: UltraScale architecture configurable logic block user guide (UG574), February 2017

31. Xilinx Inc.: Zynq-7000 SoC: DC and AC switching characteristics (DS187), December 2020

32. Zhao, M., Suh, G.E.: FPGA-based remote power side-channel attacks. In: IEEE Symposium on Security and Privacy (SP), pp. 229–244. San Francisco, CA, USA, May 2018

FLARE: An FPGA-Based Universal Large Flow Detection Engine

Arish Sateesan[1]([envelope]) [iD], Jo Vliegen[2] [iD], and Nele Mentens[2,3] [iD]

[1] INETS, RWTH Aachen University, Aachen, Germany
arish.sateesan@rwth-aachen.de
[2] COSIC-ES&S, ESAT, KU Leuven, Leuven, Belgium
{jo.vliegen,nele.mentens}@kuleuven.be
[3] LIACS, Leiden University, Leiden, The Netherlands

Abstract. Detecting large flows in high-speed networks is a persistent challenge in network security, often hampered by processing speed, memory demands, and the need for versatile handling of a range of attack vectors. The emergence of FPGA-based solutions offers promising prospects for real-time, scalable network security. Yet, precise detection of diverse large flow attacks introduces significant complexity and calls for the coordination of multiple independent detection algorithms. This paper presents FLARE, a large flow detection framework designed to address these challenges by integrating multiple detection algorithms into a unified system. FLARE can monitor network flows in real-time, handling data rates of up to 200 Gbps, and employs a shared architecture that minimizes resource usage while enhancing detection accuracy and coordination. The proof-of-concept implementation on the Alveo U250 data center accelerator shows that FLARE can process an entire packet in every clock cycle, irrespective of the throughput of the employed detection algorithms. Beyond large flow detection, FLARE provides a versatile and scalable platform applicable to a broad spectrum of network security applications.

Keywords: Large flow detection · Heavy-hitter detection · FPGA · DDoS · Network security

1 Introduction

The rapid growth in data rates in recent years has significantly raised the benchmarks for network performance. However, this growth has been paralleled by a rise in cyber threats, particularly volumetric distributed denial of service (DDoS) attacks. Mitigating these attacks, especially volumetric attacks like *large flows*, otherwise called *heavy-hitters*, has become more challenging than ever due to the surge in network speeds and diversity of attack patterns. *Large flows* refer to network flows that consume considerably larger bandwidth than the permitted

---

A. Sateesan—The author carried out this work while at KU Leuven.

R. Giorgi et al. (Eds.): ARC 2025, LNCS 15594, pp. 106–120, 2025.
https://doi.org/10.1007/978-3-031-87995-1_7

within a given time frame. These flows can degrade network performance, leading to congestion and slowdowns, and may indicate malicious activity like DDoS attacks. *Large flow detection* involves identifying and mitigating these flows, which is a fundamental problem in networking and holds significant importance in many applications, such as volumetric DDoS attack detection and traffic engineering [1–3]. This process typically relies on analyzing network traffic data to identify flows that exceed a set data volume or duration threshold.

Figure 1 shows a real-time flow-based large flow detection system. A network flow is the collection of all network packets that share the same characteristics and are identified by a unique flow identifier (Flow ID). The Flow ID is characterized by the 5-tuple, ⟨source IP address, source port, destination IP address, destination port, protocol ID⟩. In the large flow detection system, a parser extracts the flow ID from the packet header and forwards it to the mitigation and detection blocks. The real-time monitoring results or a predefined set of rules may define the mitigation policy. A commonly used mitigation policy involves both blacklisting [4,5], maintaining a list of malicious Flow IDs or their fingerprints (f), and dropping any incoming packets that match the blacklist. The detection algorithm determines whether the flow is malicious based on traffic features extracted by the flow measurement unit, where flow measurement refers to the collection and analysis of network flow data.

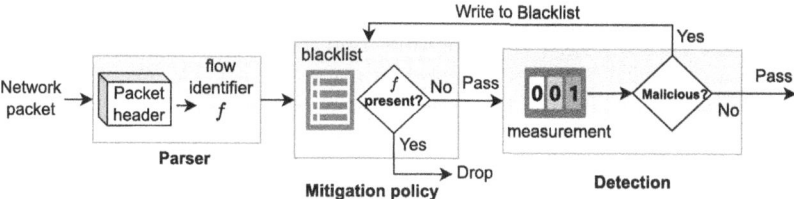

Fig. 1. Generic large flow detection system.

Previous approaches to large flow detection involve setting a predefined threshold within a specific time frame or measurement epoch. However, this approach struggles to detect a variety of these attack patterns, such as overuse flows [5], which are steady-rate flows slightly exceeding the allocated bandwidth, and burst-flood attacks, which involve periodic transmission of large data bursts within short timeframes [6]. Complete detection capabilities against such diverse patterns often require multiple independent algorithms, increasing computational complexity, resource demands, and coordination challenges. With increasing network speeds, real-time processing demands have outpaced the capabilities of existing detection frameworks. Existing research has yet to offer a universal detection framework capable of coordinating multiple algorithms to manage a broad spectrum of attacks effectively. Universal sketches such as UnivMon [1] and Light-weight Universal Sketch (LUS) [7] take advantage of dedicated measurement modules to collect flow metrics that can be utilized for various other applications. Nevertheless, this approach is orthogonal to the detection of a range of attack patterns of volumetric DDoS attacks, as it focuses only on traffic measurement tasks.

This paper introduces FLARE, an FPGA-based large flow detection engine designed for real-time monitoring and detection of large network flows on high-speed networks, capable of handling data rates up to 200Gbps. Unlike universal sketches like UnivMon and LUS, which aim to generalize detection methods across various applications, FLARE offers a specialized approach by integrating dedicated detection units to identify diverse patterns of network attacks. This positions FLARE as a comprehensive detection system for high-performance data center accelerators, while also broadening its applicability to addressing a wider range of network security challenges beyond large flow detection.

The key contributions of FLARE include:

- A versatile detection framework that effectively integrates and coordinates distinct detection units to identify a wide range of attack patterns, optimized for data center accelerator cards targeting Terabit Ethernet (data rates greater than 100 Gbps).
- A shared architecture that minimizes resource requirements and prevents redundant blacklist entries by facilitating the sharing of blacklists among detection units. Moreover, it uses a probabilistic blacklist, ensuring reduced memory requirement and constant lookup delay irrespective of the blacklist size.
- An independent detection framework and packet forwarding mechanism, which can forward a network packet in every clock cycle, ensuring that the throughput is not affected by algorithm complexity.

2   Challenges in Designing a Large Flow Detection System

Overcoming the challenges of fast and accurate detection of large flows while ensuring efficient hardware deployment involves a multitude of related problems, which will be discussed in the subsequent sections.

2.1   The Need for Dedicated Algorithms

Detecting large flows is a multi-dimensional challenge involving both detection accuracy and range, requiring tailored algorithms for different attack types. The frequent emergence of new and sophisticated attacks, such as carpet bomb attacks [8], underlines this requirement. Large flow detection algorithms typically set a detection threshold based on the average volume over a measurement period. The choice of measurement period and threshold significantly impacts detection accuracy. A long period with a high threshold might overlook potential threats, while a short period with a low threshold risks false positives. Existing algorithms [2,3,9] often target large flows that are significantly above (100 to

1000 times) the allocated bandwidth and maintain a steady sending rate. These algorithms, often using simple data structures like sketches [10], tolerate some measurement errors. While this simplicity of sketches is attributed to lower memory requirements and reduced complexity, it can be exploited by attackers who send traffic just below the high detection threshold, evading detection.

Detecting flows with non-steady rates, such as burst-flood attacks involving periodic transmission of large data bursts within short timeframes [6], introduces additional challenges. Algorithms designed for steady-rate detection may fail to identify bursts, as the average volume over a long period may fall below the threshold. Reducing the measurement period to capture bursts can lead to false positives in steady-rate flows. To accurately detect non-steady-rate flows, the detection algorithm must minimize estimation errors, which can be amplified by sketch-based methods. More sophisticated approaches, such as LOFT [5], can detect flows slightly exceeding the allocated bandwidth, termed as *low-rate overuse* flows. LOFT eliminate the need for distinct detection algorithms to detect low-rate and high-rate overuse flows. ALBUS [6] is another precise detection algorithm designed for detecting burst-flood attacks. These algorithms are less tolerant of estimation errors. However, relying solely on a single detection algorithm is insufficient for comprehensive detection, as LOFT can only detect steady-rate flows, highlighting the need for dedicated algorithms like ALBUS for detecting distinct attack vectors.

2.2 Hardware Deployment and Challenges

FPGAs offer a promising solution for deploying detection algorithms by providing significant parallelism to accelerate computational tasks and meet real-time processing requirements. While graphics processing units (GPU) excel in high-performance computing due to their high throughput design, they aren't optimized for the low-latency processing required by applications like large flow detection. This task demands consistent, real-time performance, and FPGAs can be specifically customized to provide precise, deterministic timing, and highly optimized application-specific hardware designs [11]. Moreover, large flow detection primarily involves operations like data storage and membership queries rather than heavy computations. Transferring data between the CPU and GPU can add extra latency and complexity, whereas FPGAs can be embedded directly into data paths (bump-in-the-wire architectures), thereby minimizing data movement and associated delays [12].

The applications of FPGAs in data centers and networking environment showcases their exceptional potential in high-speed networking applications [13–16]. However, deploying multiple detection units is suboptimal due to the increased resource requirements and complexity, especially in high-speed environments. With blacklisting being the mitigation policy, each detection unit requires a dedicated blacklist, consuming more memory and increasing the detection overhead. Additionally, multiple algorithms identifying the same malicious flow can create redundant blacklist entries, reducing memory efficiency and increasing query latency. The accuracy of large flow detection algorithms solely depends on the accuracy of the measurement module. Limited on-chip memory on FPGAs can reduce measurement accuracy, as sketch-based units may produce significant overestimations under limited memory. Moving to off-chip memory is not desirable due to considerable access delays, hampering real-time processing [17]. Coordinating algorithms with different throughput and query latencies further complicates hardware deployment, potentially slowing down the system and hindering parallel processing capabilities.

3   Proposed Detection Framework – FLARE

Figure 2 shows the system architecture of FLARE. FLARE is designed to function as a bump-in-the-wire, performing online flow monitoring while positioned between the external network and the protected network to filter traffic. The complete detection engine integrates a parser, a traffic filtering unit, and additional functional and control logic responsible for handling incoming traffic, in conjunction with the detection framework and blacklist module. It buffers incoming packets during processing, forwarding legitimate ones to the network and dropping malicious ones. Further elaboration on the components of FLARE is provided in the subsequent sections.

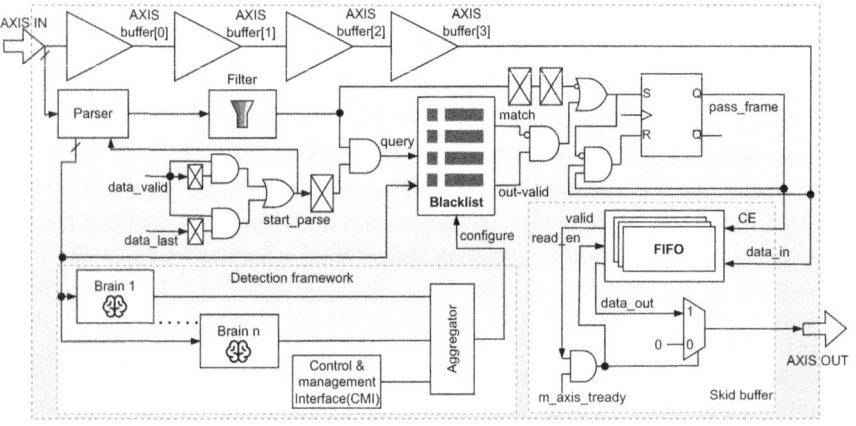

Fig. 2. System architecture of FLARE.

3.1   Parser and Network Filter

The network parser extracts the flow ID and various attributes from incoming flows, such as flow size, EtherType, and protocol. Based on these attributes, the network filter identifies and directs flows meeting the filtering criteria to the blacklist and detection framework. In FLARE, the filtering criteria are based on the EtherType and IP protocol, and it inspects flows with

EtherType=IPv4 and *Protocol=TCP/UDP*. In the proof-of-concept implementation of FLARE (Sect. 4), the protocol used is UDP. Flows that do not match these criteria are passed through without inspection. The filtering policy is configurable and can be modified during run-time using the control and management interface in the detection framework.

3.2   Detection Framework

The detection framework, the core of FLARE, comprises multiple detection algorithms (referred to as *brains*), a control and management interface (CMI), and an aggregator. Detailed descriptions of these modules are provided in subsequent sections.

Brain: The brain (detection algorithm) determines whether an incoming flow is malicious. Multiple brains can operate concurrently, each tasked with a specific detection role. While brains operate independently, they share a common blacklist, minimizing memory usage. FLARE can also support the sharing of measurement unit, given that the detection algorithms are designed that way, thereby further reducing hardware resources. In such a case, the detection algorithm can function only as a smart decision-maker.

Control and Management Interface (CMI): The CMI is an AXI-Lite module responsible for controlling and validating the detection framework and network filter. CMI also serves the purpose of a brain as it allows users to manually add entries to the blacklist while providing a user interface for testing, framework validation, and blacklist management. The CMI uses a 32-bit control register, along with dedicated data and status AXI slave registers for reading and writing to the blacklist and verifying functionality across modules. The control register also allows dynamic modification of the filtering policy.

Aggregator: The aggregator coordinates interactions among the brains, CMI, and the blacklist. It manages multiple concurrent brains and forwards flow IDs of the detected malicious flows to the blacklist. The aggregator is a smart multiplexer that prevents data loss by ensuring proper sequencing of write operations to the blacklist. The hardware architecture of the aggregator is shown in Fig. 3, which can handle three brains and is easily expandable. Data from each brain is queued into the respective data FIFOs (brain B0 is not available, hence set to zero), and the aggregator controls the flow of data to the blacklist based on FIFO status and a predefined priority using a finite state machine (FSM).

3.3   Blacklist Module

The blacklist module consists of a shared blacklist and the associated *time-to-live* (TTL) logic.

TTL Logic: The TTL logic helps to distinguish the flow IDs written to the blacklist by different brains. Each algorithm may have a distinct measurement period or epoch, resulting in varying reset periods. The expiration of each entry

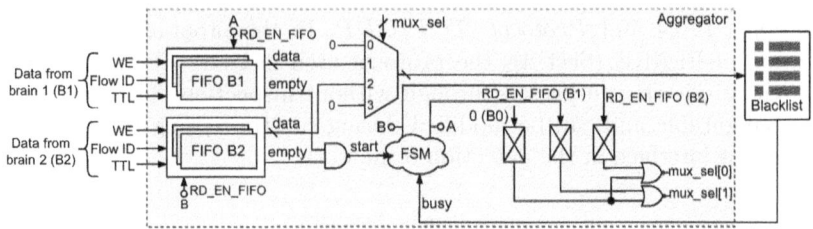

Fig. 3. Aggregator.

on the blacklist depends on the reset period of the corresponding brain. A TTL value, associated with each flow ID, indicates the expiry time of a blacklist entry with respect to a timestamp and is specific for each brain. Figure 4 illustrates the logic circuitry employed in TTL logic. A combination of a prescaler, counter, and an adder generates a value referred to as TTLT (Time-To-Live Timestamp), which is the sum of the current timestamp and the TTL value. This value is stored alongside the flow ID in the blacklist. The prescaler is a clock divider, and it drives a 16-bit counter that produces the timestamp. The size of the TTLT value is taken as 16 bits. The divisor to the prescaler is calculated based on the clock frequency and the size of the TTLT value.

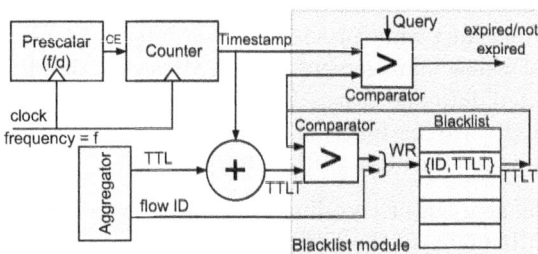

Fig. 4. TTL logic.

Blacklist: The blacklist, implemented using SPArch-based [18] content address-able memory (CAM), consists of a sketch component and a memory unit for TTL values. SPArch is a probabilistic data structure that is used as a counter array, which can be modified as a probabilistic key-value store, a faster alternative to content addressable memories. The architecture of the blacklist is shown in Fig. 5. It uses a hash function (Xoodoo-NC [19]) to map flow IDs to the sketch using hash values h_1 to h_d, where d is the number of arrays in the sketch. The size of the hash values is $log_2 m$, where m is the depth of each memory array. The blacklist stores only an 8-bit fingerprint (f) of the flow ID, which is generated using the hash value h_f. Each hash-indexed cell in the sketch stores f and the address A, which points to the TTL memory. The TTL memory stores the associated expiration information (TTLT value). For a detailed description of the update and query operations of the blacklist, we refer to the original work [18].

If a flow ID already exists in the blacklist (previously written by another brain), the existing TTLT value is compared with the new entry, and if the new value is greater, it replaces the old one. To inspect which brain added a specific flow ID to the blacklist (with the assistance of CMI), an additional identifier tag field of 1 or 2 bits (depending on the number of brains) can be added to the TTL memory. The blacklist is queried for every incoming flow that meets the filtering criteria. If the incoming flow is present in the blacklist but the TTLT value is expired, the flow is allowed to pass and the entry is removed from the blacklist. The address of the removed entry is stored in a FIFO and re-used later. If required, the blacklist can be reset periodically based on the reset periods of the brains.

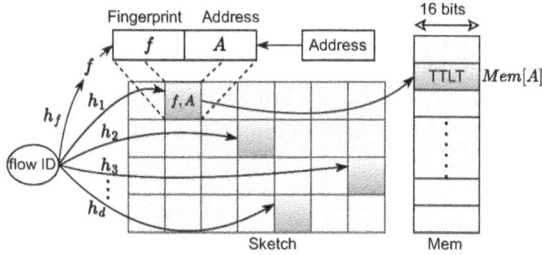

Fig. 5. Architecture of blacklist

3.4 Skid Buffer

The skid buffer, implemented using data FIFOs, buffers outgoing packets until the master AXIS interface is ready. It also handles clock domain crossing. The buffer is controlled by a *pass_frame* signal (refer to Fig. 2), which ensures that packets are transmitted only after blacklist processing. The *reset* signal of the SR flip-flop keeps the *pass_frame* signal active for one packet, guaranteeing correct transmission behaviour.

4 Implementation of a Proof of Concept

We implemented a proof of concept (PoC) for FLARE to validate its feasibility. The PoC employs the LOFT [5] detection algorithm and CMI as the brains, with LOFT handling large flow detection and CMI enabling manual additions to the blacklist. LOFT, although has a sophisticated design, is chosen due to its superior detection accuracy, which can be as low as 1.5× the allowed bandwidth. While other algorithms, like EARDet [4], also follow the blacklisting model, LOFT was chosen for its efficiency and hardware suitability as it employs sketches for flow measurement. This PoC demonstrates the efficiency of FLARE, and the implementation and hardware evaluation are detailed in this section.

4.1   Hardware Platform

The hardware evaluation was conducted on the Alveo U250 data center accelerator card [20]. Alveo U250 is a robust FPGA-based solution to accelerate data center workloads, supporting data rates up to 200Gbps. Alveo employs two QSFP28 ports as the network interface that can transmit/receive 512 bits per clock cycle. The card has extensive resources: 1,341K LUTs, 2,749K flip-flops, 11,508 DSP slices, 54MB of on-chip memory with 38TB/s bandwidth, and 64GB of off-chip DDR memory with 77GB/s bandwidth. As shown in Fig. 6, the Alveo platform is divided into static and dynamic regions. The static region establishes the fundamental framework for the platform, including essential elements such as PCIe connectivity, board management, sensors, clocking, and reset. The dynamic region is subdivided into four super logic regions (SLRs), and are available for user-programmed RTL logic. For a deeper understanding of the Alveo platform, we refer to the Alveo user guide [21].

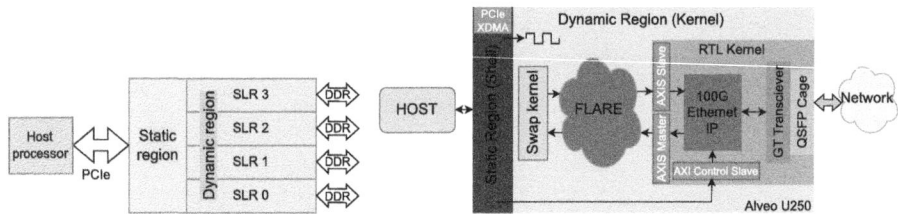

Fig. 6. Alveo U250 floorplan.   **Fig. 7.** Evaluation testbed.

4.2   Experimental Setup and Implementation Details

FLARE is integrated into the dynamic region of Alveo U250 as an AXI4-Stream IP, along with the CMAC kernel (100G Ethernet Media Access Control), using Xilinx Vivado 2022.1. The CMAC kernel is adopted from the XUP Vitis network example (VNx) [22], which uses the Ultrascale+ integrated Ethernet subsystem. The CMAC core is built around the CAUI-4 (100 Gigabit Attachment Unit Interface), which uses four lanes operating at 25.78125 Gbps each. This results in an aggregate uni-directional physical layer (PHY) raw data rate of 103.125 Gbps; however, after accounting for the 64b/66b encoding overhead, the effective payload data rate is approximately 100 Gbps. Data from the four lanes is aggregated into 512-bit wide words that are processed at a clock frequency of 322 MHz, the same frequency at which the CAUI-4 interface serializes and deserializes data. By converting high-speed serial data into these wider parallel words, the CMAC core is able to manage bursty traffic more effectively. It achieves this by buffering the data and inserting idle cycles or employing flow control, ensuring that while its instantaneous processing capability might be higher, the average throughput is maintained at the PHY's 100 Gbps limit.

The CMAC kernel offers two 512-bit AXI4-Stream interfaces to connect with FLARE. The setup, shown in Fig. 7, connects FLARE to the network via QSFP and communicates with the host computer through PCI Express. FLARE is interfaced with another AXI4-Stream IP, *Swap kernel*, to verify FLARE's functionality by echoing traffic by swapping source and destination addresses. The system architecture of FLARE is as depicted in Fig. 2. The incoming 512-bit AXI Stream data is buffered for four cycles to accommodate the blacklist query data path processing delay, which includes parsing, filtering, and blacklist query. The detection framework, containing the LOFT algorithm and CMI, processes the parsed data, with aggregator facilitating communication between the blacklist and detection components. For the details of LOFT, we refer to the original work [5]. In the implementation, LOFT uses 16,384 24-bit counters (16 bits for flow volume, 8 bits for cardinality), assuming that there are no *jumbo* frames. The size of the flow ID, consisting of the source address and port, is 48 bits. The active flow list and flow table in LOFT are implemented using the Cuckoo hash table, and both have a depth of 16384.

The blacklist, implemented with dual-port block RAM (BRAM) and controlled by two FSMs, handles simultaneous query and configure operations with a query latency of 2 cycles, ensuring processing at line rate. The sketch module of the blacklist has two arrays ($d=2$, $m=1024$) and the fingerprint size is 8 bits, adequate to provide near-hundred percent accuracy for storing up to 1024 elements (address size of 10-bits). An 8-bit fingerprint is optimal for SPArch [18], though even a 6-bit fingerprint is sufficient to reach saturation in accuracy. The update operation of the blacklist is not pipelined to conserve resources as well as to improve the operating frequency. As the update operation occurs less frequently, the aggregator can store and queue multiple update requests, making the pipelining of the update operation unnecessary.

4.3   Results

The overall resource consumption of the testbed including the static shell region is summarized in Table 1, detailing the resource usage of various modules. Although the logic resource usage of the testbed is negligible compared to the total available resources, it consumes 32% of the BRAMs. Of this, 20% is allocated to LOFT, while 10% is consumed by the memory subsystem and interconnects. The memory requirement of LOFT, ~97% of the memory consumption of FLARE, is primarily driven by its measurement module. This underscores the importance of optimizing the algorithm and designing the measurement module to be shared across multiple algorithms so that the memory footprint stays within the constraints of on-chip resources. FLARE requires only <1% of the logic resources and on-chip memory, excluding the detection algorithms.

Table 1. FPGA resource utilization.

Design	LUTs	Registers	CLB	BRAM	DSP
Testbed*	**166,646 (9.6%)**	**270,704 (7.9%)**	**46,207 (21.4%)**	**860 (32.0%)**	**9 (0.1%)**
FLARE	21,006 (1.2%)	11,761 (0.3%)	6,212 (2.9%)	547 (20.3%)	0 (0.0%)
Blacklist	1,031 (0.1%)	107 (0.0%)	178 (0.1%)	2 (0.1%)	0 (0.0%)
LOFT	18,341 (1.1%)	9,937 (0.3%)	5,717 (2.6%)	533 (19.8%)	0 (0.0%)
CMAC	9,126 (0.5%)	32,051 (0.9%)	5,838 (2.7%)	17 (0.6%)	0 (0.0%)
Swap kernel	686 (0.0%)	802 (0.0%)	253 (0.1%)	17 (0.6%)	0 (0.0%)

*Including static shell region.

FLARE has 4 pipeline stages and introduces a total propagation delay of four clock cycles per packet, covering the operations of parsing, filtering, and blacklist lookup to determine whether to forward or drop a packet. The detection framework operates independently and does not interfere with the packet-forwarding operations. The CMAC core can transmit and receive 512 bits per clock cycle at an operating frequency of 322 MHz. Assuming a minimum packet size of 64 bytes, FLARE can process one packet per clock cycle. When metadata is included, an additional clock cycle is required to transmit or receive a 64-byte packet, resulting in a total of two clock cycles for processing. This additional cycle provides enough slack time for FLARE during processing. FLARE supports bidirectional data rates up to 200Gbps, which is the maximum throughput the network interface can support (cf. 4.2). The throughput of packet forwarding remains unaffected by the throughput of detection algorithms, as the detection framework operates independently in parallel. With a network interface that can support higher data rates, FLARE can sustain the required throughput as long as the critical path delay remains sufficient. The detection framework in the PoC implementation can achieve a throughput of 400 million packets per second assuming minimum packet size, consistent with the performance of LOFT. For a detailed discussion of the experimental results of LOFT, we refer to the original work [5].

4.4   Existing Works and Comparison

Exploration of FPGA-based solutions for large flow detection remains limited, with even fewer studies available in integrating DDoS defence algorithms [23,24]. Moreover, most existing solutions are designed for Gbps link speeds, making them unsuitable for Terabit Ethernet environments. Scalability challenges in integrating multiple detection units on hardware further contribute to the under-exploration of this research area. The work proposed in [24] incorporates multiple detection techniques for DDoS defense, employing an approach analogous to FLARE. However, their approach targets Gigabit networks and employs filtering techniques rather than independent detection algorithms, making it less suitable for algorithms with variable measurement epochs. Similarly, commercial solutions like Intel's Algo-shield [25] act as an accelerated filtering mechanism that integrates only established defense methods, limiting their adaptability.

Approaches using generic sketches, such as Jaquen [26], Poseidon [27], Uni-vMon [1], LUS [7], and generalized families of sketches [28], are limited to detecting high-bandwidth flows due to the high overestimation of sketches. These approaches also suffer from high latency and computational complexity [7], hindering their applicability in high-speed environments. Collaborative DDoS defense frameworks like SENSS [29], DefCOM [30], and CoDef [31] enable resource sharing across organizations and networks but introduce coordination complexity and potential privacy risks. These solutions predominantly support Gbps networks, often neglecting algorithmic optimization crucial for low-overhead detection at Tbps speeds.

Recent advancements in FPGA-based data center accelerators, such as Alveo, showed promising trends toward Terabit Ethernet. Recent works on FPGA-based data center accelerators to accelerate workloads show promise [15,32,33], but their applications to network security and large flow detection remain under-explored. Data center accelerator card-based smart NICs [34,35] and 100Gbps network stacks [22,36] primarily target data analytics, machine learning, and cryptography [37–40]. Nevertheless, these architectures offer valuable insights and can be adapted for large flow detection, significantly reducing design time.

Advantages of FLARE: Compared to the existing solutions, FLARE offers several advantages and those are listed here:

Reduced detection overhead and real-time monitoring: FLARE reduces the detection overhead by sharing a blacklist that operates independently of the detection algorithms. Additionally, it supports sharing flow measurement modules among algorithms with similar measurement criteria, which can further reduce overhead. Since the algorithms and packet forwarding mechanism operate independently in parallel, their complexity does not affect throughput, enabling real-time processing at Tbps link speeds.

Enhanced coordination and communication: TTLT functionality enables easier coordination of individual detection algorithms with different measurement epochs, improving overall efficiency.

Scalability: FLARE can easily accommodate emerging attack detection algorithms without interfering blacklist lookups or packet forwarding throughput, ensuring scalability.

Privacy-preserving: Unlike collaborative defense frameworks, which share resources and data externally, FLARE confines resource sharing internally, addressing privacy concerns.

Robust fault prevention: Compromised detection units (brain) can be isolated and disconnected from the framework in a plug-and-play manner, maintaining robustness and operational integrity.

5 Conclusions

This paper proposed FLARE, an FPGA-based large flow detection engine targeting Terabit Ethernet capable of integrating multiple detection algorithms into a unified framework while sharing a common blacklist. We tested the functionality of FLARE on an ALveo U250 data center accelerator card using high-speed network interfaces, supporting bidirectional data rates up to 200 Gbps. The implementation validates its real-time flow monitoring capabilities and adaptability for high-speed network security applications. Future work will expand its algorithmic repertoire, focusing on shared measurement modules, and explore broader real-world deployments, solidifying its role in next-generation network security.

Acknowledgments. This work is supported by the ESCALATE project, funded by FWO (G0E0719N) and SNSF (200021L_182005), and by Cybersecurity Research Flanders (VR20192203).

References

1. Liu, Z., Manousis, A., Vorsanger, G., Sekar, V., Braverman, V.: One sketch to rule them all: rethinking network flow monitoring with UnivMon. In: Proceedings of ACM Special Interest Group Data Commun. (SIGCOMM), pp. 101–114 (2016)
2. Yang, T., et al.: Elastic sketch: adaptive and fast network-wide measurements. In: Proceedings of ACM Special Interest Group Data Communication (SIGCOMM), pp. 561–575 (2018)
3. Tang, L., Huang, Q., Lee, P.: A fast and compact invertible sketch for network-wide heavy flow detection. IEEE/ACM Trans. Networking **28**(5), 2350–2363 (2020)
4. Wu, H., Hsiao, H.C., Hu, Y.C.: Efficient large flow detection over arbitrary windows: an algorithm exact outside an ambiguity region. In: Proceedings of the 2014 Conference on Internet Measurement Conference, pp. 209–222 (2014)
5. Scherrer, S., et al.: Low-rate overuse flow tracer (loft): an efficient and scalable algorithm for detecting overuse flows. In: 2021 40th International Symposium on Reliable Distributed Systems (SRDS), pp. 265–276. IEEE (2021)
6. Scherrer, S., et al.: Albus: a probabilistic monitoring algorithm to counter burst-flood attacks. In: 2023 42th International Symposium on Reliable Distributed Systems (SRDS), IEEE (2023)
7. Xiao, Q., Cai, X., Qin, Y., Tang, Z., Chen, S., Liu, Y.: Universal and accurate sketch for estimating heavy hitters and moments in data streams. IEEE/ACM Trans. Networking (2023)
8. Carpet Bomb DDoS attacks: on the rise and evading detection. https://www.corero.com/threat-report-carpet-bomb-intro/ (2023)
9. Yang, T., et al.: Sf-sketch: a fast, accurate, and memory efficient data structure to store frequencies of data items. In: 2017 IEEE 33rd International Conference on Data Engineering (ICDE), pp. 103–106 (2017)
10. Cormode, G., Muthukrishnan, S.: An improved data stream summary: the count-min sketch and its applications. J. Algorithms **55**(1), 58–75 (2005)
11. Hoozemans, J., Peltenburg, J., Nonnemacher, F., Hadnagy, A., Al-Ars, Z., Hofstee, H.P.: Fpga acceleration for big data analytics: challenges and opportunities. IEEE Circ. Syst. Mag. **21**(2), 30–47 (2021)

12. Fu, Y.: Adaptable machine learning with alveo data center accelera-
    tion cards. https://www.xilinx.com/publications/events/machine-learning-live/
    colorado/AdaptableMachineLearning_with_Alveo.pdf (2018)
13. Chung, E., et al.: Serving dnns in real time at datacenter scale with project brain-
    wave. iEEE Micro **38**(2), 8–20 (2018)
14. Putnam, A., et al.: A reconfigurable fabric for accelerating large-scale datacenter
    services. ACM SIGARCH Comput. Archit. News **42**(3), 13–24 (2014)
15. J., Abel, F., Hagleitner, C., Herkersdorf, A.: Enabling FPGAs in hyperscale data
    centers. In: 2015 IEEE 12th International Conference on Ubiquitous Intelligence
    and Computing and 2015 IEEE 12th International Conference on Autonomic
    and Trusted Computing and 2015 IEEE 15th International Conference on Scal-
    able Computing and Communications and Its Associated Workshops (UIC-ATC-
    ScalCom), pp. 1078–1086. IEEE (2015)
16. Weerasinghe, J., Polig, R., Abel, F., Hagleitner, C.: Network-attached FPGAs for
    data center applications. In: 2016 International Conference on Field-Programmable
    Technology (FPT), pp. 36–43. IEEE (2016)
17. Hassan, M.: On the off-chip memory latency of real-time systems: Is ddr dram
    really the best option? In: 2018 IEEE Real-Time Systems Symposium (RTSS), pp.
    495–505. IEEE (2018)
18. Sateesan, A., Vliegen, J., Scherrer, S., Hsiao, H.C., Perrig, A., Mentens, N.: SPArch:
    a hardware-oriented sketch-based architecture for high-speed network flow mea-
    surements. ACM Trans. Privacy Secur. (2024)
19. Sateesan, A., Vliegen, J., Daemen, J., Mentens, N.: Hardware-oriented optimization
    of bloom filter algorithms and architectures for ultra-high-speed lookups in network
    applications. Microprocess. Microsyst. **93**, 104619 (2022)
20. Xilinx. Alveo U250 data center accelerator card. https://www.xilinx.com/
    products/boards-and-kits/alveo/u250.html (2023)
21. Xilinx. Vitis unified software platform documentation: Application accel-
    eration development (ug1393). https://docs.xilinx.com/r/en-US/ug1393-vitis-
    application-acceleration (2023)
22. Xilinx. XUP Vitis Network Example (VNx). https://github.com/Xilinx/xup_
    vitis_network_example
23. Chen, Yu., Hwang, K.: Collaborative detection and filtering of shrew ddos attacks
    using spectral analysis. J. Parall. Distrib. Comput. **66**(9), 1137–1151 (2006)
24. Pham-Quoc, C., Nguyen, B., Thinh, T.N.: Fpga-based multicore architecture for
    integrating multiple ddos defense mechanisms. ACM SIGARCH Comput. Archit.
    News **44**(4), 14–19 (2017)
25. Stop DDoS attacks before they disrupt the customer experience. https://intel.ly/
    2N9hexa (2020)
26. Liu, Z., et al.: Jaqen: a {High-Performance}{Switch-Native} approach for detecting
    and mitigating volumetric {DDoS} attacks with programmable switches. In: 30th
    USENIX Security Symposium (USENIX Security 21), pp. 3829–3846 (2021)
27. Zhang, M., et al.: Poseidon: mitigating volumetric ddos attacks with programmable
    switches. In: The 27th Network and Distributed System Security Symposium
    (NDSS 2020) (2020)
28. Zhou, Y., Zhang, Y., Ma, C., Chen, S., Odegbile, O.O.: Generalized sketch families
    for network traffic measurement. Proc. ACM on Measure. Anal. Comput. Syst.
    3(3), 1–34 (2019)
29. Ramanathan, S., Mirkovic, J., Yu, M., Zhang, Y.: Senss against volumetric ddos
    attacks. In: Proceedings of the 34th Annual Computer Security Applications Con-
    ference, pp. 266–277 (2018)

30. Oikonomou, G., Mirkovic, J., Reiher, P., Robinson, M.: A framework for a collaborative ddos defense. In: 2006 22nd Annual Computer Security Applications Conference (ACSAC 2006), pp. 33–42. IEEE (2006)
31. Lee, S.B., Kang, M.S., Gligor, V.D.: Codef: collaborative defense against large-scale link-flooding attacks. In: Proceedings of the ninth ACM conference on Emerging Networking Experiments and Technologies, pp. 417–428 (2013)
32. Falsafi, B., Dally, B., Singh, D., Chiou, D., Joshua, J.Y., Sendag, R.: FPGAs versus GPUs in data centers. IEEE Micro **37**(1), 60–72 (2017)
33. Bobda, C., et al.: The future of fpga acceleration in datacenters and the cloud. ACM Trans. Reconfigurable Technol. Syst. (TRETS) **15**(3), 1–42 (2022)
34. Wang, Z., Huang, H., Zhang, J., Wu, F., Alonso, G.: {FpgaNIC}: An {FPGA-based} versatile 100gb {SmartNIC} for {GPUs}. In: 2022 USENIX Annual Technical Conference (USENIX ATC 22), pp. 967–986 (2022)
35. AMD. AMD OpenNIC project. https://github.com/Xilinx/open-nic/blob/main/OpenNIC_manual.pdf. Accessed 2024
36. He, Z., Korolija, D., Alonso, G.: Easynet: 100 gbps network for hls. In: 2021 31st International Conference on Field-Programmable Logic and Applications (FPL), pp. 197–203. IEEE (2021)
37. Chiosa, M., Preußer, T.B., Alonso, G.: Skt: a one-pass multi-sketch data analytics accelerator. Proc. VLDB Endowment **14**(11), 2369–2382 (2021)
38. Jiang, W., Korolija, D., Alonso, G.: Data processing with FPGAs on modern architectures. In: Companion of the 2023 International Conference on Management of Data, pp. 77–82 (2023)
39. Jiang, W., et al. Fleetrec: large-scale recommendation inference on hybrid gpu-fpga clusters. In: Proceedings of the 27th ACM SIGKDD Conference on Knowledge Discovery & Data Mining, pp. 3097–3105 (2021)
40. Bex, L., Turan, F., Van Beirendonck, M., Verbauwhede, I.: Mining cryptonight-haven on the varium c1100 blockchain accelerator card. arXiv preprint arXiv:2212.05033 (2022)

Efficient AI and Stream Analytics on FPGAs

Out-of-the-Box Performance of FPGAs for ML Workloads Using Vitis AI

Deepak Kumar Athur[1]([✉]) [iD], Rutuparn Pawar[2] [iD], and Aman Arora[1] [iD]

[1] Arizona State University, Tempe, AZ 85281, USA
{dathur,aman.kbm}@asu.edu
[2] The University of Texas at Austin, Austin, TX 78712, USA
rutuparn.pawar@utexas.edu

Abstract. Field Programmable Gate Arrays (FPGAs) are an attractive choice for accelerating Machine Learning (ML) workloads due to the flexible fabric of configurable logic blocks, interconnects, and embedded memory. However, programming FPGAs is difficult for ML developers as it requires intricate hardware knowledge. Even though high-level implementation solutions such as HLS are available, they come with their own challenges and a steep learning curve. To address this issue, FPGA vendors have raised the level of abstraction by providing ready-to-deploy frameworks for ML. In this paper, we present an evaluation of the out-of-the-box performance of FPGAs using AMD/Xilinx Vitis AI, a development environment for deploying ML models on FPGAs. The study aims to assess the inference performance of Vitis AI for both edge and cloud platforms. We benchmark various popular and standard pre-trained models focusing on latency, throughput, and power efficiency. Since Google Tensor Processing Units (TPUs) are a platform for out-of-the-box acceleration of ML, we compare these results with cloud TPU and edge TPU in terms of performance, ease of use, and tool support. We discuss the experience of working with Vitis AI, the strengths and limitations of Vitis AI as a plug-and-play solution for FPGA-based ML acceleration, providing insights for developers looking to leverage FPGAs for their inference workloads.

1 Introduction

Platforms for Running ML Workloads: Deep Neural Networks (DNNs) inference has become a fundamental workload in modern applications. The high computational complexity of DNN algorithms and the stringent cost-energy-latency constraints for data center workloads necessitate efficient domain-specific hardware. With several hardware platform choices available from Graphic Processing Units (GPUs) to reconfigurable Field Programmable Gate Arrays (FPGAs) to highly specialized ASICs (Application Specific Integrated Circuits) it is important to make a meaningful hardware platform choice. GPUs are power-hungry and are optimized for throughput, hence they are less suitable for inference at the edge [8,12]. Google TPUs, on the other hand, are ASICs that must be

R. Giorgi et al. (Eds.): ARC 2025, LNCS 15594, pp. 123–139, 2025.
https://doi.org/10.1007/978-3-031-87995-1_8

redesigned when models evolve, costing a lot of time and money. However, these platforms have achieved success because they are easy to program. The vendors of TPUs and GPUs have spent considerable resources developing software stacks to easily use their hardware for DNN acceleration. Nvidia, for example, has created libraries like cuDNN and cuBLAS, which are natively supported by popular ML frameworks like Pytorch and Tensorflow, making it easy to run ML workloads optimally without any GPU programming. For the TPUs, Google provides Accelerated Linear Algebra (XLA), a domain-specific compiler that takes operations written Pytorch or Tensorflow and optimizes them for execution on the TPU. Also, the pre-configured cloud-based environments make it easy to work with TPUs.

FPGAs, Flexible and Efficient: The field of AI is rapidly evolving, with new algorithms and models being developed every week. Hardware capable of effectively running these algorithms must likewise advance at the same rate to keep up with the fast pace of algorithm development. This has led to the widespread use of reconfigurable hardware architectures such as Field Programmable Gate Arrays (FPGAs) that can easily adapt to changing requirements. Moreover, AI's computational complexity also comes with an energy cost which has become an important factor for both cloud and edge platforms. FPGA solutions are known to be more energy-efficient [7,8], by designing customized dataflows specific to the model being deployed and exploiting the inherent parallelism in DNNs. Furthermore, they avoid the overhead of fetching/decoding instructions and can use smaller data precisions.

FPGAs have a Steep Learning Curve: While FPGAs offer appealing advantages, most ML engineers are not accustomed to designing at lower abstraction levels like RTL, which involves hardware description languages like Verilog or VHDL and requires an understanding of hardware-specific concepts. High-Level Synthesis (HLS) addresses this concern by allowing engineers to describe hardware using languages like C/C++. However, it still requires some hardware knowledge and often yields less optimal results compared to expert-written RTL [14].

Out-of-the-Box DNN Deployment Frameworks for FPGAs: Overlays are intermediate hardware designs that abstract the complexity of low-level FPGA fabric, providing developers with a simpler, programmable interfaces. This abstraction gap helps users to interact at higher levels. The Deep Learning Processing Unit (DPU) [4], Deep Learning Accelerator (DLA) [2] are such overlays offered by AMD and Intel respectively for easy DNN acceleration. Vendors also provide software tools and frameworks for these overlays. AMD's Vitis AI [4], Intel's FPGA AI suite [3], and Lattice AI Suite [21] and Matlab's DNN toolbox [18] are such tools and frameworks that help users optimize and accelerate workloads on FPGAs. The goal is to make FPGAs easy to use, allowing an end-user, such as an ML practitioner, to utilize them with minimal effort-essentially achieving an "out-of-the-box" experience.

Contributions: Our intent in this work is to understand how easy it is to use modern FPGAs for DL acceleration. We wish to use this as a case study to see the maturity of FPGA tool flows for realistic deployment scenarios that do not involve experienced computer engineers who can write RTL or use HLS. We also compare the out-of-the-box performance and experiences with TPUs. To that end, we use AMD FPGAs and Vitis AI suite in this work. There is a knowledge gap about Vitis AI's capabilities and limitations, which our work tries to fill. Also, our analysis is helpful for companies to improve their solutions thereby expanding the user base of FPGAs. Specifically, our contributions are:

– Performance analysis of ML workloads on FPGAs deployed using AMD/Xilinx Vitis AI, for both edge and cloud devices.
– Comparison with Google TPUs (Edge and Cloud platforms) for out-of-the-box performance, deployment flow, and ease of use.
– Highlighting our experiences with AMD/Xilinx Vitis AI - strengths, weaknesses, and issues faced.

While some FPGA domain experts may know the experience and limitations of tools like Vitis AI, we believe it is useful for people from other domains (i.e., ML engineers) to understand the capabilities that exist with FPGA tools to make informed decisions.

2 Related Work

There are a few recent works that have focused on Vitis AI. In [24], the authors implement three different variants of ResNet that vary in number of layers, which are implemented on Zynq-7000 SoC. They compare the throughput and power consumption with GPU. In [25], the authors implement Yolov3 on ZCU104 and compare results with GPU. In [17], a course-grained accelerator using SystemVerilog, a fine-grained FINN accelerator, and a sequential Vitis AI accelerator are implemented and their performance is compared using the Zynq ZCU3EG device. In [11], the performance of FINN, Vitis AI and Jetson Nano GPU are compared for a single Resnet Model. In [6], the performance of CNNs implemented on U280 using HLS4ML and Vitis AI is studied.

FPGA overlays have grown in popularity for DNN acceleration [5]. Microsoft Brainwave provides low latency inference for neural networks in the cloud [7]. Recent works have evaluated FPGAs and GPUs for DNNs [19].

Although academic frameworks like HLS4ML [1], DNNWeaver [22], FPDNN [9], HPIPE [10], etc. exist, they have several drawbacks. These lack support for some frameworks or only limited support, inadequate profiling tools, support for multiple devices, thorough documentation, and technical support, which renders them less attractive than FPGA vendor tool options. As ML is a rapidly developing field, academic solutions might be unable to adapt and optimize architectures for these advances quickly. FPGA vendors have more extensive resources and financial incentives to overcome these challenges. Intel and Lattice have their Intel FPGA AI Suite and Lattice AI suite for out-of-the-box acceleration [3,21].

Table 1. Resource utilization and throughput for the DPUs used for our edge and cloud FPGAs

Platform	LUTs	FFs	BRAM	DSP	FPGA Peak TOPS
Edge	52161	98249	255	710	3.36
Cloud	592600	1013608	616	6569	26

In our work, we use a range of standard models that are commonly used and evaluate AMD's Vitis AI tool for implementing them on both Edge and Cloud platforms on devices marketed for ML acceleration. We also compare it with the deployment flow for Google TPUs in terms of features, performance, and ease of use.

3 Out-of-the-Box Deployment of DNNs on FPGAs

Vitis AI Overview: AMD Xilinx's Vitis AI is an open-source, comprehensive framework for the end-to-end deployment of ML inference on AMD hardware suitable for both cloud and edge applications [4]. This tool has a wide range of hardware support including Alveo data center cards, Zynq Ultrascale+ MPSoCs, Xilinx Versal Adaptive Compute Acceleration Platform (ACAP) cards, and Kria System on Modules. This tool is developed keeping the ML algorithm developers in mind who would like to develop and deploy ML applications to speed up inference deployment by abstracting the underlying hardware's intricacies. Vitis AI consists of set of IP cores, tools, libraries, models and example designs.

DPU FPGA Overlay: The DPU is an optimized overlay for DNN execution on AMD/Xilinx FPGAs. Vitis AI uses this as the core accelerator for inference. The DPU fetches and executes an optimized DPU instruction set for model inference from system memory. This helps abstract away the complex underlying hardware.

The architecture of the DPU [4] is shown in Fig. 1. The DPU is on the Programmable Logic (PL) and communicates with the host. The DPU can consists of several DPU cores which again contain several PEs which are convolution Engines. To handle interrupts and manage data transfers, an application on the host is also necessary. The instructions are fetched from off-chip memory, decoded and dispatched by the instruction scheduler to control the DPU. To attain high throughput and efficiency, input activations, intermediate feature maps, and output meta-data are buffered using on-chip memory.

There are several variants of DPUs, each targeting a particular hardware. Some features of the DPUs are parameterized to enable optimizing the design based on the user's requirements. Features such as number of cores, PEs, RAM usage etc. can be configured. However, the parameters that can be configured depend on the DPU. The two DPU architectures we use in our work for edge and cloud platforms are DPUCZDX8G and DPUCAHX8H-DWC respectively.

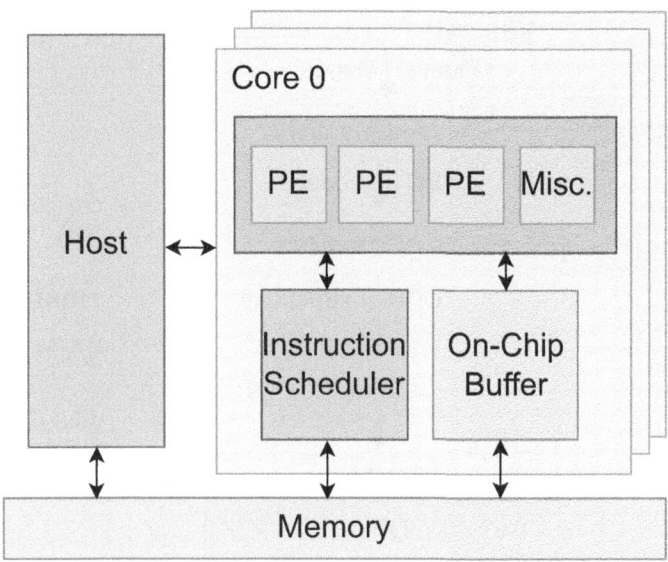

Fig. 1. High-level architecture of the DPU overlay

DPUCZDX8G is the DPU designed for Zynq Ultrascale+ MPSoC FPGAs. It comes in different configurations with varying throughput and resource usage. For our **edge FPGA platform**, we use the B4096 variant which has the highest peak throughput and resource utilization which are described in Table 1. The DPU has one core with four Processing Elements (PEs) for fundamental computation and runs at a clock frequency of 325 MHz.

DPUCAHX8H is the DPU designed for Alveo cards with HBM memory. It comes in throughput-optimized and latency-optimized variants. For our **cloud FPGA platform**, we use the latency-optimized variant DPUCAHX8H-DWC. It consists of 3 cores with 11 PEs in total and runs at a clock frequency of 300 Mhz with a peak performance of 14745 GOPs/s. To attain high throughput and efficiency, HBM is utilized to buffer weights, biases etc. The resource utilization of this DPU is mentioned in Table 1.

Vitis AI Flow: The overall flow that we follow for deploying DNNs on FPGAs is summarized in Fig. 2. To deploy a model on the DPU, it first needs to be quantized using Vitis AI quantizer. This tool quantizes the model's floating point precision weights and activations to fixed point (8-bit) with minimal loss in prediction accuracy. This can help reduce the model's memory footprint by reducing the overall size and the bandwidth for loading and unloading the data. This is particularly crucial for the deployment of these demanding models on resource-constrained edge devices. Then the binary instruction code that can be deployed on the DPU is generated using Vitis AI Compiler. Vitis AI Run Time (VART) provides APIs which are used to manage and execute AI models on the DPU. The instructions are then loaded into the DRAM.

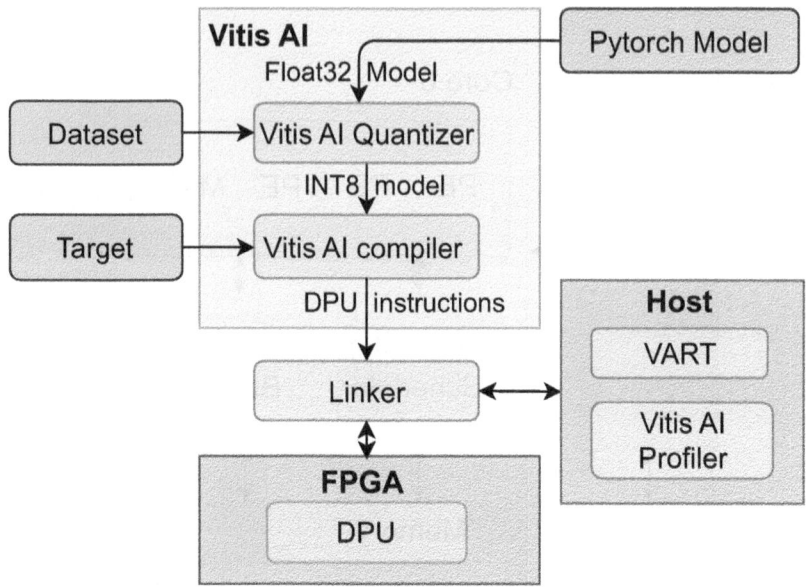

Fig. 2. Summary of DNN acceleration flow using Vitis AI

Model Zoo: Xilinx also provides a Model Zoo that contains several models several pre-trained models for different applications that are ready to be deployed on the DPU. Various versions of the same model for various hardware platforms are available. This out-of-the-box support reduces development time further. Examples of some models that are available are UNet, Inception, Yolo, and Mobilenet. Transformer-based models are not supported as of this writing.

4   Methodology

In this section, we discuss the details for our approach to evaluate Vitis AI for ML acceleration on FPGAs. This involves empirical analysis to evaluate performance.

4.1   FPGA Platforms

We sampled an edge and a cloud FPGA from the extensive number of FPGA platforms available, thereby covering both common scenarios. Additionally, these FPGAs come close in terms of specs to the Google TPUs (mentioned in the next section). Furthermore, these FPGAs are marketed for ML applications. While the experiments depicted in this paper can be performed on more FPGAs, our conclusions regarding the performance gap between out-of-the-box solutions and hand-coded solutions and showcasing the experiences of using out-of-the-box solutions, will stay the same. For the edge scenario, we use **KRIA KV260**. It

Table 2. Specifications of edge and cloud FPGA

	KV260	U55C
INT8 TOPS/s	3.36	26
DDR Bandwidth (GB/s)	9.2	460
Max power (W)	15	150
Tech node	16 nm	16 nm
On-chip memory (MB)	2.88	23
Availablility	2021	2021

Table 3. Specifications of edge and cloud TPU

	TPU v3	Edge TPU
TOPs/s	123 (BF16)	4 (INT8)
DDR Bandwidth	900 GB/s	-
Max power	262	-
Tech node	16 nm	-
On-chip memory	32 MB	8 MB
Availability	2018	2019
Clock frequency	940 Mhz	500 Mhz

targets ML application engineers and developers who have strong time to market
constraints allowing them to quickly prototype and deploy AI-driven systems.
For the cloud scenario, we use **U55C**, which is a high-performance accelerator
card for workloads like machine learning, fintech, and data search. It is equipped
with 16GB of high bandwidth memory (HBM) and fast networking capabilities.
The specifications for these FPGAs are described in Table 2. **INT8** precision is
used for executing the DNNs on both FPGA platforms.

4.2   TPU Platforms

We use the TPU for comparison because we want to compare out-of-the-box
performance and ease of deployment. The **Edge TPU** is an ASIC developed by
Google for the edge. It is designed to execute TensorFlow Lite models efficiently,
providing high-speed ML inference while maintaining low power consumption.
The Edge TPU only supports **INT8** precision. On the other hand, for the cloud
scenario, we use **TPU v3**, which is a large multi-die accelerator card for training,
fine-tuning and inference. We refer to this TPU as 'Cloud TPU' in this paper.
This TPU is closer to the U55C than TPU v2 in terms of max power. One
TPU v3 has 4 chips, and each chip has 2 cores which equals to 8 cores per card.
For our experiments, we are only using 1 core of the TPU. This version of the
TPU does not support INT8 precision. Hence, we use Google's Brain Float 16
(**BF16**) precision for our experiments. Specifications of the TPUs are mentioned

in Table 3. Some specifications are not available for the Edge TPU. Furthermore, the cloud TPU and Edge TPU do not have an inbuilt method to monitor power.

4.3   Benchmarks

The benchmarks chosen for evaluating the performance of our FPGA and TPU platforms are shown in Table 4 in descending order of the total number of compute operations. These popular DNNs have diverse computational demands that provide varied insights. *Note that these benchmarks are all Convolutional Neural Networks (CNNs). Unfortunately, Transformer-based models that form the backbone of recent DNN applications like ChatGPT are not supported by the Vitis AI flow, for FPGA devices (they are supported only for devices with AI engines). Hence, we are not able to deploy them.* Furthermore, YoloX-Nano could not be deployed on our cloud FPGA due to lack of support. All evaluations are performed at a batch size of 1 for edge devices and a batch size of 3 for cloud devices. A batch size of 1 for edge inference is a common usecase, but a higher batch size would have been more practical for cloud inference. However, the out-of-the-box DPU that we use does not support other batch sizes than a batch size of 1 for the KV260 and a batch size of 3 for U55C. Hence, our experiments were limited to these batch sizes.

Table 4. Benchmarks used in our experiments

Model	Operations	Parameter size		Input Sizes
	GOPs	M	MB	
VGG19	39.28	143.667	548.09	224 * 224 * 3
VGG16	30.96	138.358	527.79	224 * 224 * 3
Resnet-152	21.83	60.193	229.62	224 * 224 * 3
Resnet-50	8.2	25.557	97.49	224 * 224 * 3
MobileNetV1	1.14	3.505	13.37	224 * 224 * 3
YOLOX-Nano	1	0.91	2	416 * 416 * 3
EfficientNet b0	0.78	5.289	20.17	224 * 224 * 3

4.4   Software Platforms

For the edge TPU, we take the Pytorch model and convert it to Tensorflow Lite. Then, this model is run on the Edge TPU using the TPU compiler. For the Cloud TPU, we deploy the Pytorch model using XLA compiler. When it comes to both the Cloud and Edge FPGA, we go through the Vitis AI flow where the DPU instructions are generated by Vitis AI compiler executed on the DPUs. We use Vitis AI version 3.0 for KV260, but we are forced to use Vitis AI version 2.5 for U55C as the later versions have dropped support for that device.

4.5   Performance Measurement

The key metrics that we focus for evaluating the platforms are latency, through-put and energy efficiency. We measure latency using the TPU profiler and APIs for the Cloud TPU and the Edge TPU respectively, and Vitis AI Profiler and APIs the Edge FPGA and the Cloud FPGA respectively. We measure the latency of the DPU or TPU execution only. We ignore any overhead from the host. We measure utilization as a percentage ratio of peak TOPS and achieved TOPS for the TPU, and peak TOPS of the FPGA (not the DPU peak TOPS mentioned in Table 2) and achieved TOPS for the FPGA. We measure the power of the Sys-tem on Module (ARM core, FPGA, etc.) for the edge FPGA, and for the Cloud FPGA, we measure the power of the FPGA board (PCIE card). For the edge FPGA we use Xilinx's xmutil and for Cloud FPGA we use xbutil to measure power. Hence we obtained Inferences/J as shown below.

$$\text{Inferences per Joule} = \frac{\text{Inferences per second}}{\text{Power in Watts}} \tag{1}$$

Since XLA compiler works in 'lazy' mode by default (i.e. it builds the whole graph, optimizes it and then executes it), we use XLA APIs to break the graph and force the compiler to execute 'greedily' for performance debug.

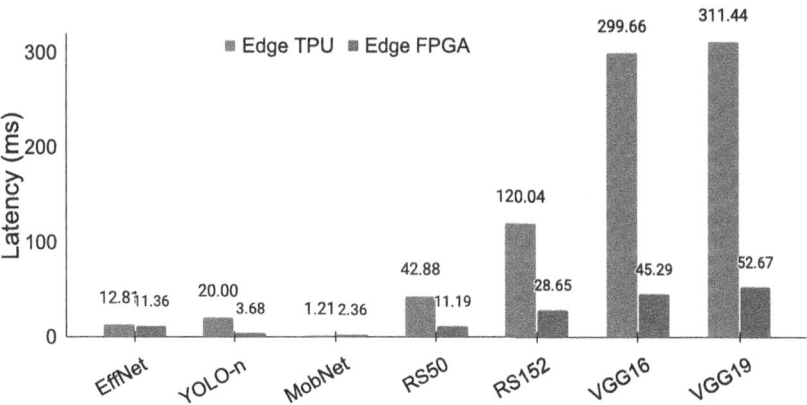

Fig. 3. Latency of edge devices for various DNNs

5   Results and Discussion

In this section, we present the performance of the various benchmarks in terms of latency, utilization, and throughput efficiency. We also present a roofline anal-ysis of these benchmarks. *Specifically, we compare the performance achieved on FPGA platforms using Vitis AI with the performance achieved on TPU* platforms, as a way to demonstrate the out-of-the-box performance of DNNs on FPGAs. The underlying assumption here is that similar efforts are spent on deploying the ML models on both the FPGA and the TPU. No extensive customizations are performed on the FPGA platforms, other than those easily achieved through the Vitis AI framework. Since this effort is difficult to quantify, we qualitatively compare our experiences deploying the DNNs on FPGAs and TPUs in the last subsection (Sect. 5.6). Note that our goal is not to compare the achievable performance of FPGAs with that of ASICs, which is done in prior work [13].

5.1 Edge Platforms: Latency and Utilization

Starting with the edge devices Kria KV260 and Edge TPU, the inference latency of benchmarks are shown in Fig. 3. The single-batch inference of **edge FPGA outperforms the edge TPU** by 5.2X on average. The largest gap is seen for VGG19. Note that we calculate utilization using peak performance of the FPGA not the DPU. From Fig. 4, we also see a trend that the Edge TPU is underutilized for most benchmarks. However, the Edge TPU seems to be optimized for MobileNet, the only benchmark where it beats Edge FPGA. Even though the peak throughput of the edge TPU is higher than that of the edge FPGA, the edge TPU being optimized for power and the lack of sufficient on-chip memory for larger models are the likely reasons for this unexpected result. Also, EfficientNet has extremely poor utilization on both the devices.

5.2 Cloud Platforms: Latency and Utilization

For the cloud devices TPUv3 and U55c, from the batch 3 inference metrics shown in Fig. 5, **the TPUv3 outperforms cloud FPGA** by an average of 1.37X. We observe that the gap is small for VGG166 and is the largest for MobileNetV1. Comparing their power consumption would have given a better

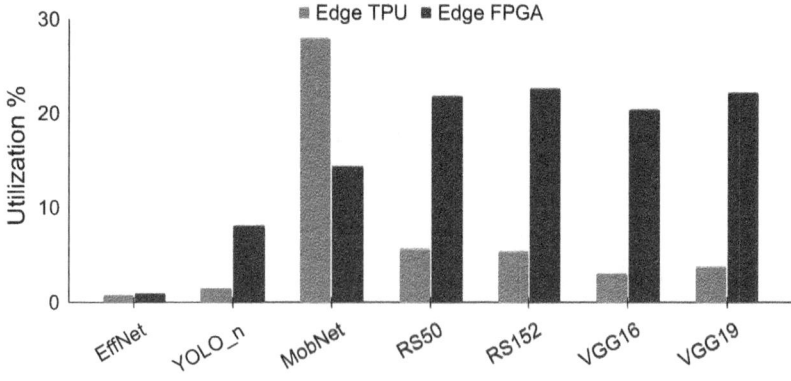

Fig. 4. Utilization of edge devices for various DNNs

insight. However, there is no means of measuring cloud TPU's power accurately. Regarding utilization (Fig. 6), for a batch size of 3, both the devices do not cross 35%. Based on Fig. 5, the DPU architecture appears to be more rigid than the TPU. We must note that this DPU supports only this batch size while the TPU supports several. When we run a Resnet50 inference with a higher batch size on the TPU, for example, a batch size of 512, the utilization of the TPU reaches 55%. An interesting point to note is that while the edge FPGA is worse in terms of latency on average (Fig. 3) compared to the cloud FPGA (Fig. 5), its performance for edge-optimized models like MobileNet and EfficientNet is very close to that of the cloud FPGA. **The cloud FPGA has much more room for optimizations.**

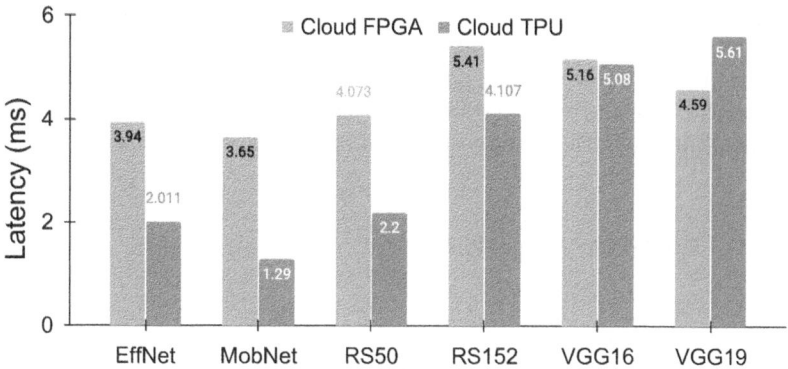

Fig. 5. Latency of cloud devices for various DNNs

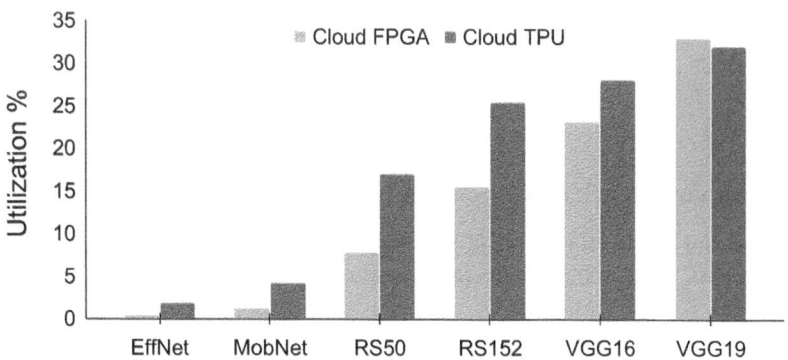

Fig. 6. Utilization of cloud devices for various DNNs

5.3   Energy Efficiency

Figure 7 shows the energy efficiency in terms of Inferences/Joule for the various benchmarks on both edge and cloud FPGAs. On average, the Edge FPGA is 4.19X more efficient for these benchmarks. But this is misleading. Although the edge FPGA provides excellent efficiency for MobileNet (17.3X) and EfficientNet(1.98x), it quickly falls off, performing much worse for more compute-intensive workloads in comparison to the cloud FPGA.

5.4   Roofline Analysis

The performance results are shown in a roofline plot in Fig. 8 for the cloud platforms. All the models except VGG16 are bandwidth-limited on the TPU. For the FPGA, EfficientNet and MobileNet are bandwidth limited, whereas others are compute bound. We see a trend that models that are optimized for edge (e.g., Efficient and MobileNet, as seen in Fig. 3) are the most memory bound in the cloud scenario. For the edge platforms, to plot the roofline chart, we could not find the peak bandwidth because of lack of documentation of these platforms.

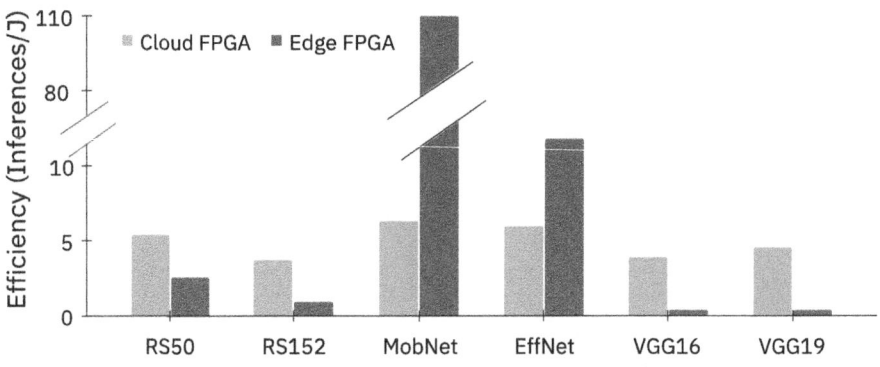

Fig. 7. Energy Efficiency for cloud and edge FPGAs

5.5   Comparison with Non Out-of-the-Box Performance

To understand how well the out-of-the-box solutions work, we compare their performance with that achieved by prior works which use hand-coded RTL-based accelerators, for the same DNNs. However, it is difficult to obtain the raw performance results for same DNNs, same FPGA devices, same precision, and same technology node from prior non-Vitis AI works. Hence, for fair comparison, we use the efficiency metric (GOPS/W) to compare our results with results from any FPGA device, for the same DNNs. For differences in technology node, we scale the results using [23] to a common value (16nm). The efficiency of non-Vitis AI works implemented using hand-coded accelerators is listed in Table 5.

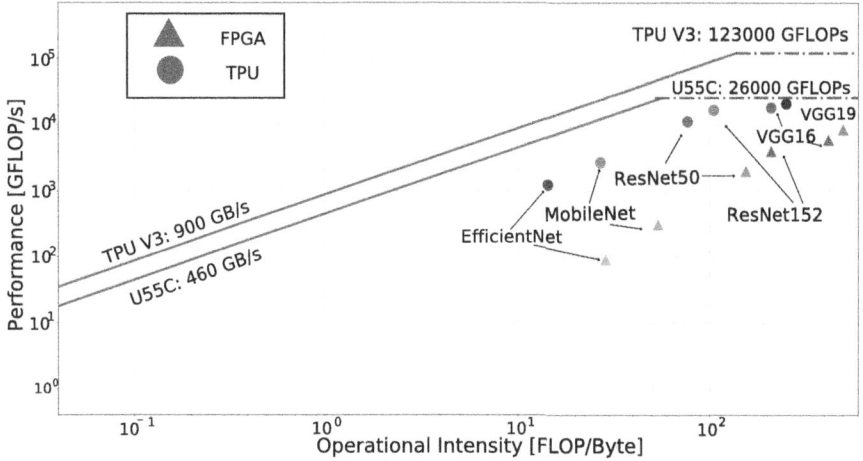

Fig. 8. Roofline plot for cloud TPU and cloud FPGA

In comparison to Vitis AI, these works achieve 2.65×, 3.52×, 1.89× higher efficiency compared to our edge platform and 1.6×, 6.4×, 16.85× compared to our cloud platform, for Vgg16, Resnet50 and MobileNetv1 respectively. We conclude that, at present, the **out-of-the-box solution provides inferior efficiency compared to hand-coded solutions.** Note that the precision of these works is larger than or equal to INT8 (the precision supported by Vitis AI). These prior works obtain a higher efficiency even with larger precision, implying that the efficiency will be even higher with a lower INT8 precision. Thus, our conclusion about the inferior efficiency of out-of-the-box solutions will not change. Since only INT8 precision is supported in Vitis AI, these results also highlight that hand-coded solutions offer higher flexibility.

Table 5. Comparison with non Vitis AI solutions

Work	Device	Model	Precision	GOPS/W
[16]	Virtex7 VX690T	VGG16	8-bit BFP	195
[20]	ZC706	Resnet50	8–16 bit	283.5
[15]	XCVU37P	MobileNetv1	8-bit	121.30

5.6 Experiences with Vitis AI

Throughout our experience with Vitis AI, we identified various strengths and challenges associated with the deployment of machine learning models utilizing this platform. Overall, Vitis AI is a great effort towards making FPGA acceleration available out-of-box. The experience was a mix. The flow shines in many places, but there is significant scope for improvement. Based on our experience, to develop an efficient ML accelerator on an FPGA using hand-coded Verilog, it would take 5–6 months of design and debug, assuming we heavily use existing IP blocks for common parts of the design. But with Vitis AI, this can be reduced to 3–4 weeks of time that includes setup, customization, deployment and debug. However, our experience was worse than this because of the issues we mention below in this section. On the other hand, for a TPU, it takes about 3–4 days to set up and run DNNs.

(1) Vitis AI repository contains a **large number of examples for different scenarios to help developers** to learn the flow quickly. However, the Vitis AI tool has a large number of capabilities and even with this large number of examples, developing some projects might be challenging. The Vitis AI model zoo consists of a diverse set of ready-to-deploy models. Several variants with various pruning ratios are present for the user to choose from, and new models are added with each release. However, **some models are available only to a particular DPU or device for a specific version of Vitis AI**.

(2) Vitis AI optimizer is a valuable tool for developers to optimize the performance of the deployed models. It provides several pruning features and techniques like Neural Architecture Search (NAS), Once-for-All (OFA), iterative and one-step pruning. The optimizer's paid license requirement has only been removed for version 3.5 at the time of this work. Also, **not all these features of the optimizer are supported by all the ML frameworks** (PyTorch, TensorFlow, etc.).

(3) Vitis Model Inspector is a handy tool that provides insights into compiled models. It provides information on which layers on CPU and which ones run on the DPU. It can present the compiled models visually similar to Netron. This can **help developers optimize and confirm DNN compatibility with a specific DPU**.

(4) Since Vitis AI runs on a docker container for cloud FPGAs, it can cause issues. We have tried running the Vitis AI flow on academic compute clusters and on Xilinx's Heterogeneous Accelerated Compute Cluster (HACC) that have Xilinx FPGAs. However, these **public clusters do not provide root access which makes it very hard or impossible to run Vitis AI flow**. The documentation also mentions that users can utilize the FPGAs in Azure or AWS. However, the documentation for this has not been updated.

(5) All the tools involved in Vitis AI flow have **strict version dependencies**. This, combined with the availability of several versions for Vitis AI and all its tools, along with documentation gaps with each release, makes it **quite confusing to set up the environment**. For example, each Vitis AI version only supports specific versions of XRT (Xilinx Run Time), DPU IP, shells (necessary infrastructure on the FPGA), OS, OS kernel, Vivado, and Vitis. It will be a great help to the developers if a dashboard could be developed, which documents models, supported FPGAs, versions of all supported tools, DPU capabilities, and download links.

(6) With each version of Vitis AI release, AMD seems to drop support for some devices. **Transformer-based models are only supported on devices with AI engines**. Recurrent Neural Networks (RNN) are not supported by Vitis AI flow but by a separate flow using the Vitis AI RNN compiler. Besides Vitis AI version 3.5, older versions **do not support precisions other than INT8**.

(7) Users can integrate custom logic along with the DPU, such as custom pre-processing blocks for specific image transformations (e.g., resizing or normal-ization) or custom post-processing blocks to handle the output of the DPU for additional operations like encoding. Even though Xilinx provides some param-eters to customize the edge DPU, **users need to rebuild the operating system with the required firmware. They cannot just load a new bit-stream and run their applications with that new DPU**. When the DPU configuration is customized, the underlying hardware design is changed. This modified hardware design requires corresponding firmware components, such as device tree files, kernel modules, and drivers, which describe the hardware con-figuration to the Linux operating system.

(8) The **cloud TPU environment is much easier to use than the FPGA overall**. Since cloud TPU is available in Google Cloud Platform (GCP), users can get started with just a few commands making it highly convenient. There is no hassle of setting up the card and environment as it is for the FPGA. Google TPUs in GCP come pre-configured, eliminating the time and technical expertise required to set up such environments. Porting your workloads to the TPU can be as easy as writing one line of code. Similar to Vitis AI's Profiler, the TPU profiler can help users identify bottlenecks and improve performance. The **Vitis AI DPU is not as flexible as the TPU**. For example, transformer-based models can be easily run on the TPU, and, in terms of batch size, the user can choose any arbitrary batch size. Though the TPUs support several data precisions, some versions, however, do not support INT8 precision.

6   Conclusion

In this paper, we evaluated the experience of out-of-the-box deployment of DNN workloads on FPGAs, using AMD/Xilinx Vitis AI suite. We focused on perfor-mance as well as ease-of-use, and compared them with TPUs. We believe that while such deployment can provide high performance, even surpassing TPUs with higher theoretical throughput in some cases, the experience leaves a lot to be desired in terms of ease-of-use. Particularly, we believe that the following efforts are essential for widespread usage of such platforms: (1) making the environment setup easier, (2) ensuring all the parts of the flow (models, tool versions, overlay versions, devices) are well supported and documented, (3) supporting state-of-the-art DNNs (such as transformer-based models) and (4) supporting all batch sizes and precisions for a wide range of devices.

References

1. Aarrestad, T., et al.: Fast convolutional neural networks on FPGAs with hls4ml. Mach. Learn. Sci. Tech. **2**(4), 045015 (2021). https://doi.org/10.1088/2632-2153/ac0ea1
2. Abdelfattah, M.S., et al.: DLA: compiler and FPGA overlay for neural network inference acceleration. In: 2018 28th International Conference on Field Programmable Logic and Applications (FPL), pp. 411–4117 (2018). https://doi.org/10.1109/FPL.2018.00077
3. Ahmad, J., Jervis, M., Venkata, R.: Intel® FPGAs and SOCs with intel® FPGA AI suite and OpenVino toolkit drive embedded/edge AI/machine learning applications
4. AMD: AMD Vitis AI (2020). https://www.amd.com/en/developer/resources/vitis-ai.html
5. Boutros, A., Nurvitadhi, E., Betz, V.: Specializing for efficiency: customizing AI inference processors on FPGAs. In: 2021 International Conference on Microelectronics (ICM), pp. 62–65. IEEE, New Cairo City, Egypt (2021). https://doi.org/10.1109/ICM52667.2021.9664938
6. Carini, D.: Comparing hls4ml and VITIS AI for CNN synthesis and evaluation on FPGA: a comprehensive study (2022)
7. Chung, E., et al.: Serving DNNs in real time at datacenter scale with project brainwave. IEEE Micro **38**(2), 8–20 (2018). https://doi.org/10.1109/MM.2018.022071131
8. Dhilleswararao, P., Boppu, S., Manikandan, M.S., Cenkeramaddi, L.R.: Efficient hardware architectures for accelerating deep neural networks: survey. IEEE Access **10**, 131788–131828 (2022). https://doi.org/10.1109/ACCESS.2022.3229767
9. Guan, Y., et al.: FP-DNN: an automated framework for mapping deep neural networks onto FPGAs with RTL-HLS hybrid templates. In: 2017 IEEE 25th Annual International Symposium on Field-Programmable Custom Computing Machines (FCCM), pp. 152–159. IEEE (2017)
10. Hall, M., Betz, V.: HPIPE: heterogeneous layer-pipelined and sparse-aware CNN inference for FPGAs. arXiv preprint arXiv:2007.10451 (2020)
11. Hamanaka, F., Odan, T., Kise, K., Van Chu, T.: An exploration of state-of-the-art automation frameworks for FPGA-based DNN acceleration. IEEE Access **11**, 5701–5713 (2023)
12. Jouppi, N.P., et al.: In-datacenter performance analysis of a tensor processing unit. In: Proceedings of the 44th Annual International Symposium on Computer Architecture, pp. 1–12 (2017)
13. Kuon, I., Rose, J.: Measuring the gap between FPGAs and ASICs. IEEE Trans. Comput. Aided Des. Integr. Circuits Syst. **26**(2), 203–215 (2007). https://doi.org/10.1109/TCAD.2006.884574
14. Lahti, S., Sjövall, P., Vanne, J., Hämäläinen, T.D.: Are we there yet? A study on the state of high-level synthesis. IEEE Trans. Comput. Aided Des. Integr. Circuits Syst. **38**(5), 898–911 (2019). https://doi.org/10.1109/TCAD.2018.2834439
15. Li, Z., et al.: A high-performance pixel-level fully pipelined hardware accelerator for neural networks. IEEE Trans. Neural Netw. Learn. Syst. 1–14 (2024). https://doi.org/10.1109/TNNLS.2024.3423664
16. Lian, X., Liu, Z., Song, Z., Dai, J., Zhou, W., Ji, X.: High-performance FPGA-based CNN accelerator with block-floating-point arithmetic. IEEE Trans. Very Large Scale Integr. (VLSI) Systems **27**(8), 1874–1885 (2019)

17. Machura, M., Danilowicz, M., Kryjak, T.: Embedded object detection with custom LittleNet, FINN and VITIS AI DCNN accelerators. J. Low Power Electron. Appl. **12**(2), 30 (2022)
18. Miller, R.: Meta Previews New Data Center Design for an AI-Powered Future. https://www.datacenterfrontier.com/data-center-design/article/33005296/meta-previews-new-data-center-design-for-an-ai-powered-future/. Accessed 12 Sept 2024
19. Nurvitadhi, E., et al.: Can FPGAs beat GPUs in accelerating next-generation deep neural networks? In: Proceedings of the 2017 ACM/SIGDA International Symposium on Field-Programmable Gate Arrays, pp. 5–14 (2017)
20. Ou, Y., Yu, W.H., Un, K.F., Chan, C.H., Zhu, Y.: A 119.64 GOPs/W FPGA-based resnet50 mixed-precision accelerator using the dynamic DSP packing. IEEE Trans. Circuits Syst. II: Express Briefs **71**(5), 2554–2558 (2024). https://doi.org/10.1109/TCSII.2024.3377356
21. Semiconductors, L.: Accelerating implementation of low power artificial intelligence at the edge. In: A Lattice Semiconductor White Paper (2018)
22. Sharma, H., et al.: DNNweaver: from high-level deep network models to FPGA acceleration. In: The Workshop on Cognitive Architectures (2016)
23. Stillmaker, A., Baas, B.: Scaling equations for the accurate prediction of CMOS device performance from 180nm to 7nm. Integration **58**, 74–81 (2017). https://doi.org/10.1016/j.vlsi.2017.02.002, https://www.sciencedirect.com/science/article/pii/S0167926017300755
24. Ushiroyama, A., Watanabe, M., Watanabe, N., Nagoya, A.: Convolutional neural network implementations using VITIS AI. In: 2022 IEEE 12th Annual Computing and Communication Workshop and Conference (CCWC), pp. 0365–0371 (2022). https://doi.org/10.1109/CCWC54503.2022.9720794
25. Wang, J., Gu, S.: FPGA implementation of object detection accelerator based on VITIS-AI. In: 2021 11th International Conference on Information Science and Technology (ICIST), pp. 571–577. IEEE (2021)

A Heterogeneous Embedded Platform for AI-Based Protocol Identification

Aymane Kharchouf[1,2]([✉])[iD], Smail Niar[2][iD], Virginie Deniau[3][iD], Rihab Hmida[1], and Christophe Gaquiere[1][iD]

[1] MC2-technologies, Villeneuve d'ascq, France
cgaquiere@mc2-technologies.com
[2] Laboratoire d'Automatique, de Mécanique et d'Informatique Industrielles et Humaines, UPHF, Valenciennes, France
{aymane.kharchouf,smail.niar}@uphf.fr
[3] Université Gustave Eiffel, Lille, France
virginie.deniau@univ-eiffel.fr
https://www.mc2-technologies.com/en/ , https://www.uphf.fr/lamih/ ,
https://www.univ-gustave-eiffel.fr/

Abstract. In today's increasingly digitalized world, wireless protocols enable seamless data transmission across devices, supporting applications in telecommunications, healthcare, transportation, and more. However, the rapid advancement of wireless technologies has introduced new challenges, particularly in areas such as network security, device interoperability, and network reliability. Therefore, it has become crucial to develop a system capable of detecting and monitoring wireless Radio-Frequency (RF) communications, providing operators with the necessary data to address these issues. This paper presents a novel embedded system architecture for robust multi-channel, multi-protocol RF detection, classification, and localization, leveraging heterogeneous platforms and deep learning (DL)-based object detection. The proposed system addresses the challenge of broadband spectrum detection while ensuring high efficiency in both throughput and energy consumption. The DL models are trained on a custom RF dataset featuring a wide range of wireless protocols, taking into account low Signal-to-Noise Ratios (SNR) and Rayleigh fading scenarios. Our results demonstrate broadband capability, achieving an instantaneous bandwidth of 983.6 MHz while maintaining a good trade-off between accuracy (92%) and throughput (55 Million Samples Per Second (Msps)). Finally, the system is compact and lightweight, making it ideal for deployment in a portable embedded device.

Keywords: Embedded systems · GPU · Hardware acceleration · RFSoC · Deep learning object detectors · Wireless protocols detection and classification · RF signal localization

R. Giorgi et al. (Eds.): ARC 2025, LNCS 15594, pp. 140–159, 2025.
https://doi.org/10.1007/978-3-031-87995-1_9

1   Introduction

The radio frequency (RF) spectrum ranges from 3 kHz to 300 GHz [7], encompassing a wide variety of wireless communication protocols. These include legacy communications technologies such as analog broadcasting and television, as well as the latest generations of mobile networks, IoT and satellite communications. The spectrum also supports short-range communication protocols like Bluetooth and extends to long-distance systems such as the Deep Space Network. In the context of wireless communication technologies being integrated into nearly every aspect of our lives, several challenges arise, including efficient spectrum utilization [20,35], communication among autonomous systems, and neutralizing cyber-attacks and other malicious RF communications [23,27]. Considering these challenges, designing an embedded system for protocol recognition can offer multiple benefits and provide significant improvements.

First, it can be used to improve spectrum efficiency and device interoperability by dynamically identifying unused frequency bands. These bands can then be allocated to other wireless devices without interfering with communications already in place. Moreover, in autonomous systems and IoT, embedded protocol detectors can enable real-time coordination and management of tasks and processes between different systems communicating with each other, eliminating the need for human intervention. To develop an efficient and capable embedded protocol identifier, several system requirements must be taken into account:

- **Detection:** It refers to the ability to accurately determine whether a captured RF signal contains the communication packet from a wireless protocol and to separate it from other interfering signals.
- **Classification:** It consists of accurately identifying the received RF signal or one of its characteristics, such as the protocol, modulation type, or transmitting physical device.
- **RF localization** [46]: This involves identifying the position of RF protocol frames on the time-frequency scale. This is a crucial step for many RF detection and classification use cases, from the design of cognitive radio devices to the implementation of intelligent jamming or anti-jamming techniques.
- **Spectrum coverage** [12]: Detecting and classifying protocols are often performed without prior knowledge of the transmitting frequency band, as transmitters do not always communicate this information to receivers. Consequently, protocol detectors must be evaluated based on their spectrum coverage, which is the ability to operate over an instantaneous frequency band wider than the one used during transmission.
- **System efficiency:** This is the performance of the system as a whole, apart from accuracy. It is evaluated using several metrics including *throughput*, *latency* and *energy efficiency*. Finally, it is important to take into account the system's *weight* and *compactness*, especially when used in embedded applications.

This paper presents **a novel end-to-end embedded system for combined protocol detection, classification, and RF localization, leveraging heterogeneous platforms and Deep-Learning object detectors.**

The proposed solution aims to improve spectrum coverage compared to state-of-the-art solutions, while providing an optimal balance between throughput and accuracy. Furthermore, the system delivers energy efficiency, compactness, and weight, ideal to be used as a portable embedded device.

The rest of the paper is organized as follows:

- Section 2 summarizes state-of-the-art in the domain of the wireless protocol detection and classification. It also shows the different categories of supporting hardware platforms. Our contributions compared to state-of-the-art are also listed in this section.
- Section 3 provides a top-level overview of the proposed embedded system solution as well as the suggested implementation plan.
- Section 4 details the methodology for designing and implementing the embedded heterogeneous platform. It describes the functional and structural architecture and presents the mapping between the functionalities and the different hardware and software components.
- Section 5 presents the algorithm based on DL object detection performing broadband detection, classification and localization.
- Section 6 evaluates the proposed solution in the specific use-case of detecting and classifying a subset of wireless communication protocols in penitentiary facilities, including Wi-Fi, Bluetooth, and LTE. and compare it to state-of-the art solutions.
- Finally, Sect. 7 concludes the paper with a summary and identifies avenues for future research.

2   State-of-the-Art and Contributions

In the field of protocol detection and classification, energy-based physical layer solution methods are proposed in [14,22] where detection and separating from environmental noise using an adaptive energy threshold. A more robust method based on goodness-of-fit statistical model is introduced in [8] achieving higher accuracy compared to adaptive threshold at very low Signal-to-Noise Ratio (SNR). While threshold-based methods are sufficient for signal detection, they do not allow signal classification. The latter can be addressed using machine learning-based methods such as Support Vector Machines (SVM) [13], XGBoost [51], Random Forest [16], or K-Nearest Neighbors (KNN) [15]. Moreover, Deep-Learning (DL) models, such as Convolutional Neural Networks (CNN) [9,24], Feed-forward Neural Networks (FNN) [16], LSTM [31,42], and GAN [38] have been shown to achieve significant improvements in detection accuracy compared to machine learning models, especially in low SNR environments.

Certain CNN-based methods enhance detection accuracy by incorporating a pre-processing phase. For instance, [41] computes the Power Spectral Density (PSD) of the RF signal while [1,2,17] uses spectrograms to combine time domain and frequency domaine features both achieving higher accuracy compared to raw time-series data. The studies in [8,26,52] perform both detection and classification using DL object detectors, addressing the issue of multi-target detection.

This solution enables combined detection and classification, while achieving high accuracy with low SNR.

Finally, several other studies address the challenges of broadband protocol detection [27,28,30,35] and RF localization [30,45,53]. However, the hardware and software platforms used in the aforementioned works are not necessarily optimized for these applications. First, they are constrained by limited spectrum coverage due to the use of commercial software-defined-radio (SDR) modules [34], which typically support restricted frequency bandwidths (Ettus USRP X310: 160 MHz) [27], Ettus USRP 2901: 56 MHz [30], ADALM-Pluto: 20 MHz [35], and AD9631 with a Xilinx Zynq [33]). The work in [27] provides significantly higher throughput and a 100 MHz spectrum coverage but uses a standard host computer, whose weight, size, and energy consumption are not suitable for embedded applications.

To address these limitations, **we introduce a novel, configurable multi-channel embedded system architecture for robust end-to-end protocol detection, classification, and localization**. The contributions of this paper are outlined as follows:

- **Broadband capabilities:** We incorporate a software-defined radio (SDR) front-end with a very wide instantaneous bandwidth, offering significantly better spectrum coverage than state-of-the-art solutions.
- **Robust detection, classification, and RF localization:** This is achieved by integrating DL object detection algorithm inspired from [8,27]. This approach was selected not only for its robustness toward noise but also for its ability to perform multiple target detection, classification and localization simultaneously and even in large bandwidth operations.
- **Improved system efficiency:** The system incorporates a heterogeneous platform that combines the parallel processing capabilities of both an RF FPGA System on Chip (SoC) platform and an embedded graphical processing unit (GPU). This architecture achieves high throughput with a good energy efficiency. Furthermore, the overall system is compact and lightweight, making it well-suited for portable embedded applications.
- Our system uses **two powerful deep learning models** to detect, classify, and localize the communication protocol. The first model is based on convolution neural network (CNN) while the second one is a Transformer model.

3 Overview of the Proposed Architecture

The top-level architecture of the embedded system is provided in Fig. 1. From a structural perspective, the proposed embedded solution is built on a heterogeneous platform that integrates two main units: the SDR front-end and the embedded accelerator. Each of these components is mapped onto a dedicated hardware processing system and performs specific tasks.

- **The SDR front-end:** This unit acquires analog RF signals from the RF front-end-i.e. the external component responsible for capturing the RF analog signals-converts them to in-phase/quadrature (IQ) representation [4], and

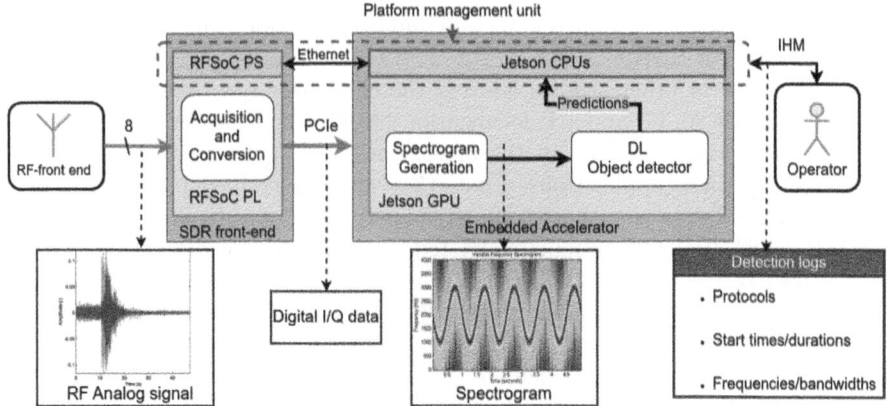

Fig. 1. Overview of the system's architecture

transfers them to the accelerator. This unit is implemented on a Xilinx FPGA UltraScale Radio Frequency System-on-Chip (RFSoC) [50], which features both a processing system (PS) and programmable logic (PL). The RFSoC includes 8 RF data converters, supports up to 4 GHz of instantaneous bandwidth, and integrates a Peripheral Component Interconnect Express (PCIe) controller for high-throughput transfer.

- **The embedded accelerator:** It is primarily used to efficiently execute the detection, classification, and RF localization algorithm. The latter consists of two sub-tasks: (1) pre-processing the transferred IQ data using Spectrogram-based [35] image generation and (2) performing inference with DL object detection models for detection, classification, and localization. Hardware accelerators [39] enhance the system's throughput and ensure real-time performance. For this study, we selected the Jetson ORIN AGX [5], a GPU-based embedded accelerator, for its versatility, ease of use, adaptability to state-of-the-art DL object detection models, and relatively high power efficiency compared to similar systems.

Furthermore, data transactions between these two units are carried out through a high-throughput PCIe interface and managed by a system management unit.

- **A high-throughput PCIe x8 link** between the RFSoC FPGA and the Jetson GPU, enabling low-latency and high-throughput direct memory access (DMA) between the two subsystems.
- **The system management unit** hosted on both the RFSoC PS and the Jetson CPUs. This unit monitors acquisitions, commands and data transfers between the SDR front-end and the accelerator while managing the User-Interface (UI)

More details on the mapping and implementation of these 4 units are given in Sects. 4 and 5.

4 System Architecture Description and Task Mapping

The following sections provide a detailed explanation of the tasks performed by the SDR front-end and the system management unit, as depicted in Fig. 1. Additionally, each task is mapped to a dedicated hardware or software module within the heterogeneous platform. Finally, a comprehensive description of the overall architecture is presented in Fig. 3.

4.1 SDR Front-End: Acquisition, Conversion and Data Transfer

The signal captured by the RF front-end undergoes conversion from analog to digital format. Next, after decomposing the target spectrum into several sub-bands, In-phase/Quadrature (IQ) demodulation is performed to extract the IQ representation of the captured signal for each sub-band. Finally, the converted IQ data is transferred to the Jetson's DRAM via the PCIe link for processing. Below, we provide a detailed description of each of these steps as well as the modules mapped to it.

- **Data conversion:** On each receiver's RF inputs, analog-to-digital conversion [21] is performed by sampling the analog RF signal captured by the RF front-end at a specified sample rate f_s. This function is performed using the Xilinx multi-channel data converter, which is hardwired into the RFSoC Programming logic. In order to prevent aliasing of information, the Shannon sampling theorem [29] represented by Eq. (1) must be respected during this operation.

$$|f|_{max} < \frac{f_s}{2}, \tag{1}$$

  where $|f|$ is the absolute value of a frequency capture by a given the channel, setting up a limit for the maximum frequency covered by each channel.

- **IQ demodulation:** In most modulation schemes used in wireless communications, IQ modulation is applied to the data. This involves encoding the information into two distinct signals, known as I (in-phase) and Q (quadrature), which represent the real and imaginary components respectively, before combining them into a single carrier signal for transmission. This operation is depicted by Eq. (2):

$$S(t) = I(t)cos(2\pi f_c t) - Q(t)sin(2\pi f_c t), \tag{2}$$

  where f_c is the carrier frequency of the modulated signal. we perform IQ demodulation to extract the I and Q components. Since we assume that the carrier frequency is unknown (as the transmitter does not necessarily provide this information), the spectrum is divided into several sub-bands, and multiple demodulation operations are applied in parallel using the central frequency of each sub-band, as illustrated in Fig. 2. This process creates a multi-channel IQ matrix representing the observed spectrum.

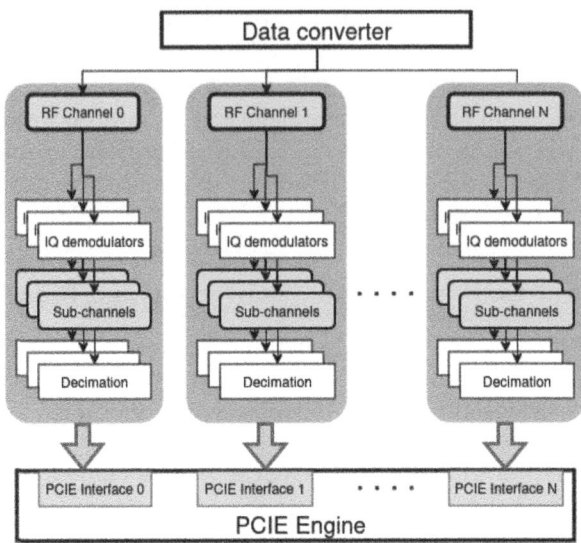

Fig. 2. Mapping of each set of IQ sub-channels to a different PCIe transfers

– *Decimation and transfer*: Before initiating transfer, down-sampling is performed using digital decimation filters [47] to align the higher sample rate of the SDR front-end with the transfer rate of the PCIe link. Each set of sub-channels is subsequently mapped to a single transfer channel, as illustrated in Fig. 2. Multiple PCIe transfers can be queued to enable efficient movement of IQ data from the RFSoC to the accelerator's DRAM. The Xilinx PCIe subsystem, shown in Fig. 3 uses Direct memory access (DMA) to perform the transfers, achieving rates of up to 1.7 Gsamples/s.

4.2   System Management Unit: Task Management

Several system management tasks are performed enabling rapid configuration and customization of the system:

– *Scheduling and configuring the acquisitions:* A Pulse Per Second (PPS) generator is implemented in the RFSoC PL to periodically provide pulses that trigger the start of each acquisition. The pulse generator is synchronized with the Global Positioning System (GPS) signal provided by an external U-blox GPS receiver module, as shown in Fig. 3. The primary function of the PPS generator is to provide a deterministic start time for each acquisition, which is crucial for accurately estimating the time coordinates of the detected protocol packets. The PPS pulse periodicity and duty cycle are adjusted through a PPS controller, while the center frequencies of the RF channels are configured dynamically via an RF data conversion (RFDC) controller before each acquisition. Both controllers are implemented on Cortex-0 of the RFSoC ARM53.

- *Monitoring the transfers:* The transfers between devices are managed by two distinct drivers: a Xilinx PCIe driver, which initiates and controls the DMA transfers between the PCIe subsystem and the Jetson's DRAM, and NVIDIA drivers, which monitor the operations between the GPU and the DRAM. Both drivers are implemented on the Jetson's Cortex-A78AE CPU cluster and share the same memory space. This unified memory scheme minimizes memory transfer overhead, saving both energy and time.
- *Managing the interfaces:* The management unit includes a user interface (UI) hosted on the Jetson, enabling the operator to view protocol identification logs and customize the system by providing commands and adjusting parameters for specific use cases. The system also incorporates an Ethernet link for inter-processor communication between the Jetson's Cortex-A78AE and Cortex-0 of the RFSoC's ARM53. This link serves as an interface for managing the controllers implemented in the RFSoC from the Jetson, thereby allowing control of the SDR front-end through the UI.

4.3   Summary of the System's Architecture

The presented software and the hardware architecture of the embedded platform are summarized in Fig. 3. All components of the SDR front-end are synchronized to a common reference clock supplied by a clock generator within the RFSoC programming logic fabric. The PL digital modules are designed using Verilog and Vivado 2022.2 [49], while PS modules such as the PPS and RFDC controllers are developed using the C\C++.

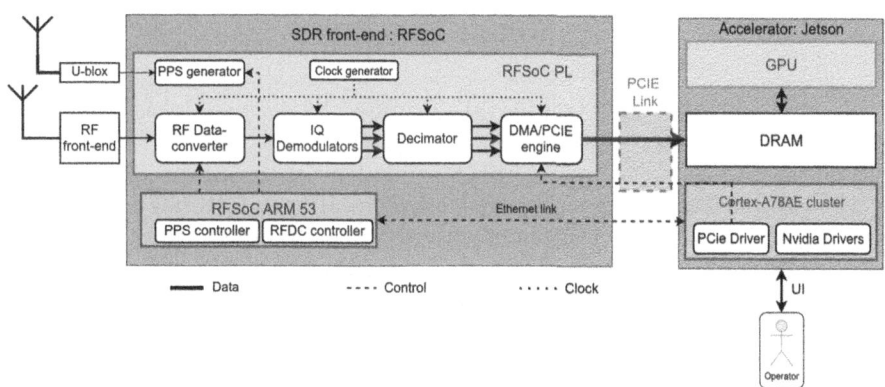

Fig. 3. Detailed block diagram of the heterogeneous embedded platform

The next section details the main task performed by the embedded accelerator, which is the inference of the DL algorithm.

5 Embedded Accelerator: Inference of the DL Recognition, and RF Localization Algorithm

As explained in Sect. 3, the embedded accelerator is primarily used to infer the DL-based detection, classification, and RF localization algorithms. The steps of this algorithm are outlined in pseudo-code 1 and enumerated as follows:

Algorithm 1. Proposed algorithm for detection, classification and localization of RF protocols

---

Input:
   $Ch = [i_1, i_2, \ldots, i_N]$: Indexes of the channels to aquire.
   K:Number of sub-channels per channel
   N_{sample}:The number of samples per sub-channel
Output:
   $Protocols$: List of predicted protocols for the detected packets
   $[f_c, t_0, b, d]$: List of frequency-time coordinates of the detected packets
   $conf$: List confidence level of each prediction.
for $i = 0$ to $N - 1$ **do**
   $CH[i] \leftarrow transfer(i, K * N_{sample})$
   for $j = 0$ to $K - 1$ **do**
      $S[i, j] \leftarrow preprocess(CH[i, j])$
   end for
   $[Protocol, conf, Boxes] \leftarrow predict(Model, S)$
   $[f_c, t_0, b, d] \leftarrow locate(Boxes)$
end for
Return $[Protocol, conf, f_c, t_0, b, d]$

- **Preprocess**: After each transfer, the captured IQ data are transformed into spectrogram images of (256×256) pixels, with one spectrogram image generated per sub-channel using the Short-Time Fourier Transform (STFT) [40]. This process is performed in parallel, using the Jetson's GPU for acceleration.
- **Predict**: The generated image batch is fed into DL object detection models to detect and predict the protocols present in the spectrogram. Several object detection models have been tested from Ultralytics' repository [44]. It includes both state-of-the-art convolution-based models series and transformer-based models. Due to their good performance trade-offs, we selected two models from this repository, namely YOLOv8 [32] and RT-DETR [54]. Simultaneous detection and classification are performed on each image in parallel using the Jetson's GPU. Additionally, bounding boxes are generated to delimit the classified frame, preparing for the *locate* step.
- **Locate:** From the coordinates of the bounding box of a given detected protocol packet P, both the central frequency f_c^P and communication's bandwidth b^P are calculated according to Eq. (3).

$$f_c^P = f_{ch} - B_{ch}/2 + \frac{B_{ch}(y_{max} + y_{min})}{2},$$
$$b^P = B_{ch}(y_{max} - y_{min}), \tag{3}$$

where (y_{min}, y_{max}) the bounding box coordinates with respect to the y-axis. f_{ch} and B_{ch} refers respectively to the central frequency and observed bandwidth of the processed sub-channel. Similarly, we extract both the initial time t_0^P and the duration of the communication packet using the formula in Eq. (4).

$$t_0^P = t_0 + x_{min}D_{acq},$$
$$d^P = (x_{max} - x_{min})D_{acq}, \tag{4}$$

where (x_{min}, x_{max}) bounding box with respect to the x-axis. t_0 and D_{acq} are respectively the starting time and the time span of the acquisition. t_0 is provided by the PPS module which deterministically schedules the start time of each acquisition by generating a triggering pulse at a period configured by the operator.

Figure 4 presents an example of the algorithm applied to Bluetooth and Wi-Fi communications. In Fig. 4a, multiple frames are detected simultaneously, and bounding boxes are generated around the frames within the image. The spectrogram is visualized on a time-frequency scale, and the bounding boxes are converted to time-frequency coordinates, as illustrated in Fig. 4b. The following section presents an example of an application of the system in penitentiary facilities.

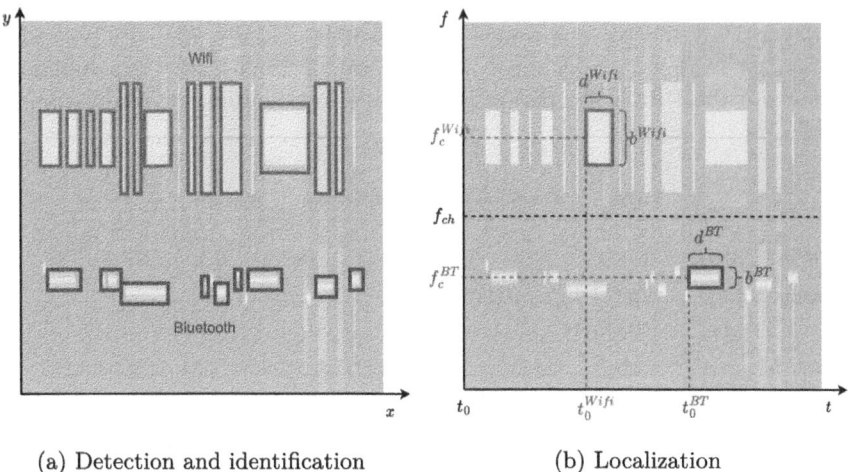

(a) Detection and identification   (b) Localization

Fig. 4. RF protocol identification and localization in a spectrogram

6   Case Study: Wireless Protocol Recognition in Penitentiary Facilities

We present a case study in which the proposed system is configured to monitor wireless communication traffic within prisons. For security purposes, identifying unauthorized devices like cell phones, drones, or other RF-emitting contraband entering prisons is important. This study focuses on the three most commonly used wireless communication protocols: Long-Term Evolution (LTE), Wireless Fidelity (Wi-Fi), and Bluetooth, and is conducted in compliance with French legislation on bandwidth allocation. This includes the 2.4 GHz and 5 GHz bands, along with their respective sub-bands for Wi-Fi [36], the 2.4 GHz ISM (Industrial, Scientific, and Medical) band for Bluetooth [10], and the 700/800 MHz bands for LTE [6], a frequency band typically used by french mobile network operators. We propose an experiment designed to evaluate our system in terms of both efficiency and accuracy. Additionally, we demonstrate the system's adaptability to the use case by comparing it with relevant works from the literature.

6.1   System Setup

Our system serves as a tool for prison staff to control and monitor wireless network traffic within the prison. Therefore, the system must be capable of detecting and processing all communication devices using the targeted wireless protocols within the frequency bands aformentioned. To achieve this, we activate 8 channels covering 122.88 MHz of bandwidth each. Additionally, we implement the configuration outlined in Table 1, which lists the central frequency of each channel. This configuration ensures minimal overlap of the channels in 5 GHz band, thereby eliminating blind spots. As a result, the selected configuration provides a total spectrum coverage of 983.5 MHz. Finally, each PCIe transfer acquires 2^{22} samples per channel, i.e., a total of 33,554,432 IQ samples per transfer and the PPS pulse period is set to 1 s, conducting one acquisition per second.

Table 1. Proposed RF channel configuration

Channels	1	2	3	4	5	6	7	8
RF bands	700 MHz 800 MHz	2.4 GHz	5 GHz					
Center frequencies (MHz)	750	2450	5089.56	5221.44	5408.56	5531.44	5653.32	5777.20

6.2   Dataset and Impairments

The MATLAB Wireless Toolbox [25] is used to generate synthetic dataset of Bluetooth, Wi-Fi, and LTE packets, as well as to introduce impairments. The dataset includes various configurations of LTE downlink and uplink, using both time and frequency division duplexing (TDD and FDD) [18], several Wi-Fi versions ranging from Wi-Fi 2 to Wi-Fi 6 [36], and both Basic Rate and Low Energy Bluetooth [10]. Building on the work in [11], we enhance the realism of dataset by emulating real-life impairments. These include adding white Gaussian noise to simulate multiple SNR levels ranging from $10\,\mathrm{dB}$ to $-7\,\mathrm{dB}$, introducing random time shifts, and applying Rayleigh fading [3]. Additionally, frequency-hopping spread spectrum (FHSS) is applied to Bluetooth signals, as it is one of their specifications. A summary of the generated protocol standards and the applied impairments is provided in Table 2. Furthermore, the spectrogram images of size (256×256) pixels are generated using the Short-Time Fourier Transform (STFT) with a Hann window [37], along with a segment size, FFT size, and overlap of 2048, 4096, and 1024. Finally, the dataset is split into a training set (20,390 images) and a validation set (5,593 images) for model evaluation, with each image containing multiple instances of the target protocols.

Table 2. Target RF Protocol Configuration

	LTE	Bluetooth	Wi-Fi
Standards	LTE Uplink	Base rate	IEEE802.11a/g/n (non-HT, HT)
	LTE Downlink	LE2M, LE1M	IEEE802.11ac (VHT)
	(FDD and TDD) [18]	LE500k, LE125k	IEEE802.11ax (VHT)
Impairments	White Gaussian noise, Rayleigh fading, frequency hopping, time shift		

6.3   Training Hyperparameters

We train both the selected RT-DETR and YOLOv8 Ultralytics models on the generated dataset with a learning rate of $lr = 0.0005$. Additionally, a batch size of 16 is chosen for the YOLO series and 8 for the RT-DETR series to address the memory intensiveness of DETR models. According to the findings in [19], the convolution-based models are optimized using the Adam optimizer, while the transformer-based models are optimized with AdamW, as this configuration has been shown to deliver the best performance for both architectures.

6.4   Accuracy Evaluation of the DL Models

On one hand, the combined detection and classification accuracy is measured and evaluated using the mean average precision (mAP) as defined in [12]. On the other hand, Intersection over Union (IoU), as defined in [45], is calculated between the predicted and the ground truth bounding boxes to assess the system's localization performance.

We present a comparative analysis of the model's accuracy across a range of SNR levels, averaged over two IoU intervals: 0.5 and [0.5 : 0.95]. This evaluation

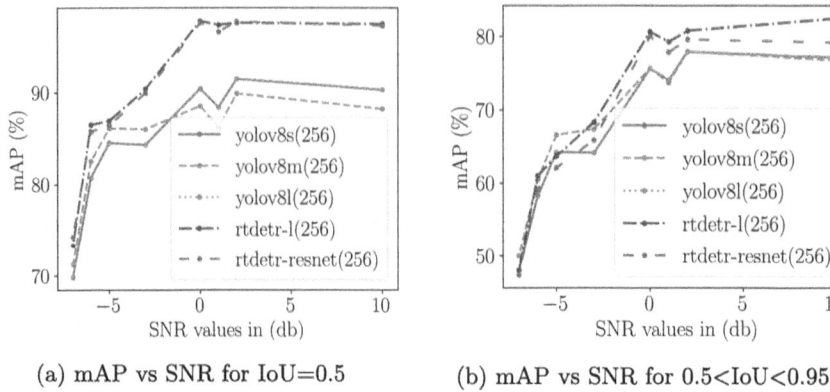

(a) mAP vs SNR for IoU=0.5   (b) mAP vs SNR for 0.5<IoU<0.95

Fig. 5. Mean average precision vs SNR

examines each solution's performance under varying SNR conditions. The RT-DETR model achieves over 95% accuracy at $SNR = 0$ with $IoU = 0.5$ (Fig. 5a), outperforming the YOLOv8 series. This result aligns with the findings in [12], as transformer-based models typically demonstrate superior accuracy compared to convolution-based object detectors.

Moreover, the proposed models are highly robust to noise and low-SNR environments, achieving an average accuracy of 85% at $SNR = -5$. Concerning localization, Fig. 5b illustrates a drop in accuracy when averaging the mAP over an IoU range of $[0.5:0.95]$. Nevertheless, RT-DETR and YOLOv8 achieve 80% and 75% accuracy, respectively, at $SNR = 0$.

Furthermore, the confusion matrix analysis, in Figures Fig. 6a and 6b, shows that RT-DETR-l outperforms YOLOv8l in terms of accuracy, particularly for low-range protocols like Wi-Fi and Bluetooth. For Bluetooth, the high accuracy

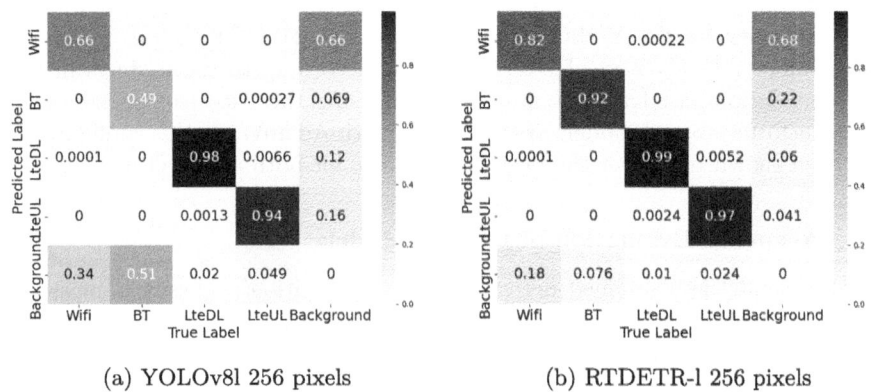

(a) YOLOv8l 256 pixels   (b) RTDETR-l 256 pixels

Fig. 6. Confusion matrix of YOLOv8l (large) and RT-DETR-l (large)

of RT-DETR can be attributed to the transformer's ability to leverage non-local features thanks to self-attention [19], such as frequency hopping, which is specific to Bluetooth and spans the entire spectrogram. Additionally, The high detection accuracy (over 94%) for LTE protocols is due to their distinct features, such as standard frame lengths in TDD and uninterrupted transmissions in FDD.

6.5 Accuracy vs Efficiency: Comparison with the State-of-the-Art

Through comparison with state-of-the-art solutions, we demonstrate that our system achieves a good trade-off between accuracy and efficiency. We selected [27] as an example of a high-throughput solution, [8] for high accuracy, and [35] for adaptability to embedded applications. We measure the throughput (T) of each solution along with ours by dividing the total number of processed samples N_{total} by the processing time $t_{processing}$ as in Eq. (5).

$$T = N_{total}/t_{processing} \qquad (5)$$

In addition, the spectrum coverage is reflected by the maximal instantaneous bandwidth support by each SDR module used in each study. Our results show that our system achieves the highest spectrum coverage of 983.6 MHz with the proposed configuration and the highest acquisition throughput leveraging a PCIe link capable of up to 1.7 Gsamples/s. While WRIST [27] shows the highest processing throughput among the selected works, it operates on a host computer equipped with an NVIDIA GeForce GTX 1080 GPU [43] yielding a power consumption of 250 W which is not suitable for embedded applications. In contrast, our system achieves the second and third highest processing speed of 58.5 Msps and 31.9 Msps respectively using YOLOv8s and RT-DETR on a Jetson platform, which is an embedded solution with less computing power. Moreover, our system demonstrates the second-highest accuracy at lower SNR (92% with RT-DETR-large) levels while delivering the best localization performance (72.2% for 0.5 < IoU < 0.95).

We measure overall the power consumption by adding up the energy consumption of its individual components. We show in Table 3 that the system's average power consumption varies depending on the inference model. Assuming continuous operation for 5 h, the required battery capacity for a 12V battery to power the system during this time is calculated. This requirement is met by several commercial embedded lithium batteries, such as LiFePO4 (12 Ah) and LiFePO4 (30 Ah) [48]. In terms of compactness, the overall system's dimensions: RFSoC + Jetson + LiFePO4 (12 Ah), are 100 mm × 150 mm × 94 mm, with a **total system weight less than 3 kg**. This compactness, energy, and weight profile further demonstrate the efficiency of the system and make it ideal for use as an autonomous, portable embedded device. In the context of the studied use case, it allows prison staff to transport and deploy it easily in various locations without relying on fixed power sources. Table 3 summarizes the performance comparison between the systems.

Table 3. Comparison with state-of-the-art solutions

Detector		YOLOv8s (Ours)	RT-DETR-l (Ours)	WRIST [27]	[8]	[35]
Accuracy (mAP)	SNR (dB)	[−7:10]		<5	< −15	-
	IoU = 50%	85.6%	92.1%	88.28%	97%	71.7%
	IoU > 50%	69.7%	72.2%	65%	-	61.3%
Spectrum Coverage (MHz)		983.6		100	100	20
Throughput (Msps)	Acquisition	1693		312.5	100	61.4
	Prediction	58.5	31.9	130.8	5.6	15.07
	Overall	58.5	31.9	130.8	5.6	15.07
Power Consumption (W)	Mean	25.75	26.5	250	-	-
	Std	0.02	0.01	-	-	-
Battery Capacity (Ah)		10.72	11.42	-	-	-
Embedded		✓	✓	✗	✗	✓

We conclude that our system achieves the optimal balance between accuracy and throughput, while providing the best spectrum coverage and being suited for embedded portable application.

7   Conclusion and Perspectives

This paper presents a novel heterogeneous embedded system architecture performing robust simultaneous detection, classification and localization of radio-frequency wireless protocols. Our solution is based on Deep-Learning object detectors executed by a programmable GPU which allows a rapid modification and adaptation to new protocols or specifications.

The system featured an 8-channel digital front-end, with the ability to expand up to 4 GHz per channel, along with an embedded Jetson GPU accelerator. We proposed a configuration that achieves a total bandwidth of 982 MHz, outperforming previous works in the literature in terms of spectrum coverage. Additionally, we evaluated the system under the same configuration on a Wi-Fi, Bluetooth, and LTE recognition in the context of wireless communication recognition in penitentiary facilities. We demonstrated that our solution provides the optimal balance between accuracy and throughput while being implemented on an embedded solution. Moreover, the system's compactness, energy efficiency, and lightweight design make it ideal for deployment as an autonomous, portable embedded device. The proposed system has potential applications across various fields, including cyber-security, autonomous vehicles, network optimization, and law enforcement.

Future work will focus on the utilization of multi-objective Hardware Aware Neural-Architectural Search (HW-NAS) for our use-case to obtain a higher-resolution spectrogram images while respecting the constrains of the system. A multi-objective approach provides multiple DL-models with different accuracy-latency-energy trade-offs. The models can be used dynamically to adapt the system to the different scenarios. In addition, the dataset will be expanded to include real-world data as well as other protocols such as DVB-S and 5G. Finally, the bandwidth will be increased to exploit the full capacity of the RFSoC and cover 4 GHz of bandwidth per channel.

References

1. Bin Sha'ameri, A.Z., Lynn, T.J.: Spectrogram time-frequency analysis and classification of digital modulation signals. In: 2007 IEEE International Conference on Telecommunications and Malaysia International Conference on Communications, pp. 113–118. IEEE, Penang, Malaysia (2007). https://doi.org/10.1109/ICTMICC.2007.4448616, http://ieeexplore.ieee.org/document/4448616/
2. Akter, R., Golam, M., Zainudin, A., Doan, V.S., Kim, D.S.: RF signal-based multipurpose UAV surveillance system using deep neural network. In: 2022 13th International Conference on Information and Communication Technology Convergence (ICTC), pp. 555–559. IEEE, Jeju Island, Republic of Korea (2022). https://doi.org/10.1109/ICTC55196.2022.9952604
3. Alan, B.: Rayleigh Fading - an overview | ScienceDirect Topics. https://www.sciencedirect.com/topics/computer-science/rayleigh-fading
4. allaboutcircuits: Understanding I/Q Signals and Quadrature Modulation | Radio Frequency Demodulation | Electronics Textbook. https://www.allaboutcircuits.com/textbook/radio-frequency-analysis-design/radio-frequency-demodulation/understanding-i-q-signals-and-quadrature-modulation/
5. Antonakakis, M., et al.: Real-time object detection using an ultra-high-resolution camera on embedded systems. In: 2022 IEEE International Conference on Imaging Systems and Techniques (IST), pp. 1–6 (Jun 2022). https://doi.org/10.1109/IST55454.2022.9827742, https://ieeexplore.ieee.org/document/9827742, ISSN 1558-2809
6. arcep: Le grand dossier 4G (2018). https://www.arcep.fr/la-regulation/grands-dossiers-reseaux-mobiles/la-4g.html
7. TeraSense Terahertz-technology/radio-frequency bands: Radio Frequency Bands | TeraSense, https://terasense.com/terahertz-technology/radio-frequency-bands/
8. Basak, S., Rajendran, S., Pollin, S., Scheers, B.: Combined RF-based drone detection and classification. IEEE Trans. Cogn. Commun. Network. **8**(1), 111–120 (2022). https://doi.org/10.1109/TCCN.2021.3099114
9. Berian, A., Aykin, I., Krunz, M., Bose, T.: Deep learning based identification of wireless protocols in the PHY layer. In: 2020 International Conference on Computing, Networking and Communications (ICNC), pp. 287–293 (2020). https://doi.org/10.1109/ICNC47757.2020.9049732, ISSN 2325-2626
10. Bluetooth: Bluetooth Technology Overview. https://www.bluetooth.com/learn-about-bluetooth/tech-overview/
11. Boegner, L., et al.: Large Scale Radio Frequency Signal Classification (2022). http://arxiv.org/abs/2207.09918, arXiv:2207.09918 [cs, eess]
12. Boegner, L., et al.: Large Scale Radio Frequency Wideband Signal Detection & Recognition (2022). https://doi.org/10.48550/arXiv.2211.10335, http://arxiv.org/abs/2211.10335, arXiv:2211.10335 [eess]

13. Chen, S., Xie, F., Chen, Y., Song, H., Wen, H.: Identification of wireless transceiver devices using radio frequency (RF) fingerprinting based on STFT analysis to enhance authentication security. In: 2017 IEEE 5th International Symposium on Electromagnetic Compatibility (EMC-Beijing), pp. 1–5 (2017). https://doi.org/10.1109/EMC-B.2017.8260381

14. Chiper, F.L., Martian, A., Vladeanu, C., Marghescu, I., Craciunescu, R., Fratu, O.: Drone detection and defense systems: survey and a software-defined radio-based solution. Sensors **22**(4), 1453 (2022). https://doi.org/10.3390/s22041453, https://www.mdpi.com/1424-8220/22/4/1453, Number: 4 Publisher: Multidisciplinary Digital Publishing Institute

15. Dubey, N., Sai Nithin, N.M., Tripathi, S.: Analysis and comparison of image-based UAV detection and identification. In: 2022 IEEE 9th Uttar Pradesh Section International Conference on Electrical, Electronics and Computer Engineering (UPCON), pp. 1–6 (2022). https://doi.org/10.1109/UPCON56432.2022.9986447, https://ieeexplore.ieee.org/document/9986447, ISSN 2687-7767

16. Fontaine, J., et al.: Towards low-complexity wireless technology classification across multiple environments. Ad Hoc Netw. **91**, 101881 (2019). https://doi.org/10.1016/j.adhoc.2019.101881, https://www.sciencedirect.com/science/article/pii/S1570870518309685

17. Glüge, S., Nyfeler, M., Ramagnano, N., Horn, C., Schüpbach, C.: Robust Drone Detection and Classification from Radio Frequency Signals Using Convolutional Neural Networks, pp. 496–504 (2024). https://www.scitepress.org/Link.aspx?doi=10.5220/0012176800003595

18. Signals research group: the_lte_standard_whitepaper_-_april_2014.pdf. https://www.qualcomm.com/content/dam/qcomm-martech/dm-assets/documents/the_lte_standard_whitepaper_-_april_2014.pdf

19. Guo, M.H., et al.: Attention mechanisms in computer vision: a survey. Comput. Vis. Media **8**(3), 331–368 (2022). https://doi.org/10.1007/s41095-022-0271-y, http://arxiv.org/abs/2111.07624, arXiv:2111.07624 [cs]

20. Guo, W., Yang, K., Stratigopoulos, H.G., Aboushady, H., Salama, K.N.: An end-to-end neuromorphic radio classification system with an efficient sigma-delta-based spike encoding scheme. IEEE Trans. Artif. Intell. **5**(4), 1869–1881 (2024). https://doi.org/10.1109/TAI.2023.3306334, https://ieeexplore.ieee.org/document/10224321, Conference Name: IEEE Transactions on Artificial Intelligence

21. Haraoubia, B.: 2 - Analog-to-digital and digital-to-analog converters. In: Haraoubia, B. (ed.) Non-linear Electron. **2**, 99–190. Elsevier (2019). https://doi.org/10.1016/B978-1-78548-301-1.50002-7, https://www.sciencedirect.com/science/article/pii/B9781785483011500027

22. Hassan, E.S.: Adaptive threshold to guarantee both detection and false alarm probabilities in multi-taper based spectrum sensing. J. Franklin Inst. **356**(3), 1640–1657 (2019). https://doi.org/10.1016/j.jfranklin.2018.10.028

23. Hong, S., Kim, K., Lee, S.H.: A hybrid jamming detection algorithm for wireless communications: simultaneous classification of known attacks and detection of unknown attacks. IEEE Commun. Lett. **27**(7), 1769–1773 (2023). https://doi.org/10.1109/LCOMM.2023.3275694, https://ieeexplore.ieee.org/document/10123966, Conference Name: IEEE Communications Letters

24. Huynh-The, T., Pham, Q.V., Nguyen, T.V., Costa, D.B.D., Kim, D.S.: RF-UAVNet: high-performance convolutional network for RF-based drone surveillance systems. IEEE Access **10**, 49696–49707 (2022). https://doi.org/10.1109/ACCESS.2022.3172787, https://ieeexplore.ieee.org/document/9768809, Conference Name: IEEE Access
25. Mathworks: WLAN Toolbox (2024). https://fr.mathworks.com/products/wlan.html
26. Nelega, R., Turcu, R.V.F., Belean, B., Puschita, E.: Radio frequency-based drone detection and classification using deep learning algorithms. In: 2023 International Conference on Software, Telecommunications and Computer Networks (SoftCOM), pp. 1–6 (2023)
27. Nguyen, H.N., Vomvas, M., Vo-Huu, T., Noubir, G.: Spectro-Temporal RF Identification using Deep Learning (2021). https://doi.org/10.48550/arXiv.2107.05114, http://arxiv.org/abs/2107.05114, arXiv:2107.05114 [cs]
28. Olesiński, A., Piotrowski, Z.: A radio frequency region-of-interest convolutional neural network for wideband spectrum sensing. Sensors **23**(14), 6480 (2023). https://doi.org/10.3390/s23146480, https://www.mdpi.com/1424-8220/23/14/6480, Number: 14 Publisher: Multidisciplinary Digital Publishing Institute
29. Picard, R.: Fourier analysis. In: Smelser, N.J., Baltes, P.B. (eds.) International Encyclopedia of the Social & Behavioral Sciences, pp. 5754–5760. Pergamon, Oxford (2001). https://doi.org/10.1016/B0-08-043076-7/00603-3, https://www.sciencedirect.com/science/article/pii/B0080430767006033
30. Prasad, K.N.R.S.V., D'souza, K.B., Bhargava, V.K.: A downscaled faster-RCNN framework for signal detection and time-frequency localization in wideband RF systems. IEEE Trans. Wirel. Commun. **19**(7), 4847–4862 (2020). https://doi.org/10.1109/TWC.2020.2987990, https://ieeexplore.ieee.org/document/9075413, Conference Name: IEEE Transactions on Wireless Communications
31. Rajendran, S., Meert, W., Giustiniano, D., Lenders, V., Pollin, S.: Deep learning models for wireless signal classification with distributed low-cost spectrum sensors. IEEE Trans. Cogn. Commun. Network. **4**(3), 433–445 (2018). https://doi.org/10.1109/TCCN.2018.2835460, https://ieeexplore.ieee.org/document/8357902, Conference Name: IEEE Transactions on Cognitive Communications and Networking
32. Reis, D., Kupec, J., Hong, J., Daoudi, A.: Real-time flying object detection with YOLOv8 (2023). https://doi.org/10.48550/arXiv.2305.09972, arXiv: 2305.09972 [cs] Number: arXiv:2305.09972
33. Restuccia, F., Melodia, T.: Big data goes small: real-time spectrum-driven embedded wireless networking through deep learning in the RF loop. In: IEEE INFOCOM 2019 - IEEE Conference on Computer Communications, pp. 2152–2160 (2019). https://doi.org/10.1109/INFOCOM.2019.8737459, https://ieeexplore.ieee.org/document/8737459, ISSN 2641-9874
34. Rischke, J., Salah, H.: Chapter 6 - Software-defined networks. In: Fitzek, F.H.P., Granelli, F., Seeling, P. (eds.) Computing in Communication Networks, pp. 107–118. Academic Press (2020). https://doi.org/10.1016/B978-0-12-820488-7.00018-9, https://www.sciencedirect.com/science/article/pii/B9780128204887000189
35. Rojas, A., Liñán-Cembrano, G., Dolecek, G.J., de la Rosa, J.: Deep learning-based architecture for RF frame detection for CR applications using spectrograms. In: 2024 IEEE 67th International Midwest Symposium on Circuits and Systems (MWSCAS), pp. 122–125 (Aug 2024). https://doi.org/10.1109/MWSCAS60917.2024.10658885, https://ieeexplore.ieee.org/document/10658885, ISSN 1558-3899

36. Ruth, C.: The Evolution of Wi-Fi Technology and Standards (2023). https://standards.ieee.org/beyond-standards/the-evolution-of-wi-fi-technology-and-standards/
37. Braun, S.: Hanning Window - an overview | ScienceDirect Topics. https://www-sciencedirect-com.ezproxy.uphf.fr/topics/engineering/hanning-window
38. Shrivastava, N., Hanif, M.A., Mittal, S., Sarangi, S.R., Shafique, M.: A survey of hardware architectures for generative adversarial networks. J. Syst. Archit. **118**, 102227 (2021). https://doi.org/10.1016/j.sysarc.2021.102227, https://www.sciencedirect.com/science/article/pii/S1383762121001582
39. Silvano, C., et al.: A Survey on Deep Learning Hardware Accelerators for Heterogeneous HPC Platforms (2023). arXiv: 2306.15552 [cs] Number: arXiv:2306.15552
40. Sturmel, N., Daudet, L.: Signal Reconstruction from STFT Magnitude: A State of the Art (2011)
41. Swinney, C.J., Woods, J.C.: RF detection and classification of unmanned aerial vehicles in environments with wireless interference. In: 2021 International Conference on Unmanned Aircraft Systems (ICUAS), pp. 1494–1498 (2021). https://doi.org/10.1109/ICUAS51884.2021.9476867, https://ieeexplore.ieee.org/document/9476867, ISSN 2575-7296
42. Tamizhelakkiya, Chandhar, P., Gauni, S.: Comparison of deep architectures for indoor RF signal classification. In: 2021 International Conference on Emerging Techniques in Computational Intelligence (ICETCI), pp. 107–112 (2021). https://doi.org/10.1109/ICETCI51973.2021.9574083, https://ieeexplore.ieee.org/document/9574083
43. techpowerup: NVIDIA GeForce GTX 1080 Ti Specs (2024). https://www.techpowerup.com/gpu-specs/geforce-gtx-1080-ti.c2877
44. Ultralytics: Ultralytics | Revolutionizing the World of Vision AI (2024). https://www.ultralytics.com/
45. Vagollari, A., Schram, V., Wicke, W., Hirschbeck, M., Gerstacker, W.: Joint detection and classification of RF signals using deep learning. In: 2021 IEEE 93rd Vehicular Technology Conference (VTC2021-Spring), pp. 1–7 (2021). https://doi.org/10.1109/VTC2021-Spring51267.2021.9449073, ISSN 2577-2465
46. Vartiainen, J., Lehtomäki, J., Saarnisaari, H., Juntti, M., Umebayashi, K.: Two-dimensional signal localization algorithm for spectrum sensing. IEICE Trans. **93-B**, 3129–3136 (2010). https://doi.org/10.1587/transcom.E93.B.3129
47. Wanhammar, L.: 1 - DSP integrated circuits. In: Wanhammar, L. (ed.) DSP integrated circuits, pp. 1–29. Academic Press Series in Engineering, Academic Press, Burlington (1999). https://doi.org/10.1016/B978-012734530-7/50001-5, https://www.sciencedirect.com/science/article/pii/B9780127345307500015
48. Eco Worthy: Batterie lithium LiFePO4 12V 30Ah | ECO-WORTHY. https://fr.eco-worthy.com/products/batterie-lithium-lifepo4-12v-30ah
49. Xilinx: AMD Vivado™ Design Suite. https://www.amd.com/en/products/software/adaptive-socs-and-fpgas/vivado.html
50. Xilinx, A.: Xilinx ZYNQ UltraScale+ RFSoC Development Board (2024). https://www.hitechglobal.com/Boards/Zynq_RFSoc.htm
51. Zhang, Y.: RF-based drone detection using machine learning. In: 2021 2nd International Conference on Computing and Data Science (CDS), pp. 425–428. IEEE, Stanford, CA, USA (2021). https://doi.org/10.1109/CDS52072.2021.00079, https://ieeexplore.ieee.org/document/9463220/
52. Zhao, R., Li, T., Li, Y., Ruan, Y., Zhang, R.: Anchor-free multi-UAV detection and classification using spectrogram. IEEE Internet Things J. **11**(3), 5259–5272 (2024). https://doi.org/10.1109/JIOT.2023.3306001

53. Zhao, R., Ruan, Y., Li, Y.: Cooperative time-frequency localization for wideband spectrum sensing with a lightweight detector. IEEE Commun. Lett. **27**(7), 1844–1848 (2023). https://doi.org/10.1109/LCOMM.2023.3280249, https://ieeexplore.ieee.org/document/10136798, Conference Name: IEEE Communications Letters
54. Zhao, Y., et al.: DETRs beat YOLOs on real-time object detection (2024). https://doi.org/10.48550/arXiv.2304.08069, http://arxiv.org/abs/2304.08069, arXiv:2304.08069 [cs]

Counting Heavy Items in Filtered Data Streams Using an HLS-Generated FPGA Kernel

Ali Ebrahim[(✉)] [iD]

University of Bahrain, Sakhir Campus, Zallaq, Bahrain
ahasan@uob.edu.bh

Abstract. This paper presents a novel circuit architecture for counting frequently occurring items (aka Heavy Items) in filtered data streams. The circuit is designed as a kernel in a multi-kernel system that can be synthesized with High-Level Synthesis (HLS) tools for Field Programmable Gate Arrays (FPGAs). The proposed kernel serves as an interface between a frequency estimation sketch configured as a data stream filter and a host processor that monitors the items in the filtered data stream. While recent work has focused on demonstrating high-throughput implementations of generic standalone frequency estimation sketches using FPGAs, the proposed work addresses the need for efficient interfacing between these sketches and a host processor. In particular, this paper demonstrates how the frequency of thousands of heavy items can be monitored entirely on-chip using an FPGA optimized key-value store circuit architecture. Implementing this architecture using the FPGA Support Package for the Intel OneAPI compiler showed good scalability and high throughput that easily matches or surpasses the throughputs of existing state-of-the-art FPGA implementations of frequency estimation sketches.

Keywords: Data Stream · Heavy Hitters · High-Level Synthesis · FPGA

1 Introduction

Extracting high-frequency items from large datasets is a fundamental operation in many applications. For example, these high-frequency items, commonly referred to as Heavy Hitters, can represent heavy flows in network traffic, bestselling products in e-commerce data, and trending stocks in financial data. Given the massive size of data in such applications, the data is usually modeled as a "stream" that must be processed very quickly in a single pass before permanent deletion [1]. There are many approximate algorithms targeting the heavy hitter detection problem in data streams [2].

Sketching techniques have gained popularity in recent years (examples in [3–6]). Sketching is based on summarizing the data stream using a probabilistic data structure called the "sketch". Some sketches are invertible, which means that heavy item keys are stored in the sketch structure and can be recovered along with estimates of the item frequencies by traversing the sketch [3–5]. Hardware accelerators based on such sketches did not gain popularity due to the complex process required to insert items in the structure, preventing meaningful gains in throughput. However, hardware implementations that are based on simple sketches such as the Count-Min sketch in [6] have shown great throughput gains compared to software (see Sect. 2). The Count-Min sketch has a very simple item update/query operation. This allowed for simple yet effective hardware solutions to resolve memory dependencies when updating the sketch. Such implantations have benefited from the flexibility of Field Programmable Gate Arrays (FPGAs). With the on-chip memory capacities available in modern mid-density and high-density FPGAs, practical sketch sizes can be implemented entirely on-chip. Embedded memory blocks can be easily configured with different geometries to alter the properties of the sketch. In addition, optimized concurrent memory accesses can be realized with the proper banking of the dual-port RAM blocks.

The Count-Min sketch does not inherently store item keys. To be used for heavy item detection in data streams, it must be paired with another data structure such as a hash map. This approach is known as data stream filtering, where the sketch functions as a filter, allowing only heavy items with counts exceeding a certain threshold to pass through to the hash map [7]. Generally, hardware implementations of generic key-value store data structures are slow, and do not meet the throughput requirements of a filtered data stream generated from a very fast hardware sketch.

This paper presents a circuit architecture specifically tailored to be paired with a sketch filter. The circuit is intended to monitor as much as possible of the high frequency items on-chip at high speed, leaving the less frequent items for a slower, but larger, software data structure. Using a multi-kernel High Level Synthesis (HLS) design flow, the circuit acts as an interface between a sketch filter and the host processor that implements the slower data structure in main memory. This paper details the design of this interface using the FPGA support package for Intel OneAPI DPC++/C++ compiler [8]. Full hardware compilations using a midrange Arria 10 GX 1150 FPGA as a target device, showed that monitoring 1000 to 3000 items with key sizes ranging from 32-bit to 128-bit requires 13% to 39% of the available logic resources and 1% to 3% of the embedded memory resource. This resource utilization distribution pairs very well with prior implementations of frequency estimation sketches that rely mainly on embedded memory resources. In addition, the achieved throughputs can easily match or surpass the throughput of the fastest available reconfigurable sketches. The remainder of this paper is organized as follows: Sect. 2 briefly introduces the Count-Min sketch as a data stream filter and summarizes existing FPGA implementations. Section 3 details the proposed architecture along with the HLS optimizations used in the design. Sections 4 and 5 evaluate the implementation results and finally, Sect. 6 draws conclusions and highlights future research plans.

2 Background and Related Work

2.1 The Count-Min Sketch

Heavy item detection involves processing skewed data containing millions of items, however, most of these items are insignificant or infrequent, and only a small subset of the items is of interest. Such data is typically aggregated from multiple sources and arrives at a very high speed. To be processed efficiently, filtering techniques can be used to filter out the insignificant items before counting the heavy items.

A sketch is a data structure that can be used to estimate how many times a given item key is inserted into the data structure. The Count-Min sketch is a popular sketch used for heavy hitter detection [6]. The sketch consists of multiple tables of equal sizes (see Fig. 1). Each table has a distinct hash function to map item keys to its entries, which represent integer count values. When an item key is inserted, the key is hashed using the different hash functions and the relevant table entries are incremented.

To query the frequency of a given item, the Count-Min outputs the minimum out of the count values in the relevant table entries. This count value is an overestimate of the actual count, and it is located in the table entry with the least number of collisions. Frequency estimation sketches, such as Count-Min, can be configured as a data stream filter to filter out infrequent items in a data stream [7]. By specifying a threshold value to the filter, any item hit with estimated count smaller than the threshold is blocked. The result is a filtered stream with a significantly smaller number of items that can be handled with key-value storage (see Fig. 1).

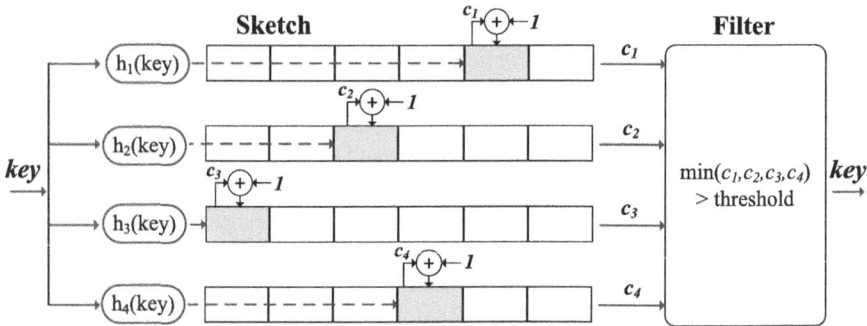

Fig. 1. The Count-Min sketch configured as a data stream filter

2.2 FPGA Implementations of the Count-Min Sketch

Sketches are probabilistic data structures usually requiring small memory to achieve good approximate results. The on-chip memory capacities available in modern mid-density and high-density FPGAs are ideal for implementing practical high-speed sketches. In fact, several FPGA implementations of the Count-Min sketch have recently emerged. Table 1 presents selected implementations of Count-Min. These implementations have primarily focused on architectural optimizations of a generic Count-Min sketch that does not specifically target heavy item detection in data streams. However, they can be easily modified to function as a sketch filter similar to the one in Fig. 1.

We can see from Table 1 that the sketches achieve very high throughputs. Sketches used for heavy hitter detection typically process skewed data streams, meaning that a significant portion of the stream comes from frequent items. A filtered data stream generated from such sketches would still have a high throughput and cannot be efficiently managed by a secondary data structure implemented in software. The filtered data stream would require a secondary hardware data structure implemented on-chip alongside the sketch.

Another observation from Table 1 shows that the overall FPGA resource utilization of hardware sketches is dominated by embedded RAM, reaching up to 90% in some implementations. Logic resources are significantly underutilized. Consequently, any secondary on-chip data structure to be paired with the sketches in Table 1 should primarily utilize the logic resources of the FPGA.

Table 1. Selected FPGA implementations of the Count-Min sketch

Sketch	FPGA	Throughput (M Item/s)	Resource Utilization (%)	
			RAM	Logic
[9]	Virtex UltraScale	325–479	1–93	1–4
[10]	Kintex-7	300	1–15	1
[11]	Virtex UltraScale +	300	25–87	2–8
[12]	Arria 10	255–312	80	5–18

3 Item Counting in Filtered Data Streams

3.1 Architecture Overview

As described in Sect. 2, a secondary data structure is needed to count the occurrences of items in a filtered data stream. It is not practical to assume that a host processor can perform item counting at the rate of the filtered data stream. Additionally, we cannot assume that it is always possible to store and count all the item keys appearing in the filtered data stream entirely on-chip using a hardware data structure. A sketch should be paired with a hardware data structure that aims to significantly reduce the filtered data stream rate by counting as much as possible the heavy items on-chip and leaving the less frequent items to be handled by the host.

The main building blocks of a proposed solution are shown in Fig. 2. The solution is designed as an HLS FPGA kernel in a multi-kernel system. The remainder of this paper may use technical terminology specific to the HLS flow in Intel OneAPI compiler [8].

The kernel is to be paired with a generic Count-Min sketch similar to the sketches in Table 1 (not implemented in this paper). The kernel consists of three sub-kernels: the sketch interface, Content Addressable Memory (CAM), and key-value store sub-kernels. A host processor invokes the sub-kernels separately through a slave interface, which is also used for passing arguments through memory mapped registers. The sub-kernels are interconnected through the "Pipe" interface specification, which supports both blocking and non-blocking read/write operations. In Fig. 2, arrows between sub-kernels represent pipes with the default capacity of zero.

The kernel returns results after processing N item hits, where each hit is a Count-Min sketch output representing the key and the estimated count of the current item in the stream.

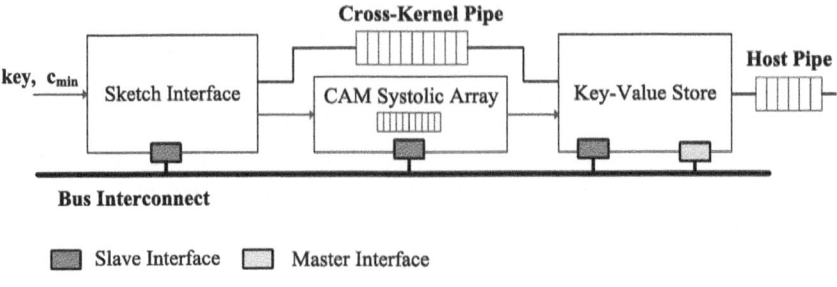

Fig. 2. HLS multi-kernel system

3.2 Sketch Interface

The sketch interface sub-kernel is invoked for $N+1$ iterations. Figure 3 shows a simplified view of the main loop pipeline in the sketch interface. N is generally large, representing an entire dataset, or the size of an observation window in a data stream. For the first N iterations, item objects packed as key-count integer pairs are read from the sketch through a pipe. A threshold value is passed to this sub-kernel to filter out keys with smaller counts. Any key with a count larger than the threshold belongs to a heavy item that needs to be monitored.

To expand the number of item keys that can be monitored using the logic resources in the FPGA, a smaller fingerprint is generated to serve as an item identifier in the CAM sub-kernel (FP in Fig. 3). Fingerprinting is particularly important if the keys are large. The sketch interface sub-kernel writes to two pipes, one to pass the item fingerprints to the CAM sub-kernel, and the other to pass the item keys to the key-value store sub-kernel. Since infrequent items are blocked in this sub-kernel, the size of the filtered data stream is unknown at run-time. In the last loop iteration, an "end" flag is asserted and passed to the other sub-kernels to indicate the end of the filtered data stream.

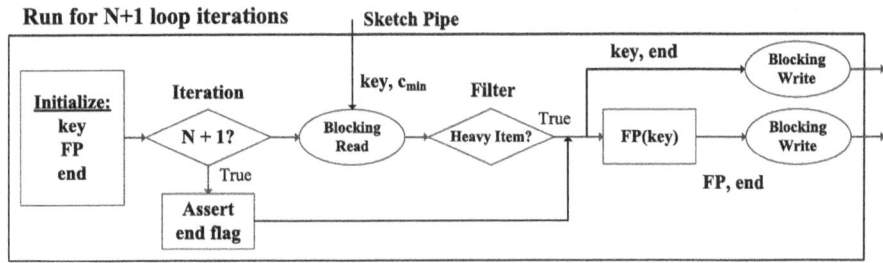

Fig. 3. Main loop pipeline in the sketch interface

There are no specific requirements for the fingerprint hash function other than the ability to be implemented as an HLS loop with an Initiation Interval (II) of 1 (II is the number of clock cycles between the launch of successive loop iterations). We opted for the simple, non-cryptographic FNV-1 hash function [13], which generates a 32-bit hash from an arbitrary key. This hash function performs multiplication and XOR operations on key bytes. An HLS implementation is shown in Fig. 4. Unrolling the hash function loop results in a pipeline with an II of 1 (one key per loop iteration). The latency of the pipeline and the number of 8-bit multipliers depends on the key size. After a key is hashed, an XOR fold operation is performed to extract the smaller fingerprint.

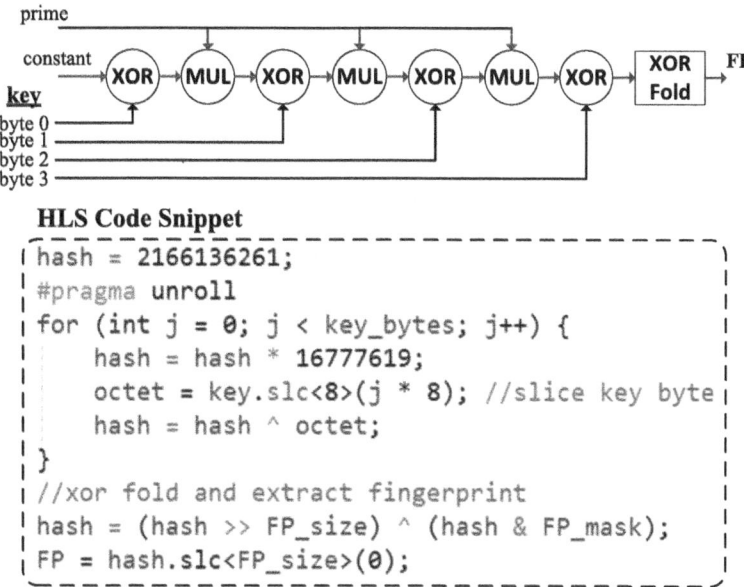

HLS Code Snippet

```
hash = 2166136261;
#pragma unroll
for (int j = 0; j < key_bytes; j++) {
    hash = hash * 16777619;
    octet = key.slc<8>(j * 8); //slice key byte
    hash = hash ^ octet;
}
//xor fold and extract fingerprint
hash = (hash >> FP_size) ^ (hash & FP_mask);
FP = hash.slc<FP_size>(0);
```

Fig. 4. HLS implementation of the FNV-1 hash function (32-bit keys)

3.3 Content Addressable Memory (CAM)

This sub-kernel reads item fingerprints from the sketch interface and assigns a unique address to each distinct fingerprint. The assigned addresses are used later by the key-value store sub-kernel to update the key counts. A simplified pipeline view of the main loop is shown in Fig. 5. A loop iteration starts with a non-blocking read from the input pipe. The non-blocking read operation asserts a "valid" flag indicating a valid fingerprint. When the pipe is empty, invalid null fingerprints are still allowed to propagate through the pipeline, as this is necessary to flush the pipeline and calculate the exit condition of the loop. The exit condition is determined by a flag asserted when the last fingerprint has reached the end of the pipeline.

The main part in the pipeline is a systolic array CAM implemented using the FPGA logic resources. The systolic array is basically an array with associated logic that performs the following: store a new fingerprint in the first empty location in the array, compare any incoming fingerprint to the stored fingerprint and, in case of a match, append the array index where the fingerprint is matched. In addition to calculating the address of a given fingerprint, the CAM also asserts two flags that are imported for correct operation in later stages. The first flag is the "update" flag, which indicates that a match of the relevant fingerprint has been found in the array. The second flag is the "insert" flag, which indicates that a new fingerprint has been inserted in the array. These flags along with the calculated addresses are passed to the key-value store sub-kernel through pipe.

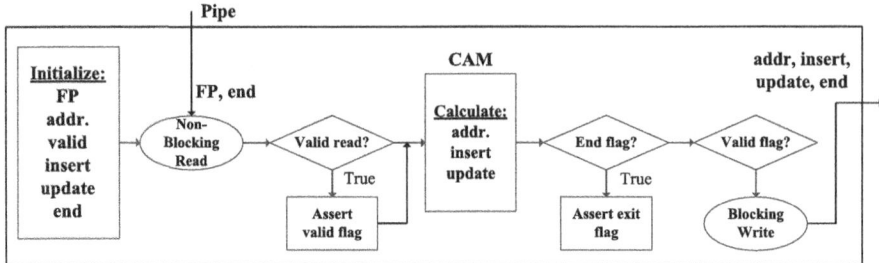

Fig. 5. Main loop pipeline for the CAM

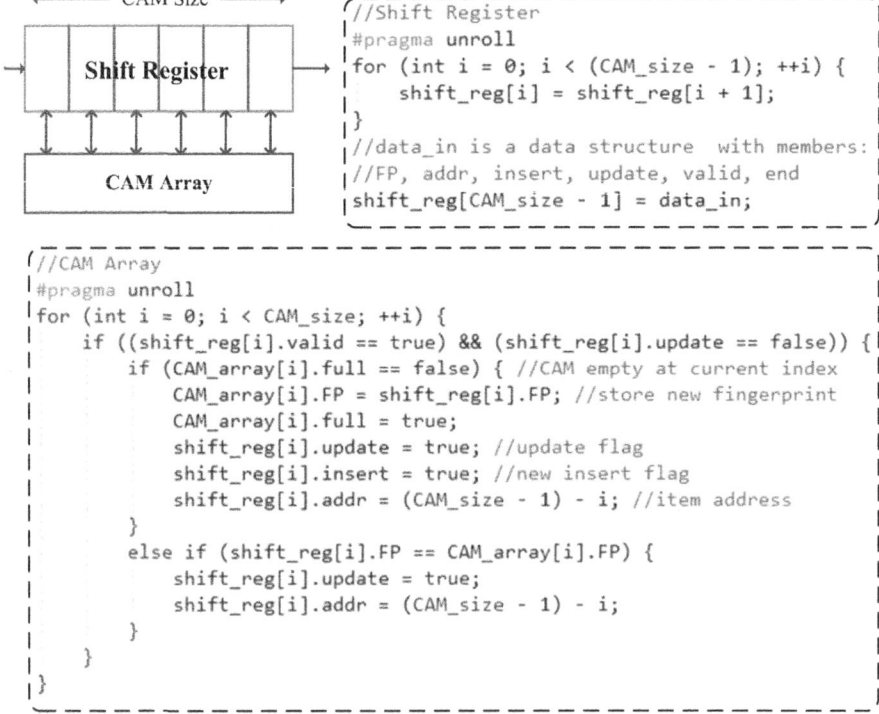

```
//Shift Register
#pragma unroll
for (int i = 0; i < (CAM_size - 1); ++i) {
    shift_reg[i] = shift_reg[i + 1];
}
//data_in is a data structure with members:
//FP, addr, insert, update, valid, end
shift_reg[CAM_size - 1] = data_in;
```

```
//CAM Array
#pragma unroll
for (int i = 0; i < CAM_size; ++i) {
    if ((shift_reg[i].valid == true) && (shift_reg[i].update == false)) {
        if (CAM_array[i].full == false) { //CAM empty at current index
            CAM_array[i].FP = shift_reg[i].FP; //store new fingerprint
            CAM_array[i].full = true;
            shift_reg[i].update = true; //update flag
            shift_reg[i].insert = true; //new insert flag
            shift_reg[i].addr = (CAM_size - 1) - i; //item address
        }
        else if (shift_reg[i].FP == CAM_array[i].FP) {
            shift_reg[i].update = true;
            shift_reg[i].addr = (CAM_size - 1) - i;
        }
    }
}
```

Fig. 6. HLS implementation of the systolic array CAM

Implementing the CAM with HLS is accomplished with two loops (see Fig. 6). The first loop implements a shift register, whereas the second loop implements the fingerprint array, and the logic needed to calculate the addresses. These two loops are implemented using the logic resources of the FPGA. The larger the CAM size, the larger the logic resource utilization.

Several item-counting systolic array architectures have been proposed previously (examples in [14, 15]). These arrays operate directly on keys. In addition, a counter for each item key is implemented as part of the array's Processing Elements (PEs). This has limited the total number of items that can be monitored with these arrays, despite being designed and optimized at the Register Transfer Level (RTL).

A unique feature of the proposed systolic array architecture is that it operates on fingerprints rather than keys. By using a fixed fingerprint size, scaling the array becomes independent of the key size. Moreover, by not implementing the item counters as part of the systolic array logic, the scalability is further enhanced compared to previous work. These architectural optimizations should offset any overhead incurred from opting for an HLS design flow.

Another important architectural optimization is the technique used for calculating the exit condition in the main CAM loop. An alternative simple solution would be to run the loop for N loop iterations, and perform a blocking read from the sketch interface pipe at the beginning of each loop iteration. This requires the sketch interface sub-kernel to write N words to the pipe, consisting of heavy item fingerprints and null words accounting for the filtered-out items. By having null words in the pipeline (also known as pipeline bubbles), the cross-kernel pipe capacity should match the latency of the CAM to guarantee stall-free operation. This is not the case in the proposed system, as the infrequent keys are not replaced with bubbles, but rather completely blocked at the sketch interface using a conditional output pipe write. This means that the cross-kernel pipe capacity does not need to match the full latency of the CAM sub-kernel to sustain a high throughput. This is particularly important when the keys are large as the pipe can account for a significant portion of the total resource utilization. The cross-kernel pipe capacity should be selected according to the CAM systolic array size, as well as the expected item filtering rate achieved by the sketch filter. For example, if a 50% filtering rate is expected, a pipe capacity equals to half the CAM latency is sufficient to sustain an average throughput of one item per clock cycle.

It is noted that collisions between item fingerprints are possible in the CAM. This issue is rectified as the number of heavy hitter items that pass the filter is a small subset of the total number of distinct items in the data stream. This reduces collision probability. However, it is important to account for collisions, or at least be able to detect collisions in the CAM. Later sections of the paper explain how the proposed system deals with collisions.

3.4 Key-Value Store

The purpose of this sub-kernel is to count heavy item keys. Results are stored in the embedded memory of the FPGA as key-count pairs. The embedded memory is configured as simple dual-port RAM (one load port and one store port). This allows for concurrent load/store operations. The number of memory locations allocated for the key-count pairs must be equal to the CAM size.

The pipeline of this sub-kernel consists of two main loops (see Fig. 7). The first loop is the item counter loop. This loop is responsible for updating the heavy item counts in memory. A loop iteration starts with non-blocking read from the CAM pipe to read addresses and flags generated from the CAM. A valid read will trigger another blocking read from the cross-kernel pipe to append the item keys to the associated addresses. Further ahead in the pipeline, a counter circuit updates the relevant memory locations in the embedded memory as follows:

1) If a key arrives with the "insert" flag asserted, the key is stored in the relevant address and the associated count is initialized.
2) If a valid key arrives with the "update" flag asserted, this key is compared to the key stored in the relevant address, if the two keys match, a "success" flag is asserted, and the associated count is updated.
3) Valid item keys that fail to update a memory location in the embedded memory are propagated to the next stage of the pipeline, where they are passed to the host processor through a host pipe. These keys are then processed by the host in software. Keys that are processed by the host are either keys that failed to register in the CAM due to array overflow, or keys that generated the same hashes to preceding item keys in the CAM (item collision).

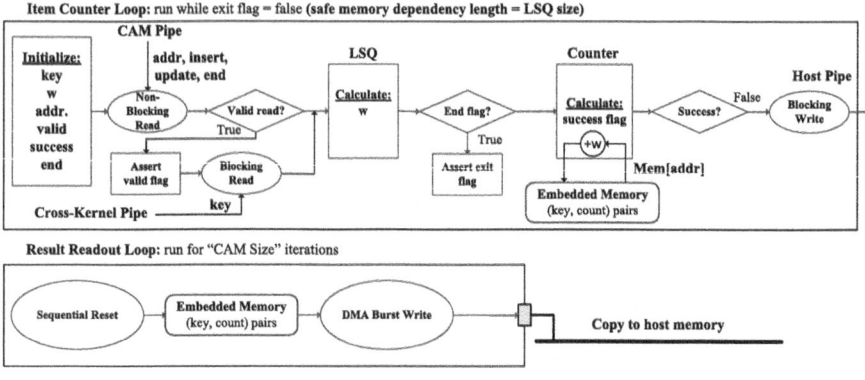

Fig. 7. The two main loops in the key-value store sub-kernels

When compiling the HLS code of the aforementioned item counter, the compiler will fail to achieve an II of 1 in the item counter loop. This is due to memory dependencies associated with the embedded memory update process. The compiler will insert stalling logic to account for the RAM latency and the read-after-write hazard caused by possible consecutive load/store operations to the same address. The compiler will basically raise the II to a value larger than the latency of the RAM resource used in the embedded memory block (a minimum of 1 clock cycle). This means that without countermeasures, an II of 2 is the best achievable II for the loop pipeline. One might argue that an II of 2 is acceptable in this sub-kernel as it operates on a filtered data stream that can be substantially smaller than the original unfiltered stream. If the sketch filter blocks at least 50% of the data stream, the overall average throughput of the multi-kernel system will be close to one item per clock cycle. While this is true for some input data distributions, the overall performance can still be affected in different ways by this bottleneck. When assuming a filtering rate of 50% and forcing the compiler to schedule the pipeline with an II of 2, the maximum clock frequency (fmax) of the sub-kernel can be significantly affected. The compiler will not be able to optimize the pipeline by performing register replication between load and store operations. The load and store operations will be scheduled one clock cycle apart in the pipeline. This bottleneck can significantly limit fmax, especially if the embedded memory block is large, consisting of many RAM primitives that are physically distanced apart in the FPGA chip. In multi-kernel HLS systems, it is desirable to avoid working with multiple clock domains. We aim for all sub-kernels to achieve high fmax close to the fmax achieved by the FPGA implementations of a sketch data structure (see Table 1).

HLS tools usually support high-level pragmas to instruct the compiler to ignore memory dependencies in loops to be able to achieve an II of 1. These pragmas can be used to completely ignore memory dependencies, or to specify a safe dependence distance, where a read-after-write hazard is guaranteed not to happen. In addition to achieving an II of 1, the compiler will be able to schedule load and store operations further apart in the pipeline to achieve a higher fmax. Obviously, using such pragmas without implementing the proper solution to resolve memory dependencies can result in functional failure. There are several solutions that have been previously proposed for breaking memory dependency when counting heavy items [9, 11, 12, 16]. In this work, we opt for a custom Load Store Queue (LSQ) that can be easily implemented with HLS (see Fig. 8).

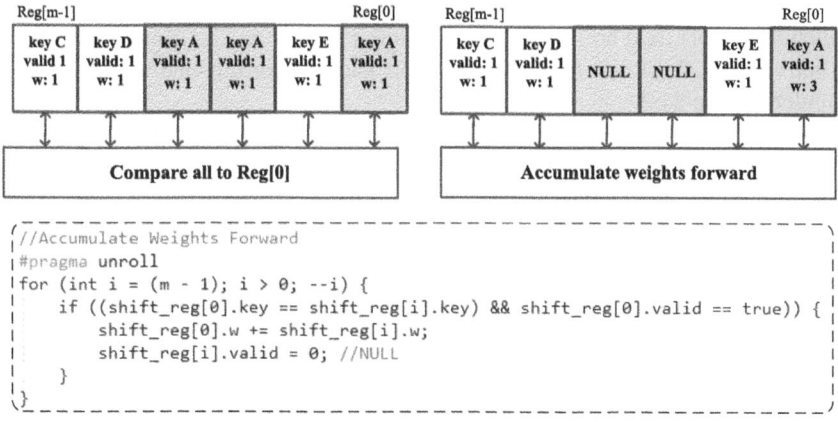

Fig. 8. Resolving memory dependency with a Load Store Queue (LSQ)

Implementing the LSQ in HSL is straightforward. The LSQ consists of two loops. The first is a shift register of size m (omitted in Fig. 8), and the second implements what we refer to as the "item weight accumulator". Items are inserted into the register with index $m - 1$ before eventually exiting the shift register through the register with index 0. When inserting items into the shift register, a weight variable is appended to the item. The weight is initialized with the value 1. The accumulator logic basically compares the item key in the first register to all proceeding keys in the shift register. If any of the proceeding keys are the same, the total weight is accumulated in the first register, and the redundant keys are replaced with a null (invalid key). By ignoring invalid keys and only updating the embedded memory block with the valid key weights, we effectively break memory dependency for m clock cycles.

Similar to the main loop in the CAM sub-kernel, the exit condition of the item counter loop is calculated when the "end" flag is detected at the end of the pipeline, which basically indicates that a total of N items in the data stream has been processed by the kernel. Following the exit of the first loop in Fig. 7, the "result readout loop" is triggered. This loop performs two operations. It basically copies the content of the embedded memory block to a buffer located in the host memory through a master interface (this can be easily implemented in different ways using SYCL specification in Intel OneAPI [8]). At the same time, the loop sequentially resets the memory locations in the embedded memory block through the write port of the memory. The reset operation is necessary to allow for consecutive invocations of the kernel without re-loading the entire kernel's bitstream into the FPGA.

4 Implementation Results

This section presents the FPGA implementation results of the proposed kernel. In particular we evaluate the maximum throughput and the FPGA resources utilization. We select the midrange Altera/Intel Arria 10 GX 1150 FPGA as a target device. This is the largest chip from the Arria 10 family with 427200 Adaptive Logic Modules (ALMs), 1518 Digital Signal Processing (DSP) blocks and 2713 M20K embedded RAM blocks. The development tools used are Intel Quartus Prime Pro version 23.4, Intel OneAPI base tool kit version 25.0.1 and the FPGA Support Package for the OneAPI DCP++/C++ Compiler version 24.2.

There are many parameters that can be varied in the kernel's configuration. We fix the following parameters to simplify the evaluation: 20-bit hash values, 32-bit count values, 5-bit item weight values, and finally we fix the LSQ size to 32 (safe memory dependence distance).

Three parameters are varied when evaluating the kernel: the key size is varied from 32 to 128 bits. The CAM size is varied from 1000 to 3000 (the CAM size reflects the maximum number of heavy items that can be monitored on-chip). As the latency of the CAM is unknown at compile time, the depth of the cross-kernel pipe is tentatively fixed to 20% of the CAM size. Table 2 shows the implementation results for different configurations of the kernel using the default settings of the HLS compiler. All results in Table 2 are post-fit results. We ran a single compilation for each configuration. All compilations achieved an II of 1. The compiler became extensively slow in configurations with CAM size of 3000, therefore, no larger CAM sizes were considered.

From Table 2 we can see that the average fmax is high and can be considered optimal for the selected device family. In addition, fmax does not seem to drop when increasing the CAM and key sizes. In fact, the reported fmax of some of the larger arrays seems to be slightly higher than some of the smaller arrays. This is attributed to natural margins in the synthesis tool.

Another important observation is that the CAM latency reported by the compiler is almost half of the CAM systolic array size. This is actually an advantage of the implicit

Table 2. FPGA implementation results (Arria 10 GX 1150)

CAM Size	CAM Latency (clock cycles)	Key (bits)	F_{max} (MHz)	Resource Utilization	
				ALM	M20K
1000	507	32	375	55,799 (13%)	13 (1%)
		64	346	57,182 (13%)	13 (1%)
		128	364	61,267 (14%)	24 (1%)
2000	1007	32	394	109,454 (26%)	18 (1%)
		64	345	110,812 (26%)	23 (1%)
		128	348	114,844 (27%)	40 (1%)
3000	1506	32	380	160,283 (38%)	34 (1%)
		64	343	161,223 (38%)	49 (2%)
		128	360	165,475 (39%)	79 (3%)

HLS systolic array design technique [17]. By using unrolled loops rather than explicit replication of a PE function to form the systolic array (see Fig. 6), we allow the compiler to optimize the array for the best results. In our case, the compiler seems to perform two fingerprint comparisons per PE.

The resource utilization breakdown in Table 2 shows that the kernel mainly utilizes the ALM resources of the FPGA. No DSP resources were used as the compiler used ALMs to implement the 8-bit multipliers in the hash function. Up to 3000 items with 128-bit keys can be monitored on-chip using 39% of the ALM resources and only 3% of the M20K memory resources. The results obtained show that the proposed kernel pairs very well with the Count-Min FPGA implementations (Table 1), that mainly utilize the embedded RAM resources of the FPGA.

The idea of using fingerprints rather than directly operating on item keys can be further exploited to monitor keys consisting of larger data structures. For example, heavy hitter detection is particularly of interest in network flow monitoring applications. In such applications, analytics are performed on data structures containing several network flow attributes. Typically, a 5-tuple data structure is used to characterize a network flow [18]. A 5-tuple encapsulates the attributes: source IP address, source port, destination IP address, destination port and transport protocol. Using IPv6 (128-bit IP addresses), a 5-tuple is 296 bits in size. This is significantly larger than the keys considered in Table 2. Table 3 shows the results from two compilations of the kernel when the key size is set to 296-bit. The sizes used for the CAM are 500 and 1000 respectively. The capacity of the cross-kernel pipe is set to 50% of the CAM size, which matches the latency of the CAM sub-kernel. This ensures stall-free operation regardless of the data stream filtering rate. We compare our HLS kernel to a previously proposed RTL systolic array architecture that serves a similar purpose [14]. We replicate the work in [14] to create an RTL systolic array that monitors up to 1000 296-bit keys using the same Arria 10 FPGA chip. We can see form Table 3 that the throughput of the HLS kernel is very close to the RTL systolic array. However, the chip utilization is significantly smaller in the HLS kernel.

In fact, the logic needed to implement the proposed HLS kernel is three times less than the RTL systolic array when both are configured to monitor 1000 heavy items. This is a significant improvement in logic utilization at the expense of only 2% memory overhead.

Table 3. FPGA implementation results (Arria 10 GX 1150, 5-tuple network flow keys)

Design	Array Size	Throughput (M items/s)	Resource Utilization	
			ALM	M20K
RTL [14]	500	322	108,164 (25%)	-
	1000	309	216,543 (51%)	-
HLS (proposed)	500	297	48,307 (11%)	29 (1%)
	1000	284	74,639 (17%)	46 (2%)

5   Further Discussion

As discussed earlier, alongside a sketch filter, the proposed kernel can be used to extract heavy items from a dataset of size N in a single pass or monitor the heavy items in an unbounded data stream by dividing the stream into consecutive observation windows of size N. We can set the sketch filter threshold value to limit the number of filtered item keys to the range allowed by the CAM. When the threshold is set to a value equal to or larger than $N/CAMSize$, the number of filtered keys will most likely fit within the kernel without causing the CAM to overflow. This is because, in any stream of size N, there will be at most x items with count equal to or larger than N/x. Of course, there is a small possibility of more items passing the sketch filter because of the sketch count overestimation error.

It is reasonable, and sometimes desirable, to set the threshold value to much smaller threshold values to deliberately saturate the CAM and make sure that the kernel is monitoring as much as possible of the items on-chip. In fact, the kernel is designed to overflow allowing the host to count the excess items using a slower software data structure. Assuming there are no fingerprint collisions in the CAM, most heavy items will be registered in the kernel, limiting the rate of items reaching the host pipe.

Section 4 demonstrated how using smaller fingerprints generated by a hash function can significantly reduce the resource utilization of the proposed kernel, especially for larger key sizes (see Table 3). In the experiments in Sect. 4, 20-bit fingerprints were used. While this provides a reasonable hash space, the possibility of collisions must still be evaluated. In particular, we need to make sure that the rate of items reaching the host pipe can be handled by the host, even in the case of collisions. The worst case will be when the highest frequency items collide with each other. To evaluate the effect of such collisions on the host pipe data rate, we set up a testbed for a kernel with a CAM size of 1000. We paired the kernel with a Count-Min sketch filter consisting of 4 tables each containing 2^{17} counters. This is in line with the FPGA implementations in Table 1. We simulated the kernel with synthetic data following a Zipf distribution [19], varying the skew parameter α from 1 to 1.5. The sketch filter threshold was set to $N/1000$. In each simulation run, we examine the valid keys that exit the LSQ in Fig. 7. In Fig. 9, we report the rate at which the most frequent items update the embedded memory block. This rate would be equivalent to the data rate at the host pipe in case of imaginary collisions causing these items to fail getting registered in the kernel.

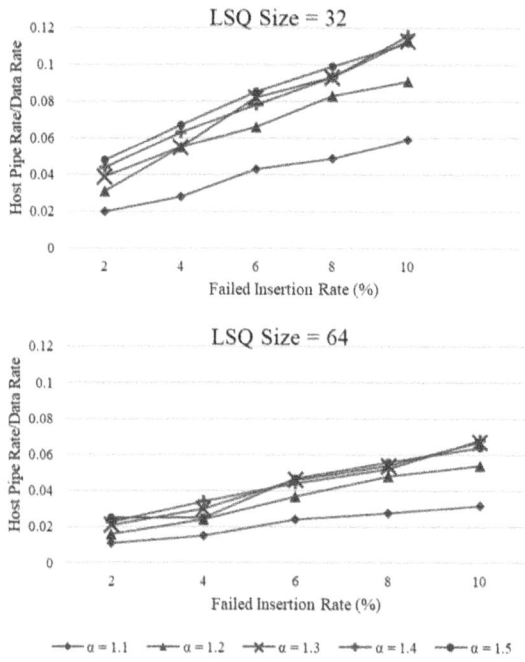

Fig. 9. The host pipe rate as a function of item collision rate (worst case)

It is noted that the LSQ size will affect the host pipe rate since using larger LSQs allows for more bubbles to be inserted in the pipeline. In the case of an LSQ size of 32, when the top 2% of the total number of filtered items fails to register in the kernel, the average data rate at the host pipe is only 4% of the data stream rate. This data rate is even halved when an LSQ of size 64 is used.

The numbers in Fig. 9 are worst case projections that are far from the expected collision rate in real applications. Nevertheless, a minor tweak to the hardware hash function can also be applied as an extra layer of protection against item collisions. Rather than hardcoding the hash seed value into the kernel, the hash seed can be passed to the sketch interface sub-kernel as a memory mapped argument by the host. This way, the hash seed can be changed in later invocations of the kernel if the host detects a high collision rate in the current observation window.

6 Conclusions and Future Work

This paper introduced a novel circuit architecture for counting frequently occurring items (Heavy Items) in filtered data streams. The circuit is designed as a kernel within an HLS multi-kernel system that acts as a host processor accelerator. The kernel operates on the output of a hardware sketch data stream filter. Using the proposed kernel, thousands of frequent items can be monitored on-chip. Implementation results showed that the proposed kernel can be paired with the fastest existing FPGA frequency estimation sketches without affecting the throughput. Furthermore, the kernel is much more scalable compared to existing systolic array item counters, allowing for large item keys to be monitored efficiently. To achieve better scalability compared to existing solutions, several design optimizations have been deployed such as item fingerprinting and item weigh accumulation using a Load Store Queue (LSQ). In addition to more extensive testing, detailed analysis and fine tuning, future work will focus on integrating the proposed kernel into a complete hardware system.

References

1. Muthukrishnan, S.: Data streams: algorithms and applications. Found. Trends® Theor. Comput. Sci. **1**, 117–236 (2005)
2. Cormode, G., Hadjieleftheriou, M.: Methods for finding frequent items in data streams. VLDB J. **19**, 3–20 (2010)
3. Huang, J., et al.: ChainSketch: an efficient and accurate sketch for heavy flow detection. IEEE/ACM Trans. Network. **31**, 738–753 (2022)
4. Yang, T., et al.: HeavyKeeper: an accurate algorithm for finding Top-$ k $ elephant flows. IEEE/ACM Trans. Network. **27**, 1845–1858 (2019)
5. Tang, L., Huang, Q., Lee, P.P.: Mv-sketch: a fast and compact invertible sketch for heavy flow detection in network data streams. In: IEEE INFOCOM 2019-IEEE Conference on Computer Communications, pp. 2026–2034. IEEE (2019)
6. Cormode, G., Muthukrishnan, S.: An improved data stream summary: the count-min sketch and its applications. J. Algorithms **55**, 58–75 (2005)
7. Estan, C., Varghese, G.: New directions in traffic measurement and accounting. In: Proceedings of the 2002 Conference on Applications, Technologies, Architectures, and Protocols for Computer Communications, pp. 323–336 (2002)
8. Intel® oneAPI DPC++/C++ Compiler Handbook for FPGAs. https://www.intel.com/content/www/us/en/docs/oneapi-fpga-add-on/developer-guide/2025-0/fpga-handbook.html
9. Tong, D., Prasanna, V.K.: Sketch acceleration on FPGA and its applications in network anomaly detection. IEEE Trans. Parallel Distrib. Syst. **29**, 929–942 (2017)
10. Saavedra, A., Hernández, C., Figueroa, M.: Heavy-hitter detection using a hardware sketch with the countmin-cu algorithm. In: 2018 21st Euromicro Conference on Digital System Design (DSD), pp. 38–45. IEEE (2018)
11. Chiosa, M., Preußer, T.B., Alonso, G.: SKT: a one-pass multi-sketch data analytics accelerator. Proc. VLDB Endow. **14**, 2369–2382 (2021)
12. Ebrahim, A.: High-level design optimizations for implementing data stream sketch frequency estimators on FPGAs. Electronics **11**, 2399 (2022)
13. Fowler, G., Noll, L.C., Vo, K.-P., Eastlake, D., Hansen, T.: The FNV non-cryptographic hash algorithm. In: IETF-draft: Fremont, CA, USA (2011)

14. Ebrahim, A., Khalifat, J.: Fast approximation of the top-k items in data streams using FPGAs. IET Comput. Digit. Tech. **17**, 60–73 (2023)

15. Sun, Y., et al.: Accelerating frequent item counting with FPGA. In: Proceedings of the 2014 ACM/SIGDA International Symposium on Field-Programmable Gate Arrays, pp. 109–112 (2014)

16. Preußer, T.B., Chiosa, M., Weiss, A., Alonso, G.: Using DSP slices as content-addressable update queues. In: 2020 30th International Conference on Field-Programmable Logic and Applications (FPL), pp. 121–126. IEEE (2020)

17. Kastner, R., Matai, J., Neuendorffer, S.: Parallel programming for FPGAs. arXiv preprint arXiv:1805.03648 (2018)

18. Tang, L., Huang, Q., Lee, P.P.: A fast and compact invertible sketch for network-wide heavy flow detection. IEEE/ACM Trans. Network. **28**, 2350–2363 (2020)

19. Zipf, G.K.: Human Behavior and the Principle of Least Effort: An Introduction to Human Ecology. Ravenio Books (2016)

Fast and Adaptive AI on FPGAs

Ultra-Low Latency and Extreme-Throughput Echo State Neural Networks on FPGA

Atousa Jafari[✉] and Marco Platzner

Computer Science Department, Paderborn University, Paderborn, Germany
{atousa.jafari,platzner}@uni-paderborn.de

Abstract. Echo state networks, as a popular form of reservoir computing models, are recurrent neural networks that consist of three layers, and only the output layer needs to be trained. Compared to other recurrent neural network models, echo state networks offer comparable performance for many tasks but lead to reduced computational requirements, making them highly suitable for resource-constrained edge implementations. In this paper, we present and compare two streamlining dataflow accelerators for echo state networks on FPGA. Our accelerators rely on a direct logic implementation style with fully unrolled computations and are fully quantized to avoid floating-point calculations. After proposing a taxonomy of DNN implementation styles on FPGA, we present a tool flow to automatically create such FPGA accelerators for echo state networks. We then discuss two accelerator versions, one employing DSP blocks available in FPGAs and the other one converting multiplications into add/shift operations mapped solely to LUTs. We evaluate our accelerators on three time-series forecasting tasks and report the achieved accuracy as well as the resource requirements, the latency, the throughput, and the required energy. Our designs achieve extreme-throughput and ultra-low latency, reaching up to 100 Megasamples/s and 9.5 ns, respectively, which significantly outperforms related FPGA-based implementations.

1 Introduction

With the growing spread of edge computing, the requirements concerning performance and energy efficiency for machine learning on resource-limited edge devices increase [5]. Many edge computing applications process sequential sensor data, e.g., time series, and rely on recurrent neural networks (RNNs) as machine learning models. Standard RNNs such as Long Short-Term Memories (LSTMs) and Gated Recurrent Units (GRUs) tend to incur high computational and memory costs, which poses challenges for edge implementation. In addition, training RNNs is computationally extremely costly and suffers from gradient vanishing when increasing the number of layers [13].

Reservoir computing (RC) is an alternative RNN model, and its most popular variant, the echo state network (ESN), comprises an input layer, a reservoir of

© The Author(s), under exclusive license to Springer Nature Switzerland AG 2025
R. Giorgi et al. (Eds.): ARC 2025, LNCS 15594, pp. 179–195, 2025.
https://doi.org/10.1007/978-3-031-87995-1_11

neurons, and an output layer. All parameters of the input layer and the reservoir remain fixed after random initialization. Only the parameters of the output layer need to be trained by using simple regression techniques. This eliminates the need for complex training algorithms and significantly reduces the computational demand for both training and inference. Recent research has demonstrated how ESN can efficiently solve time-series problems and address the drawbacks of standard RNNs [12], while achieving comparable accuracy for AI applications, especially for non-linear time series forecasting [18], pattern classification, and biosignal processing, such as multivariate time series classification for ECGs and blood samples [2].

The three-layer architecture of ESNs makes them highly suitable for resource-constrained edge implementations. In particular, streaming dataflow architectures mapped to FPGAs are known to achieve low latency and high throughput [5,21]. In this paper, we present and compare two ESN accelerators that follow the direct logic implementation style, where computations are fully unrolled to eliminate memory accesses for weights. Further, our accelerators quantize all layers of an ESN and completely avoid floating-point calculations. We discuss two accelerator versions, one employing DSP blocks available in FPGAs and the other one converting multiplications into add/shift operations mapped solely to LUTs.

The novel contributions of this paper are as follows:

– We propose a fully quantized RC model, where quantization is applied to all parameters and activation functions using the Brevitas framework [15].
– We present a streamlined dataflow architecture for ESN following the direct logic implementation approach and a corresponding tool flow that leads to ultra-low latency and extreme-throughput compared to other implementation styles. We show two accelerator versions, one employing DSP blocks available in FPGAs, and the other one converting multiplications into add/shift operations mapped solely to LUTs. Our accelerators fully quantize all layers of the RC model and eliminate all floating-point calculations.
– We validate our designs in terms of accuracy, resource requirements, latency and throughput, and energy efficiency on three popular time-series forecasting benchmarks: The Mackey-Glass chaotic oscillator prediction, the NARMA10 test, and the Sunspot time series. We further compare our designs to a 32-bit floating-point reference software implementation and previous FPGA-accelerators for RC.

The remainder of this paper is structured as follows: Sect. 2 discusses background and related work on FPGA-based RC. Section 3 elaborates on the details of our proposed fully quantized and fully unrolled dataflow architecture. An experimental evaluation is presented in Sect. 4. Section 5 concludes the paper.

2   Background and Related Work

This section first provides background in RC, in particular echo state networks (ESN), then presents a taxonomy of approaches that map RC models to FPGAs, and finally discusses related work in RC implementations on FPGAs.

2.1   Echo State Networks

Within RC, several network models exist, such as the echo state network (ESN), the liquid state machine (LSM), and the time-delayed reservoir (TDR) [17]. Our work bases on ESN, since this model is particularly suitable for low-latency and high-throughput implementations in hardware due to its simple structure, fixed reservoir weights, and low resource usage [10].

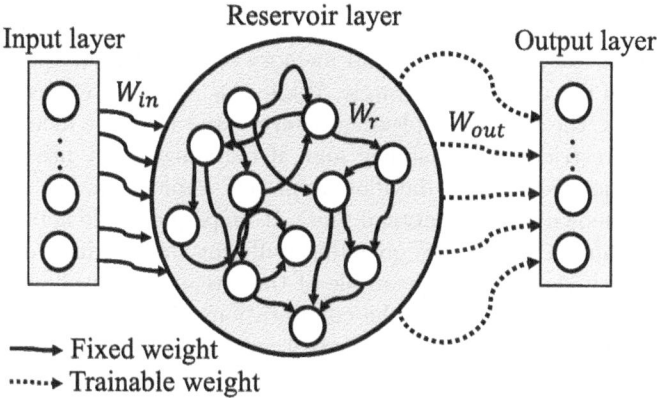

Fig. 1. Reservoir computing architecture for the echo state network (ESN) model, consisting of three layers.

An ESN consists of a three-layer structure: an input layer, a reservoir layer, and a readout or output layer [18]. As depicted in Fig. 1, the input layer feeds data into the reservoir layer via the weight matrix W_{in}. The reservoir essentially consists of a large pool of interconnected neurons with random connections, where the weight matrix W_r represents the reservoir weights. The matrix W_{out} connects the reservoir neurons to the output layer. Importantly, both W_{in} and W_r are randomly generated and fixed during model setup time. Only W_{out} needs to be trained to minimize the error between the expected target output and the model's output. Training the output layer can be done with rather simple linear regression or ridge regression approaches. The reservoir system can be characterized as [18]:

$$s(t) = f(W_{in} \times u(t) + W_r \times s(t-1)) \tag{1}$$

$$y(t) = f_{out}(W_{out} \times s(t)) \tag{2}$$

In Eqs. 1 and 2, $u(t)$ represents the input, $s(t)$ the state of the reservoir, and $y(t)$ the output at time t. W_{in}, W_r, and W_{out} represent the weight matrices, and f denotes the non-linear activation function of the reservoir node, usually $Tanh$ or $ReLU$. For the output nodes, f_{out} is mostly implemented as identity function.

2.2   Approaches for Mapping Neural Networks to FPGA

In Fig. 2, we present a taxonomy of different approaches for mapping DNN inference phases to FPGA. There are two main approaches, the *PE-based* and the
streamline dataflow approach. PE-based approaches employ arrays of processing
elements (PE) to compute the layers of the network model in a time-sequential
manner [3,6,7,9]. They have a fixed set of functional units, e.g., matrix multiplication units, non-linear activation functions, etc., which are reused for the layers
of the same network. This kind of neural network mapping requires control units
to manage the computation flow. Moreover, the network parameters and intermediate outputs are stored in external memory and must be frequently fetched
for each layer of the network separately. While this approach can compute large
network models, the time-multiplexing of layers and frequent memory accesses
impose severe restrictions on latency and, if batching is not possible, also on
throughput. The streamlining dataflow approach implements each layer of the
network with its own set of functional units. It maps the whole network to hardware as a pipeline of such layers, avoiding buffering intermediate data between
layers in memory. A prominent example of the streamline dataflow approach is
the FINN framework [21]. When the computations of the individual layers are
either not or only partially unrolled, control units are still required to multiplex
the arithmetic units and the weights still need to be stored in memory. When
fully unrolling computations, there is no time-multiplexing and, therefore, no
control units are needed and weights can be stored on the FPGA. This approach
has been termed *direct logic implementation* and is the enabler for ultra-low
latency and extreme-throughput DNN implementations on FPGA.

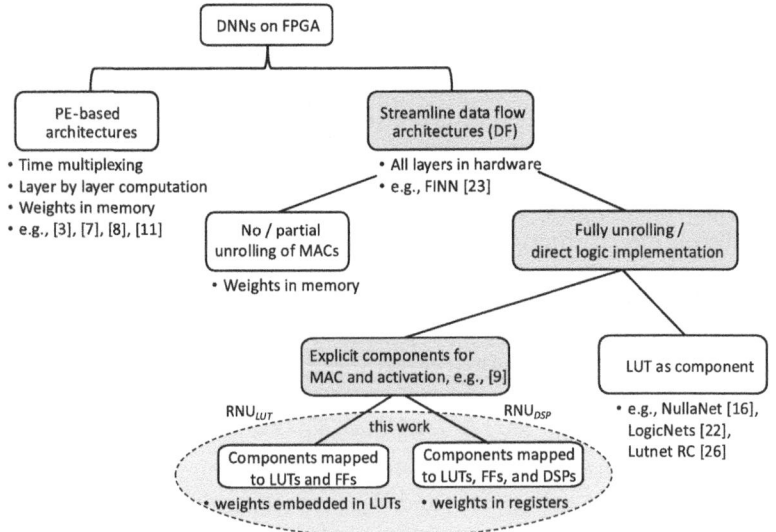

Fig. 2. Taxonomy of DNN inference implementation approaches for FPGA.

Obviously, for direct logic implementations, the available hardware resources limit the size of DNN that can be mapped. Huge DNNs with billions of parameters are thus *not* the targets of such an approach. For many embedded applications of RC networks, however, small to medium-capacity FPGAs are sufficiently large. Moreover, research is being conducted to reduce the DNN models by compression techniques such as pruning and strong quantization of weights and activation functions.

Direct logic implementations can be further differentiated into two variants: In the first variant, the neuron architecture datapath is mapped at the RTL level to explicit arithmetic components for multiply-accumulate (MAC), activation, etc. An example is [8], where a feed-forward neural network is mapped using Booth encoding and computation sharing for interconnect cost reduction. FPGA synthesis tools can then convert these components into sets of LUTs, FFs, and DSP blocks, subject to designer constraints. If DSP blocks implement the MAC operations, weights must be stored in registers. For MACs implemented in LUTs, the weights will also be embedded in LUTs. The second variant views the LUT as the only component at the RTL level, i.e., it maps the whole functionality of neurons into LUTs [14,20,23]. FPGA synthesis tools will then split those LUTs into smaller-input LUTs available on the targeted FPGA. Since this approach quickly leads to a combinatorial explosion in the number of required LUTs, activations need to be extremely quantized, typically to one or very few bits.

2.3   Related Work on FPGA RC Implementation

Several FPGA implementations have been proposed for RC networks so far [3, 4,6,16,23], and the majority of these works focus on the time-sharing PE-based approach. For instance, [4] proposes a PE-based design using a bit-serial matrix multiplication architecture. Bit-serial designs save hardware but also lead to low performance in terms of latency and throughput. The work presented in [6] utilizes the DSP blocks available in many FPGAs to reduce the need for LUTs for creating a PE-based architecture. The authors implement an ESN model and verify it for a prediction task on the NARMA10 dataset. A PE-based pipelined architecture is discussed in [3] for forecasting and modeling chaotic time series.

Only a few works are focusing on the streamlining dataflow approach or even direct logic implementation of RC. Some studies, e.g., [1], rely on probabilistic concepts such as stochastic computing. To achieve satisfying accuracy, these architectures require long numbers, leading to many clock cycles for processing them. As a result, such approaches suffer from high latency and low throughput. A very recent study presents a direct logic RC implementation on FPGA [23] following the second variant that converts complete reservoir neurons into LUTs. Activations are extremely quantized down to one bit to control resource requirements, resulting in distinct models for both training and inference. Moreover, the implementation uses the direct logic implementation approach only for the reservoir layer, while the other layers are done in a PE-based design, requiring memory access.

Our work differs from related approaches in several key aspects: We present the first FPGA implementation for RC network models using variant two of the direct logic implementation approach (see Fig. 2). Then, unlike most previous RC implementations that use fixed-point number representations, we quantize weights and activations to use only integer operations and apply that scheme to all layers of the network model for efficient deployment to hardware. We propose and compare two designs, RNU$_{LUT}$ that implements multipliers with add/shift and maps them to LUTs and FFs and, as a consequence, embeds weights into the LUTs, and RNU$_{DSP}$ which employs DSP blocks for multiplications.

3   Proposed Dataflow Design for FPGA-Based RC

Figure 3 shows an overview of our proposed RC tool flow. We start by selecting the dataset, defining the reservoir size, and initializing weight matrices. We then tune crucial hyperparameters, such as input connectivity, reservoir connectivity, leaking rate, spectral radius, etc., to create the RC model using the ReservoirPy framework [19]. Next, we assess the accuracy of the selected dataset with the reference FP-32 software implementation. Once the accuracy target is met, we quantize all layers of the RC model with the Brevitas [15] framework and apply the streamline algorithm [22] discussed in Subsect. 3.1 to implement the design in hardware. Then, we create the logic implementation for all layers of RC. In this step, we present two variants for RC hardware implementations. Both approaches quantize the entire network using the streamlining algorithm, but they differ in how they synthesize neuron computations into logic. Subsequently, we develop two distinct code generators to convert the logic implementation of RC model layers into Verilog RTL (Register Transfer Level) files for each design approach. Finally, we synthesize each RC model's direct logic implementation into hardware using the Xilinx Vivado tool and evaluate designs in terms of accuracy, resource usage, latency, throughput, etc. The rest of this section provides more detailed information on the quantization and dataflow architectures.

3.1   Quantization and Streamlining for RC Implementation

In this step, we explain the quantization procedures for the RC layers in detail and show how to apply the streamlined algorithm to the RC model for efficient hardware implementation. Equation 3 demonstrates how we linearly quantize floating point numbers [11]:

$$r = Scale \times (Q - Z) \tag{3}$$

In this equation, r is the original floating point number, $Scale$ is the scaling factor in floating point format, Z is the chosen zero-point, and Q is the quantized integer for r. By applying linear quantization to all RC layers separately, we obtain integer values (Q) and scaling factors ($Scale$) for all parts of the RC model: $Q_{u(t)}$ and $Scale_{u(t)}$ for the inputs, $Q_{W_{in}}$ and $Scale_{W_{in}}$ for the input weights, Q_{W_r} and $Scale_{W_r}$ for the reservoir weights, $Q_{s(t)}$ and $Scale_{s(t)}$ for the reservoir

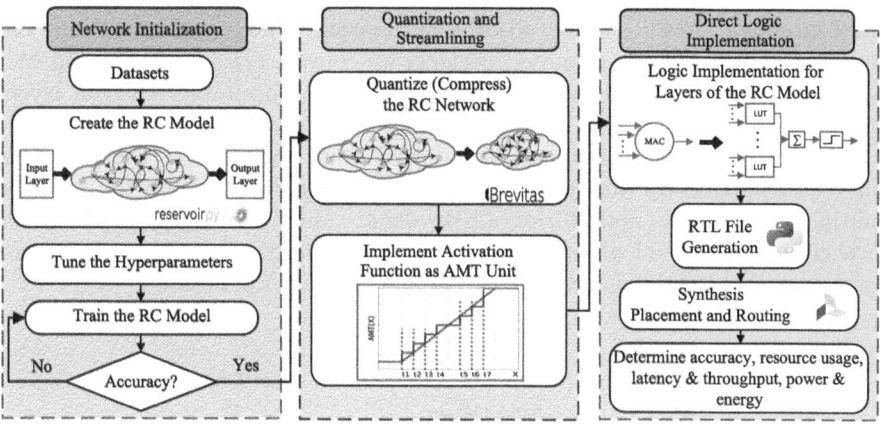

Fig. 3. Overview of the proposed tool flow for mapping the trained RC into the FPGA.

states, and $Q_{W_{out}}$ and $Scale_{W_{out}}$ for the output weights. We approximate the nonlinear activation function $Tanh$ by $HardTanh$, as depicted in Fig. 4 (a), and apply linear quantization to result in $Q_{HardTanh}$. The zero point for all quantized parameters is set to zero.

To eliminate all floating-point scaling factors extracted from linear quantization, we use the successive multi-threshold streamlining algorithm detailed in [22]. This algorithm converts the quantized activation function layer to a multi-threshold (MT) layer by dividing the range of the activation function into $2^K - 1$ levels, where K is the bit-width of the quantized activation function. The difference between levels in the MT layer, known as a *step*, is equal to the scale factor of the activation function.

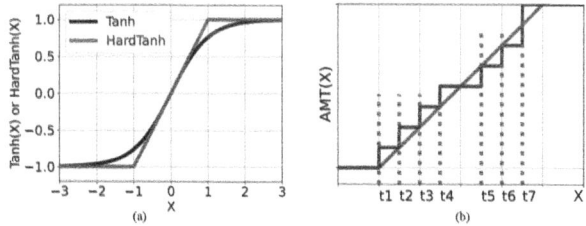

Fig. 4. (a) $HardTanh$ as approximation for the $tanh$ activation function.(b) Example for the functionality of the absorbing multi-threshold (AMT) unit with $K=3$-bit multi-thresholds where $Q_{HardTanh}$ is divided into 7 thresholds (t1-t7).

In the multi-threshold method, the input value is compared with all threshold values, and the result is the nearest threshold index. However, the floating-point scaling factor still exists. So, to eliminate this as well, we divide each threshold level by $Scale$ and round it to the nearest integer. This step is known as *absorbing multi-threshold* (AMT), which absorbs all floating point calculations into the multi-threshold. For our proposed designs, we convert $Q_{HardTanh}$ into an MT layer as shown in Fig. 4 (b) and then absorb *Scale* of input and reservoir layers into it.

The hardware implementation of the AMT unit is detailed in Fig. 5. It uses only two comparators (implemented as multiplexers) to eliminate the need for multiple comparisons and storing all threshold values. The threshold level for each given input is calculated efficiently by summing the outputs of two comparators with $1/Scale$ and then applying a K-bit shift operation.

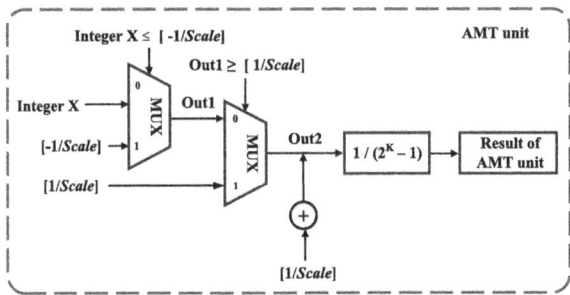

Fig. 5. Proposed AMT unit for our streamline dataflow implementation. K denotes the bit-width of the quantized activation function.

To apply the streamlining approach to our RC model, we begin by replacing the activation function with an AMT unit. We separate the activation function into two parts, input and reservoir layers (cmp. Eq. 1). Then we substitute the activation function with the AMT unit, as shown in Eq. 5, where AMT_{Input} and $AMT_{Reservoir}$ represent the AMT units applied to the input and reservoir layers, respectively.

$$s(t) = (AMT_{Input}(Q_{W_{in}} \times Q_{u(t)}) + AMT_{Reservoir}(Q_{s(t-1)} \times Q_{W_r})) \times step) \quad (4)$$

$$Q_{s(t)} = (AMT_{Input}(Q_{W_{in}} \times Q_{u(t)}) + AMT_{Reservoir}(Q_{s(t-1)} \times Q_{W_r})) \quad (5)$$

According to Eq. 4, the sum of two AMT results needs to be multiplied by a floating-point *step* to calculate the new state in the RC model. The floating-point *step* propagates to the output layer, so the integer part of Eq. 4 can be represented as shown in Eq. 5. To measure the final result of the system, Eq. 2 can be re-written as Eq. 6a. By merging $Scale_{W_{out}} \times step$ to S_{final}, we result in Eq. 6b. In summary, with the help of the streamlining approach, all calculations required to compute the next reservoir state can be done completely in integer format, and there is only one floating point number, S_{final}.

$$y(t) = Q_{W_{out}} \times Scale_{W_{out}} \times Q_{s(t)} \times step \quad (6a)$$

$$y(t) = Q_{W_{out}} \times Q_{s(t)} \times S_{final} \quad (6b)$$

3.2   Dataflow Direct Logic Implementation for RC

This subsection details our dataflow architecture for RC. We propose two designs; both are fully unrolled and fully quantized with respect to all RC layers. Moreover, we apply the streamlining approach to both designs, converting all operations into integers by using AMT as described in Sect. 3.1. Figure 6(a) depicts an overview of the designs, consist of an input, reservoir and output layers. The quantized input is connected to the neurons with the input weights W_{in}. The reservoir layer consists of a pool of connected neurons. We denote the compute unit responsible for calculating the next state of a neuron with *Reservoir Neuron Unit LUT* (RNU). The results of an RNU are passed to other connected neurons and to the *Output Neuron Unit* (ONU) in the output layer to generate the system's final output. The structure of the RNU and ONU varies between the two RC designs.

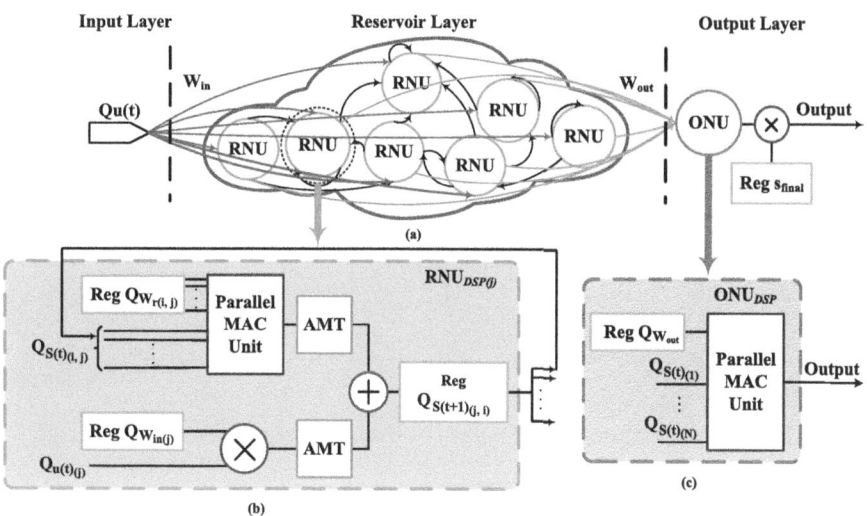

Fig. 6. (a) Overview of our dataflow architecture for RC. (b) Architecture for RNU_{DSP}. (c) Design for output layer (ONU_{DSP}).

Figure 6(b) shows the RNU structure for our first design RNU_{DSP}, based on dedicated multipliers. To calculate the new state, each RNU multiplies the quantized input by the corresponding quantized input weight. Simultaneously, it performs the multiply-accumulate (MAC) operation between the current quantized states of connected neurons and the reservoir weights for that neuron. We then pass the results from each unit to the corresponding AMT, which applies the activation function by multi-thresholding and absorbing the floating-point scales.

Finally, we add the outputs of the two AMTs to update the neuron state. Each RNU stores its final result in a register to be used for updating the next state of others connected RNU. Additionally, the RNU's final result propagates to the output layer for further calculation. Figure 6(c) shows the ONU for the first design, which multiplies and accumulates the calculated states from all neurons in the reservoir layer by using the corresponding quantized output weights. The system then generates the final result by multiplying the output from the MAC unit by S_{final}.

Figure 7 (a) sketches the RNU structure for our second design, RNU$_{LUT}$, based on add/shift operations mapped to LUTs. To achieve this design, we start by replacing each multiplication operation with a shift and add operations across all layers. Since we know the weight values in advance, we can hard-wire the weights into the logic operators, eliminating the need for weight registers. As depicted in Fig. 7 (a), the RNU$_{LUT}$ has the same functionality as the RNU$_{DSP}$, but it updates the new system's state solely using logic operations (shift and add) rather than multiplications. The concept of add/shift operation is extended to the output layer for multiplies and accumulates, as shown in Fig. 7 (b).

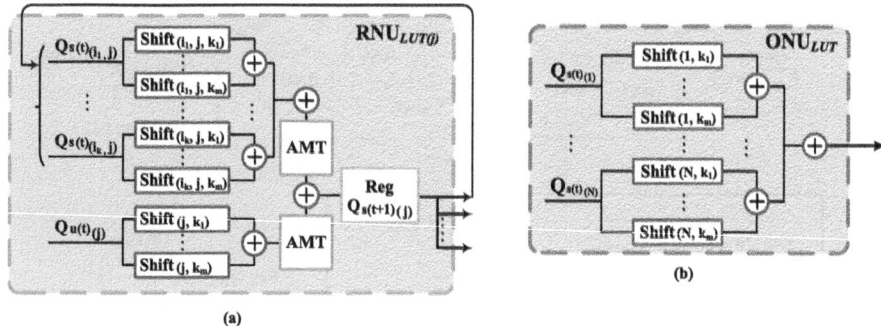

(a)

Fig. 7. (a) Architecture for RNU$_{LUT}$. (b) Design for output layer (ONU$_{LUT}$).

4   Experimental Evaluation

In this section, we describe our experimental setup and then present results concerning the accuracy in dependence of ESN hyperparameters, followed by results comparing resource and performance parameters of our designs with related work.

4.1   Experiment Setup

To set up the RC models and initialize their hyperparameters, we use the ReservoirPy framework [19]. With the help of the hyperopt optimization library, we set hyperparameters such as the connectivity ratio for the input matrix and the reservoir-internal matrix, which represent the connectivity of the input and the connectivity of the reservoir, respectively. The output matrix is fully populated in the RC model. The output layer uses trainable linear regression nodes to map reservoir states to the output. For quantizing the resulting RC models, we employ the Brevitas framework [15].

For hardware implementation, we have developed two distinct code generators to automatically convert the trained ReservoirPy models into Verilog netlists. The generated Verilog code is synthesized using Xilinx Vivado 2022.2 to a Virtex UltraScale VCU108 FPGA. The reported energy values are derived from the Vivado power report, which is estimated by generating the Switching Activity Interchange File (SAIF) for each benchmark through simulation. These SAIF files are subsequently injected into Vivado for detailed power measurement.

For evaluation, we rely on the three widely-used RC benchmarks: (i) Mackey-Glass (MG) chaotic oscillator prediction, (ii) Nonlinear Autoregressive Moving Average of order 10 (NARMA10), and (iii) the Sunspot time series. The Sunspot dataset spans solar activity observations from 1749 to 2019, comprising 3242 data points. These time-series benchmarks aim to predict future values based on previously observed ones. We validate our designs on selected data sets comprising 7000 training samples T_{Train} and 3000 test samples T_{Test}, respectively. To evaluate the achieved accuracy for the benchmarks, we report on the measured error metrics *root mean squared error (RMSE)* and *normalized RMSE (NRMSE)*.

4.2   Quantitative Accuracy Evaluation

Table 1 presents the error analysis between a 200 neuron 32-bit floating-point software reference implementation, our proposed RC architecture with 200 neurons and weights, inputs, states, and activations quantized to 8-bit integer, and hardware implementations from related work.

Table 1. Error analysis for the selected benchmarks comparing a floating-point (FP-32) software implementation as a baseline, to our proposed quantized designs, and–where available–hardware implementations for related work. N denotes the reservoir size in number of neurons.

	Software FP-32 (baseline) N = 200		Our 8-Bit Quant. Accelerator N = 200		[6] N = 100	[7] N = 200	[16] N = 300	[23] N = 1500
Dataset	RMSE	NRMSE	RMSE	NRMSE	NRMSE	RMSE	NRMSE	NRMSE
MG	0.0064	0.0032	0.0091	0.0054	-	-	0.0764	-
NARMA10	0.0381	0.0850	0.0401	0.0856	0.353	0.0974	-	0.137
Sunspot	0.0620	0.0687	0.0295	0.0353	-	-	-	-

Figure 8 compares the prediction results between the baseline FP-32 software reference and our proposed hardware design for the benchmark MG. Visually, the two signals are very close, which supports the quantitative data of Table 1 and the insight that 8-bit quantization has little to no impact on the accuracy. The same holds true for the NARMA10 and Sunspot time series benchmarks. As for any neural network, the hyperparameters and the model size affect the error in RC models. Figure 9(a) and Fig. 9(b) analyze the relation between RMSE vs. input and reservoir connectivity ratios for the chosen benchmarks.

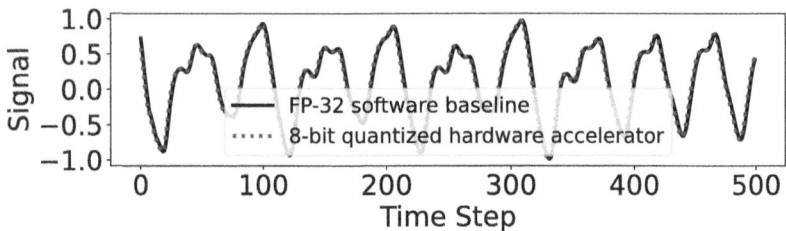

Fig. 8. Predicted signals for the FP-32 software implementation (baseline) and our 8-bit quantized hardware accelerator for 500 time steps.

To measure the RMSE, we leverage hyperopt library for optimizing input and reservoir connectivity over multiple independent experiments.

Figure 9 shows that the RMSE does not depend much on the input and reservoir connectivity ratios. This holds for all three benchmarks. Even with low connectivity, i.e., high sparsities of W_{in} and W_r, it is possible to achieve a low error. This sparse structure is a notable feature of the RC model, which makes it very suitable for direct logic implementation.

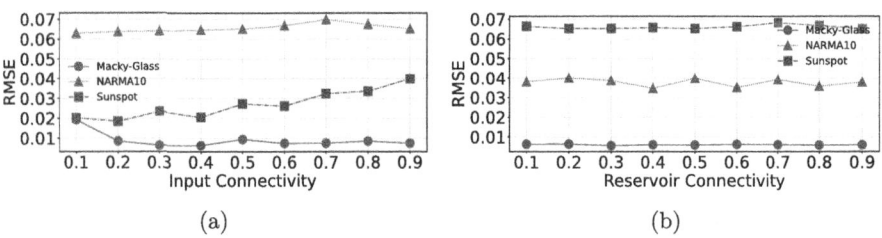

Fig. 9. RMSE vs. (a) input neuron connectivity ratio and (b) reservoir neuron connectivity ratio for a 200-neuron RC model and all three benchmarks.

Figure 10 plots the achieved RMSE in dependency of the reservoir size for all three benchmarks MG, NARMA10, and Sunspot time series, for both the FP-32 baseline and the 8-bit quantized models. The RMSE values are obtained by averaging the results over multiple independent experiments for each size. Figure 10 indicates that across all benchmarks, the RMSE values of the FP-32 and the quantized design show different behaviors, but remain in comparable ranges. In particular, a higher number of reservoir neurons does not necessarily

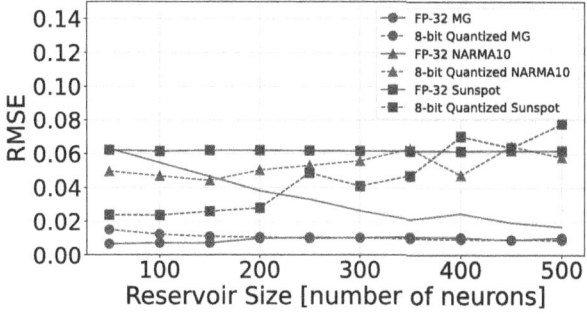

Fig. 10. RMSE vs. reservoir size for the FP-32 baseline and 8-bit quantized models for all three benchmarks.

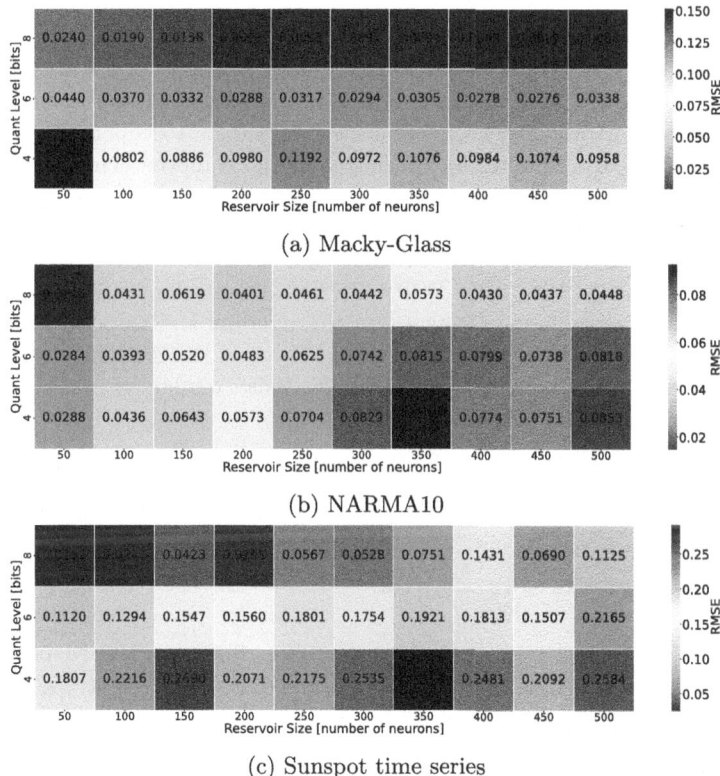

Fig. 11. RMSE in dependency of quantization level and reservoir size.

lead to a lower RMSE. For example, there is a saturation beyond 200 neurons for the MG dataset. In the quantized NARMA10 and sunspot experiments, smaller reservoir sizes can even achieve better RMSE compared to larger ones.

In Fig. 11, we depict the results of a more detailed study of the RMSE and its dependence on the reservoir size and the quantization level. We have varied the reservoir size between 50 and 500 neurons, and the quantization in [4, 6, 8] bit. To obtain the RMSE values, multiple trials have been conducted for each specific combination of network size and quantization level.

The averaged RMSE values are plotted in the cells of the tables. Clearly, reducing the quantization level leads to a degradation in accuracy. However, the choice of the reservoir size is benchmark-dependent, as already shown in Fig. 10. While the Macky-Glass dataset achieves higher RMSE with larger reservoir sizes, the NARMA10 and Sunspot datasets both require fewer reservoir neurons to reach better accuracy.

4.3 Comparison of Our Accelerator Designs and Prior Works

Obviously, larger reservoir sizes and higher connectivity ratios lead to increasing hardware requirements. Thus, for further experiments, we have quantized weights, inputs, states, and activations to 8-bit integers and set the connectivity ratios for the input and reservoir connectivity to 0.1. A deeper exploration of the impact of hyperparameter optimization on the achieved error and resource requirements for our RC accelerators is part of future work.

Table 2 presents a detailed comparison between both our designs RNU_{DSP} and RNU_{LUT}, along with prior work. The table lists for all designs the required hardware resources (LUTs, FFs, DSPs, BRAMs), the achieved clock frequency, the performance parameters latency and throughout, and the energy in terms of the power-delay product. [6,7,9] propose PE-based RC implementations with restrictions on latency and throughput due to issues explained in Sect. 2.2.

Table 2. Quantitative analysis of our proposed quantized designs and related work. Throughput is measured in Kilo samples per second (Ksps) and Mega samples per second (Msps).

	Reservoir Size	LUTs [K]	FFs [K]	DSPs	BRAMs	F_{clk} [MHz]	Latency [ns/µs]	Throughput [Ksps/Msps]	PDP
RNU_{LUT}	200	229.4	4.7	0	0	100	**9.5 ns**	**100 Msps**	72 nWs
RNU_{DSP}	200	257.9	4.9	746	0	33	**29 ns**	**34 Msps**	86 nWs
[6]	16	11.0	7.2	162	12	100	3.2 µs	1.2 Msps	26 µWs
[7]	100	28.9	44.0	20	48	200	200 µs	200 Ksps	4.4 µWs
[9]	16	2.1	6.0	16	0	100	830 ns	26 Msps	-
[23]	1500	17.9	15.2	0	4	100	84 ns*	1.2 Msps	-

* Latency is limited by output layer and type of multiply-accumulation (S-DMACC).

Our designs as first full logic implementations are clearly superior to all related works in terms of throughput and latency. Additionally, compared to [23], where only the reservoir layer is a direct logic implementation using LUTs as components (cmp. Fig. 2), our designs achieve 8.3× and 2.25× higher throughput with fewer neurons. To maintain an accuracy similar to the conventional reservoir model, the design in [23] requires 1500 neurons, which significantly impacts the performance parameters. On the other hand, our designs come with an increased resource usage compared to previous work. This is to be expected due to the direct logic implementation style, where all operations are fully unrolled and weights are hardwired or kept in registers rather than being stored in memory, such as BRAMs. It also leads to an increase in power consumption compared to PE-based designs, but our PDP is much better due to decreased latency, as shown in Table 2.

The table also shows the trade-off between RNU_{LUT} and RNU_{DSP}. In terms of resources, RNU_{DSP} obviously requires DSP blocks but does not at all save on LUTs and FFs, mainly because weights need to be explicitly stored. RNU_{LUT} can increase the throughput up to 2.9× over RNU_{DSP} by turning multipliers into shift/add operators and embedding weights into the logic. Additionally, RNU_{LUT} achieves lower latency compared to RNU_{DSP}, a trend seen across all neuron sizes as shown in Fig. 12. Our fully unrolled architectures use only one register layer in the dataflow path to store the calculated reservoir states, resulting in a one-cycle latency. With that, we could achieve a maximum clock frequency of 100 MHz for our RNU_{LUT} design, which is comparable to related work. For RNU_{DSP}, however, the single cycle constraint leads to a rather low clock frequency. In turn, the low clock frequency also hurts the power-delay product for RNU_{DSP}, although this design excels over RNU_{LUT} in power consumption by a factor of three. Optimizations of the RNU_{DSP} design, for example through pipelining, that sacrifice some latency for an overall improved energy efficiency are part of future work.

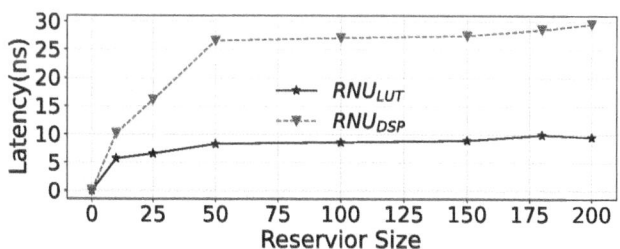

Fig. 12. Latency vs.—reservoir size for RNU_{LUT} and RNU_{DSP}.

Overall, our fully unrolled and fully quantized streamlining dataflow architecture for RC on FPGA offers a compelling balance between accuracy, resource utilization, and throughput/latency, making it a promising design for extreme-throughput and ultra-low latency implementations.

5   Conclusion and Future Work

In this paper, we have presented two variants of FPGA-based dataflow accelerators for ESN and a corresponding tool flow. The accelerators follow the direct logic implementation style, that fully unrolls computations. In addition, we fully quantize all layers of the ESN model. Experimental results show that our 8-bit accelerator designs exhibit similar accuracy as an FP-32 software baseline but excel in latency, throughput, and energy efficiency over previous FPGA-based accelerators, albeit at the cost of increased resource usage. Further work includes a deeper study on hyperparameter optimization, further optimization of the accelerators in terms of clock frequency, power, and resource requirements, and application studies for more complex time-series forecasting tasks. We will also make available our tool flow as open source.

Acknowledgments. This work is supported by the German Federal Ministry for the Environment, Nature Conservation, Nuclear Safety, and Consumer Protection under grant no. 67KI32004A.

References

1. Alomar, M.L., Canals, V., Perez-Mora, N., Martínez-Moll, V., Rosselló, J.L.: FPGA-based stochastic echo state networks for time-series forecasting. Comput. Intell. Neurosci. 15–15 (2016). https://doi.org/10.1155/2016/3917892
2. Bianchi, F.M., Scardapane, S., Løkse, S., Jenssen, R.: Reservoir computing approaches for representation and classification of multivariate time series. IEEE Trans. Neural Netw. Learn. Syst. **32**(5), 2169–2179 (2020). https://doi.org/10.1109/TNNLS.2020.3001377
3. Dai, Z., et al.: A scalable small-footprint time-space-pipelined architecture for reservoir computing. IEEE Trans. Circuits Syst. II Express Briefs **70**(8), 3069–3073 (2023). https://doi.org/10.1109/TCSII.2023.3252802
4. Denton, M., Schmit, H.: Direct spatial implementation of sparse matrix multipliers for reservoir computing. In: 2022 IEEE International Symposium on High-Performance Computer Architecture (HPCA), pp. 1–11. IEEE (2022). https://doi.org/10.1109/HPCA53966.2022.00009
5. Duarte, J., et al.: Fast inference of deep neural networks in FPGAs for particle physics. J. Instrum. **13**(07), P07027 (2018). https://doi.org/10.1088/1748-0221/13/07/P07027
6. Gan, V.M., Liang, Y., Li, L., Liu, L., Yi, Y.: A cost-efficient digital ESN architecture on FPGA for OFDM symbol detection. ACM J. Emerg. Technol. Comput. Syst. (JETC) **17**(4), 1–15 (2021). https://doi.org/10.1145/3440017
7. Honda, K., Tamukoh, H.: A hardware-oriented echo state network and its FPGA implementation. J. Robot. Network. Artif. Life **7**(1), 58–62 (2020). https://doi.org/10.2991/jrnal.k.200512.012
8. Huang, Y.S., Jiang, J., Mishchenko, A.: Quantized neural network synthesis for direct logic circuit implementation. IEEE Trans. Comput. Aided Des. Integr. Circuits Syst. **42**(2), 473–482 (2023). https://doi.org/10.1109/TCAD.2022.3183547
9. Kleyko, D., Frady, E.P., Kheffache, M., Osipov, E.: Integer echo state networks: efficient reservoir computing for digital hardware. IEEE Trans. Neural Netw. Learn. Syst. **33**(4), 1688–1701 (2020). https://doi.org/10.1109/TNNLS.2020.3043309

10. Lin, C., Liang, Y., Yi, Y.: FPGA-based reservoir computing with optimized reservoir node architecture. In: 2022 23rd International Symposium on Quality Electronic Design (ISQED), pp. 1–6. IEEE (2022). https://doi.org/10.1109/ISQED54688.2022.9806247
11. Liu, S., Liang, Y., Gan, V., Liu, L., Yi, Y.: Accurate and efficient quantized reservoir computing system. In: 2020 21st International Symposium on Quality Electronic Design (ISQED), pp. 364–369 (2020). https://doi.org/10.1109/ISQED48828.2020.9136986
12. Lukoševičius, M., Jaeger, H.: Reservoir computing approaches to recurrent neural network training. Comput. Sci. Rev. **3**(3), 127–149 (2009). https://doi.org/10.1016/j.cosrev.2009.03.005
13. Mittal, S., Umesh, S.: A survey on hardware accelerators and optimization techniques for RNNs. J. Syst. Architect. **112**, 101839 (2021). https://doi.org/10.1016/j.sysarc.2020.101839
14. Nazemi, M., Pasandi, G., Pedram, M.: Energy-efficient, low-latency realization of neural networks through Boolean logic minimization. In: Proceedings of the 24th Asia and South Pacific Design Automation Conference. pp. 274–279 (2019). https://doi.org/10.1145/3287624.3287722
15. Pappalardo, A.: Xilinx/brevitas (2023). https://doi.org/10.5281/zenodo.3333552
16. Skibinsky-Gitlin, E.S., Alomar, M.L., Isern, E., Roca, M., Canals, V., Rossello, J.L.: Reservoir computing hardware for time series forecasting. In: 2018 28th International Symposium on Power and Timing Modeling, Optimization and Simulation (PATMOS), pp. 133–139. IEEE (2018). https://doi.org/10.1109/PATMOS.2018.8463994
17. Soures, N., Merkel, C., Kudithipudi, D., Thiem, C., McDonald, N.: Reservoir computing in embedded systems: three variants of the reservoir algorithm. IEEE Consum. Electron. Mag. **6**(3), 67–73 (2017). https://doi.org/10.1109/MCE.2017.2685159
18. Tanaka, G., et al.: Recent advances in physical reservoir computing: a review. Neural Netw. **115**, 100–123 (2019). https://doi.org/10.1016/j.neunet.2019.03.005
19. Trouvain, N., Pedrelli, L., Dinh, T.T., Hinaut, X.: Reservoirpy: an efficient and user-friendly library to design echo state networks. In: International Conference on Artificial Neural Networks, pp. 494–505. Springer, Cham (2020). https://doi.org/10.1007/978-3-030-61616-8_40
20. Umuroglu, Y., Akhauri, Y., Fraser, N.J., Blott, M.: Logicnets: co-designed neural networks and circuits for extreme-throughput applications. In: 2020 30th International Conference on Field-Programmable Logic and Applications (FPL), pp. 291–297 (2020). https://doi.org/10.1109/FPL50879.2020.00055
21. Umuroglu, Y., et al.: Finn: a framework for fast, scalable binarized neural network inference. In: Proceedings of the 2017 ACM/SIGDA International Symposium on Field-Programmable Gate Arrays, pp. 65–74 (2017). https://doi.org/10.1145/3020078.3021744
22. Umuroglu, Y., Jahre, M.: Streamlined deployment for quantized neural networks (2018). https://doi.org/10.48550/arXiv.1709.04060
23. Yoshioka, K., Tanaka, Y., Tamukoh, H.: Lutnet-RC: look-up tables networks for reservoir computing on an FPGA. In: 2023 International Conference on Field Programmable Technology (ICFPT), pp. 170–178 (2023). https://doi.org/10.1109/ICFPT59805.2023.00024

A Reconfigurable Stream-Based FPGA Accelerator for Bayesian Confidence Propagation Neural Networks

Muhammad Ihsan Al Hafiz[1]([✉])(iD), Naresh Ravichandran[1](iD),
Anders Lansner[1,2,3](iD), Pawel Herman[1,3,4,5](iD), and Artur Podobas[1,3]([✉])(iD)

[1] KTH Royal Institute of Technology, Stockholm, Sweden
{miahafiz,nbrav,ala,paherman,podobas}@kth.se
[2] Stockholm University, Stockholm, Sweden
[3] Swedish e-Science Research Centre (SeRC), Stockholm, Sweden
[4] Digital Futures, Stockholm, Sweden
[5] International Research Centre for Neurointelligence, University of Tokyo,
Tokyo, Japan

Abstract. Brain-like algorithms are attractive and emerging alternatives to classical deep learning methods for use in various machine learning applications. Brain-like systems can feature local learning rules, both unsupervised/semi-supervised learning and different types of plasticity (structural/synaptic), allowing them to potentially be faster and more energy-efficient than traditional machine learning alternatives. Among the more salient brain-like algorithms are Bayesian Confidence Propagation Neural Networks (BCPNNs). BCPNN is an important tool for both machine learning and computational neuroscience research, and recent work shows that BCPNN can reach state-of-the-art performance in tasks such as learning and memory recall compared to other models. Unfortunately, BCPNN is primarily executed on slow general-purpose processors (CPUs) or power-hungry graphics processing units (GPUs), reducing the applicability of using BCPNN in Edge systems, among others. In this work, we design a reconfigurable stream-based accelerator for BCPNN using Field-Programmable Gate Arrays (FPGA) using Xilinx Vitis High-Level Synthesis (HLS) flow. Furthermore, we model our accelerator's performance using first principles, and we empirically show that our proposed accelerator (full-featured kernel non-structural plasticity) is between 1.3x - 5.3x faster than an Nvidia A100 GPU while at the same time consuming between 2.62x - 3.19x less power and 5.8x - 16.5x less energy without any degradation in performance.

Keywords: BCPNN · Neuromorphic · FPGA · HLS

1 Introduction

Deep Learning (DL) [15] has emerged as one of the most essential machine learning approaches in the past decades. DL approaches are used in everything

R. Giorgi et al. (Eds.): ARC 2025, LNCS 15594, pp. 196–213, 2025.
https://doi.org/10.1007/978-3-031-87995-1_12

from image recognition [2] and time-series prediction [16] to natural language processing [11]. Since their inception around 2012, the size of DL systems has been growing at an exponential rate, demanding more and more computational resources and power [27]. In particular the latter, energy consumption, has been identified as a challenge to overcome since training a modern DL system can take several months and can be very energy-consuming (ChatGPT4 consumed 50 GWh [8]). In short, there is a growing need to research alternative machine learning methods in order to satisfy performance demands without needlessly taxing the environment. One such direction is to draw inspiration from biology and investigate `brain-like` systems.

A `brain-like` system is a system that solves machine learning problems in a way abstracted but derived from theories of the brain in computational neuroscience. A brain-like system can be either spiking [18] (often called neuromorphic system [26]) or rate-based (non-spiking). Brain-like systems typically have several traits that make them attractive to use, such as: (i) they can be very sparse and energy-efficient, (ii) they have local (non-propagating) learning rules, and (iii) supports one- and few-shot learning. There are multiple brain-like machine learning models, but few are as salient and with such mature theory as the *Bayesian Confidence Propagation Neural Network (BCPNN)* [3].

BCPNN is a biologically plausible model that is derived from the organization of the human cortex [19], where the basic building blocks are hypercolumns and minicolumns. Bayesian Confidence Propagation Neural Network (BCPNN) supports multiple different forms of learning, including learning of synaptic strengths [5] (based on Bayes theorem) as well as structural plasticity [12] that rewire the connections between building blocks. More importantly, BCPNN supports supervised, semi-supervised, and unsupervised learning [24], making it a strong choice for systems with a limited amount of labeled data. While BCPNN has shown state-of-the-art training and inference performance [23] in multiple data sets using general-purpose Central Processing Unit (CPU) and Graphics Processing Unit (GPU) implementation, these devices are typically too expensive (e.g., in terms of power consumption) to deploy on Edge computing devices that could leverage the properties of BCPNN.

In this work, we propose the first high-performance hardware accelerator for BCPNN. We have described our data-flow accelerator using the Xilinx Vitis High Level Synthesis (HLS) [20] toolchain and executed it on state-of-the-art Alveo U55C Field Programmable Gate Array (FPGA). We claim the following contributions:

1. We describe and implement the first reconfigurable high-performance BCPNN FPGA accelerator for use in data centers and edge systems that support both inference as well as online (unsupervised) learning,
2. We apply the BCPNN theory on two new datasets: detecting Pneumonia and Breast cancer,
3. We develop an analytical performance model (based on first principles) to provide insight into the performance of our hardware accelerator and

4. We empirically quantify the performance of our accelerator, positioning it against a Tesla-class Nvidia A100 GPU and an Intel Xeon server-class CPU, showing an advantage in both performance and power consumption of our FPGA accelerator.

2   Related Work

BCPNN has a long lineage of research work dating back to the 1980s [13]. Since then, several research works have extended the use of BCPNN to drug reaction signal generation [3], pattern recognition [21], spike-based formulation [30], investigated support for fixed-point arithmetic [9], and several machine learning applications [24,25,29] and more. Motivated by the success and versatility of BCPNN, several groups have proposed hardware accelerators to improve performance and reduce the energy consumption of BCPNN. In 2020, Yang et al. [38] optimized the BCPNN learning rule with respect to memory accesses, showing how non-coalesced column-wise memory access patterns in lazy-based methods can be eliminated, which can result in significant speed-ups. In 2020, Liu et al. [17] implemented an FPGA-based hardware accelerator for a spiking-based BCPNN model. This architecture employs a 'lazy update mode', efficiently updating eight local synaptic state variables by optimizing parallelism and decomposing calculations based on inherent data dependencies. These optimizations reduce the computation and bandwidth by more than two orders of magnitude, which makes efficient implementation of BCPNN for real-time brain simulation engine [17]. This approach led to a substantial acceleration in processing time, with an update time of 110 ns on an FPGA, compared to 25800 ns on a CPU [17]. Podobas et al. introduced StreamBrain [22] in 2021, a framework that enables the deployment of the rate-based BCPNN in High-Performance Computing (HPC) systems. StreamBrain is a domain-specific language (DSL) that supports various backends, including CPUs, GPUs, and FPGAs. The authors demonstrate the practical capabilities of StreamBrain by training the MNIST dataset within seconds and showing the result of BCPNN in higher-dimension problems with STL-10 networks. Additionally, the paper explores the use of custom floating-point formats and the impact when using FPGAs. However, unlike the present paper, StreamBrain only accelerated a small subset of the BCPNN algorithm on the FPGA platform. Wang et al. [32] showed that the BCPNN local learning rule could be mapped and executed using an analog memristor model, showing that the device could have a correlation coefficient as high as 0.98 and showing that it could learn the MNIST benchmark. Wang et al. [31] presented an FPGA-based HPC design specifically optimized for a BCPNN-based associative memory system. Their approach incorporates several optimizations, including shared parallel computing units, hybrid-precision computing for a hybrid update mechanism, and the globally asynchronous, locally synchronous (GALS) strategy. Using the Xilinx Alveo U200 FPGA accelerator card, the design achieved a maximum network size of 150×10 and a peak frequency of $100\,\text{MHz}$. The FPGA-based solution outperformed its Nvidia GTX 4090 counterpart, demonstrating a maximum latency reduction of 33.23x and a power consumption reduction of over 6.9x. The study underscores the potential of FPGA-based accelerators to significantly enhance both speed and energy efficiency in neuromorphic computing implementations. However, the scope of their work is limited to a small network size and omits evaluation of real-world datasets. Contrary to the related work, which has been shown either in-parts [22,32,38] or at a low Technology Readiness Level (TRL) (omitting real use-cases) [31], our work is the first that provides an FPGA accelerator for BCPNN that is high-performance (outperforms Nvidia A100) and that can handle real-life use-case with a low-latency, encourage its deployment in data-centers and on-edge premises. We are also the first to show BCPNN with the (more complicated) use cases, such as detecting pneumonia or breast cancer.

3   Bayesian Confidence Propagation Neural Network

BCPNN is a brain-like machine learning model that utilizes the principles of Bayesian statistics to derive the synaptic and neuronal update operations. It has two types of formulation: spike-based and rate-based. In this paper, we design a hardware accelerator for the rate-based BCPNN. The work is based on the latest work in [23], which is a feedforward BCPNN that integrates cortical column, divisive normalization, Hebbian synaptic plasticity, structural plasticity, sparse activity, and sparse, patchy connectivity.

The BCPNN divides its computational units into *minicolumns*, which form part of larger modules known as *hypercolumns* [23]. Each hypercolumn encodes a particular input attribute, while its constituent minicolumns represent discrete, mutually exclusive values of that attribute. This arrangement echoes the columnar structure of the primate neocortex, where functionally similar neurons are grouped vertically, creating a sparse and energy-efficient coding scheme [6,7].

A basic feedforward BCPNN consists of at least two layers: an input layer and a hidden layer. The input layer's minicolumns capture discrete feature values provided by the data, and the hidden layer's minicolumns encode internal representations derived from these inputs [23]. Connecting these layers are weighted projections that undergo synaptic plasticity, an unsupervised learning mechanism analogous to Hebbian-Bayesian updates. This rule adapts the network parameters online, using local statistics of neuronal activities.

At the core of BCPNN lie three key probability traces, incrementally updated at each training step: the probability of an input minicolumn being active (p_i), the probability of a hidden minicolumn being active (p_j), and their joint probability (p_{ij}). These traces support a learning rule where biases (b_j) and connection weights (w_{ij}) are computed as logarithms of conditional probabilities:

$$b_j = \log p_j, \quad w_{ij} = \log \frac{p_{ij}}{p_i p_j}. \tag{1}$$

This formulation expresses the hidden unit's bias as the self-information and the synaptic weight as the mutual information between pre- and post-synaptic activities. Conceptually, it transforms observed co-occurrences of events into updated parameters that influence network activity. The activation of each hidden minicolumn is determined by a softmax function applied to support values derived from weighted input signals. This ensures that minicolumns in the same hypercolumn compete, resulting in a probability distribution across features. Consequently, a BCPNN hypercolumn provides a discrete probability estimate that closely resembles the cortical microcircuit behavior, where excitatory and inhibitory interactions lead to sparse, distributed coding patterns. Finally (and importantly), BCPNN also supports structural plasticity where the network changes as a function of time, complementing the synaptic learning rule described above.

In short, BCPNN integrates neuroscientific principles-cortical microcircuitry, local learning, and probabilistic coding-into a neural computation framework. It encodes probability distributions directly within its weights and biases, learns online from streaming data, and yields a compact, high-level representation of complex inputs.

4   High-Performance Stream-Based BCPNN Accelerator

Figure 1 illustrates our complete development workflow. We start with a C-level simulation to verify correctness, then proceed to C-level synthesis to obtain a preliminary estimate of hardware resources. Next, we perform C/Register Transfer Level (RTL) cosimulation to finalize First In First Out (FIFO) depths and confirm that no deadlocks can occur. If we encounter resource constraints, we adjust model sizes or parameters. After ensuring the design meets our resource and timing requirements from the adjustment of FIFO depth, we transition to the Vitis development flow. This process packages the RTL into an extensible platform, performs synthesis and implementation, and generates the FPGA bitstream. By leveraging Vitis flow, we can concentrate on optimizing the BCPNN kernel, as low-level tasks such as Peripheral Component Interconnect Express (PCIe) or Direct Memory Access (DMA) configuration are handled automatically (Fig. 1).

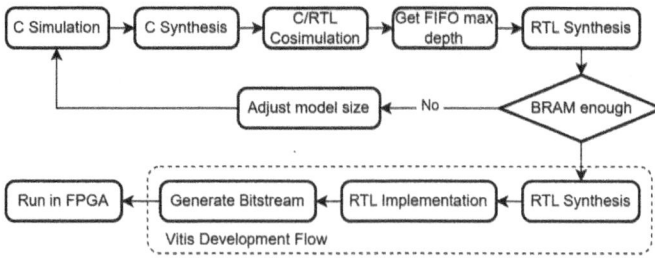

Fig. 1. Design workflow

4.1   Accelerator Design Using HLS

The BCPNN kernel comprises three interconnected population layers: input, hidden, and output. Each population layer represents a group of neurons that encodes and processes probabilistic relationships. These layers communicate through projection layers, with the input-hidden projection connecting the input population to the hidden population and the hidden-output projection linking the hidden population to the output population. A projection refers to the connections in which information is transmitted from one population of neurons to another. To simplify FPGA optimization, we set key dimensions (e.g., hidden layer sizes) to powers of two or multiples of four. This choice eases unrolling and data partitioning during HLS.

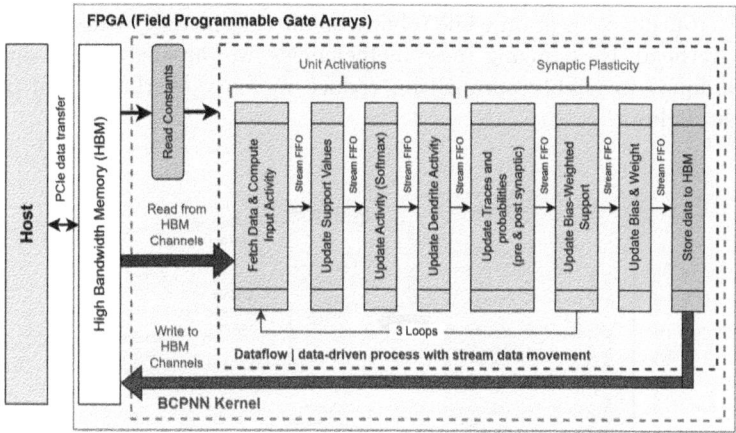

Fig. 2. Block diagram connection host to FPGA

Building on these structural decisions, we designed the BCPNN kernel as a stream-based, data-driven architecture, as shown in Fig. 2. Starting from a C/C++ specification, the HLS flow generates RTL that covers both unit activations and synaptic plasticity, which are the most computationally demanding. Although some routines in the BCPNN kernel depend on each other's outputs and thus execute sequentially, operations associated with separate populations and projections are inherently independent. This independence enables parallelization through multiple streaming pipelines.

Expanding on the range of functionalities, the complete kernel supports unsupervised, supervised, and inference modes, with or without structural plasticity. Although each mode reuses the same streaming pipeline, there is a key exception in the inference-only design. Inference does not require synaptic plasticity updates (weights, biases, and activity probabilities remain fixed), which reduces Block Random Access Memory (BRAM) usage and allows for higher clock frequencies. This inference-specific configuration is particularly beneficial for energy-sensitive edge deployments. Although the final kernel design takes advantage of parallel streaming and specialized inference-only configurations, this level of efficiency and resource utilization was not achieved in a single step. Our development process began with a straightforward sequential implementation. Starting from this initial baseline allowed us to identify bottlenecks in computation and memory access, paving the way for the subsequent optimization strategies described below.

Initial Unoptimized Sequential Implementation. As illustrated in Fig. 3, our initial implementation processed each sub-task sequentially. This approach wasted resources because the hardware allocated for other steps remained idle during the execution of the current step. It also introduced challenges in handling data: storing all data on-chip consumed an excessive amount of BRAM and led to routing congestion while relying on off-chip memory caused significant latency overhead. Recognizing these inefficiencies, we pursued several optimization techniques to enable parallelism, reduce memory overhead, and improve overall throughput.

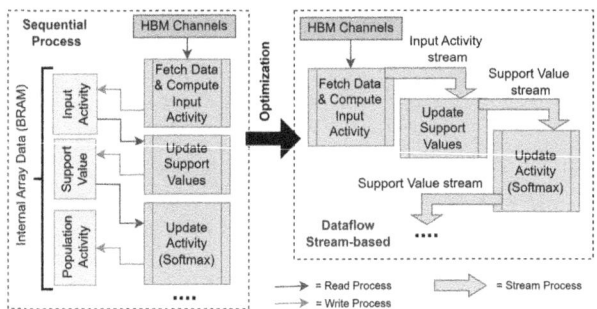

Fig. 3. Optimization from sequential process to dataflow stream-based

Optimization #1: Stream-Based FIFO Data. The first step was to adopt a stream-based data transfer model, where data elements are packaged into fixed-size segments and forwarded continuously through FIFOs. Rather than using static arrays in BRAM, we defined FIFO channels with a fixed depth to control data flow dynamically. We found that this approach reduces on-chip memory usage, mitigates routing complexity, and provides a foundation for task-level parallelism. However, streams alone are insufficient; we still need to break the sequential execution pattern.

Optimization #2: Dataflow Process. Dataflow directives in HLS enable task-level pipelining, allowing multiple sub-tasks to run concurrently as long as they are not interdependent. As shown in Fig. 3, each stage of the computation can begin processing as soon as partial data is ready, passing intermediate results through FIFO streams. This setup lets independent operations, such as those performed on different populations and projections, proceed in parallel, significantly increasing throughput. When combined with stream-based FIFOs, dataflow introduces backpressure to maintain synchronization, preventing writes when FIFOs are full and reads when they are empty. Certain operations, such as the softmax computation for updating activity levels, require waiting until all relevant data arrives. To avoid deadlocks and ensure every stage has the data it needs, we carefully size the FIFO depths. Figure 1 illustrates our systematic approach to determining optimal FIFO configurations without resorting to trial and error. By applying dataflow directives alongside stream-based data transfers, our BCPNN kernel achieved roughly 70% performance improvement compared to the initial sequential implementation.

Optimization #3: Spread Memory Mapping in HBM with Data Partitioning and Data Merging. As shown in Fig. 4, we further improve performance by leveraging multiple High Bandwidth Memory (HBM) channels through data partitioning and merging. Large arrays from the input-hidden projection layer (e.g., joint probability and weight data) are divided into four segments, and each is streamed to a separate HBM channel. On the FPGA, we use 512-bit burst reads, equivalent to fetching 16 floating-point values at a time from each channel. Although HBM natively supports 256-bit access, its higher frequency (450 MHz) allows this effective doubling to 512 bits at our lower clock rate (<300 MHz) [34]. The data from all four channels is then merged into a single stream packet of 64 floating-point values. Aligning indexing between pre-/post-synaptic activities allows these large packets to be processed in parallel using HLS unroll directives. For the hidden-output projection, we apply a similar burst-read strategy without partitioning, producing 16-value packets to maintain efficient data flow. Since the input-hidden and hidden-output projections operate in parallel, this optimization reduces latency by a factor of 64. A similar approach is used for write operations.

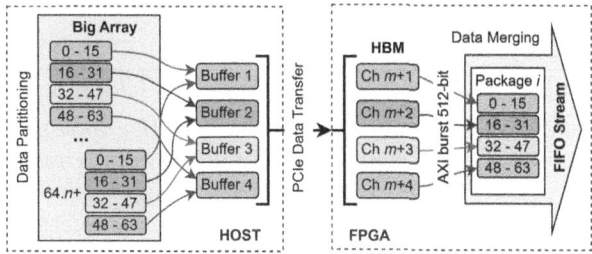

Fig. 4. Parallel HBM Access with Data Partitioning and Merging

4.2 Performance Analysis

We conducted an internal performance analysis to guide platform-specific optimizations. To accomplish this, we employ a roofline model that highlights bottlenecks and helps us refine the design for a given hardware. The Roofline Model [33] helps us visualize whether an application is limited by compute resources or memory bandwidth. It does so by plotting achievable performance (in FLOP/s) against arithmetic intensity (I, defined as the ratio of floating-point operations to bytes of data moved). On conventional architectures, if I is lower than the machine balance M_b, the application is memory-bound; otherwise, it is compute-bound [4, 10, 28].

Adapting this model to FPGAs is non-trivial. Unlike fixed architectures, an FPGA's theoretical peak compute performance C_{FPGA} depends on how many operations can be mapped onto its available resources and the operating frequency f_{imp}. We start with the number of available resources R_A and the resource requirement per operation R_O. The ratio R_A/R_O indicates how many such operations can run in parallel. Incorporating a utilization factor U_R^i (to account for routing congestion and practical limits, often around 80%), and the implemented frequency f_{imp}, we have:

$$C_{FPGA} = f_{imp} \times \min_i \left(\frac{R_A^i}{R_O^i} \times U_R^i \right) \tag{2}$$

If we focus on Digital Signal Processors (DSPs) and Look-Up Tables (LUTs) as the primary resources for floating-point operations, this simplifies to:

$$C_{FPGA} = f_{imp} \times \min \left(\frac{R_A^{LUT}}{R_O^{LUT}} \times U_R^{LUT}, \frac{R_A^{DSP}}{R_O^{DSP}} \times U_R^{DSP} \right) \tag{3}$$

Next, we determine the FPGA's memory bandwidth B_{HBM} by considering the HBM frequency f_{HBM}, data width W_{HBM}, and the number of channels Ch_{HBM}:

$$B_{HBM} = f_{HBM} \times W_{HBM} \times Ch_{HBM} \tag{4}$$

Finally, the machine balance M_b for the FPGA is given by:

$$M_b = \frac{C_{FPGA}}{B_{HBM}} = \frac{f_{imp} \times \min \left(\frac{R_A^{LUT}}{R_O^{LUT}} \times U_R^{LUT}, \frac{R_A^{DSP}}{R_O^{DSP}} \times U_R^{DSP} \right)}{f_{HBM} \times W_{HBM} \times Ch_{HBM}} \tag{5}$$

By placing our kernel's arithmetic intensity I on the Roofline plot and comparing it to M_b, we can determine if it is operating in a memory-bound or compute-bound region for our particular FPGA implementation. This helps guide subsequent optimizations, either by increasing arithmetic intensity (e.g., reusing data to reduce memory traffic) or by improving the resource utilization and frequency (to push C_{FPGA} closer to its theoretical peak).

Theoretical Performance and Bandwidth. In this work, we implemented the kernel with single floating-point precision, albeit future work can easily use other number representations with certain adjustments on data arrangement. The theoretical peak performance can be estimated by using a multiply-accumulation operation that consists of one addition and one multiplication. This method is similar to the evaluation in [4]. Based on the report resource utilization for floating-point by Xilinx [35] for our FPGA, the addition operation requires 192 LUTs and 2 DSPs, whereas the multiplication operation requires 74 LUTs and 3 DSPs. On the other hand, Xilinx Alveo U55C consists of 1146240 LUTs and 8376 DSPs. Therefore, the computation performance C for frequency implementation 100 MHz with an assumption utilization maximum of 80% is 288.77 GFLOPs/s. Moreover, the Xilinx Alveo U55C HBM has 32 pseudo channels with bit-width 256 and runs normally at 450 MHz. so the maximum bandwidth of HBM is 460 GB/s [34].

5 Experimental Setup

We implemented the BCPNN kernel with three distinct models, each with a different dataset and network configuration, to demonstrate its reconfigurability (albeit, nothing limits our framework for creating accelerators with other models). As shown in Table 1, these models differ in the input size, hidden layers, output classes, dataset scale, and unsupervised training epochs. The parameter *nactHi* defines the sparsity of the input for both with and without structural plasticity. We used a semi-unsupervised setup: the listed epochs are for unsupervised training, while supervised training runs once per configuration. MNIST comprises 28×28 grayscale images of handwritten digits from 0 to 9 [14]. The Pneumonia and Breast dataset are part of the MedMNIST dataset [36,37]. The Pneumonia dataset includes pediatric chest X-ray images and focuses on a binary classification task: distinguishing healthy (normal) cases from pneumonia-infected lungs [36]. The Breast dataset contains ultrasound images originally split into three classes (normal, benign, and malignant). In our binary classification, we used the dataset as provided by [36], where normal and benign cases were combined into a single positive category, and malignant cases were treated as negative. *This is the first time the BCPNN theory has been applied to pneumonia and medical breast use cases.*

Table 1. Model Configurations and Dataset Details

Model	Dataset	Input size	Hidden Layer		nactHi	Out	Data size		Epoch
			Hyper	Mini			Train	Test	
Model 1	MNIST	28×28	32	128	128	10	60000	10000	5
Model 2	Pneumonia	28×28	32	256	128	2	4708	624	20
Model 3	Breast	64×64	32	128	128	2	546	156	100

To benchmark performance, we deployed our BCPNN kernel on an AMD Xilinx Alveo U55C FPGA, using the AMD Vitis Unified software platform v2023.2 and Xilinx Runtime library (XRT) v2.16.204. For comparison, we ran equivalent CPU and GPU implementations with identical configurations. The CPU experiments were conducted on an Intel Xeon Silver 4514Y, compiled with g++ 11.4.0 and optimized using the -O3 flag on a single CPU core. For the GPU, we used Nvidia A100 and compiled it with CUDA 12.6.0 with optimization (-O3). We utilized the GPU node from the High-Performance Computer Alvis [1]. Moreover, we compared the three implementations in terms of latency, power, and energy. GPU power was recorded using the visualization tools provided by the Alvis cluster [1]. The FPGA measurements relied on real-time reporting through the XRT tool, ensuring accurate and direct observation of power usage.

Our reference implementation, written by domain experts, is in C/C++ with a CUDA backend for GPU acceleration. We modified the code to rely solely on the Bayesian Confidence Propagation (BCP) layer for supervised learning and selected model sizes that align both with FPGA resource constraints and dataset requirements. The GPU implementation was similarly optimized using standard techniques and restricted to a single GPU, ensuring a balanced comparison and a clear understanding of the efficiency gains offered by our FPGA-based solution.

6   Experimental Results

6.1   Correctness

As shown in Table 2, the FPGA implementation achieves virtually the same accuracy as the reference CPU and GPU versions, confirming that the stream-driven dataflow architecture preserves the correctness of the C++ reference code. Across all models, accuracy differences are negligible, typically fractions of a percentage point. These minor discrepancies are primarily due to compiler optimizations (e.g. `unsafe-math-optimizations`) and slight variations in random number generation. Such factors can introduce small floating-point rounding differences and nonidentical data sampling patterns compared to CPU and GPU platforms. Importantly, these variations do not affect the underlying BCPNN algorithm or its probabilistic learning rules. The FPGA-based accelerator still accurately replicates the intended model behavior. Moreover, the important takeaway is that the test accuracy for the Pneumonia and Breast dataset is comparable with the accuracy from the CNN-based models that are reported in [36]. Figure 5 shows the receptive field of one hypercolumn unit (HCU) and how it evolves with time, indicating that structural plasticity works as intended and in line with prior work [24] (Fig. 5).

6.2   Performance

Table 2 compares the performance of each model across CPU, GPU, and FPGA platforms, focusing on execution time, energy consumption per image, and average power usage. The FPGA implementation consistently achieves a lower average processing time per image (latency) for both training and inference compared

Table 2. Comparison of Model Implementations on Different Platforms (**infer**= inference only, **train**=w/training, **struct**=w/train+structural plasticity,**acc.**= accuracy, -=not available)

Model	Type	Metric	Unit	CPU	GPU	FPGA	Impr.(over GPU)
Model 1	Infer	Latency	ms	2.644	1.495	0.280	5.3x
		Energy/img	mJ	-	124.4	7.5	16.5x
	Train	Latency	ms	13.610	1.497	0.422	3.54x
		Energy/img	mJ	-	124.6	11.3	11.02x
		Total time	s	4302.9	572.2	314.9	1.81x
	Struct	Latency	ms	40.362	1.520	0.508	2.99x
		Energy/img	mJ	-	126.5	13.7	9.23x
		Total time	s	13286.8	621.6	473.9	1.31x
	Other	Train acc.	%	94.5	94.6	94.5	-
		Test acc.	%	94.6	94.5	94.5	-
		Power (W)		-	83.2	27.0	3.08x
Model 2	Infer	Latency	ms	4.721	1.633	0.504	3.24x
		Energy/img	mJ	-	146.6	14.2	10.32x
	Train	Latency	ms	27.4	1.646	0.552	3.03x
		Energy/img	mJ	-	147.8	15.5	9.53x
		Total time	s	2608.5	166.1	126.7	1.31x
	Struct	Latency	ms	55.258	1.631	0.609	2.63x
		Energy/img	mJ	-	146.5	17.1	8.56x
		Total time	s	5333.3	174.9	234.3	0.75x
	Other	Train acc.	%	91.5	91.0	91.5	-
		Test acc.	%	85.4	85.6	85.3	-
		Power (W)		-	89.8	28.1	3.19x
Model 3	Infer	Latency	ms	2.649	1.541	0.540	2.75x
		Energy/img	mJ	-	105.4	14.1	7.48x
	Train	Latency	ms	13.507	1.554	0.702	2.11x
		Energy/img	mJ	-	106.3	18.3	5.8x
		Total time	s	740.4	87.3	66.9	1.30x
	Struct	Latency	ms	38.319	1.556	0.690	2.26x
		Energy/img	mJ	-	106.4	18.0	5.91x
		Total time	s	2107.6	91.6	95.1	0.96x
	Other	Train acc.	%	89.1	89.7	89.7	-
		Test acc.	%	76.9	80.1	80.1	-
		Power (W)		-	68.4	26.1	2.62x

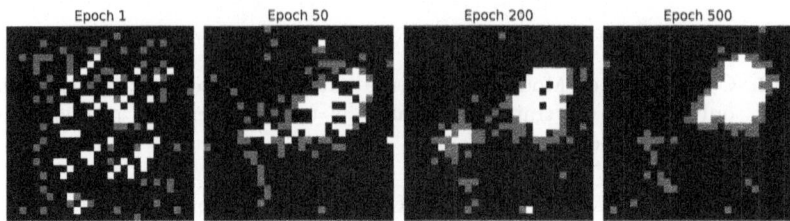

Fig. 5. Structural plasticity can modify HCUs receptive (or visual) field to extract the most information from the data. Here, we show how one receptive field in an HCU changes as a function of time from a random (left) to a more refined (right) field.

to the CPU and GPU in all the models. This reduction in latency translates to shorter total execution times, defined here as the sum of unsupervised training with the defined epoch, one epoch supervised training, and inference for training and testing data. However, the improvement in total time execution is less pronounced than that of the per-image latency. This is primarily due to overheads, such as data transfers between the host and the FPGA. Moreover, when structural plasticity is enabled, the system periodically computes the plasticity on the host, adding significant overhead. For smaller datasets, this computation occurs relatively more frequently, which explains why models 2 and 3 exhibit slightly slower overall execution times on the FPGA compared to the GPU in the structural plasticity configuration. In contrast, the FPGA still outperforms the GPU even when structural plasticity is enabled for larger datasets such as model 1.

In terms of power and energy consumption, the FPGA demonstrates a substantial advantage over the GPU. While the GPU draws between 68.4–89.8 W, the FPGA's power consumption remains around 26.1–28.1 W. Additionally, energy consumptions per image are reduced by factors ranging from 5.8x to 16.5x compared to the GPU. This combination of energy efficiency and competitive performance underscores the FPGA's suitability for energy-constrained environments. Consequently, the implementation of BCPNN in an FPGA with stream-based reconfigurable architecture shows promising potential for deployment in edge applications.

6.3 Analysis

Figure 6 illustrates the roofline model for three BCPNN variants, each implemented using a stream-based FPGA approach, both with and without structural plasticity. It provides valuable insights into their computational performance and memory access efficiency. Each model's peak (theoretical) performance is computed assuming up to 80% LUT and DSP utilization at the chosen operating frequency. It shows only the full version of BCPNN model implementation, which is the model that can handle training and inference.

None of the models achieve peak performance due to less than 80% resource usage and specific algorithmic constraints. The design process has optimized the flow of data with stream-based FIFO to make sure every resource will be maximally occupied during the operation. Using data partitioning for large arrays mapped to four pseudo-channels in the HBM helps push the BCPNN models closer to peak performance. However, because the BCPNN algorithm requires accumulation operations on certain arrays, the concurrency and, thus, overall performance is limited.

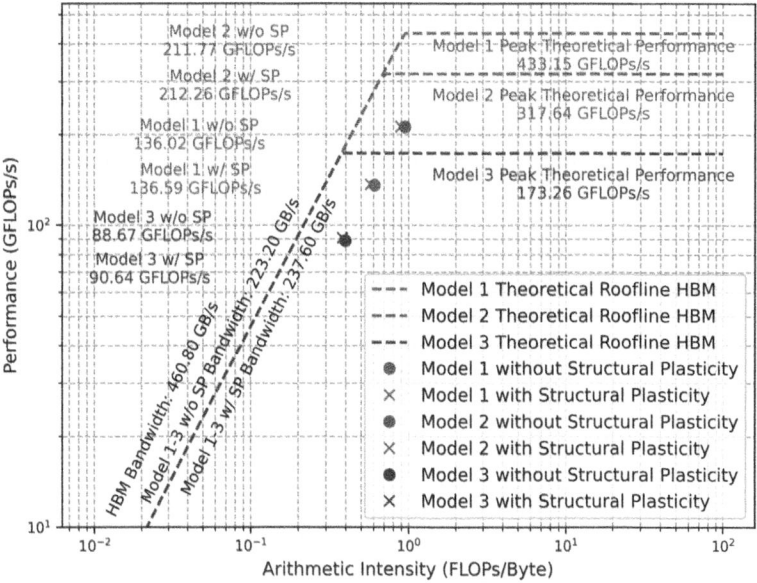

Fig. 6. Roofline model plot of our accelerators (for the different models), showing the performance (y-axis) as a function of arithmetic intensity (x-axis) for our accelerators, revealing how optimized our accelerators are (given theoretical upper limit).

The three models have distinct peak theoretical performances due to differences in their operating frequencies. Each model's measured performance is compared against its own theoretical maximum. Model 1 shows a lower measured GFLOPs/s than its theoretical peak relative to other models. This is because network configuration limits its concurrency and parallelism within the compute pipeline. In contrast, by doubling the number of mini-columns in the hidden layer, Model 2 maximizes parallelism and achieves performance closer to its theoretical limit. Although Model 3 shares a hidden layer size similar to Model 1, its larger input layer increases overall parallelism, allowing it to reach a performance closer to its peak. However, Model 3 also requires more hardware resources, which lowers its operating frequency and thus reduces its theoretical peak compared to the other models.

In summary, the FPGA-based BCPNN implementation balances resource constraints and computational efficiency through a dataflow streaming approach and memory partitioning strategies. While the FPGA may not always outperform a well-optimized GPU in total execution time for every model, it consistently delivers lower power consumption and often competitive or superior per-image processing rates. The roofline analysis confirms that while current optimizations have moved the design closer to its theoretical limits, some algorithmic and architectural constraints remain.

6.4   Resource Consumption

We evaluated the three versions (*Infer, Train, Struct*) of resource consumption of the BCPNN kernel from every model. *Infer* is an inference-only kernel. *Train* is a full-featured kernel supporting unsupervised, supervised, and inference modes but without structural plasticity. *Struct* is a full-featured kernel with structural plasticity. The inference kernel's reduced complexity enables higher operating frequencies and lower resource utilization. This design choice makes it suitable for edge applications, where hardware resources, power, and execution time are often constrained.

Table 3. FPGA Utilization (**infer**=inference only, **train**=w/training, **struct**=w/ train+structural plasticity)

	Version	LUT	FF	DSP	BRAM	Frequency
Model 1	Infer	174400 (15%)	257462 (11%)	550 (7%)	327.5 (18%)	200.0 MHz
	Train	454024 (40%)	546419 (24%)	3573 (43%)	437.5 (25%)	150.0 MHz
	Struct	475074 (41%)	574657 (25%)	3765 (45%)	473.5 (27%)	147.3 MHz
Model 2	Infer	177201 (15%)	261754 (11%)	644 (8%)	701.5 (40%)	160 MHz
	Train	459419 (40%)	488973 (21%)	3573 (43%)	862.5 (49%)	110 MHz
	Struct	479801 (42%)	513057 (22%)	3765 (45%)	898.5 (51%)	107.8 MHz
Model 3	Infer	180365 (16%)	259592 (11%)	640 (8%)	1419 (80%)	84.4 MHz
	Train	463580 (40%)	406798 (18%)	3573 (43%)	1568.5 (88%)	60.0 MHz
	Struct	481731 (42%)	430927 (19%)	3765 (45%)	1604.5 (90%)	60.0 MHz

Table 3 presents the FPGA utilization for the three models evaluated, offering a clear comparison of their resource demands. Among the three, the inference-only kernel stands out, consuming fewer resources and achieving higher operating frequencies compared to the full kernel. This highlights its effectiveness and suitability for edge application scenarios, where inference speed and hardware efficiency are critical. Notably, the addition of the structural plasticity feature introduces a slight increase in resource consumption, demonstrating the trade-off between utilizing the feature and resource efficiency.

7   Conclusion

In this paper, we introduced a reconfigurable stream-based FPGA accelerator for BCPNN, demonstrating its viability as a high-performance and energy-efficient platform for neuromorphic computing. *This accelerator is currently the most power-efficient and fastest single-node implementation of the BCPNN theory,* opening up opportunities in deploying BCPNN for use in edge computing use-case as well as exploring computational neuroscience aspects of the theory. We achieved substantial gains over CPU and GPU equivalent implementations by leveraging a range of optimizations, such as stream-based FIFO, dataflow parallelization, and strategic HBM channel partitioning. We evaluated our accelerator on three BCPNN model sizes using the MNIST, Pneumonia, and Breast Medical datasets. In all cases, the FPGA-based system maintained comparable accuracy while substantially reducing latency, power, and energy consumption. For example, on the MNIST dataset, the training time per image decreased from 1.497 ms on the GPU to 0.422 ms on the FPGA, while energy consumption for the train fell from 124.6 mJ to 11.3 mJ. Similar improvements were observed across the other datasets, underscoring the robustness and scalability of our design. Overall, our FPGA accelerator achieves speedups of 1.3x to 5.3x over an NVIDIA A100 GPU for total time execution in a full-featured kernel without structural plasticity while reducing power consumption by 2.62x to 3.19x and energy consumption by 5.8x to 16.5x. These results indicate that an optimized FPGA-based approach can extend BCPNN deployments into resource-constrained environments where power, energy, and latency are critical. By bridging neuromorphic principles with specialized hardware design, this work moves brain-like models closer to real-world applications in edge and energy-sensitive systems.

Acknowledgments. This work was funded by the European Commission Directorate-General for Communications Networks, Content and Technology grant no. 101135809 (EXTRA-BRAIN), the Swedish Research Council grant no. 2021-04579 (Building Digital Brains), and the Swedish e-Science Research Centre (SeRC). The computations were enabled by resources provided by the Chalmers e-Commons at Chalmers and National Academic Infrastructure for Supercomputing in Sweden (NAISS), partially funded by the Swedish Research Council through grant agreement no. 2022-06725.

Disclosure of Interests. The authors have no competing interests to declare that are relevant to the content of this article.

References

1. Alvis - C3SE. https://www.c3se.chalmers.se/about/Alvis/
2. Alzubaidi, L., et al.: Review of deep learning: concepts, CNN architectures, challenges, applications, future directions. J. Big Data **8**, 1–74 (2021)
3. Bate, A., et al.: A bayesian neural network method for adverse drug reaction signal generation. Eur. J. Clin. Pharmacol. **54**, 315–321 (1998)

4. Calore, E., Schifano, S.F.: FER: a benchmark for the roofline analysis of FPGA based HPC accelerators. IEEE Access **10**, 94220–94234 (2022). https://doi.org/10. 1109/ACCESS.2022.3203566
5. Citri, A., Malenka, R.C.: Synaptic plasticity: multiple forms, functions, and mechanisms. Neuropsychopharmacology **33**(1), 18–41 (2008)
6. Douglas, R.J., Martin, K.A.: Neuronal circuits of the neocortex. Annu. Rev. Neurosci. **27**(1), 419–451 (2004). https://doi.org/10.1146/annurev.neuro.27.070203. 144152
7. Douglas, R.J., Martin, K.A., Whitteridge, D.: A canonical microcircuit for neocortex. Neural Comput. **1**(4), 480–488 (1989). https://doi.org/10.1162/neco.1989.1.4. 480
8. Jia, Y.: Analysis of the impact of artificial intelligence on electricity consumption. In: 2024 3rd International Conference on Artificial Intelligence, Internet of Things and Cloud Computing Technology (AIoTC), pp. 57–60. IEEE (2024)
9. Johansson, C., Lansner, A.: BCPNN Implemented with Fixed-Point Arithmetic. Department of Numerical Analysis and Computer Science, Royal Institute of Technology, Stockholm (2004)
10. Mccalpin, J.: Memory bandwidth and machine balance in current high performance computers. In: IEEE Computer Society Technical Committee on Computer Architecture (TCCA) Newsletter, pp. 19–25 (1995)
11. Kalyan, K.S., Rajasekharan, A., Sangeetha, S.: AMMUS: a survey of transformer-based pretrained models in natural language processing. arXiv preprint arXiv:2108.05542 (2021)
12. Lamprecht, R., LeDoux, J.: Structural plasticity and memory. Nat. Rev. Neurosci. **5**(1), 45–54 (2004)
13. Lansner, A., Ekeberg, Ö.: A one-layer feedback artificial neural network with a bayesian learning rule. Int. J. Neural Syst. **1**(01), 77–87 (1989)
14. Lecun, Y., Bottou, L., Bengio, Y., Haffner, P.: Gradient-based learning applied to document recognition. Proc. IEEE **86**(11), 2278–2324 (1998). https://doi.org/10. 1109/5.726791
15. LeCun, Y., Bengio, Y., Hinton, G.: Deep learning. Nature **521**(7553), 436–444 (2015)
16. Lindemann, B., Müller, T., Vietz, H., Jazdi, N., Weyrich, M.: A survey on long short-term memory networks for time series prediction. Procedia Cirp **99**, 650–655 (2021)
17. Liu, L., et al.: A FPGA-based hardware accelerator for bayesian confidence propagation neural network. In: 2020 IEEE Nordic Circuits and Systems Conference (NorCAS), pp. 1–6 (2020). https://doi.org/10.1109/NorCAS51424.2020.9265129
18. Maass, W.: Networks of spiking neurons: the third generation of neural network models. Neural Netw. **10**(9), 1659–1671 (1997)
19. Mountcastle, V.B.: The columnar organization of the neocortex. Brain: J. Neurol. **120**(4), 701–722 (1997)
20. Nane, R., et al.: A survey and evaluation of FPGA high-level synthesis tools. IEEE Trans. Comput. Aided Des. Integr. Circuits Syst. **35**(10), 1591–1604 (2015)
21. Orre, R., Bate, A., Norén, G.N., Swahn, E., Arnborg, S., Edwards, I.R.: A bayesian recurrent neural network for unsupervised pattern recognition in large incomplete data sets. Int. J. Neural Syst. **15**(03), 207–222 (2005)
22. Podobas, A., et al.: StreamBrain: an HPC framework for brain-like neural networks on CPUs, GPUs and FPGAs. In: Proceedings of the 11th International Symposium on Highly Efficient Accelerators and Reconfigurable Technologies, pp. 1–6. HEART

2021, Association for Computing Machinery, New York, NY, USA (2021). https://doi.org/10.1145/3468044.3468052

23. Ravichandran, N., Lansner, A., Herman, P.: Unsupervised representation learning with Hebbian synaptic and structural plasticity InBrain-like feedforward neural networks. Neurocomputing, p. 129440 (2025). https://doi.org/10.1016/j.neucom.2025.129440

24. Ravichandran, N.B., Lansner, A., Herman, P.: Brain-Like approaches to unsupervised learning of hidden representations - A comparative study. In: Farkaš, I., Masulli, P., Otte, S., Wermter, S. (eds.) ICANN 2021. LNCS, vol. 12895, pp. 162–173. Springer, Cham (2021). https://doi.org/10.1007/978-3-030-86383-8_13

25. Ravichandran, N.B., Lansner, A., Herman, P.: Brain-like combination of feedforward and recurrent network components achieves prototype extraction and robust pattern recognition. In: International Conference on Machine Learning, Optimization, and Data Science, pp. 488–501. Springer (2022). https://doi.org/10.1007/978-3-031-25891-6_37

26. Schuman, C.D., et al.: A survey of neuromorphic computing and neural networks in hardware. arXiv preprint arXiv:1705.06963 (2017)

27. Sevilla, J., Heim, L., Ho, A., Besiroglu, T., Hobbhahn, M., Villalobos, P.: Compute trends across three eras of machine learning. In: 2022 International Joint Conference on Neural Networks (IJCNN), pp. 1–8. IEEE (2022)

28. Siracusa, M., et al.: A comprehensive methodology to optimize FPGA designs via the roofline model. IEEE Trans. Comput. **71**(8), 1903–1915 (2022). https://doi.org/10.1109/TC.2021.3111761

29. Svedin, M., Podobas, A., Chien, S.W., Markidis, S.: Higgs boson classification: brain-inspired BCPNN learning with StreamBrain. In: 2021 IEEE International Conference on Cluster Computing (CLUSTER), pp. 705–710. IEEE (2021)

30. Tully, P.J., Lindén, H., Hennig, M.H., Lansner, A.: Spike-based bayesian-hebbian learning of temporal sequences. PLoS Comput. Biol. **12**(5), e1004954 (2016)

31. Wang, D., et al.: FPGA-based HPC for associative memory system. In: 2024 29th Asia and South Pacific Design Automation Conference (ASP-DAC), pp. 52–57 (2024). https://doi.org/10.1109/ASP-DAC58780.2024.10473880, iSSN: 2153-697X

32. Wang, D., et al.: Mapping the BCPNN learning rule to a memristor model. Front. Neurosci. **15**, 750458 (2021)

33. Williams, S., Waterman, A., Patterson, D.: Roofline: an insightful visual performance model for multicore architectures. Commun. ACM **52**(4), 65–76 (2009). https://doi.org/10.1145/1498765.1498785

34. Xilinx, Inc: AXI high bandwidth memory controller LogiCORE IP product guide (PG276) (2022). https://docs.amd.com/r/en-US/pg276-axi-hbm/HBM-Topology

35. Xilinx, Inc.: Performance and resource utilization for floating-point v7.1. Tech. Rep. Vivado Design Suite Release 2023.2, Xilinx, San Jose (2023). https://download.amd.com/docnav/documents/ip_attachments/floating-point.html

36. Yang, J., Shi, R., Ni, B.: MedMNIST classification decathlon: a lightweight AutoML benchmark for medical image analysis. In: 2021 IEEE 18th International Symposium on Biomedical Imaging (ISBI), pp. 191–195 (2021). https://doi.org/10.1109/ISBI48211.2021.9434062

37. Yang, J., et al.: MedMNIST v2 - A large-scale lightweight benchmark for 2D and 3D biomedical image classification. Sci. Data **10**(1), 41 (2023). https://doi.org/10.1038/s41597-022-01721-8

38. Yang, Y., Stathis, D., Jordão, R., Hemani, A., Lansner, A.: Optimizing BCPNN learning rule for memory access. Front. Neurosci. **14**, 878 (2020)

Real-Time Multi-object Tracking Using YOLOv8 and SORT on a SoC FPGA

Michal Danilowicz$^{(\boxtimes)}$ and Tomasz Kryjak

Embedded Vision Systems Group, Computer Vision Laboratory, Department of Automatic Control and Robotics, AGH University of Science and Technology, Krakow, Poland
{danilowi,tomasz.kryjak}@agh.edu.pl

Abstract. Multi-object tracking (MOT) is one of the most important problems in computer vision and a key component of any vision-based perception system used in advanced autonomous mobile robotics. Therefore, its implementation on low-power and real-time embedded platforms is highly desirable. Modern MOT algorithms should be able to track objects of a given class (e.g. people or vehicles). In addition, the number of objects to be tracked is not known in advance, and they may appear and disappear at any time, as well as be obscured. For these reasons, the most popular and successful approaches have recently been based on the tracking paradigm. Therefore, the presence of a high quality object detector is essential, which in practice accounts for the vast majority of the computational and memory complexity of the whole MOT system. In this paper, we propose an FPGA (Field-Programmable Gate Array) implementation of an embedded MOT system based on a quantized YOLOv8 detector and the SORT (Simple Online Realtime Tracker) tracker. We use a modified version of the FINN framework to utilize external memory for model parameters and to support operations necessary required by YOLOv8. We discuss the evaluation of detection and tracking performance using the COCO and MOT15 datasets, where we achieve 0.21 mAP and 38.9 MOTA respectively. As the computational platform, we use an MPSoC system (Zynq UltraScale+ device from AMD/Xilinx) where the detector is deployed in reprogrammable logic and the tracking algorithm is implemented in the processor system.

Keywords: Multi-object tracking · MOT · Object detection · AI · SoC FPGA · FINN · YOLOv8

1 Introduction

Multi-object tracking (MOT) is one of the most important issues in computer vision, due to its key role in the perception systems of Autonomous Vehicles (AV), Advanced Driver Assistance Systems (ADAS) or Advanced Video Surveillance Systems (AVSS). It allows to predict the trajectories of moving objects, such as pedestrians around a car. Nowadays, most MOT methods are based on the tracking-by-detection paradigm: in the first step, the tracked objects are detected in the image, and in the second step, current detections are matched

© The Author(s), under exclusive license to Springer Nature Switzerland AG 2025
R. Giorgi et al. (Eds.): ARC 2025, LNCS 15594, pp. 214–230, 2025.
https://doi.org/10.1007/978-3-031-87995-1_13

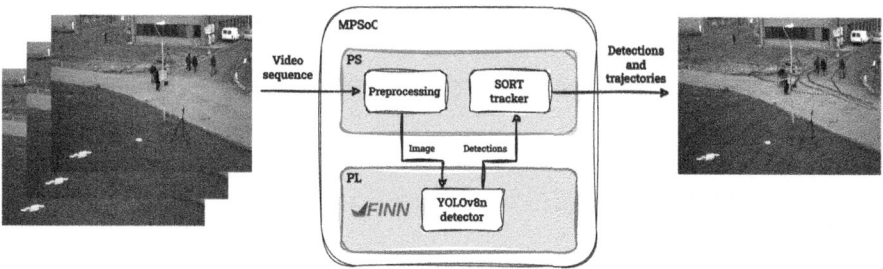

Fig. 1. Top-level diagram of our multi-object tracking system implemented in SoC FPGA.

to the history of the previously tracked objects. It should be noted that in the above scheme, the role of the detector is crucial – it is the element on which the final effectiveness of the algorithm largely depends. Moreover, this step it is usually also the most computationally and memory-intensive.

Currently, a deep neural network is usually used as the detection module. On the one hand, this provides good results, but on the other hand, it requires a powerful computing platform – e.g. a modern GPU (Graphic Processing Unit). If the MOT system is to be applied to, for example, mobile robotics, it needs to run on a suitable embedded platform with a limited energy budget. One of these are FPGA SoCs, for example Zynq UltraScale+ MPSoC (Multi-Processor System on Chip).

This paper presents the design and implementation of a hardware-software tracking system in an SoC FPGA device (Fig. 1). A quantised YOLOv8 object detector is trained on the COCO [16] dataset to provide the system with precise detections. It is implemented in the programmable logic (PL) using the FINN framework, which was adapted for implementation of the YOLOv8 architecture and to properly utilise external RAM for model parameters. For the tracking part of the system, the SORT (Simple Online Real-time Tracking) algorithm computed on the processing system (PS) of the SoC is used.

The main contribution of the paper can be summarised as allows:

- We present an implementation of a real-time, embedded multi-object tracking-by-detection system with modular hardware and software architectures as a baseline for future research. We have achieved detection speed of 195.3 fps.
- We emphasise the importance of a comparable evaluation of an embedded multi-object tracking system and evaluate our proposal on the commonly used and challenging MOT15 [14] and COCO datasets, where we achieve 38, 9 MOTA and 0.21 mAP respectively.

The reminder of this papers is organised as follows. Section 2 summarises previous work on multi-object tracking algorithms and their implementation in FPGAs. Section 3 describes the proposed algorithm. Section 4 presents the proposed computational architecture on the SoC FPGA device. Section 5 discusses the appropriate evaluation approach for embedded multi-object tracking systems and presents the results of detection and tracking quality of the proposed embedded tracker. Section 6 summarises the work and indicates directions for future research.

2   Previous Work

Multi-object tracking algorithms, due to their usefulness, are currently being intensively developed [2, 19]. As many solutions are currently being presented, there have also been many papers and challenges on datasets and metrics for MOT evaluation [3, 18, 21, 25]. What all solutions and challenges have in common, however, is that a multi-object tracking system needs as input a set of detections of objects of a specific class present in the scene. In challenges based on the MOTChallenge sets [6, 14, 22], the task is to track only pedestrians, while challenges using the BDD100k set [36] require tracking and classification of a total of eight object classes (pedestrian, rider, car, bus, truck, train, motorbike, bicycle). The detections in the MOT system are necessary to initialise the actual tracking algorithm, and many successful methods rely solely on the association of the input detections to the corresponding motion trajectories – so-called tracking-by-detection approach [23].

Hardware Implementations. Existing work on multi-object tracking on FPGA platforms often lacks a high-quality detector capable of indicating the presence and position of objects of a specific class. In papers [26–28], due to the absence of a detector, the systems cannot autonomously initialise the tracking algorithm, so they can only be used as some part of a larger perception system. In the work [8], only objects on which a special marker has been placed can be tracked. In the papers [11, 17], background modelling and subtraction algorithms are used for detection (so-called foreground object segmentation and detection). This method of detection, however, excludes its use in autonomous robots/vehicles, which require perception in a dynamically changing environment and in moving camera scenario. In addition, it is characterised by losing objects that stop moving, high detection noise and, by themselves, do not offer any object classification.

Some of the existing works, lack adequate evaluation of tracking and detection quality using standardised datasets and metrics, making it impossible to effectively compare a given solution with existing ones. FPGA implementations require certain trade-offs, like fixed-point computations or the use of a more compact neural network model, in the tracking algorithm and it is necessary to evaluate their impact on tracking quality. Without proper evaluation, it is difficult to draw conclusions about what platform, computing power and power consumption are needed to achieve the desired quality of an embedded multi-object tracking system. A further discussion on evaluation of embedded MOT systems is presented in Sect. 5.

Table 1. A summary of existing implementations of MOT systems in FPGAs.

Paper	Tracking speed	Detection algorithm	Tracking algorithm	Evaluation
2011 [26]	–	not included in the system, targets initialized by user	three algorithms that can be reconfigured in runtime: correlation tracker, brightest spot tracker, centroid tracker	not reported
2013 [11]	60 fps	moving object detection by background modeling and subtraction	particle filter per target	qualitative results on own sequences
2015 [28]	around 10 - 3 fps depending on the number of objects (10-50)	not included in the system, using previously generated regions	partition of bipartite graph representing targets and detections, based on region features like position and shape	not reported
2015 [17]	1.3 fps	moving object detection by background modeling and subtraction	Kalman filter per target	qualitative results on own sequences
2017 [8]	152 fps	color and shape recognition of predefined markers	targets are not distinguishable	precision and recall rates of 98% on own sequences
2019 [35]	11.1 fps	single-scale, 5-anchor YOLO with depthwise separable convolution backbone	a single detection with highest confidence score is considered a tracking output	IoU metric on a single object detection dataset DAC SDC [34]
2021 [10]	36.2 fps	SSD detector every N frames, trained on the VOC dataset	per-target KCF tracker between detection frames	single object tracking performance on OTB-10 dataset and detection performance on VOC
2023 [37]	91.65 fps	2-scale YOLOv3-tiny detector	Deepsort [33]	detection and MOT performance evaluated on chosen sequences using mAP and CLEARMOT metrics from the ua-detrac [32] dataset.
2023 [29]	45 fps	YOLOv4 detector	Deepsort [33]	detection and MOT evaluation not reported
2023 [27]	30 fps	not included	auction-based assignment algorithm	MOT performance evaluated on the MOT15 dataset
Ours	195.3 fps for detection, 24 fps for whole system	YOLOv8n detector	SORT [33]	detection and MOT performance evaluated on COCO, ua-detrac and MOT15 datasets using mAP and CLEARMOT metrics

The papers [10,35] contain a high quality detector, however, the effectiveness of the first system is only evaluated in terms of single object detection quality on the DAC SDC [34] set, while the second system is evaluated on the single object tracking set. It is therefore impossible to compare with these publications in terms of performance on a multi-object tracking task. In the paper [27], the authors do not present any evaluation of detection or tracking quality. They present a hardware implementation of the YOLOv4 detector and a similarity matrix calculation system for the Deepsort [33] algorithm. The paper, however, points out that there is no processor system to handle the hardware acceleration.

In summary, excluding solutions that are not complete MOT tracking systems, do not have a suitable detector and those that cannot be directly compared with due to the lack of MOT evaluation, only the work [37] should be considered a direct competitor of our proposal. The authors present an embedded MOT system based on the Deepsort algorithm, which uses a YOLOv3-tiny 2-scale detector. The processing speed allows real-time perception at 91.65 fps, and its multi-object tracking performance is demonstrated on three selected sequences from the UA-DETRAC [32] set representing traffic. In Sect. 5, we will present a comparison of our solution with the above. A review of existing solutions is summarised in Table 1.

3   The Proposed MOT Algorithm

As a baseline for our tracking system we have adapted the original implementation of the SORT (Simple Online Real-time Tracking) algorithm which was first presented in the paper [4]. The method utilises the Kalman filter, in which the prediction of the state of each tracked object obtained from a linear motion model is corrected by a measurement of the object's position obtained from the detector. The challenge is then to appropriately assign new detections in each image frame to the currently tracked objects. One of the simplest ways to solve this problem is to use the Hungarian algorithm, using the IoU (Intersection over Union) metric between detections and objects as the assignment weights. SORT is the basis for many of the more advanced methods (DeepSORT [33], BoT-SORT [1], ByteTrack [38]), and in itself offers very good tracking results at a relatively low computational cost.

3.1   Detector

The YOLOv8_n (nano) detector (3.2M parameters), which is one of the latest detectors in the YOLO (You Only Look Once) family, was used in this study. It is a representative of the one-step detectors "family", in which the convolutional features of the whole image serve as input to a box predictor, and the class membership classification and regression of surrounding rectangles is performed for each pixel. Unlike previous versions of detectors of this kind, YOLOv8 is an anchor-free detector, i.e. it does not require a predefined set of bounding boxes. Instead, a probability distribution is predicted for each of the four parameters of

the bounding box, the expected value of which is the result of the detection of
[15]. Another difference introduced in YOLOv8 is the use of a single joint representation score instead of separately predicting the probability of class membership and objectness score. The detector architecture is shown in Fig. 2. After
adapting the original implementation [12] for quantised training, the model was
trained on the COCO using the procedure discussed in Sect. 3.2.

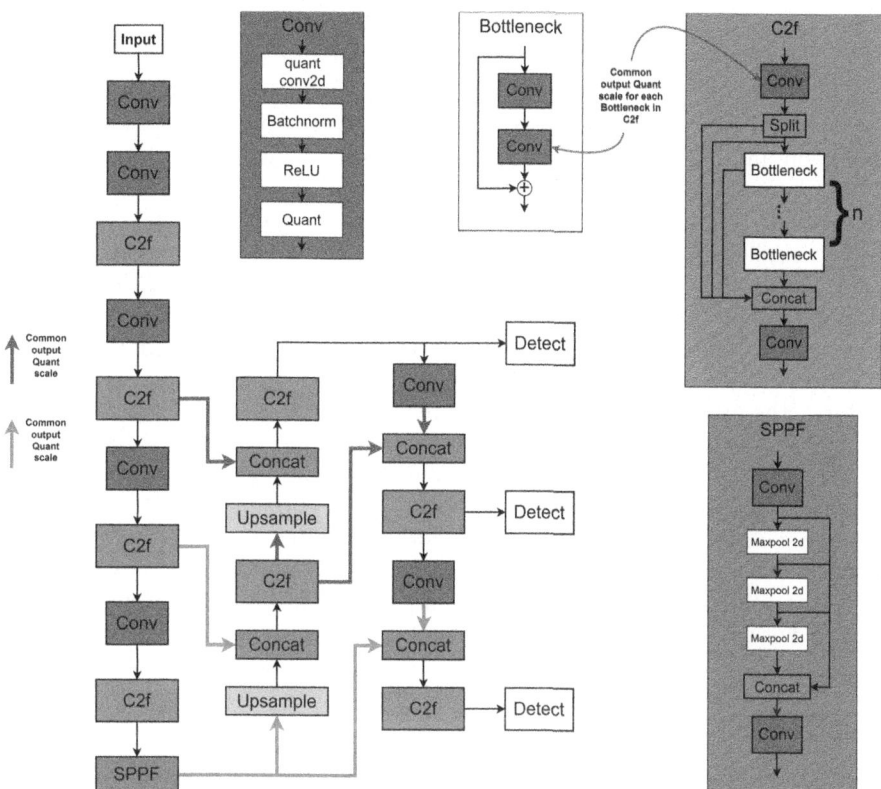

Fig. 2. Topology of the YOLOv8 detector used in the proposed MOT system. The `Conv`
block contains a quantised 2d convolution, batch normalisation, ReLU and activation
quantiser. Red arrows and green arrows represent two groups of quantised tensors,
that, each share a common quantisation scale. This was necessary to properly simplify
the computational graph – more details this in Sect. 4.1

3.2   Quantization

The implementation of such deep models in full 32bit floating-point precision
may not be possible on embedded platforms due to limited computational and
memory resources. For this reason, quantisation of parameters and intermediate
results (activations) to an integer representation with fewer bits is usually used.

A smaller number of bits saves resources for storing model parameters (or reading from external memory) and for multiplication and accumulation operations. In addition, operations performed on integers are much less complex than operations on floating point numbers. However, these savings usually come at the expense of accuracy [9,13].

The simplest approach is post-training quantisation, in which the parameters of a full-precision learned model are quantised to an appropriate representation before deployment. This approach usually gives worse results than including quantisation during training (so-called Quantisation-Aware Training, QAT) [13]. With QAT training, the model parameters are stored at full precision, however, during forward propagation, they are quantised with the input of each layer to the appropriate numerical representation before performing multiplication and accumulation operations. In this way, integer operations of the target platform are simulated. During back-propagation, full-precision weights are modified based on the gradients of the quantised operations.

The applied in this work QAT implementation uses the `Brevitas` library, which is a wrapper for the popular PyTorch library and supports the operations discussed above. It is important to remember to quantise the intermediate results after each convolution layer, as the operations of multiplication and accumulation of integers increases the number of bits for their representation.

First, the model was trained to full precision on the COCO set until convergence. An SGD (Stochastic Gradient Descent) optimiser was used with an initial learning rate of 0.01, which decreased to 0.0001 for 300 epochs. The input image was scaled to 320 pixels for the longer edge. Then, starting with the weights at full precision, the model was fine-tuned with quantisation enabled to 4 bits per weight and activation. During fine-tuning, a constant learning rate of 0.0001 was applied and the EMA (Exponential Moving Average) of all model parameters was tracked. For evaluation, the model was loaded with these averaged parameters.

4   Hardware Implementation

Since in the adopted multi-object tracking algorithm, the detection step is performed independently of the tracking result, it is possible to separate these tasks into the programmable logic (PL) and the processor system (PS) of the FPGA SoC device (Fig. 3). Preprocessing involves scaling the input image to the appropriate size and sending it via DMA to the accelerator in the PL. During postprocessing, the three feature maps obtained from the three detection heads are interpreted into boudning boxes, which are subjected to NMS (Non-Maximal Suppression) filtering. The SORT algorithm step is also regarded as a postprocessing step. The top-level diagram of the entire system is shown in Fig. 4.

4.1   FPGA Architecture

The FINN framework [30] was used to implement the detector architecture in the FPGA logic of the SoC FPGA device. It is a framework that includes Python libraries such as *finn-hlslib*, *finn-rtllib*, *brevitas* and *qonnx*. With FINN, it is

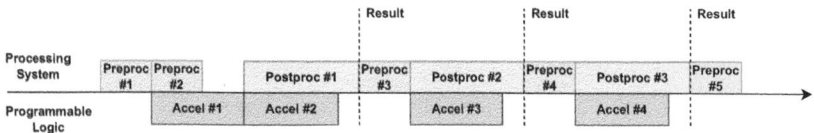

Fig. 3. Parallel task sharing between PS and PL in the SoC FPGA device. The length of tasks here is not precise, it only illustrates that the PL part is faster than the PS part in our case.

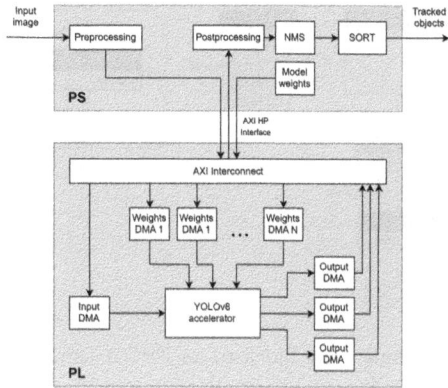

Fig. 4. Hardware-software system implemented in the ZCU102 SoC FPGA.

possible to conveniently perform operations on *qonnx* graph nodes such as moving some operation past another and folding repeated neighbouring operations into one. FINN also provides templates to call the appropriate *finn-hlslib* library function (or RTL module from the *finn-rtllib library*) for each node in the graph representation of the *onnx* model.

The following steps of the procedure for implementing the `conv` block used in YOLOv8 are shown in Fig. 5. Graph 5a represents a block imported directly from the Python code used for network training. The multiplication operation `Mul` results from quantisation and transforms an integer into a real-valued representation. The scaling factor of `Mul` depends on the adopted range of real numbers to be quantised and the number of quantisation thresholds ($2^N - 1$ for the uniform N bit quantisation used here). The `MultiThreshold` block implements the requantisation. The module performs three functions: it implements a quantiser; an activation function; and it allows to implicitly compute the preceding affine operation [31]. The input of the module is compared against a set of thresholds $T = \{t_0, t_1, \dots t_n\}$ and the output is the index of the smallest t_i that is bigger than the input. The calculation of an affine operation $ax + b$ can be omitted and implicitly performed by the `MultiThreshold` by substituting $t_i \leftarrow (t_i - b)/a$.

The `conv` block is decomposed into padding, context generation and matrix-vector multiplication operations (Respectively, `FMPadding_Batch`,

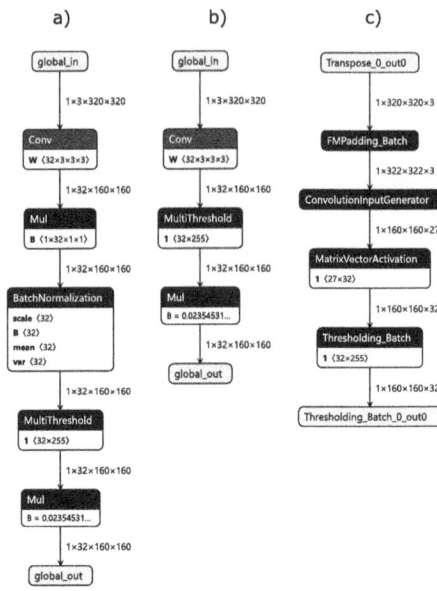

Fig. 5. Deployment of a single `conv` block to an FPGA using the FINN library. First, the block is loaded from *brevitas* code to graph representation **a)**. Then, affine transformations are collapsed into the MultiThreshold operation and the Mul node at the end can be moved past the following convolution in the network or delegated to postprocessing on the PS if this is the end of the accelerator **b)**. Finally, each node is represented by IP from *finn-hlslib* library (convolution is a sequence of padding, context generation and matrix multiplication) **c)**.

`ConvolutionInputGenerator` and `MatrixVectorActivation` blocks in Fig. 5c). The operation performed by the convolution layers is in practice a matrix multiplication operation (an example for a 2×2 convolution for a 2×3 input is shown in Fig. 6). The processed channels are interleaved, thus avoiding the caching of scalar products from individual input channels to be later summed to obtain a single output channel.

The balance between the degree of parallelization and the accelerator's resource consumption can be controlled by selecting the number of input channels processed in parallel (SIMD – Single Instruction Multiple Data) and the number of computational elements (PE). The rows of the filter matrix (Fig. 6) are distributed in parallel between the PEs (hence the number of output channels must be a multiple of the PEs), while the columns are distributed between the SIMD input lines (hence the number of input channels is a multiple of the SIMD).

The affine operations resulting from batch normalisation and quantisation can be directly moved past the convolution operation due to its linear nature. In blocks with skip-connections, like `C2f`, affine operations can be shifted behind the fork node by copying the node to the beginning of each branch. In the

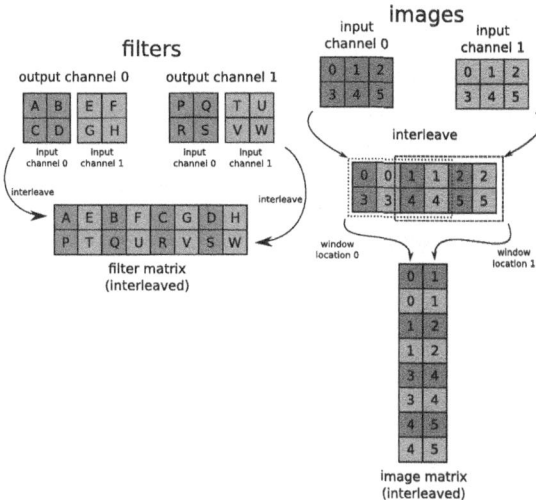

Fig. 6. The diagram shows the computation of a standard convolution of 2×2 with two input and output channels for an input of 2×3. Each row of the filter matrix corresponds to the weights needed to compute one output channel. In contrast, each column of the image matrix is composed of the input data located in one position of the filter context [20].

case of a join node behind a bottleneck block, the operations must be identical before being moved past the join. This condition was met by restricting the quantization scales of some activations to be the same during training. To be specific, in each C2f block, the scale of the quantised output of the first `Conv` block and the second `Conv` inside each `Bottleneck` need to be the same. For the same reason, some tensors at the highest level of the YOLOv8 topology also share common quantisation scale – denoted by the same colour in Fig. 2. These affine operations are moved down the computational graph until all have been removed from the graph by joining them with `MultiThreshold` nodes using method described earlier.

To enable acceleration of the YOLOv8 detector in the FINN framework, the library has been enhanced with the channel split operation `Split`, and the channel concatenation operation `Concat` has been updated to accept inputs with different data types. This situation occurs in the `C2f` block, where 4-bit activations from the `Split` block need to be concatenated with 5-bit activations from the `Bottleneck` block.

One of the challenges of the pipelined accelerator architecture used here is that certain adjacent operations in the pipeline – even though they have the same throughput – may not work fully efficiently. This is due to the fact that for certain operations (matrix multiplication, for example), the "producer" accumulates input data for a while and then wants to send a lot of output data in one burst. This burst may be too large to be read quickly enough by the "consumer", causing the pipeline to stop temporarily. To avoid this, a FIFO queue deep enough to accommodate the burst in question should be placed between the "producer" and the "consumer".

Another problem is the need to balance the parallel branches of the graph also by placing FIFOs with appropriate depths. This avoids deadlocks, in which one branch halts all processing before a stream addition operation because the data from the other branch is not yet ready (because the stream is halted). The appropriate FIFO depths needed for smooth accelerator operation are selected by placing deep FIFOs in front of each branch of the graph and then simulating to check the largest saturation of each FIFO. Our detector in the reprogrammable logic uses one static configuration for input image shape of 320×192 pixels.

4.2   Processing System

The processor part of the system receives data from the detector in the form of three feature maps - one for each detection head (Fig. 2). Each pixel location on those feature maps contains 84 channels - 4 for the regression of the bounding box, and the classification distribution for all 80 classes from the COCO dataset. The resulting detections are thresholded by the probability score and then subjected to non-maximum suppression filtering. The detections of the selected object classes are passed to the SORT algorithm. As the AMD PYNQ operating system was used on the SoC FPGA platform, it was possible to program the processor system in the Python language and using popular implementations of the Kalman filter and the Hungarian algorithm from the `filterpy` and `scipy` libraries.

It is also the task of the processor system to handle the DMA modules appropriately, as a dedicated DMA is assigned for each `MatrixVectorActivation` module to send convolutional layer weights. All filter parameters need to be sent by the DMA for each convolutional filter position on the input feature tensor.

5   Evaluation

For the evaluation of state-of-the-art MOT methods, the most commonly used datasets are MOT15, MOT16, MOT17 and MOT20 [2] using HOTA [18] and CLEARMOT [3] metrics. To isolate the impact of detector quality on tracking performance during MOT evaluation, the set of detections in each frame of the sequence is fixed for all algorithms tested. This is an evaluation using so-called public detections and, thanks to this approach, multi-object tracking studies can be focused on the association algorithm itself.

However, in practical MOT applications, it is necessary to take into account the presence of a detector in the system – especially in embedded systems, as the detection algorithm is responsible for the vast majority of the computational complexity of the entire system. It is also worth noting that the tracking algorithm is only able to predict the trajectories of those objects that the detector is able to detect – so-called private detections. For these reasons, in order to correctly infer the effectiveness of a given embedded MOT system solution against others, it is necessary to evaluate MOT on popular datasets from the MOTChallenge using private detections.

In addition to MOT evaluation using private detections, the evaluation of the stand-alone detector used in the system is also needed for a comprehensive analysis of the embedded solution. For some specific application of the embedded MOT system, it may be helpful to additionally train the detector on a set containing sequences representing objects under the conditions in which the system will ultimately operate [11,17,37]. However, reporting results on such datasets does not allow for an effective comparison of the system among state-of-the-art. In order to be able to absolutely assess the ability of a given system to detect the objects to be tracked, popular datasets such as MS COCO [16] should be used for evaluation and training. For evaluating detection quality, we use the primary metric in the COCO challenge - mAP (mean average precision). It describes detection precision averaged over all object categories and 10 IoU thresholds between 0.5 and 0.95.

The detector architecture shown in Fig. 2 was trained on COCOtrain and evaluated on COCOval, the results are summarised in Table 2.

Table 2. Detection evaluation of our quantized YOLOv8 detection on the COCOval dataset. 4w4a denotes 4 bits for weights and 4 bits for activations.

Model	Our full precision	Our 4w4a	Faster-RCNN [24] full precision	2018 [7] 8w8a
Hardware	CPU	FPGA	CPU	FPGA
COCOval mAP	0.28	0.21	0.21	0.20
Model size	96.4Mb	12.0Mb	1404Mb	25.5Mb

The well-known Faster-RCNN [24] two-stage detector and a sequential model of similar complexity implemented in FPGA in [7] are also listed for comparison. Faster-RCNN is used for generation of public detections used to evaluate state-of-the-art MOT algorithms in MOT Challenge. Note that the proposed detector achieves an mAP value of 0.21, which is at the same level as the more computational complex Faster-RCNN using floating-point computations and surpassed the result of [7] with 8-bit quantisation for weights and activations. However, with respect to the original floating-point model the drop in mAP is substantial – around 25%.

In competitions, the MOTA metric described by the Equation (1), is used.

$$MOTA = 1 - \frac{\sum_t (FN_t + FP_t + IDSW_t)}{\sum_t g_t} \tag{1}$$

It penalises the tracker for missed detections (FN_t), incorrect detections (FP_t) and a number of identity switches of tracked objects ($IDSW_t$) in each frame

t. The number of ground-truth objects in frame t is denoted by g_t. For the implemented 4-bit detector, an evaluation was performed on MOT15 set using CLEARMOT metrics. Although there are no FPGA implementations of MOT systems evaluated with such methodology, we can compare our results with the original, non-embedded implementation of the SORT algorithm with Faster-RCNN detector evaluated on the train split of the MOT15 dataset in [4]. We achieved combined MOTA of 0.389, while the baseline SORT is reported to reach 0.340. Existing state-of-the-art algorithms offer higher quality tracking; however, their computational complexity does not allow application to embedded real-time systems.

In order to compare with the work [37], an evaluation was performed on the same three sequences from the ua-detrac set. The results are presented in Table 3. We achieve comparable multi-object tracking quality using a significantly simpler MOT algorithm. The FPGA detection processing speed of our detector was 195.3fps for 300MHz FPGA clock. The performance was measured by clock cycles counting. The running time of the SORT and NMS algorithm on the PS ZCU102 limits the speed of the overall system to around 24 fps. However, there is still room for improvement, as the operations are currently implemented in Python.

Table 3. Comparison of tracking performance for the sequences using in the paper [37]. MOTA metrics are presented.

sequence name	MVI_40701	MVI_40701	MVI_40701
Ours	0.666	0.756	0.337
[37]	0.675	0.696	0.405

Qualitative results of our system for example MOT15 sequences are shown in Fig. 7.

Fig. 7. Visualized tracking result for TUD-Stadtmitte (left) and PETS09-S2L1 (right) sequences. MOT15 groundtruth is denoted by red and tracking output by green. (Color figure online)

The resource consumption of the implemented detector for 4-bit quantisation is shown in Table 4. The advantage of pipelined fine-grained architectures is the high processing speed due to the full parallelization of all operations during video stream processing.

Table 4. FPGA resources utilisation for the whole design with axi_interconnects and DMA modules and just for the detector. Absolute and relative to all available resources on the ZCU102 developement board. We also include utilisation reported in [37], where the relative utilisation is for Zynq-700 device.

	LUT	FF	BRAM	DSPs
Full design	205k (74.71%)	246k (44.94%)	421 (46.16%)	486 (19.29%)
Detector only	105k (38.24%)	72k (13.08%)	293 (32.13%)	482 (19.13%)
Work [37]	38k (22.2%)	43k (12.5%)	132.5 (26.5%)	144 (16.2%)

Disadvantages, however, include the high computing resource requirements for the DMA modules and the interconnect modules connecting them to the PS-PL AXI4 bus of the SoC. This applies in the case of using the RAM of the processor system to store the weights of the detector in reprogrammable logic as in this work. Due to the need to place FIFO queues in the pipeline (for reasons described in Sect. 4.1 and the need to requantise the activation after each convolution, the depth of the model also translates into a direct increase in memory resource requirements (BRAM, LUTRAM).

6 Conclusion

This paper presents a multi-object tracking system implemented on a heterogeneous SoC FPGA device. The FINN library was used to implement the 4-bit quantised YOLOv8 nano detector architecture in reprogrammable logic, which was adapted to support external memory for storing the model parameters. Thanks to FINN's modular fine-grained accelerator architecture, the resources allocated to individual operations can be selected. For example, the way the parameters are stored (BRAM, URAM – only for the Zynq UltraScale+ devices, LUTRAM or external memory) for the MultiThreshold, MatrixVectorActivation modules or the way multiplication and accumulation (LUT, DSP) are implemented for the MatrixVectorActivation module. The degree of computational parallelization can also be selected depending on the hardware platform chosen. To save memory resources, the requantisation operation MultiThreshold (which accounts for around 35% BRAM utilisation) could be implemented by multiplication using DSP resources which are currently underutilised (Table 4). This will be part of the future work which would enable targeting smaller devices.

In addition to external memory management, the SORT algorithm was implemented in the processor system, which forms the basis of multi-object tracking algorithms using tracking-by-detection paradigm. We achieve state-of-the art detection and tracking quality at high processing speed of the detector accelerator - 195.3 fps. This speed overhead could be utilised for processing bigger images for even higher detection quality. Python implementation of the software being run on the processing system will be optimised in the future work.

The tracking algorithm in the processor system can be extended with more sophisticated association mechanisms based on the appearance features of the objects [33] or use correlation filters [5] to predict the trajectory if the detection of the tracked object fails. The additional computation resulting from the network computing embeddings or correlation filter responses can then also be accelerated in reprogrammable logic.

References

1. Aharon, N., Orfaig, R., Bobrovsky, B.Z.: Bot-sort: robust associations multi-pedestrian tracking (2022). https://arxiv.org/abs/2206.14651
2. Bashar, M., Islam, S., Hussain, K.K., Hasan, M.B., Rahman, A.B.M.A., Kabir, M.H.: Multiple object tracking in recent times: a literature review (2022)
3. Bernardin, K., Stiefelhagen, R.: Evaluating multiple object tracking performance: the clear mot metrics (2008)
4. Bewley, A., Ge, Z., Ott, L., Ramos, F., Upcroft, B.: Simple online and realtime tracking. In: 2016 IEEE International Conference on Image Processing (ICIP). IEEE (2016). https://doi.org/10.1109/icip.2016.7533003
5. Danilowicz, M., Kryjak, T.: Real-time embedded object tracking with discriminative correlation filters using convolutional features. In: Gan, L., Wang, Y., Xue, W., Chau, T. (eds.) Applied Reconfigurable Computing. Architectures, Tools, and Applications, pp. 166–180. Springer Nature Switzerland, Cham (2022). https://doi.org/10.1007/978-3-031-19983-7_12
6. Dendorfer, P., et al.: Mot20: a benchmark for multi object tracking in crowded scenes. arXiv:2003.09003cs (2020). http://arxiv.org/abs/1906.04567, arXiv:2003.09003
7. Fan, H., et al.: A real-time object detection accelerator with compressed SSDLite on FPGA. In: 2018 International Conference on Field-Programmable Technology (FPT), pp. 14–21 (2018). https://doi.org/10.1109/FPT.2018.00014
8. Irwansyah, A., Ibraheem, O.W., Hagemeyer, J., Porrmann, M., Rueckert, U.: FPGA-based multi-robot tracking. J. Parallel Distrib. Comput. **107**, 146–161 (2017). https://doi.org/10.1016/j.jpdc.2017.03.008, https://www.sciencedirect.com/science/article/pii/S0743731517300965
9. Jacob, B., et al.: Quantization and training of neural networks for efficient integer-arithmetic-only inference. CoRR abs/1712.05877 (2017). http://arxiv.org/abs/1712.05877
10. Ji, Q., Dai, C., Hou, C., Li, X.: Real-time embedded object detection and tracking system in Zynq SoC. EURASIP J. Image Video Process. **2021**(1), 1–16 (2021). https://doi.org/10.1186/s13640-021-00561-7
11. Jin, J., Lee, S., Jeon, B., Nguyen, T.T., Jeon, J.W.: Real-time multiple object centroid tracking for gesture recognition based on FPGA. ICUIMC 2013, Association for Computing Machinery, New York, NY, USA (2013). https://doi.org/10.1145/2448556.2448636, https://doi.org/10.1145/2448556.2448636
12. Jocher, G., Qiu, J., Chaurasia, A.: Ultralytics YOLO (2023). https://github.com/ultralytics/ultralytics

13. Krishnamoorthi, R.: Quantizing deep convolutional networks for efficient inference: a whitepaper. CoRR abs/1806.08342 (2018). http://arxiv.org/abs/1806.08342
14. Leal-Taixé, L., Milan, A., Reid, I.D., Roth, S., Schindler, K.: Motchallenge 2015: towards a benchmark for multi-target tracking. CoRR abs/1504.01942 (2015). http://arxiv.org/abs/1504.01942
15. Li, X., et al.: Generalized focal loss: learning qualified and distributed bounding boxes for dense object detection. CoRR abs/2006.04388 (2020). https://arxiv.org/abs/2006.04388
16. Lin, T.Y., et al.: Microsoft coco: Common objects in context (2015)
17. Liu, W., Chen, H., Ma, L.: Moving object detection and tracking based on ZYNQ FPGA and arm SOC. In: IET International Radar Conference 2015, pp. 1–4 (2015). https://doi.org/10.1049/cp.2015.1356
18. Luiten, J., et al.: Hota: a higher order metric for evaluating multi-object tracking (2021)
19. Luo, W., Xing, J., Milan, A., Zhang, X., Liu, W., Kim, T.K.: Multiple object tracking: a literature review. Artif. Intell. **293**, 103448 (2021). https://doi.org/10.1016/j.artint.2020.103448, http://dx.doi.org/10.1016/j.artint.2020.103448
20. Machura, M., Danilowicz, M., Kryjak, T.: Embedded object detection with custom LittleNet, FINN and Vitis AI DCNN accelerators. J. Low Power Electron. Appl. **12**(2) (2022). https://doi.org/10.3390/jlpea12020030, https://www.mdpi.com/2079-9268/12/2/30
21. Manohar, V., Soundararajan, P., Raju, H., Goldgof, D., Kasturi, R., Garofolo, J.: Performance evaluation of object detection and tracking in video. In: Narayanan, P.J., Nayar, S.K., Shum, H.-Y. (eds.) ACCV 2006. LNCS, vol. 3852, pp. 151–161. Springer, Heidelberg (2006). https://doi.org/10.1007/11612704_16
22. Milan, A., Leal-Taixé, L., Reid, I., Roth, S., Schindler, K.: MOT16: a benchmark for multi-object tracking. arXiv:1603.00831 (2016). http://arxiv.org/abs/1603.00831, arXiv: 1603.00831
23. Rakai, L., Song, H., Sun, S., Zhang, W., Yang, Y.: Data association in multiple object tracking: a survey of recent techniques. Expert Syst. with Appl. 192, 116300 (2022). https://doi.org/10.1016/j.eswa.2021.116300, https://www.sciencedirect.com/science/article/pii/S0957417421016031
24. Ren, S., He, K., Girshick, R.B., Sun, J.: Faster R-CNN: towards real-time object detection with region proposal networks. CoRR abs/1506.01497 (2015). http://arxiv.org/abs/1506.01497
25. Ristani, E., Solera, F., Zou, R.S., Cucchiara, R., Tomasi, C.: Performance measures and a data set for multi-target, multi-camera tracking (2016)
26. Rümmele-Werner, M., Perschke, T., Braun, L., Hübner, M., Becker, J.: A FPGA based fast runtime reconfigurable real-time multi-object-tracker. In: 2011 IEEE International Symposium of Circuits and Systems (ISCAS), pp. 853–856 (2011). https://doi.org/10.1109/ISCAS.2011.5937700
27. Shemonaev, D., Gal, B.L., Jego, C., Besseau, A.: Implementation of an assignment algorithm for object tracking on a FPGA MPSOC. In: 2023 26th Euromicro Conference on Digital System Design (DSD), pp. 373–380 (2023). https://doi.org/10.1109/DSD60849.2023.00059
28. Strotov, V., Alpatov, B., Babayan, P.: The implementation of multiple objects tracking algorithm based on partition of bipartite graph in FPGA-based onboard vision systems (2015). https://doi.org/10.1117/12.2193882
29. Szántó, P., Kiss, T., Sipos, K.J.: FPGA accelerated deepsort object tracking, pp. 423–428 (2023). https://doi.org/10.1109/ICCC57093.2023.10178935

30. Umuroglu, Y., et al.: Finn: a framework for fast, scalable binarized neural network inference. In: Proceedings of the 2017 ACM/SIGDA International Symposium on Field-Programmable Gate Arrays, pp. 65–74. FPGA 2017, ACM (2017)
31. Umuroglu, Y., Jahre, M.: Streamlined deployment for quantized neural networks (2018)
32. Wen, L., et al.: DETRAC: a new benchmark and protocol for multi-object tracking. CoRR abs/1511.04136 (2015). http://arxiv.org/abs/1511.04136
33. Wojke, N., Bewley, A., Paulus, D.: Simple online and realtime tracking with a deep association metric (2017)
34. Xu, X., et al.: DAC-SDC low power object detection challenge for UAV applications. CoRR abs/1809.00110 (2018). http://arxiv.org/abs/1809.00110
35. Yang, L., He, Z., Fan, D.: Binarized depthwise separable neural network for object tracking in FPGA. In: Proceedings of the 2019 on Great Lakes Symposium on VLSI, pp. 347-350. GLSVLSI 2019, Association for Computing Machinery, New York, NY, USA (2019). https://doi.org/10.1145/3299874.3318034
36. Yu, F., et al.: Bdd100k: a diverse driving dataset for heterogeneous multitask learning (2020)
37. Zhai, J., Li, B., Lv, S., Zhou, Q.: FPGA-based vehicle detection and tracking accelerator. Sensors **23**(4) (2023). https://doi.org/10.3390/s23042208, https://www.mdpi.com/1424-8220/23/4/2208
38. Zhang, Y., et al.: ByteTrack: multi-object tracking by associating every detection box (2022). https://arxiv.org/abs/2110.06864

Short Paper

Dynamic Function Exchange in FPGA to Redefine RISC-V Multicore Architectures at Runtime

Téo Sobrino Alves$^{(\boxtimes)}$ (iD) and Vanderlei Bonato (iD)

Institute of Mathematical and Computing Sciences, The University of São Paulo,
São Carlos, São Paulo, Brazil
{teo.sobrino.alves,vbonato}@usp.br
https://www.icmc.usp.br/

Abstract. Dynamic Partial Reconfiguration is a powerful feature available in some FPGAs that enables the reconfiguration of specific regions within the FPGA fabric without halting the whole system. This capability opens new opportunities for more efficient utilization of the available FPGA resources since the hardware can be configured dynamically to better fit the demands of varying workloads. In this work, we investigate the Dynamic Partial Reconfiguration available from Xilinx/AMD FPGAs as Dynamic Function Exchange in multicore RISC-V systems, focusing on maximizing area utilization while minimizing execution time for a set of testbenches. This approach leverages the modularity of the RISC-V architecture that goes beyond the traditional customization provided by the RISC-V processor extensions. As a result for a testbench composed of CNN, Linked List, and Simplex Method, we could notice an improvement from 0.15% to 6% in execution time by dynamically reconfiguring the RISC-V in relation to the number of cores and configurations of each core regarding cache size and availability of FPU.

Keywords: DFX · RISC-V · Multicore

1 Introduction

Field-Programmable Gate Arrays (FPGAs) are extensively utilized as hardware accelerators in both academic research [4,21] and industrial applications [23]. A notable feature of modern FPGAs is Dynamic Partial Reconfiguration (DPR), also referred to by Xilinx/AMD as Dynamic Function Exchange (DFX). DFX facilitates the reconfiguration of predefined partitions within the FPGA fabric at runtime, without disrupting the operation of the entire system [3,18].

As the downscaling of the transistor is slowing its pace and the computational demands for edge computing, artificial intelligence (AI) and cloud-based systems are accelerating, the significance of area efficiency has become a key factor for the current hardware designs. For example, convolutional neural networks (CNNs) can be implemented directly on FPGAs as a hardware-based solution, and when

R. Giorgi et al. (Eds.): ARC 2025, LNCS 15594, pp. 233–243, 2025.
https://doi.org/10.1007/978-3-031-87995-1_14

available DPR can be exploited to dynamically adapt the network architecture to maximize resource efficiency [24].

However, FPGA-based designs are inherently more time-consuming, expensive, and complex to develop, debug, and maintain compared to ordinary software solutions [19]. A potential compromise lies in adopting general-purpose architectures capable of adapting to varying workloads. Such architectures enable development to remain primarily software-oriented while preserving efficiency in terms of resource utilization.

The emergence of open architectures such as RISC-V introduces new opportunities for dynamic reconfiguration. The customizable nature of RISC-V's instruction set architecture (ISA) and it's open microarchitecture are particularly appealing for exploring reconfigurable systems as pointed out by [15]. In this work, we investigate the impact of architectural reconfiguration on the performance and area efficiency of a RISC-V multicore system. Specifically, we examine the effects of varying the availability of Floating Point Units (FPUs), cache sizes, and the number of cores on execution time and resource utilization.

2   Related Work

This section outlines key research in the application of DPR to soft-core processors, highlighting their use as flexible accelerators and their integration into main processing units.

The use of soft-core co-processors as runtime-reconfigurable accelerators represents a compelling application of dynamic reconfiguration. Studies such as [5,10] demonstrate this approach effectively. Both works employ RISC-V-based soft cores as runtime-customizable accelerators, achieving reductions in execution time and energy consumption.

In addition to using soft cores as accelerators, a promising direction involves utilizing RISC-V cores as actuators for dynamic reconfiguration. This concept is explored in [6], where RISC-V cores are employed to reconfigure coupled accelerators. The study highlights the performance benefits of this approach, leveraging new processor instructions specifically designed for reconfiguration tasks.

Applying dynamic reconfiguration directly to main processors is not a novel concept but remains an area of active research. For instance, [17] focuses on resource optimization in soft-core processors through dynamic reconfiguration, while [15] exploits DPR to integrate specialized accelerators. The latter demonstrates notable improvements in area utilization and energy efficiency, showcasing the potential of reconfigurable architectures for optimized resource management.

Further advancing this concept, [7] introduces a customizable instruction set architecture (ISA) using Dynamic Partial reconfiguration, enabling the dynamic modification of core capabilities at runtime. This approach illustrates the potential for creating adaptable processing units tailored to specific workloads.

A critical challenge associated with dynamic reconfiguration is determining the optimal timing for reconfiguration. This issue is addressed in [2], which employs a machine learning algorithm to identify the most opportune moments for reconfiguring accelerators in RISC-V cores. This method demonstrates the potential of intelligent decision-making frameworks to enhance the performance and efficiency of reconfigurable systems.

There are also alternative ways to address this issue, such as analyzing the workload, in order to dynamically schedule tasks to predefine the optimal moments of reconfiguration, as it was successfully done by [9].

3   Background

In this section, we provide a brief overview about DFX, FPGA framework, and the RISC-V processor employed in this work.

3.1   DFX

DFX is restricted to predefined partitions within the design implemented in the reconfigurable region of an FPGA. These partitions are referred to as Reconfigurable Partitions (RP). Each RP can host multiple predefined designs, known as Reconfigurable Modules (RM). A default RM is assigned to every RP, but each RP can support up to 255 additional RMs. Each RM is associated with a partial bitstream (a .bit file), which is stored on the FPGA and used to dynamically reconfigure only the respective RP.

Various methodologies exist for reconfiguring an RP [25]. In this study, we employed PYNQ, a framework developed by AMD that facilitates reconfiguration through the Internal Configuration Access Port (ICAP) [8]. PYNQ provides a high-level Python interface for managing reconfiguration and treats each RM as an instance of an overlay class [16]. Each overlay instance must be associated with its respective partial bitstream.

In this study, the ZCU104 Development Kit was utilized, which incorporates a Zynq UltraScale+ XCZU7EV FPGA for the Programmable Logic (PL) and a quad-core ARM Cortex-A53 processor for the Processing System (PS). The PYNQ framework operates on the PS and provides functionalities to monitor and control the design deployed in the PL.

3.2   BlackParrot Processor

The processor employed in this work is BlackParrot, an open-source, multicore processor designed for flexibility and scalability [20]. A high-level overview of the BlackParrot tile, showcasing the integration of both the processor cores and their associated peripherals in the multicore system can be found at [13], and a detailed depiction of the microarchitecture of a single BlackParrot core can be found at [12].

At the time of this work, BlackParrot was still under active development. A stable version supporting the RV64IMAFDMSU[1] ISA was used, enabling the processor to run a broad range of programs on Linux.

---

[1] Each letter represents an ISA extension. Their definitions can be found in [22].

For this study, some components of the BlackParrot processor were modified. These modifications included changes to the data and instruction cache slices, and the number of cores and FPUs interconnected via an NoC.

4   System Architecture

The system comprises implementations in both PL and PS, as depicted in Fig. 1. In the PL, a modified version of the BlackParrot soft processor has been implemented to support DFX. This processor consists of a static master core (not dynamically reconfigurable) and two to four reconfigurable worker cores. The master core operates on BlackParrot Linux [14], enabling it to oversee system operations, assign threads, and manage the context and usage of its worker cores.

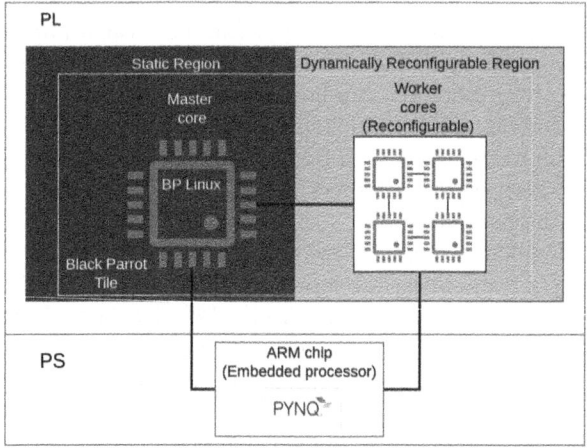

Fig. 1. Overview of the system architecture.

The PS hosts the PYNQ framework, which monitors specific metrics in the worker cores to trigger automatic dynamic reconfigurations. These triggers include cache hit rate, Floating Point Unit (FPU) utilization, and CPU usage (the number of instructions that each core has completed), all of which are accessible through register file reads from the BlackParrot worker cores. Heuristics for performing the reconfigurations were developed and are further elaborated in the results section. The process of automatic reconfiguration is illustrated in Fig. 2.

4.1   Designed Architectures

As previously discussed, RPs and their associated RMs must be predefined. In this system, the RP encompasses the entirety of the worker cores. This choice

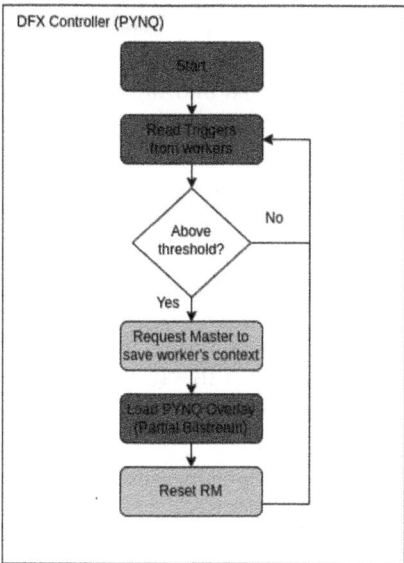

Fig. 2. Flowchart representing the process of automatic DFX. Darker gray represent activities performed by the PS, and lighter gray by the PL.

simplifies the design process and facilitates a shared resource view, enabling operations such as removing two FPUs across different cores with a single reconfiguration step.

While a more modular RP design could allow for greater architectural flexibility, it would significantly increase reconfiguration time, potentially offsetting its benefits, because multiple reconfiguration would be required in order to make any significant change in the architecture. For the experiments, we configured the four predefined RMs as follows:

i)   Standard: three worker cores;
ii) Extra core with reduced FPUs: four worker cores, with only one core featuring FPU;
iii) Increased cache with one fewer core: two worker cores, each with one FPU, and a 35% cache size increase;
iv) Increased cache with reduced FPUs: three worker cores with a 41% cache size increase and FPUs removed from two cores.

Architecture (i) represents the baseline, a three worker-core BlackParrot system, that performs no reconfiguration, suffers no overhead and is therefore the standard static architecture.

The rationale for Architecture (ii) stems from the observation that FPU utilization can often be minimal or even nonexistent across certain workloads. By removing two out of the three FPUs in the worker cores, the system retains compatibility with the ISA while optimizing resource usage by reducing unused logic area. The addition of an extra core to replace the FPUs is advantageous in scenarios where parallelization is feasible, where the workload can benefit from high utilization of multiple cores and minimal floating point computation is required, as it is common practice in some embedded applications such as CNNs [11].

For Architecture (iii), the design targets the opposite scenario. This config-uration is optimized for programs that heavily utilize the FPU, have significant cache demands, and exhibit lower overall core utilization.

Architecture (iv) is designed for scenarios characterized by high cache and CPU usage but minimal FPU requirements.

These architectures plus the master core utilize approximately 63% of the total FPGA area, as summarized in Table 1. Note that no testbench computa-tions are performed in the master core.

Table 1. Area usage for all the possible architectures, including the master core. LRAM stands for LUT RAM, and BR for Block RAM.

Area usage										
Config	Cores	FPUs	L1 Cache	LUTs	LRAMs	FFs	BR36	BR18	DSP48	Total Area (%)
i	4	4	4932	68.412	2.750	26.820	12	250	24	63.3
ii	5	3	6156	70.514	2.902	26.034	15	312	24	63.4
iii	3	3	6660	61.419	1.314	29.817	9	352	28	63.1
iv	4	3	7002	65.596	1.789	31.009	12	365	26	63.2
Available (total)	–	–	–	230.400	–	460.800	336	672	1728	100

5   Results

This section presents the adopted testbenches and the results obtained from three execution approaches, as follows:

1. Separate execution with fixed reconfiguration: each testbench was executed individually with a fixed reconfiguration applied shortly after the program began;
2. Joint execution with fixed reconfiguration: all testbenches were executed sequentially within a single binary file, with a fixed reconfiguration applied shortly after the start of each program;
3. Joint execution with automatic reconfiguration: all testbenches were exe-cuted sequentially within a single binary file, with reconfiguration determined dynamically using a heuristic-based approach to optimize the reconfiguration timing.

   Context saving is critical to ensuring the correctness of execution during reconfiguration. However, since the time required for context saving is two orders of magnitude smaller than the reconfiguration time, it was excluded from the time measurements presented in the next sections.

5.1 Testbenches

The selected testbenches were a Convolutional Neural Network (CNN), a doubly linked list, and a linear programming Simplex solver.

CNN was selected due to its high cache usage, potential for parallelization, and absence of FPU usage (the implemented version employs fixed-point arithmetic). A pre-trained CNN with 5 layers was evaluated using the MNIST dataset.

Doubly linked list has poor cache efficiency, and it was configured to create a doubly linked list with 300k nodes performing 50k random insertions and deletions.

Finally, Simplex solver has a significant FPU usage, and it was set to solve a linear problem involving 517 variables and 302 constraints[2].

5.2 Individual Testbenches Running on Fixed Reconfiguration

This analysis involved applying a single, predefined reconfiguration to each possible architecture at an early stage of execution for each testbench, in order to force and observe how the system would behave under each architectural possibility. The results are summarized in Tables 2, 3, and 4, showing the total execution time and the cache hit rate.

Table 2. Execution time and cache hit for CNN testbench.

CNN TB				
Config	Exec Time (ms)	Rec Time (ms)	Total time (ms)	Cache Hit (%)
i	3,991.949	0	3,991.949	65
ii	3,784.713	12.218	3,796.931	63
iii	3,785.466	11.127	3,797.593	82
iv	3,543.320	12.510	3,555.830	83

Table 3. Execution time and cache hit for double linked list testbench.

Double Linked List TB				
Config	Exec_Time (ms)	Rec_Time (ms)	Total_time (ms)	Cache_Hit (%)
i	567.301	0	567.301	34
ii	439.845	12.218	452.064	33
iii	598.057	11.127	609.180	29
iv	575.219	12.510	587.731	37

---

[2] Problem named agg2, available at https://www.netlib.org/lapack/index.html.

Table 4. Execution time and cache hit for Simplex testbench.

Simplex TB				
Config	Exec Time (ms)	Rec Time (ms)	Total time (ms)	Cache Hit (%)
i	1,493.372	0	1,493.372	57
ii	1,517.229	12.219	1,829.448	56
iii	1,343.487	11.125	1,354.612	78
iv	1,709.986	12.508	1,702.494	79

The results indicate that not single configuration outperformed all others for every testbench, underscoring the importance of flexibility for heterogeneous workloads.

For the CNN testbench, the hardware configuration (iv) was the best performer, likely due to the high data locality and temporal cache access patterns inherent to CNN workloads. The removal of one core reduced cache contention, resulting in fewer cache misses and better execution time.

While for the doubly linked list, configuration (ii) performed best, as the addition of an extra core fully exploited the parallelizable nature of the workload. The standard cache size introduced only a minimal penalty for cache misses, which dominate memory access patterns in this program.

Finally, for Simplex solver, configuration (iii) outperformed others due to the availability of FPUs in all worker cores and its ability to maintain a high cache hit rate. Configurations (i) and (ii) suffered from limited cache availability, while (iv) exhibited reduced performance due to having only one FPU across the worker cores.

5.3 Joint Testbenches Running on Fixed Reconfiguration

In this analysis, a single, predefined reconfiguration was applied to each architecture and the entire joint testbenches was run. The results are summarized in Table 5. The reconfigurable architectures (iii) and (iv) outperformed the static architecture (i), demonstrating their ability to adapt to specific workload requirements and achieve better performance on tasks like CNN and Simplex solver workloads, that accounted for the majority of execution time.

5.4 Automatic Reconfiguration for Heterogeneous Applications

This analysis used automatic reconfiguration based on the flowchart presented in Fig. 2. We defined the following heuristic: if the cache hit rate exceeds 50%, FPU usage is below 40%, and CPU usage is above 60%, reconfigure to (ii); if the cache hit rate is below 40%, FPU usage exceeds 40%, and CPU usage is below 60%, reconfigure to (iii); and, if both the cache hit rate and FPU usage are below 40%, reconfigure to (iv), regardless of CPU usage.

Table 5. Execution time and cache hit for joint testbenches.

Joint TB				
Config	Exec Time (ms)	Rec Time (ms)	Total time (ms)	Cache Hit (%)
i	6,052.622	0	6,052.622	60
ii	6,341.787	12.218	6,354.005	58
iii	5,727.010	11.125	5,738.135	79
iv	5,828.525	12.508	5,841.033	79

This automatic configuration is identified as (v). The testbench consisted of the three workloads, put sequentially and compiled into a single binary. The results are presented in Table 6.

Table 6. Execution time and cache hit for joint testbench.

Full TB				
Config	Exec Time (ms)	Rec Time (ms)	Total time (ms)	Cache Hit (%)
i	6.052,622	0,000	6.052,622	60
v	5.693,151	35,855	5.729,006	69

The reconfiguration (v), by employing the described heuristic achieved the best overall performance, with a 5.3% improvement over the static architecture (i), despite requiring three reconfigurations during execution.

6 Conclusion

This work aimed to explore the potential of reconfigurable multicore systems to balance flexibility and processing power, enabling efficient performance across heterogeneous workloads by leveraging DFX for dynamic system reconfiguration. For the chosen testbenches, the results demonstrated that reconfigurable architectures can provide processing time gain over static ones. For heterogeneous workloads, multiple reconfigurations proved effective, illustrating that no single architecture could match the performance of a system dynamically reconfigured to adapt to workload changes. It is important to notice that the advantage of using dynamic hardware reconfiguration may not be present if the total application execution time is too small to overcome the reconfiguration overhead and the application demands for hardware are too similar between different applications or between application execution stages.

Future work could explore additional configurations, necessitating a deeper investigation into the heuristics for reconfiguration. Moreover, varying levels of modularity for the RPs could also be examined to further enhance flexibility and efficiency.

All code developed in this work and results obtained should be reproductible using the files available here [1].

Acknowledgments. This study was financed in part by the São Paulo Research Foundation (FAPESP), Brazil, process number 2023/15719-2. I also would like to thank Dan Petrisko who helped me to better understand the BlackParrot processor.

References

1. Alves,   T.S.:   Github   repository.   https://github.com/TeOSobrino/IC_code. Accessed 21 Dec 2024
2. Angioli, M., Barbirotta, M., Mastrandrea, A., Jamili, S., Olivieri, M.: Automatic hardware accelerators reconfiguration through linearucb algorithms on a RISC-V processor. In: 2023 18th Conference on Ph.D Research in Microelectronics and Electronics (PRIME), pp. 169–172. IEEE (2023)
3. Bendou, Y.: FPGA dynamic function eXchange. Ph.D. thesis, Politecnico di Torino (2020)
4. Bobda, C., et al.: The future of FPGA acceleration in datacenters and the cloud. ACM Trans. Reconfig. Technol. Syst. (TRETS) **15**(3), 1–42 (2022)
5. Castro, J.W.A., Morales-Villanueva, A.: Exploring dynamic partial reconfiguration in a tightly-coupled coprocessor attached to a RISC-V Soft-processor on a FPGA. In: 2021 IEEE XXVIII International Conference on Electronics, Electrical Engineering and Computing (INTERCON), pp. 1–4. IEEE (2021)
6. Charaf, N., Kamaleldin, A., Thümmler, M., Göhringer, D.: RV-CAP: enabling dynamic partial reconfiguration for FPGA-based RISC-V system-on-chip. In: 2021 IEEE International Parallel and Distributed Processing Symposium Workshops (IPDPSW), pp. 172–179. IEEE (2021)
7. Dao, N., Attwood, A., Healy, B., Koch, D.: Flexbex: a RISC-V with a reconfigurable instruction extension. In: 2020 International Conference on Field-Programmable Technology (ICFPT), pp. 190–195. IEEE (2020)
8. Devices), A.A.M.: PYNQ | Python Productivity to AMD Adaptive Computing. https://www.pynq.io/. Accessed 19 Nov 2024
9. Diessel, O., ElGindy, H., Middendorf, M., Schmeck, H., Schmidt, B.: Dynamic scheduling of tasks on partially reconfigurable FPGAs. In: IEE Proceedings-Computers and Digital Techniques, vol. 147, no. 3, pp. 181–188 (2000)
10. Drewes, C.: Rethinking CPU-FPGA Interfaces: A Reconfigurable RISC-V Co-Processor
11. Goyal, R., Vanschoren, J., Van Acht, V., Nijssen, S.: Fixed-point quantization of convolutional neural networks for quantized inference on embedded platforms. arXiv preprint arXiv:2102.02147 (2021)
12. group, B.: BlackParrot Core Micro Architechture Overview. https://github. com/black-parrot/black-parrot/blob/master/docs/microarchitecture_guide.md. Accessed 18 Dec 2024
13. group, B.: BlackParrot Platform Guide Tile Taxonomy. https://github.com/black-parrot/black-parrot/blob/master/docs/platform_guide.md. Accessed 18 Dec 2024
14. Group, B.: Linux on BlackParrot. https://github.com/black-parrot-sdk/bp-linux. Accessed 18 Dec 2024
15. Jamili, S., et al.: Implementation of dynamic acceleration unit exchange on a RISC-V soft-processor. In: International Conference on Applications in Electronics Pervading Industry, Environment and Society, pp. 300–306. Springer, Cham (2022)

16. Janßen, B., Zimprich, P., Hübner, M.: A dynamic partial reconfigurable overlay concept for PYNQ. In: 2017 27th International Conference on Field Programmable Logic and Applications (FPL), pp. 1–4. IEEE (2017)
17. Kirchhoff, M., Kerling, P., Streitferdt, D., Fengler, W.: A real-time capable dynamic partial reconfiguration system for an application-specific soft-core processor. Int. J. Reconfig. Comput. **2019**(1), 4723838 (2019)
18. Koch, D.: Partial Reconfiguration on FPGAs; Architectures, Tools and Applications. Springer, Cham (2013)
19. Koch, D., Hannig, F., Ziener, D.: FPGAs for Software Programmers. Springer, Cham (2016)
20. Petrisko, D., et al.: BlackParrot: an agile open-source RISC-V multicore for accelerator SoCs. IEEE Micro **40**(4), 93–102 (2020)
21. Reichenbach, M., Holzinger, P., Häublein, K., Lieske, T., Blinzer, P., Fey, D.: Heterogeneous computing utilizing FPGAs: a new and flexible approach integrating dedicated hardware accelerators into common computing platforms. J. Sig. Process. Syst. **91**, 745–757 (2019)
22. RISCV-Foundation: List of RISCV standard ratified extensions. https://gist.github.com/dominiksalvet/2a982235957012c51453139668e21fce. Accessed 16 Dec 2024
23. Saday, A.: A review of FPGA-based applications and FPGA usage in the industrial area. Innov. Technol. Eng. 171 (2022)
24. Shi, K., Wang, M., Tan, X., Li, Q., Lei, T.: Efficient dynamic reconfigurable CNN accelerator for edge intelligence computing on FPGA. Information **14**(3), 194 (2023)
25. Vipin, K., Fahmy, S.A.: ZyCAP: efficient partial reconfiguration management on the Xilinx Zynq. IEEE Embed. Syst. Lett. **6**(3), 41–44 (2014). https://doi.org/10.1109/LES.2014.2314390

Author Index

The manufacturer's authorised representative in the EU is Springer
Nature Customer Service Centre GmbH, Europaplatz 3, 69115 Heidelberg,
Germany. If you have any concerns regarding our products, please
contact ProductSafety@springernature.com

Printed and bound by CPI Group (UK) Ltd, Croydon, CR0 4YY

24/04/2026

02096367-0008